Third Edition

Fire Department Company Officer

**Edited By
Carl Goodson
Marsha Sneed**

Validated by the International Fire Service Training Association
Published by Fire Protection Publications, Oklahoma State University

RECYCLABLE

The International Fire Service Training Association

The International Fire Service Training Association (IFSTA) was established in 1934 as a "nonprofit educational association of fire fighting personnel who are dedicated to upgrading fire fighting techniques and safety through training." To carry out the mission of IFSTA, Fire Protection Publications was established as an entity of Oklahoma State University. Fire Protection Publications' primary function is to publish and disseminate training texts as proposed and validated by IFSTA. As a secondary function, Fire Protection Publications researches, acquires, produces, and markets high-quality learning and teaching aids as consistent with IFSTA's mission.

The IFSTA Validation Conference is held the second full week in July. Committees of technical experts meet and work at the conference addressing the current standards of the National Fire Protection Association and other standard-making groups as applicable. The Validation Conference brings together individuals from several related and allied fields, such as:

- Key fire department executives and training officers
- Educators from colleges and universities
- Representatives from governmental agencies
- Delegates of firefighter associations and industrial organizations

Committee members are not paid nor are they reimbursed for their expenses by IFSTA or Fire Protection Publications. They participate because of commitment to the fire service and its future through training. Being on a committee is prestigious in the fire service community, and committee members are acknowledged leaders in their fields. This unique feature provides a close relationship between the International Fire Service Training Association and fire protection agencies which helps to correlate the efforts of all concerned.

IFSTA manuals are now the official teaching texts of most of the states and provinces of North America. Additionally, numerous U.S. and Canadian government agencies as well as other English-speaking countries have officially accepted the IFSTA manuals.

ISBN 0-87939-161-8   Library of Congress LC# 98-88704

Third Edition, First Printing, January 1999   Printed in the United States of America
Second Printing, July 1999
Third Printing, November 1999

If you need additional information concerning the International Fire Service Training Association (IFSTA) or Fire Protection Publications, contact:

Customer Service, Fire Protection Publications, Oklahoma State University
930 North Willis, Stillwater, OK 74078-8045
800-654-4055   Fax: 405-744-8204

For assistance with training materials, to recommend material for inclusion in an IFSTA manual, or to ask questions or comment on manual content, contact:

Editorial Department, Fire Protection Publications, Oklahoma State University
930 North Willis, Stillwater, OK 74078-8045
405-707-3020   Fax: 405-707-0024   E-mail: editors@ifstafpp.okstate.edu

Table of Contents

PREFACE vii
INTRODUCTION 1
   Responsibilities of a Company Officer 1
   Duties of a Company Officer 1
   Purpose and Scope 3
   Note on Gender Usage 3

SECTION I   GENERAL

1 ASSUMING THE ROLE OF COMPANY OFFICER 7
   Making the Transition 7
   Knowledge, Skills, and Abilities 8
   Summary 11

2 FIRE DEPARTMENT STRUCTURE 12
   Types of Fire Departments 13
     Public Fire Departments 13
     Private Fire Departments 16
   Personnel 17
     Career (Full-Time) 17
     Volunteer 18
     Combination 18
     Paid-On-Call 18
     Public Safety 18
   Purposes of Fire Protection Agencies 18
   Response Considerations 19
     Automatic Aid 19
     Mutual Aid 20
     Outside Aid 21
   Fire Department Organizational Principles 21
     Unity of Command 22
     Span of Control 23
     Division of Labor 24
     Discipline 25
   Fire Department Organizational Structure 26
     Scalar Organizational Structure 26
     Line and Staff 26
     Authority to Implement 29
     Company Organizational Structure 29
   Summary 30

3 COMPANY OFFICER'S LEGAL RESPONSIBILITIES AND LIABILITY 31
   Governmental Immunity 31
   Sources of Law 33
     Common Law 33
     Constitutional Law 33
     Statutory Law 33
     Administrative Law 33
     Case Law 34
   Criminal and Civil Law 34
     Criminal Liability 34
     Civil Liability 34
     Fireman's Rule 36
   Federal Laws 37
     Occupational Safety and Health Administration (OSHA) 37
     Environmental Protection Agency (EPA) 37

     Title VII 38
     Equal Employment Opportunity Commission (EEOC) 38
     Americans with Disabilities Act (ADA) 40
     Fair Labor Standards Act (FLSA) 41
   National Standards 41
     National Fire Protection Association (NFPA) ... 42
     American National Standards Institute (ANSI) ... 42
     Standards Council of Canada (SCC) 43
   Summary 43

SECTION II   HUMAN RESOURCES MANAGEMENT

4 THE COMPANY AS A GROUP 46
   Groups Defined 47
   Group Dynamics 48
     Common Binding Interests 48
     Vital Group Image 48
     Sense of Continuity 49
     Common Values 49
     Roles Within the Group 49
     Roles of the Company Officer 49
     Role Expectations 49
     Rules and Guidelines 51
     The Group as Individuals 51
   Maslow's Hierarchy of Needs 52
     Basic Physiological Needs 52
     Safety and Security 52
     Belonging and Social Activity 52
     Esteem and Status 53
     Self-Actualization and Fulfillment 53
     Applying Maslow's Needs Model 53
   Vroom's V.I.E. Theory 54
   Strokes and Stamp Collecting 55
   Cultural Diversity as a Group Factor 56
   Summary 56

5 LEADERSHIP AS A GROUP INFLUENCE 58
   Types of Power 59
     Reward Power 59
     Coercive Power 60
     Identification Power 60
     Expert Power 60
     Legitimate Power 60
   Theories of Leadership 61
     Theory X and Theory Y 61
     Theory Z 61
     The Managerial Grid 62
   Leadership Styles 64
     Autocratic Leadership 64
     Democratic Leadership 64
     Laissez-Faire Leadership 64
   Dimensions of Leadership 65
     Making People Feel Strong 65
     Building Trust in the Leader 65

Cooperating to Achieve Common Goals 65
Confronting Conflicts 65
Differences in Those Being Lead 66
Value Systems 66
Gender and Leadership 66
Summary 67

6 ELEMENTS OF SUPERVISION AND MANAGEMENT **68**
Theories of Supervision/Management 69
Scientific Theory of Management 69
Human Relations Theory 70
Hygiene Theory 70
Theory X/Y 71
Management by Objectives 71
Leadership Continuum 72
Modern Management 73
Total Quality Management (TQM) 73
Theory Z 74
Responsibilities of a Supervisor 75
Getting the Job Done 75
Keeping the Work Area Safe and Healthy 76
Encouraging Teamwork and Cooperation 76
Developing Member Skills 76
Keeping Records and Making Reports 76
Supervisory Skills 77
Motivation 77
Delegation 78
Decision-Making 78
Communication 79
Training 80
Resource Management 80
Time Management 81
Discipline 82
Coaching and Counseling 84
Summary 85

7 COMPANY-LEVEL TRAINING **86**
Education 87
Preparation 88
Presentation 88
Application 89
Evaluation 89
Training 89
Mastery Learning 90
Traditional Training 93
Prescriptive Training 94
Summary 94

SECTION III COMMUNITY AND GOVERNMENT RELATIONS

8 GOVERNMENT STRUCTURE **96**
Local Government 97
Municipal (City) Government 97
Township Government 100
County/Parish Government 100
Fire Districts 101
Impact of Local Governments on Fire Protection Agencies 101
Lawmaking Process of Local Governments 101
Agencies of Local Governments 102
State and Provincial Governments 103

State Governments 103
Provincial and Territorial Governments............. 104
Agencies of State and Provincial Governments .. 104
Federal Government 106
Structure of the United States Federal Government 106
Lawmaking Process of the United States Federal Government 107
U.S. Federal Agencies Involved in Fire Protection 108
Structure of the Canadian Federal Government 111
Lawmaking Process of the Canadian Federal Government 112
Canadian Agencies Involved in Fire Protection 112
Private and Professional Organizations 114
Congressional Fire Services Caucus 114
Congressional Fire Services Institute 114
International Fire Service Accreditation Congress (IFSAC) 114
International Fire Service Training Association (IFSTA) 114
International Municipal Signal Association (IMSA) 114
International Society of Fire Service Instructors (ISFSI) 115
National Board on Fire Service Professional Qualifications (NBFSPQ) 115
National Volunteer Fire Council (NVFC) 115
International Association of Arson Investigators (IAAI) 115
International Association of Black Professional Fire Fighters (IABPFF) 116
International Association of Fire Chiefs (IAFC) 116
International Association of Fire Fighters (IAFF) 117
National Registry of Emergency Medical Technicians (NREMT) 117
Underwriters Laboratories Inc. 117
Factory Mutual Research Corporation (FMRC) 117
Building and Fire Research Laboratory (BFRL) 118
Society of Fire Protection Engineers (SFPE) 118
Summary 118

9 COMMUNITY AWARENESS AND PUBLIC RELATIONS **120**
Community Awareness 121
Public Relations 122
Group Presentations 122
Media Programs 122
Handling Citizen Concerns 123
Handling Public Inquiries 125
Summary 127

10 PUBLIC EDUCATION PROGRAM DEVELOPMENT AND IMPLEMENTATION **128**
Company-Level Participation 129
The Five-Step Planning Process 130
Identification 130
Selection 131

Design 132
Implementation 133
Evaluation 135
Summary 136

SECTION IV ADMINISTRATION

11 LABOR RELATIONS 138
History of Labor Relations 139
Norris-La Guardia Act 139
National Industrial Recovery Act (NIRA) 140
Wagner-Connery Act 140
Fair Labor Standards Act (FLSA) 140
Taft-Hartley Act 140
Landrum-Griffin Act 141
Public-Sector Unions 141
Firefighter Unions 141
International Association of Fire Fighters 141
Contracts and Agreements 142
Collective Bargaining 142
Contract Issues 143
Conflict Resolution 145
Conflict Communication 145
Mediation 145
Arbitration 145
Fact-Finding 146
Job Actions 146
Relationship-by-Objectives (RBO) 147
MFD Model 148
Summary 149

12 BUDGETING 150
Types of Budgets 151
Capital Budgets 151
Operating Budgets 153
Types of Operating Budgets 153
Line-Item Budgets 153
Program Budgets 154
Performance Budgets 154
Zero-Base Budgets 154
The Budget Process 154
Planning 154
Preparation 156
Internal Review 156
External Review 157
Implementation 157
Grants and Gifts 157
Summary 157

13 INFORMATION MANAGEMENT 158
Written Communication 159
Report Writing 159
Letter Writing 164
Record Keeping 169
Maintenance Records 169
Activity Records 169
Personnel Records 171
Electronic Data Storage/Retrieval 171
Hardware 174
Software 174
The Internet 175
Summary 175

14 FIRE DEPARTMENT COMMUNICATIONS 176
Communication as a Process 177
The Sender and Receiver 177
The Message 178
The Medium 178
Listening and Hearing 179
Formal Communications 180
Written Policies and Procedures 180
Standard Operating Procedures 181
Orders and Directives 181
Face-to-Face Communications 181
Firefighter-Officer Relationships 182
Selective Listening 182
Semantics 182
Emotional Context 182
Physical Barriers 183
Cultural Differences 183
Communicating With Victims 183
Public Speaking 183
Presentations 184
Media Relations 184
News and Press Releases 185
Informal Communications: The Grapevine 185
Summary 186

SECTION V INSPECTION AND INVESTIGATION

15 FIRE AND LIFE SAFETY INSPECTIONS 188
Authority 189
Ordinances, Codes, and Standards 189
Company-Level Inspection Responsibilities 190
Preparing for Inspections 191
Conducting Inspections 193
General Inspection Categories 194
Occupancy Classifications 198
Hazard of Contents 203
Closing Interview 203
Documentation 204
Conducting Exit Drills 204
Inspecting/Testing Fire Protection Systems 204
Fire Detection/Signaling Systems 205
Water Supplies 206
Stationary Fire Pumps 206
Public Fire Alarm Systems 207
Standpipe Systems 207
Fire Extinguishing Systems 208
Summary 214

16 FIRE INVESTIGATION 216
Fire Investigation 217
Locating the Point of Origin 217
Securing the Scene 219
Determining the Cause of the Fire 220
Accidental Fires 220
Smoking-Related Fires 221
Pyrophoric Ignition 221
Electrical Fires 221
Natural Fires 222
Lightning-Related Fires 222
Earthquake-Related Fires 222
Other Natural Fires 223
Incendiary Fires 223
Preparing the Documentation 225

Summary 226

SECTION VI EMERGENCY SERVICE DELIVERY

17 PRE-INCIDENT PLANNING 228
The Pre-Incident Survey 229
   Facility Survey Equipment 230
   Scheduling Pre-Incident Surveys 230
   Public Relations During the Survey 231
Conducting The Pre-Incident Survey 231
   Basic Building Construction 234
   Fuel Loading 239
   Fire Protection Systems 240
   Water Supply 240
   Property Conservation 241
Developing Pre-Incident Plans 242
   Facility Survey Drawings 242
   Written Report 246
Managing Pre-Incident Data 246
Summary 247

18 INCIDENT SCENE COMMUNICATIONS 248
Communications Equipment 249
   Radios 249
   Pagers 252
   Alternative Communications Methods 252
   Advanced Technology Communications Systems 254
Communications Procedures 255
   Radio Communications 255
   The Five Cs of Communication 256
Summary 257

19 INCIDENT SCENE MANAGEMENT 258
Objectives of Scene Management 259
   Life Safety 259
   Incident Stabilization 259
   Property Conservation 259
Phases of Scene Management 260
   Scene Assessment 260
Elements of Scene Management 260
   Traffic Control 261
   Perimeter Control 262
   Crowd Control 263
   Witness Control 264
   Occupant Services 264
   Evacuation 265
Termination of the Incident 268
   Equipment Retrieval 268
   Investigation 268
   Release of Scene 268
   Critical Incident Stress Debriefing 269
Summary 270

20 SIZE-UP AND INCIDENT PLANS 270
Size-Up Defined 271
   Traditional Size-Up 272
   Three-Step Process 273
Application 274
   Pre-Incident 274
   On Arrival 276
   During the Incident 276
   Priorities 277

   RECEO 277
  Incident Plans 278
   Pre-Incident Survey Data 279
   Operational Plans 279
   Incident Action Plans 280
  Summary 280

21 ACTION PLAN IMPLEMENTATION 282
Action Plan Implementation 283
   Defensive Mode 284
   Offensive Mode 285
   Rescue Mode 286
Incident Command 286
   Common Terminology 287
   Modular Organization 288
   Common Communications 288
   Unified Command Structure 289
   Incident Action Plans 292
   Manageable Span-of-Control 292
   Predesignated Incident Facilities 292
   Comprehensive Resource Management 292
Personnel Accountability 293
Summary 294

SECTION VII SAFETY

22 FIREFIGHTER SAFETY AND HEALTH 296
Safety Standards 297
   OSHA Regulations 297
   NFPA 1500 298
   Other Safety Standards 297
Safety and Health Policies and Procedures 298
   Safety and Health Program 299
   Infectious Disease Control Program 299
Firefighter Injuries 300
   Incident Safety 300
   Workplace Safety 303
Stress 305
   Physical, Environmental, and
    Psychological Stressors 306
   Reducing Physical and Environmental Stress 306
   Psychological Stress — Signals and Reduction .. 307
Critical Incident Stress 308
   Symptoms of Critical Incident Stress 308
   Critical Incident Stress Debriefings (CISD) 309
Substance Abuse 309
Accident Investigations 309
   Conducting Accident Investigations 310
   Understanding Human Factors 310
Analyzing Accident/Injury Reports 311
   Who Was Involved? 311
   What Was Involved? 311
   What Were the Circumstances? 311
   What Was the Root Cause? 311
   Conclusions 311
Wellness Programs 312
   Medical Program 312
   Physical Fitness Program 312
   Member Assistance Program 313
Summary 313

GLOSSARY 315

INDEX 320

This third edition of **Fire Department Company Officer** has been updated to conform to the requirements of NFPA 1021, *Standard for Fire Officer Professional Qualifications*, 1997 Edition, Levels I and II. Based on information from a variety of sources, this edition of **Company Officer** retains the best of the previous edition and adds new material to make it more relevant to the roles and responsibilities of first-line supervisors today.

Acknowledgment and special thanks are extended to the members of the IFSTA validation committee who contrib uted their time, wisdom, and knowledge to this manual.

IFSTA Validation Committee

Chair
James A. McSwain
Lawrence Fire and Rescue
Lawrence, Kansas

Vice-Chair
Chris Neal
Stillwater Fire Department
Stillwater, Oklahoma

Secretary
Geoff Miller
Sacramento County Fire District
Rancho Cordova, California

Committee Members

Lou Amabili
Delaware State Fire Training (Ret.)
Hockessin, Delaware

Harold McCoy
Tulsa Fire Department
Tulsa, Oklahoma

Sherry Arasim
Tualatin Valley Fire & Rescue
Aloha, Oregon

Hugh Pike
U.S. Air Force Fire Protection
Tyndall AFB, Florida

Veldora Arthur
Miami Fire-Rescue Department
Miami, Florida

Joe Plumlee
DeSoto Fire Rescue
DeSoto, Texas

Bill Bingham
Bell Buckle Volunteer Fire Dept.
Bell Buckle, Tennessee

Jeff Scott
Boone County Fire Protection Dist.
Columbia, Missouri

Steve George
Oklahoma State Fire Service Training
Stillwater, Oklahoma

Alan Walker
Louisiana State University
Baton Rouge, Louisiana

Robert Giorgio
Cherry Hill Fire Department
Cherry Hill, New Jersey

Michael Ward
Fairfax County Fire/Rescue
Fairfax, Virginia

Chuck Holman
Palisades Nuclear Power Plant
Covert, Michigan

Thomas Wilson
Maryland Fire and Rescue Institute
Princess Anne, Maryland

Acknowledgment and thanks are also extended to the following individuals who reviewed the material but did not participate in the committee's deliberations:

William Goswick, Tulsa (OK) Fire Department

Rudy Horist, Elgin (IL) Fire Department

Lee Ireland, Egg Harbor, NJ

Joseph Johnson, Kern County (CA) Fire Department

James O'Brien, Clark County (NV) Fire Department

Lenny Perez, Brownsville (TX) Fire Department

The following individuals and organizations contributed information, photographs, and other assistance that made the completion of this manual possible:

Fire Chief Darryl Anderson and the personnel of the Tamalpais (CA) Fire Protection District — especially Assistant Chief Mike Stone and Captain Jack Thomas

Captain Steven Braun, Larkspur (CA) Fire Department

Fire Division Commander Robert Cassel and the personnel of the Rohnert Park (CA) Department of Public Safety — especially Sergeant Duane Rosengren

Fire Chief Ron Collier and the personnel of the Windsor (CA) Fire Protection District

Dennis Compton, Mesa (AZ) Fire Department

Al Da Cunha, San Francisco (CA) Fire Department (Ret.)

Battalion Chief Jim Eastman and the personnel of Battalion 14 of the Sacramento County (CA) Fire Protection District

Assistant Chief Hank Gilliam, West Sacramento (CA) Fire Department

Division Chief John Hawkins, California Department of Forestry and Fire Protection

Ron Jeffers, New Jersey Metro Fire Photographers Association

Fire Chief Terry Krout and the personnel of the Petaluma (CA) Fire Department — especially Battalion Chief Dan Simpson

Bill Lellis, Larkspur (CA) Fire Department (Ret.)

Patrick McDonald and the personnel of Redwood Empire Air Care Helicopter (REACH), Santa Rosa, CA

Monterey County (CA) Training Officers

National Interagency Fire Center, Boise, ID

Fire Chief Chris Neal and the personnel of the Stillwater (OK) Fire Department

Fire Chief Tony Pini and the personnel of the Santa Rosa (CA) Fire Department — especially Division Chief Charles Hanley and Battalion Chiefs Mark Basque, Jack Piccinini, and Owen Wilson

Ed Prendergast, Chicago (IL) Fire Departmment

Fire Chief John Rentz and the personnel of the Novato (CA) Fire Protection District — especially Battalion Chiefs Al Arendell, Wayne Hinrichs, and Dan Northern, and Fire Marshal Forrest Craig

Sonoma County (CA) Department of Fire Services — especially Assistant Chiefs Barry Gaab and Sophia Galifaro

Sonoma-Lake-Napa Ranger Unit, California Department of Forestry and Fire Protection — especially Battalion Chiefs Kim Thompson and Don Uboldi

Fire Chief Robert Taylor and the personnel of the Healdsburg (CA) Fire Department

Fire Chief Ron Tougas (interim) and the personnel of the Fairfield (CA) Fire Department — especially Battalion Chiefs Ron Glantz and Vince Webster

Roger Valinoti, Hewlett-Packard Company, Santa Rosa (CA) Facility

Carlton Williams, Los Medanos Community College, Pittsburg CA

Fire Chief Doug Williams and the personnel of the Northbay Fire Authority (CA)

Wilmar (CA) Volunteer Fire Company

Last, but certainly not least, gratitude is also extended to the following members of the Fire Protection Publications staff whose contributions made the final publication of this manual possible:

Mike Wieder, Senior Publications Editor

Cindy Brakhage, Associate Editor

Don Davis, Coordinator, Publications Production

Ann Moffat, Graphic Design Analyst

Desa Porter, Senior Graphic Designer

Connie Nicholson, Senior Graphic Designer

Susan F. Walker, Fire Service Programs Librarian

Kevin Dillow, Research Technician

Kayla Moorman, Library Assistant

Introduction

Along with the rest of the fire service, the role of the company officer has changed and continues to change. This is natural and inevitable in the ever-changing world we inhabit. Today's company officers must know about and be able to deal with concepts such as *gender equity* and *cultural diversity.* They must know about *planning, budgeting,* and *time management.* In short, today's company officer must be a much more versatile and better informed supervisor than in the past.

Today — more than ever — company officers are in the "people business." In many departments, a small percentage of a company officer's time is spent dealing with emergencies. The majority of their on-duty time is spent dealing with people.

As someone once said, the more things change, the more they stay the same. In spite of the many and varied changes that have taken place in the fire service as a whole — and in the company officer's role in particular —some things remain unchanged. For example, dedication to duty and courage in the face of adversity are as necessary for company officers today as they ever were. Company officers, regardless of their specific rank or title, are on the cutting edge of service delivery to the public. Day or night, summer or winter, when there is a difficult or dangerous job to do, the company officer and his crew are often the ones called upon to get it done. So, on balance, some parts of the company officer's job have changed while other parts remain the same.

Responsibilities of a Company Officer

Regardless of whether they are career officers or volunteers and whether they are called fire officers, company officers, or whatever, according to the International City Management Association (ICMA), first-line supervisors (company officers) are responsible for the following:

- Getting the job done (meeting the organization's goals/objectives)
- Keeping the work area free of health and safety hazards

- Building teamwork and cooperation
- Developing members' skills
- Keeping records and making reports

Even though these general responsibilities have not changed in most fire departments, other aspects of the company officer's job have changed significantly. Most fire departments are being asked by their governing bodies to do more with less. Many fire departments are performing duties today that were formerly not provided or were the responsibility of some other agency.

A generation ago, many fire departments did not provide emergency medical services, and the terms *universal precautions* and *bloodborne pathogens* were not a part of the average company officer's vocabulary. Most firefighters were neither trained nor equipped to safely and effectively handle a hazardous materials incident. In most fire departments, staffing levels on fire apparatus were higher than is typical today. Few fire departments now respond with more personnel than they did in the past, and some use alternative staffing schemes that vary the number of personnel on duty at different times of the day and night. In response to declining revenues, some departments have had to close fire stations and spread that workload among the remaining companies. Likewise, as other departments of local government experienced revenue reductions, some of their duties and responsibilities were reassigned to the fire department. Career fire departments are now doing everything from enforcing the building codes to reading utility meters. Regardless of whether these additional services are an appropriate use of fire department resources, fire departments are being asked to provide them, and most of these additional duties are performed by firefighters at the company level.

Duties of a Company Officer

Despite all the changes in the roles and responsibilities of fire departments, the specific duties of the company officer have, in general, remained the same or expanded. While there are variations from department to department and from volunteer departments to career departments, the general responsibilities mentioned earlier translate into the following specific duties:

- Maintaining company health and safety
- Enforcing departmental rules and regulations
- Managing company activities
- Collecting pre-incident plan data
- Conducting company fire inspections
- Conducting company training evolutions
- Facilitating company communications
- Building company motivation
- Implementing departmental goals and objectives
- Performing career counseling and problem solving
- Keeping departmental records and making reports

Clearly, the most important duty of a company officer is to protect all members of the company from injury or illness. A company officer or firefighter who is incapacitated for any reason is of no use to the public or to the other members of the company. The company officer must know the department's safety rules and must follow and enforce them conscientiously. One of the most effective ways that a company officer can promote safety within the company is by setting a good example — that is, by being a positive role model.

Just as setting a good example helps the company officer promote safety, it is also an essential part of enforcing departmental rules and regulations. A company officer cannot expect the other members of the company to abide by the rules if he does not. A company officer who knowingly ignores departmental rules or allows his subordinates to do so sets a precedent that will erode the foundation of discipline on which the company and the department depend. A company officer must be willing to follow and enforce all departmental rules and regulations, even those with which he disagrees.

As mentioned earlier, one of the company officer's major responsibilities is to get the job done. More than anything else, this means managing the time and activities of the company. Because of the many and varied assignments that most fire companies have today and because of the time spent responding to emergencies, there are not enough hours in the day to complete them all. Therefore, the company officer must apply time management principles to prioritize and schedule the company's activities. However, the fire officer must also realize that the most carefully planned schedule may be changed or entirely eliminated by one or more emergency calls during the shift.

One of the assignments that must be managed along with all the other company activities is collecting pre-incident plan data. Collecting this information has a number of benefits for the company. By visiting the target hazards within the response district, the crew becomes more familiar with the potential problems they may have to handle during an emergency. Using the data collected to identify the resources that would be needed in various scenarios also helps in developing contingency plans.

Many career fire departments require their companies to conduct inspections in a wide variety of occupancies to identify potential fire and life safety hazards, and they are to apply the appropriate codes to get the problems corrected. Conducting these inspections in a thorough and conscientious manner requires that fire department personnel inspect every room, compartment, or void space in a building and in the process, identify hidden or obscure hazards that can be corrected before they cause a problem.

Helping company members acquire and maintain the knowledge, skills, and abilities they need to safely and effectively perform their jobs is certainly a critical duty of company officers. In some departments, a full-time training staff delivers most of the skill development training (new skills/information) while the company officers use repetitive drills and other techniques to help members maintain their skills. In other departments, company officers are responsible for both skill development and skill maintenance training.

In order to facilitate company communications, company officers must understand the principles of effective communication as well as be adept at selecting and using the most appropriate communications medium in each situation. Communications at the company level may involve everything from face-to-face oral communication to hand-written reports and records, to fax machines and cellular phones, to mobile and portable radios, and to E-mail and sophisticated computerized communications programs. Regardless of how basic or sophisticated the available communications equipment may be, its skillful operation requires hands-on training and regular reinforcement through the use of simulations and actual emergencies.

Keeping company members motivated on a long-term basis can be a significant challenge for most company officers. At a relatively quiet station, there may be long periods between emergency calls. During these long periods of relative inactivity, it is easy for company members to divert their attention to more stimulating activities such as playing games or watching television. The challenge for the company officer is to find ways to keep the members interested in and focused on their jobs.

One way of maintaining the members' focus is by involving them in the planning and execution of programs designed to fulfill company-level objectives that contribute to the achievement of departmental goals. If the members clearly understand the relationship of an assignment to the goals of the department, then they are often self-motivated. So, one of the keys for a company officer is to be able to translate departmental goals into company assignments.

Because a company officer has demonstrated enough education and experience to have been promoted, firefighters interested in earning a promotion often turn to their company officer for advice about their own careers. Providing this advice is a legitimate and important duty of every company officer. Company officers should know their subordinates' professional strengths and weaknesses and should be willing and able to offer constructive suggestions when asked. In addition to career counseling, company officers are sometimes asked for advice on more personal problems. The company officer must know what professional counseling services are available through member assistance programs and how to access them.

Even in this electronic age, fire departments still require a great deal of paperwork. While some data can be reported and stored electronically, many hard-copy forms and records must still be submitted and maintained to satisfy federal and state or provincial mandates. Many company officers spend a good deal of their on-duty time filling out forms and writing reports. A certain amount of this paperwork can and should be delegated, but much of it is privileged or confidential information such as performance evaluations or disciplinary documentation. The company officer is responsible for the completion of these records and reports. Therefore, regardless of who writes the report, the company officer will be judged by the grammar, spelling, and punctuation used, as well as the content. Considering that any report may someday be used in court, the company officer must make sure that all reports submitted by his company are as accurate, complete, and well-written as possible.

While many of the traditional roles and responsibilities of fire departments and company officers remain unchanged, new and different ones have been and continue to be added. Today's company officer must be at least as physically fit, emotionally strong, and mentally agile as company officers have ever been. In addition, to cope with today's new challenges and tomorrow's un-known ones, current and aspiring company officers must work harder than ever to keep up with changes in technology and changes in society that directly or indirectly impact the fire service.

Purpose and Scope

Fire Department Company Officer is written for firefighters and driver/operators who aspire to the position of company officer; for company officers determined to remain versed in essential and innovative management, leadership, and human relations concepts; and for training officers responsible for teaching and developing officers and officer candidates. A knowledge of fire behavior and essential fire fighting skills is assumed.

Each chapter addresses one or more of the objectives contained in Levels I and II of NFPA 1021, *Standard for Fire Officer Professional Qualifications*, 1997 Edition. What it means to assume the role of a company officer is discussed, along with how that role relates to the department and the community, and what liability and legal responsibilities attach to the position. Also discussed are some of the classic and contemporary theories of human resource management. Discussions of labor relations, budgeting, information management, and fire department communications are included. Company-level inspections, investigations, and training are discussed along with emergency service delivery. Finally, the company officer's responsibilities relating to firefighter safety and health are discussed.

Two additional educational resources to supplement this manual are planned for development. One of these is a study guide with which individuals may increase the breadth and depth of their knowledge of the contents of this manual. The second is a professionally developed curriculum with which trainers can teach the concepts and techniques described in this manual. The curriculum will contain an instructor's guide, lesson plans, visual aids, and lesson tests.

Notice on Gender Usage

In order to keep sentences uncluttered and easy to read, this text has been written using the masculine gender, rather than both the masculine and female gender pronouns. Years ago, it was traditional to use masculine pronouns to refer to both sexes in a neutral way. This usage is applied to this manual for the purposes of brevity and is not intended to address only one gender. Please note that the included photos and artwork reflect the diversity of today's firefighters.

Chapter 1

Assuming the Role of Company Officer

Having served for some years as a member of a fire company, you have probably become highly skilled at using the tools of the firefighter's trade. You may feel that your skill and experience also qualify you to function as a company officer. However, the job requirements for a company officer are far different than those for a firefighter or driver/operator. If you have decided that you would like to be a company officer, then you need to know what becoming one entails. This chapter discusses the transition from firefighter to company officer and the knowledge, skills, and abilities that a fire officer must possess to be successful in the company officer's role.

Making the Transition

The transition from firefighter to company officer is perhaps the most important and potentially the most difficult change in your entire fire service career. This transition is important to the department because the company officer is the vital connecting link between the fire company and the rest of the organization. It is important to you because it represents a major step in your career. However, as mentioned earlier, this transition also can be one of the most difficult.

As a firefighter or driver/operator, you are in a very responsible position that is extremely important to the overall success of your company and the department. However, in both of these roles you function as a member of a team, and you employ tools and equipment to accomplish your assigned tasks. As a company officer, you will be the leader of a team and will employ other people to accomplish the organization's goals and the team's assigned tasks. Performing your duties as a company officer can be far more difficult than accomplishing your tasks as a firefighter. As a company officer, you will still be an integral part of the team, and you often will have to perform the same tasks as your subordinates. But in addition to performing those tasks, you will be responsible for supervising the other members of your team and for making decisions for the team, and you will be held accountable for the team's performance. More than any other position in the fire department organization — whether career or volunteer — the role of the first-level supervisor (company officer) is that of player/coach.

Working and living closely together on duty helps to bond the individual members of the company into a team. The team trains together, works together, lives together, and in some cases, socializes together off duty. Working together, the team produces a synergistic effect — that is, it accomplishes more as a team than the sum of what the individual members could accomplish working separately. However, this very closeness and unity can make the company officer's job extremely difficult at times.

If one or more members of the team cannot or will not perform up to standard, some corrective action is necessary. If the performance problem results from a skill deficiency, the problem can be resolved through training. But if the substandard performance results from a lack of motivation or other attitude problem, progressive discipline may be required to improve the performance. Imposing discipline on those with whom you work as part of a team can be very difficult, especially if you also socialize together off duty or if you worked together as fellow firefighters in the recent past. There are few things more difficult than having to discipline a friend. Establishing a new relationship with your former peers can be an extremely uncomfortable thing to do. However, if you are to do your job as a company officer, you *must* do so.

When you accept the badge of office as a company officer, you must be willing to assume the responsibilities that go along with that position. You must be willing to accept responsibility for your company's performance in both routine and emergency situations. You must be willing to make decisions — even difficult or unpleasant ones — and to do what you believe to be the right thing under the circumstances. You must be willing to comply with and enforce all departmental rules and regulations, including unpopular ones. You must be willing to set aside personal preferences and feelings and think and act objectively. In other words, you must be willing to *lead*. You must also realize that, more than ever before, you represent the organization in a highly visible way; therefore, you must be willing to renew your commitment to the organization. One of the best ways to manifest this level of commitment and to succeed as a fire officer is to lead by example and apply the following six rules:

- **Learn your job, be sincerely interested in it, and be dedicated to it**. In most cases, what you are able to contribute to and achieve in the fire service is limited only by the degree of your personal commitment. You must assume responsibility for the duties assigned to you. Do your best to analyze and profit by your mistakes and the mistakes of others. Learning from past mistakes will allow you to use your experience to contribute to the success of your company and the department. Fire departments use the combined resources and productivity of each company to accomplish departmental goals. Every firefighter and every company must do their part in order for tasks to be accomplished efficiently and effectively. Every company officer must promote this cooperation among the members of the company and with other companies within the department.

- **Be loyal to the department**. You are a part of the department, and it is a part of you. Criticism of the department is, in fact, a criticism of yourself. You must strive to understand and be prepared to advocate the policies, procedures, and functions of the department. Always be aware that you represent yourself, your company, and your department. Your appearance, conduct, and statements are a direct reflection on the fire department. The image of the department must be preserved and protected.

As a company officer, you must also be loyal to and supportive of your coworkers in general and the members of your company in particular. This is a critical element in building and maintaining team cohesion. However, this does not mean that you are obligated to cover up for your coworkers or to support them when they are clearly wrong. While mutual support is desirable, each individual member is ultimately responsible for his own conduct.

- **Be aggressive in the pursuit of education and training opportunities**. Training is an ongoing process throughout your career. The attainment of each educational objective will reveal even more knowledge with which you must be familiar if you are to excel in this challenging profession. As a company officer, you must function simultaneously at three levels:

  — As a steward of the position to which you are assigned

  — As a teacher of those whom you supervise

  — As a student of any position to which you aspire

- **Guard your speech both on and off duty**. As a company officer, you must always be willing to discuss the purposes and functions of your fire department and be an advocate for it; however, you must also be careful to not reveal privileged or confidential information. Because you are expected to speak for the department in the areas of fire prevention, fire protection, and fire fighting, be careful to say only those things that you know to be correct and consistent with the department's position.

- **Lead by example**. To be a positive role model, you must be scrupulously honest, fair, and trustworthy in the discharge of your duties. You have an obligation to yourself and those for whom you work to continually try to improve your knowledge, skills, and abilities. Dependability is an asset that many employers value and that will enhance your personal and professional reputations. You must also keep your personal affairs in order so that if they are made public, they will not reflect badly on you or the department.

- **Accept criticism graciously; accept praise, honors, and advancement modestly**. Everyone makes mistakes — be willing to admit those that you make and to take responsibility for them. If you are striving for advancement, be sure that your actions in this pursuit are ethical. Assume that all of your decisions and actions will be observed and evaluated. How you conduct yourself will reflect on you both personally and professionally.

Knowledge, Skills, and Abilities

As a company officer, you must possess certain knowledge, skills, and abilities and be able to apply them. Specifically, you must:

- Understand the structure, policies, and procedures of the fire department and the larger governmental entity of which it is a part.

- Know how to communicate effectively in both routine and emergency situations.

- Know the fundamentals of human resources management and how the law applies to you as a supervisor.

- Know how to protect the safety and health of those assigned to your company.

- Have an understanding of planning, inspection procedures, investigation techniques, and public education.

- Know how to deliver the emergency services that the department provides at the company level.

- Know how to develop, evaluate, and maintain your crew's knowledge, skills, and abilities in order to provide both emergency and nonemergency services in a safe and efficient manner.

As a company officer, it is important for you to understand how your department is structured, why it is structured the way it is, and how it fits into the overall governmental structure of your city or district. These structures and relationships are the result of a series of cultural, economic, political, and practical decisions. These decisions are based on an evaluation of what level of protection the community needs, how this protection can be provided most efficiently, and what the citizens are willing and able to spend for these services (Figure 1.1). These topics are discussed in greater detail in Chapter 2, "Fire Department Structure," and Chapter 8, "Government Structure."

To be successful as a company officer, you must be able to communicate effectively in a variety of situations. You must be able to receive and understand verbal and written orders and directives from your immediate su-

pervisor. In turn, you must be able to translate these orders into assignments for your company and effectively communicate them to your subordinates (Figure 1.2). You must be able to use the best means available to communicate through the chain of command in both routine, day-to-day activities and during minor and major emergency operations.

As a company officer, you must also know and be able to apply the principles of human resources management and the elements of supervision. In fact, the majority of your on-duty time will be spent using "people skills" in one form or another. You will have to deal with group dynamics, motivation, career counseling, and problem solving. You must know what professional counseling services are available to company members and must know how to access these services. As a company officer, you will be responsible for helping your subordinates to function safely and effectively. To do this, the members of your team must be well-trained, and one of your most important roles as a fire officer is that of trainer or coach (Figure 1.3). You will have to help them to acquire and develop new knowledge, skills, and abilities and to maintain what they already know.

In our highly litigious society, knowledge of your legal responsibilities and your personal liability as a fire officer can be very important to your effectiveness as a supervisor, as well as to your personal financial security. Supervisors and managers have been and will continue to be sued by their subordinates, special interest groups, and the public at large. To protect yourself and the department, you must know and fulfill your legal obligations as a company officer (Figure 1.4). One of your most basic and most important responsibilities as a fire officer is for

Figure 1.1 Officials must structure the department to meet community needs.

Figure 1.2 Company officers must be effective communicators.

Figure 1.3 Teaching is one of a company officer's most important duties.

Figure 1.4 Company officers must know and follow applicable laws.

Figure 1.5 Safety is a company officer's most important responsibility.

Figure 1.6 Company officers must manage their budgets carefully.

Figure 1.7 Conducting fire and life safety inspections is an important company function.

the health and safety of your subordinates, yourself, and others. Knowing and applying the requirements of NFPA 1500, *Standard on Fire Department Occupational Safety and Health Program*, as well as other recognized safe operating techniques and procedures is fundamental (Figure 1.5). Failing to know and apply the applicable laws and regulations could result in your being held personally liable, subjecting you to severe financial penalties.

Your responsibilities as a company officer include different forms of planning. You must be able to devise appropriate plans for a variety of anticipated contingencies. One of the most important of these plans is the company budget request. Using the budget as a planning tool can significantly increase your productivity and that of your company (Figure 1.6). Other plans will assist in preparing for various possible emergencies such as fires,

floods, and other natural disasters. Pre-incident plans can reduce the number of decisions required after a major incident begins and can reduce the time necessary to get the needed resources on scene.

Chapter 15, "Fire and Life Safety Inspections," and Chapter 16, " Fire Investigations," discuss the company officer's responsibilities in the areas of fire prevention and investigation and how these relate to public education, community awareness, and public relations. As a career fire officer, the majority of your time during normal business hours may be spent planning and conducting fire prevention inspections (Figure 1.7). Other time during and after the normal business day may be devoted to preparing and delivering public fire safety education programs within the community (Figure 1.8). At any hour of the day or night you may be conducting a fire investigation, the results of which could result in civil or criminal prosecution of those responsible for setting the fire and/or could form the basis for a public fire safety education program (Figure 1.9).

Last, but certainly not least, your responsibilities in the delivery of emergency services are discussed in the final chapters. Being or having been one of those directly involved in performing these duties, you should be intimately familiar with what these services are. As a company officer you are responsible for making decisions and supervising those who actually deliver these services. However, your department's staffing levels and operating procedures may require you to participate directly in the delivery of these services as well (Figure 1.10).

Summary

If you have decided to become a company officer, you should consider what becoming one entails. You must be willing to make the most important and possibly the most difficult transition of your entire fire service career. You must be willing to establish a new relationship with your fellow firefighters and the department. You must also be willing and able to switch from the role of follower to the role of leader.

As a company officer, you must also be willing to develop and maintain the knowledge, skills, and abilities that the position demands. This will require extra time and effort (and perhaps extra expense) for you to maintain your current knowledge and skills and to acquire new ones. You must maintain your current skills because you may have to continue to apply them as a member of the team. Even if you do not have to use your firefighter or driver/operator skills during actual emergencies, you will have to supervise those who do. And, at least as important, you will have to act as a coach to help your subordinates develop and maintain their job skills.

Obviously, deciding to become a company officer requires an even higher level of personal and professional commitment than has been expected of you. If you are not willing to make that commitment fully and enthusiastically, you would do yourself, the department, and your coworkers a favor if you decided to remain in your present position — and there is nothing wrong with that. But if you still truly want to become a professional company officer, the first step is to read and be ready to apply the material contained in this book, and we wish you the best of luck in your pursuit of becoming a company officer!

Figure 1.8 Company officers can be effective advocates for fire and life safety.

Figure 1.9 The origin and cause of every unfriendly fire should be investigated.

Figure 1.10 Company officers may have to participate as well as supervise.

This chapter provides information that will assist the reader in meeting the following job performance requirements from NFPA 1021, *Standard for Fire Officer Professional Qualifications*, 1997 edition. The colored portions indicate the topics addressed in the chapter. The numbers of the job performance requirements are also noted directly in the sections of text where they are addressed. Those in the following list that are denoted with an asterisk (*) are global in nature and are covered by reading the chapter in its entirety.

Fire Officer I

2-1.1 **General Prerequisite Knowledge**. The organizational structure of the department; departmental operating procedures for administration, emergency operations, and safety; departmental budget process; information management and record keeping; the fire prevention and building safety codes and ordinances applicable to the jurisdiction; incident management system; socioeconomic and political factors that impact the fire service; cultural diversity; methods used by supervisors to obtain cooperation within a group of subordinates; the rights of management and members; agreements in force between the organization and members; policies and procedures regarding the operation of the department as they involve supervisors and members.

2-2.1 Assign tasks or responsibilities to unit members, given an assignment at an emergency operation, so that the instructions are complete, clear, and concise, safety considerations are addressed and the desired outcomes are conveyed.

(a) *Prerequisite Knowledge:* Verbal communications during emergency situations, techniques used to make assignments under stressful situations, methods of confirming understanding.

(b) *Prerequisite Skills:* The ability to condense instructions for frequently assigned unit tasks based upon training and standard operating procedures.

2-2.2 Assign tasks or responsibilities to unit members, given an assignment under nonemergency conditions at a station or other work location, so that the instructions are complete, clear, and concise; safety considerations are addressed; and the desired outcomes are conveyed.

(a) *Prerequisite Knowledge:* Verbal communications under nonemergency situations, techniques used to make assignments under routine situations, methods of confirming understanding.

(b) *Prerequisite Skills:* The ability to issue instructions for frequently assigned unit tasks based upon department policy.

2-2.4 Recommend action for member-related problems, given a member with a situation requiring assistance and the member assistance policies and procedures, so that the situation is identified and the actions taken are within the established policies and procedures.

(a) *Prerequisite Knowledge:* The signs and symptoms of member-related problems, causes of stress in emergency services personnel, adverse effects of stress on the performance of emergency service personnel.

(b) *Prerequisite Skills:* The ability to recommend a course of action for a member in need of assistance.

2-2.5* Apply human resource policies and procedures, given an administrative situation requiring action, so that policies and procedures are followed.

(a) *Prerequisite Knowledge:* Human resource policies and procedures.

(b) *Prerequisite Skills:* The ability to communicate verbally and in writing and to relate interpersonally.

2-2.6 Coordinate the completion of assigned tasks and projects by members, given a list of projects and tasks and the job requirements of subordinates, so that the assignments are prioritized, a plan for the completion of each assignment is developed, and members are assigned to specific tasks and supervised during the completion of the assignments.

(a) *Prerequisite Knowledge:* Principles of supervision and basic human resource management.

(b) *Prerequisite Skills:* The ability to plan and to set priorities.

Fire Officer II

3-2.1 Initiate actions to maximize member performance and/or to correct unacceptable performance, given human resource policies and procedures, so that member and/or unit performance improves or the issue is referred to the next level of supervision.

(a) *Prerequisite Knowledge:* Human resource policies and procedures, problem identification, organizational behavior, group dynamics, leadership styles, types of power, and interpersonal dynamics.

(b) *Prerequisite Skills:* The ability to communicate verbally and in writing, to solve problems, to increase team work, and to counsel members.

3-2.2 Evaluate the job performance of assigned members, given personnel records and evaluation forms, so each member's performance is evaluated accurately and reported according to human resource policies and procedures.

(a) *Prerequisite Knowledge:* Human resource policies and procedures, job descriptions, objectives of a member evaluation probram, and common errors in evaluating.

(b) *Prerequisite Skills:* The ability to communicate verbally and in writing and to plan and conduct evaluations.

Fire Department Structure

Fire departments are diverse and sometimes complex groups of people that are organized in a manner intended to provide the highest level of service to their customers at the lowest possible cost. Company officers are responsible for directing the members of their companies in a way that achieves this high level of service. In order to accomplish this task, the company officer must understand the department's organizational structure and where he fits into it. The company officer must also understand all the other parts of the governmental structure and how they affect the officer's role.

Whether a fire department is organized as public or private, career or volunteer, full-time or on-call, or in some other manner, it must have some sort of structure. Such organizational structures provide a management framework for the department and define how it will plan and operate to meet its mission. This structure also determines how the department will interact with other organizations, including other government agencies. This chapter discusses the types of fire departments, ways in which fire departments may be structured, the purposes of fire protection agencies, and the organizational principles on which they operate.

Types of Fire Departments

[NFPA 1021: 2-1.1]

There are many ways of classifying fire departments, such as by who actually employs the firefighters — if and how firefighters are compensated — their relationship to other agencies, and other methods. At the broadest level, fire departments can be classified as either *public* or *private*. Public fire departments are the more common form and include city and county fire departments, fire protection districts, volunteer fire departments, fire bureaus, and other organizations that serve the general public. Private fire protection agencies generally fall into one of two categories: (1) fire protection agencies that

serve a very limited area, such as a single business (fire brigade) or a military installation or (2) private agencies that contract with other entities to provide fire protection services. The following sections describe some of the more common forms of public and private fire departments.

Public Fire Departments

The term *fire department* has come to be applied to virtually any fire protection agency. However, a more precise meaning of the term refers to the fact that the organization is a departmental division of a larger body, such as a municipal government or county, parish, or borough commission. Other departments may include law enforcement, water and sanitation, utilities, streets and highways (Figure 2.1). There are more than 30,000 public fire departments in the United States. The two most common ways of classifying public fire departments are:

- By the type of jurisdiction in which the department operates
- By whether personnel are paid and fire stations are normally staffed around the clock

Jurisdiction

In this context, the term *jurisdiction* has two distinct connotations. First, it refers to the area served by a fire protection agency. But it also refers to the authority that gives the agency the legal right to provide such services and to take the actions necessary to ensure adequate protection. In some cases, the jurisdiction of a fire protection agency is clearly tied to a level of government, such as a municipal fire department operating within the boundaries of its city and with the authorization of its city government. However, because fires and other emergencies do not recognize territorial and legal boundaries, and often require greater resources than a local government can provide on its own, fire protection agencies are

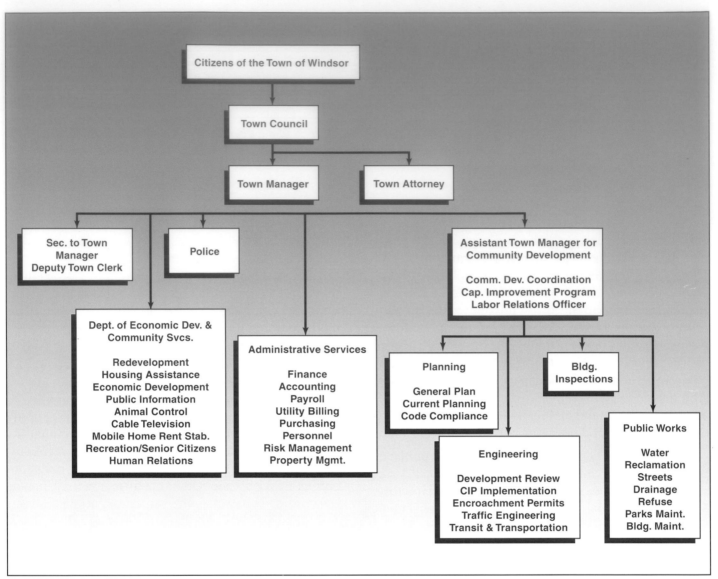

Figure 2.1 Organizational structure of a small town protected by a fire protection district. *Courtesy of Town of Windsor, CA.*

often organized across jurisdictional boundaries. Some of the more common public jurisdictions that provide fire protection include:

- Municipal
- Public safety
- County/parish/borough
- Fire district
- Fire protection district

Municipal

As used here, the term *municipal fire department* refers to a functional division of the lowest level of local government, such as a city, town, township, village, or incorporated or unincorporated community, that is authorized at the state or provincial level to form a fire department. This is the most common jurisdiction for fire depart-

ments. The municipal fire department — whether full-time, part-time, career, volunteer, or a combination — operates as part of the local government and receives funding, authority, and oversight from that body. Typically, the personnel who staff career departments are municipal employees.

Virtually every city in the United States and Canada with a population of more than 100,000 and the majority of cities with populations between 50,000 and 100,000 maintain full-time fire departments. Of those cities and towns with populations of less than 50,000, nearly half maintain full-time fire departments.

As a departmental agency within municipal government, most full-time public fire departments exhibit an organizational structure that reflects the local governmental structure. The department head generally oversees the operation of the department and serves as the principal interface between the fire department and the rest of the municipal government. In most public fire departments in North America, this official carries the title of chief or, in some cases, commissioner. The chief must ensure that the department has an adequate organizational structure and management system, including required policies and procedures, to govern the operation of the department in support of its mission.

The size of the public fire department depends primarily on the population, area of the municipality served, other factors such as special fire protection requirements (heavy industry, use and transportation of hazardous materials, etc.), and level of services to be provided as determined by the local governing body. All departments maintain one or more fire stations — sometimes called *houses* or *halls* — from which personnel and equipment respond, while larger departments may operate several stations throughout their service area as well as separate facilities for administration, training, and other functions. In small departments, personnel may be called upon to serve in multiple roles to provide a full range of services, such as hazardous materials response, technical rescue, emergency medical care, arson investigation, and fire safety/code enforcement inspections. Larger departments may have personnel who specialize in such areas as well as response personnel who are certified as driver/operators of the apparatus they drive. To provide this wide variety of services, larger departments may have administrative and functional subdivisions, such as districts, divisions, battalions, companies, and special squads or teams. These subdivisions may be under the supervision of officers with a variety of titles or ranks such as chief officers, captains, or lieutenants. A small percentage of fire departments use different military ranks/titles such as majors, sergeants, and so on.

Funding to support operation of a full-time, career fire department is part of the municipal budget and is usually obtained through the collection of taxes. However, some communities also charge subscription fees for fire services or bill users for at least part of the cost of providing an emergency response — particularly for emergency medical responses and nonemergency transfers. The department's budget generally is set on an annual basis and must cover all department expenses, including equipment purchases and maintenance, operating expenses, and funding for personnel.

Public Safety

Another type of municipal fire protection agency is the public safety department. Sometimes called *fire bureaus*, these organizations are typically under the direction of a single department head who is responsible for both po-

lice and fire protection within the jurisdiction. Public safety departments resemble combination fire departments in that some of the personnel are full-time career firefighters whose numbers are supplemented by full-time career police officers when there is a fire. Public safety departments usually train and equip their police officers to function as firefighters under the supervision of fire department company officers and command officers who have no law enforcement duties or training.

County/Parish/Borough

The second tier in local government is normally the county, parish, or borough. Fire departments at this level are becoming more common. Often these departments start as part of the mutual aid agreements of communities in the county and through the establishment of shared fire prevention, fire communications, and hazardous materials response plans and systems. Occasionally, departments are consolidated because of shared county facilities, such as county airports or industrial complexes. Such agreements and common facilities may lead to cooperation in the acquisition of specialized equipment, personnel, and other resources. For example, one community may acquire a hazardous materials response unit, while its neighboring community builds a regional training center and while a third town invests in a new mobile command post. Hazardous materials specialists and emergency medical technicians may be strategically located in towns across the county, while a single arson investigator serves on the county staff. In this way, small towns and suburban areas benefit from the availability of sophisticated fire protection resources without each individual community having to bear the expense alone. The county fire department may exist to augment small town and rural fire departments, or it may consolidate them into a single response organization.

Fire District

In some states, a fire district serves the same purpose as the county fire department but is not directly related to a single county, parish, or borough. Fire districts may be formed as a portion of a county or may overlap county lines to serve a special shared need, such as a large manufacturing plant on the border between two counties. In effect, the district is a special government body authorized by the state or province to exist and operate in order to provide fire protection to an area. Generally, the district operates under a board of trustees or commissioners who represent the residents of the district. The board oversees the fire department, administers funding, sets policy, and otherwise determines its operation. Funding may come from a district tax or subscription fee or may be taken from city, county, or state taxes. In most cases, the district is established through a vote of the people living in the district, frequently with board members being elected and taxes approved at the same time. The department itself may have a full-time, paid staff; a volunteer staff; a combination staff; or some stations that function in one way while others function differently, especially when the district absorbs local fire protection organizations during its creation. In some cases, the fire protection organization truly is a department because the district board may be responsible for administering other services, such as rural water delivery and law enforcement. However, in most cases, the district deals almost exclusively with fire protection, fire suppression, hazardous materials incidents, emergency medical services, and related activities. Even so, it is customary to refer to the organization as a fire department although the district may not have other departments.

Unlike municipal fire departments, fire districts do not have the support services provided by a municipal services center for apparatus maintenance, station maintenance, etc. Fire districts must provide these services themselves or contract with private providers.

Fire Protection District

In some states, a fire protection district is less formal than a fire district in that it does not exist as a separate government entity; in others, they are virtually the same. Fire protection districts may be established when a group with shared interests petitions an established fire department to provide fire protection services. For example, the owners of a group of lakeside cabins may find it difficult to obtain fire protection service because they are not an incorporated community and because a volunteer department is impractical since the owners are normally at their cabins only on weekends and during vacations. One option is for them to form a homeowners' association and request a nearby community to provide fire protection services for their cabins. If the community agrees, the town's government officials will sign a contract with the homeowners' association to establish the fire protection district and define the terms and conditions of the services. The town will collect money under the contract, which may then be used to buy additional apparatus or to meet other expenses. The state or province may formally recognize the district and may even provide some funding for the contract through earmarked taxes. In other instances, the only legal recognition will be through the contract itself, with the homeowners' association and community serving as legal entities.

Private Fire Departments

There are two major types of private fire departments. First, some industrial complexes and military installa-

tions may choose to maintain fire fighting resources to protect their property rather than relying solely or partially on the local public fire department for such protection. The second type of private fire protection is a business that owns fire fighting equipment and hires firefighters to provide fire protection for the public under contract with government agencies. There is a third type of private fire department, but this is the smallest category of all types of fire protection services — the private nonprofit fire department.

Industrial Fire Departments

Many commercial facilities, such as oil refineries and airports (both public and private), maintain fire brigades or other emergency response teams (Figure 2.2). There are many reasons for this, including:

- The inability or unwillingness of the local community to provide the needed resources

- The need to have a more immediate response than the local public fire department can or will provide

- The need to protect special hazards that requires capabilities beyond those of the local public fire department

- Remoteness from any public fire department

- Reduced insurance rates

- Reduction of potential liabilities

- Compliance with Federal Aviation Administration regulations at airports

Consequently, these businesses may choose to maintain their own facilities, personnel, and equipment to respond to fires and other incidents. Often, such firms are willing to enter into mutual aid agreements and are generally willing to work with public fire officials to develop fire and haz mat protection plans involving their facilities. Consequently, company officers may be re-

Figure 2.2 Some industrial facilities are protected by private fire brigades.

quired to work with private departments and corporate organizations in order to provide fire protection for these facilities and the surrounding area. Company officers should become acquainted with the facility personnel and procedures that might be involved in such a response.

Military Fire Departments

The U.S. Department of Defense operates more than 200 fire departments on military installations in the continental United States. These departments provide structural fire protection on military installations, airport crash/rescue services, or both. In addition, these military fire departments may also provide fire protection off base under mutual aid agreements with local civilian fire departments.

The Canadian Defense Department oversees military and civilian fire service agencies operating in 35 installations in and around North America. These departments provide structural protection, airfield rescue and fire fighting (ARFF), auto extrication, and hazardous materials response for land-based installations. They also provide fire fighting teams for maritime vessels that carry aircraft. These agencies operate with neighboring communities through mutual aid agreements.

Commercial Fire Protection Services

The private sector is delivering more and more services — from delivering mail to collecting refuse to operating correctional facilities — that were once considered to be government functions. An increasing number of entities are finding it less expensive or more convenient to contract with private industry to provide these services. This includes emergency services. While still not the norm, it is not uncommon for cities to contract with private industry to provide some services that public fire departments provide elsewhere, such as fire, rescue, and emergency medical services. This trend is likely to continue, and public fire departments must realize that their very survival as an entity may depend on their ability to deliver their services to their customers more efficiently.

Airport Fire Departments

Some public, nonmilitary airports depend entirely or partially on the local municipal fire department for fire protection services. However, a significant number of airports have their own fire departments or contract with commercial fire departments for these services. Regardless of how the departments are funded and organized, they must provide both crash/fire/rescue services and structural protection for the buildings on the facility.

Private Nonprofit Fire Departments

These departments operate primarily on a subscription basis — that is, property owners within the area served by the department are offered the opportunity to pay an annual subscription for fire protection services. If a subscriber has a fire, the department responds and extinguishes the fire as any other fire department would. The department will also respond to fires in nonsubscribing properties, but the property owner is then assessed a fee for service that may be as much as ten times the annual subscription. At the time of this manual's publication, there were fewer than two dozen fire departments of this type in the United States.

Personnel

Regardless of which type of fire department is maintained and whether the jurisdiction is public or private, the department must be staffed in order to function. Some firefighters receive pay for their work and are commonly called *career* firefighters while others serve on a strictly voluntary basis. In this context, the term *professional* refers to a level of competence or expertise and may apply equally to those firefighters who are paid for their services and to volunteers. A department may be fully staffed with career personnel, with volunteer personnel, or with a combination of career and volunteer personnel.

Career (Full-Time)

Most larger cities and some private industries operate full-time, career fire departments — that is, the municipality maintains facilities and equipment to support fire protection and employs firefighters and other personnel to provide fire protection and related services. The firefighters are paid, and they work for the department as their principal place of employment. In addition to salary, personnel in career fire departments are likely to receive benefits that may include life and medical insurance, retirements plans, paid vacation and sick leave, and other entitlements. Some or all of the department staff may work for the city under a periodically renewed contract, which is often negotiated on behalf of the workers by a labor union.

Another characteristic of full-time, career fire departments is that their fire stations are staffed around the clock. Emergency response personnel live in the fire stations while they are on duty. Some career departments employ personnel on a part-time basis to supplement the response force during peak emergency periods based on the time of day, the day of the week, or the season. The department may also maintain administrative offices that work more conventional business hours.

Volunteer

Another classification of fire department is the volunteer organization. This type of structure is principally found in smaller towns and rural communities but may be found in remotely located industrial facilities. These organizations operate with volunteers who perform all the required functions without pay. A volunteer organization may operate as a department of the local government, but most are totally independent from government agencies within the areas they serve. In some cases, a town may provide a facility to be used as a fire station and may even buy and maintain fire-suppression equipment. In other cases, the volunteer organization meets its expenses without support from municipal funds. Money may come from donations, subscription fees paid by people in the community, billing for all or part of response costs, and fund-raising events, such as bake sales, pancake breakfasts, dinners, dances, or fairs.

Oversight of the volunteer organization comes from the local entity that supports the department or from an independent association or governing board. However, some volunteer organizations are corporations governed by boards of directors. In most cases, volunteer organizations do not maintain staffed fire stations, and firefighters respond from home or work to emergencies when summoned by pagers, telephone calls, or a community signal. Designated personnel go to the fire station and drive the apparatus to the emergency scene, while others may report to the fire station or directly to the scene. Most communities in the United States provide fire protection through volunteer fire organizations.

Combination

By definition, a *combination department* is one in which some of the firefighters receive pay while other personnel serve on a voluntary basis. These fire departments, whether public or private, function with a combination of both paid personnel and volunteers. For example, a mostly volunteer organization may pay drivers or may pay part of the salary of a dispatcher that they share with law enforcement. A full-time career department may also maintain a cadre of volunteers trained in fire suppression, rescue, emergency medical care, scene control, or other areas. In some combination departments, there are more paid firefighters than unpaid firefighters. In some, the highest ranking officer is a volunteer and exerts primary control over the department; in others, control is exercised by a full-time paid chief. So, the distribution of responsibilities and the relative percentages of paid and unpaid personnel can vary greatly from one combination department to another.

Combination departments provide staffing and receive funding in accordance with the dominant aspect of their organization — that is, combination departments that are operated primarily as full-time, career departments tend to staff their stations around the clock and use budgeted tax dollars to fund their operations, while those that are primarily volunteer organizations tend to have no one or only limited numbers of personnel residing in their fire stations.

Paid-On-Call

Some firefighters work on an on-call basis. Under this method, a firefighter does not reside at the fire station but is summoned to the fire station or emergency scene by means of a telephone call, pager, or community signal (Figure 2.3). Personnel are paid for responding, usually with an hourly wage or with a set fee per response. This approach to compensation may also be used to pay part-time personnel in full-time, paid departments or in combination departments or to pay compensated personnel in volunteer departments. In some cases, departments are actually operated on a paid-on-call basis. Functionally, the paid-on-call department resembles a volunteer organization in that the fire stations are minimally staffed and fire suppression personnel are normally summoned to the emergency scene or fire station by pagers, telephones, or community signals. Fiscally, it resembles a full-time, paid department because most or all paid-on-call department funding comes from a local government agency or association.

Public Safety

In most public safety departments, the fire command/management officers, company officers, and apparatus driver/operators are full-time, career fire personnel, while the firefighters are police officers who are trained and equipped to function as firefighters. In a sense, public safety officers are similar to volunteer firefighters in combination departments. Public safety officers perform their normal police patrol duties until a fire is reported. Then, if they carry their fire fighting personal protective equipment (PPE) in their patrol cars, they respond directly to the fire scene and work under the supervision of a company officer (Figure 2.4).

Purposes of Fire Protection Agencies

Whether a public fire department, an industrial fire brigade, a military fire department, or a private service, all fire protection agencies share several common purposes. Some of the more important purposes include:

Figure 2.3 Some departments use rooftop air horns or sirens to alert their volunteers.

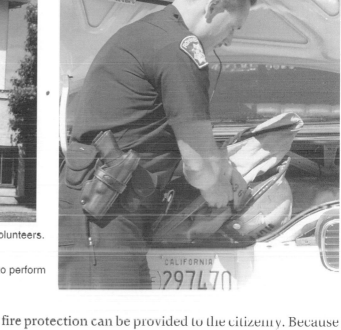

Figure 2.4 Public safety officers are trained and equipped to perform law enforcement and fire protection duties.

- Providing adequately equipped and trained fire suppression capabilities appropriate to customer requirements and reasonable budgetary allocations

- Conducting fire safety and fire prevention programs and other efforts to improve customer awareness

- Investigating fires to determine cause and to detect possible arson

- Coordinating the customer's total fire protection system to include review of new construction and development to ensure that materials and designs provide adequate suppression systems, hydrants, apparatus access, adequate separations, and means of egress

- Providing other emergency services, such as emergency medical care, technical rescue, and hazardous materials response, as required by the customer

- Advising local government in matters of fire protection and public safety, including resources needed and laws and ordinances required to support fire protection and life safety

- Establishing and maintaining agreements with public and private entities for coordinated responses and mutual aid

Response Considerations

Many factors affect the degree to which a fire department is able to provide all of the services required by a community. A primary consideration for most departments is fiscal limitations. Many communities face financial constraints that make it necessary for government leaders to evaluate the extent to which and the methods by which fire protection can be provided to the citizenry. Because fire protection is just one of the many services that a local government's budget must support, government leaders have to determine the distribution of funds to satisfy these different requirements. This frequently results in compromises in the individual services to provide a reasonable overall balance in meeting the community's various needs.

Consequently, one of the roles of the company officer and other fire department leaders is to make the best possible use of available resources. This involves not only protecting personnel and equipment and conserving supplies but also planning that will minimize the level of funding needed to fulfill the department's mission. One of the most common techniques for extending the department budget has two parts. One part is to fund only the minimum number and types of resources needed to deal with those emergencies most likely to occur within the jurisdiction. The other part is to use agreements with other agencies to supplement departmental resources for unusually large or exceptional incidents. These agreements are normally formal, written plans that define the roles of the participants and can be categorized as *automatic aid*, *mutual aid*, or *outside aid* agreements.

Automatic Aid

Automatic aid is a formal, written agreement between fire departments that share a common boundary. Automatic aid occurs whenever certain predetermined conditions occur. For example, automatic mutual aid may be initiated whenever an emergency is reported along a mutual jurisdictional boundary, especially in areas where the actual boundary line is unclear (Figure 2.5). The agreement may provide for automatic aid in the event of any fire involving a given number of alarms. Automatic aid agreements may also be required at specific facilities such as airports, oil refineries, or chemical manufacturing plants (Figure 2.6). A major incident at one of these facilities may virtually assure that the resources of the primary jurisdiction will be exceeded so that any incident involving that facility will lead to an automatic response by other agencies. An adjoining department may automatically assume a backup response role if a company in a neighboring department is deployed.

Mutual Aid

Mutual aid is a reciprocal agreement between two or more fire protection agencies. The agreements may be local, regional, statewide, or interstate so the agencies may or may not have contiguous boundaries. The agreement defines how the agencies will provide resources in various situations and how the actions of the shared resources will be monitored and controlled. Responses under a mutual aid agreement are usually on an on-request basis. As the name implies, on-request assistance is provided only when an agency asks for assistance, such as when its resources are depleted by an unusually large incident or a number of simultaneous small incidents. Under these agreements, the requested agency may, at its option, dispatch the requested aid. But if the agency receiving the request has or is likely to have to commit its resources within its own boundaries, the request for mutual aid may be denied.

There are a number of reasons why fire departments enter into mutual aid agreements. The most common reasons are as follows:

- To allow sharing of limited or specialized resources between neighboring fire protection agencies
- To address the need for neighboring fire protection agencies to assist each other when a response requirement exceeds the primary jurisdiction's capabilities
- To allow departments to meet National Fire Protection Association (NFPA), Insurance Services Office (ISO), and other requirements for staffing, apparatus available, response times, etc., through shared resources
- To provide quicker responses when other departments are closer to the emergency site than the primary jurisdiction's resources
- To define responses for areas on the boundaries between adjacent jurisdictions
- To define response methods for fire protection agencies within a jurisdiction, such as a military base or corporate fire protection agency within a city's limits
- To define response methods for areas that lie between neighboring jurisdictions

As mentioned earlier, a fire department is likely to require the assistance of neighboring agencies for any of several reasons. Adjoining fire departments or districts will sometimes work together to acquire selected apparatus or personnel resources that are required to support their overall mission but whose utilization is limited to the point that none of the individual cooperating departments could justify the expenditure. The departments may fund the resource jointly and share it, or they may agree that one or more of a number of such limited-need resources be acquired by each of the departments and shared with the others.

A department may also require assistance from another because of the size or nature of an emergency.

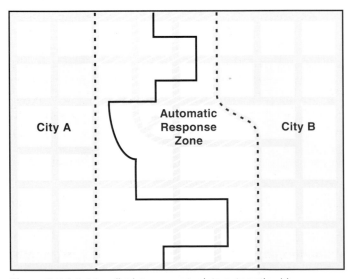

Figure 2.5 Adjoining districts may enter into automatic aid agreements.

Figure 2.6 Automatic aid may be needed at industrial complexes or major airports.

Some fires may involve such a large area or structure that they exceed the response capabilities of the responsible jurisdiction, or an emergency may result in more casualties than the primary jurisdiction can evacuate and treat.

Some occupancies within a jurisdiction may be considered such high-risk facilities that they warrant mutual aid agreements. For example, the facility may store and use substances that could pose a serious health risk to the public. If the facility is located near the boundary of another jurisdiction or if prevailing winds or waterways are likely to transport contaminants into an adjoining jurisdiction, the affected departments may choose to establish mutual aid agreements.

An agency may also require assistance if its resources are deployed at an incident when a second, simultaneous emergency occurs. In effect, a second agency may provide backup response for subsequent emergencies in the event that the primary jurisdiction's resources are already committed.

Company officers may be asked to assist in the development and maintenance of mutual aid plans. At a minimum, these plans should:

- Define roles of each agency, including incident management and chains of command.

- Establish operating guidelines.

- Define lines and methods of communications.

- Include common terminology, references, specifications, adapter requirements, and other factors that may directly affect the effectiveness of the different agencies in working with each other.

- Provide maps, evacuation routes, hydrant locations and data, details of potentially affected systems (sewers, railroads, waterways, etc.), and similar information useful in a response outside of one's jurisdiction.

- Address insurance and legal considerations that may affect the agreement.

- Establish additional nonemergency agreements, such as training and routine communications, as desired.

Additionally, mutual aid plans should undergo periodic review to ensure that they remain current and up-to-date. Both the creation and maintenance of mutual aid agreements are likely to require department personnel to work with other agencies, including their own and other community governments. In some cases, implementation of new city policies or ordinances may be necessary to support the mutual aid agreements. To be most effective, all departments participating in these agreements should conduct joint training exercises so that differences in equipment and procedures may be identified and rectified prior to a major incident occurring.

Outside Aid

Outside aid is similar to mutual aid except that payment rather than reciprocal aid is made by one agency to the other. Outside aid is normally addressed through a signed contract under which one agency agrees to provide aid to another in return for an established payment, which is normally an annual fee but which may be on a per-response basis. Otherwise, the outside agreement differs little from the mutual aid agreement. It should define the conditions under which support will be provided (automatic or on request) and the terms for conducting the response (command and communication, standard operating procedures [SOPs], legal considerations, etc.).

Fire Department Organizational Principles

A fire department is made up of individuals, each with different backgrounds, experiences, and ideas about life. The success of a fire department depends on the willingness of these individuals to put aside their differences and work together for the benefit of the department's customers — the citizens. It is the role of the fire chief to ensure that the fire department fits into the entity of which it is a part and that the department meets the needs of its customers. It is also the fire chief's responsibility to articulate the mission of the department, identify its goals and objectives, and establish the organizational climate within it. It is the company officer's role to see that his company does its part to achieve those goals and objectives. To do this, each company officer must mold a group of individuals into a company — an effective emergency response team (Figure 2.7). Company officers must recognize and respect individual differences, but individual differences must be subordinated to the mission of the department and the company.

All fire chiefs strive for unity within the department. To ensure that department members work together effectively, written operating guidelines are required (Figure 2.8). These guidelines are used to define organizational policy and describe behavioral and performance expectations of department members. However, cooperation among company members is based not only on following organizational guidelines but also on the trust that results from the consistent application of sound organizational principles.

To fulfill the department's mission, fire officers must use sound organizational principles to administer the department, manage its programs, and supervise its per-

Figure 2.7 Company officers must help their subordinates work together effectively.

Figure 2.8 SOPs are a vital part of the organizational structure.

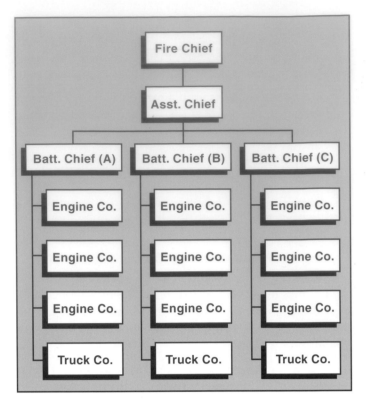

Figure 2.9 A typical small department organization.

sonnel. The most common principles used by well-run fire departments are as follows:

• Unity of command

• Span of control

• Division of labor

• Discipline

Unity of Command

Sound organizational theory dictates that each member should report to only one supervisor. If an employee is required to report to more than one supervisor, the employee and the supervisors may face a number of difficult situations. The most common of these situations are the following:

• The employee follows the last order received, even if the previous order has not been carried out. This leaves the first assignment uncompleted but with the supervisor who ordered it thinking that it has been done.

• The employee executes the task poorly because he is trying to do two (perhaps conflicting) things at once.

• The employee plays the supervisors against each other so that neither supervisor knows exactly what the employee is doing, and the employee may do little or no work. The employee may also spend time working on unauthorized, personal projects.

• The employee becomes frustrated while attempting to follow the conflicting orders of different supervisors and gives up.

As each of these scenarios illustrates, violation of the unity of command principle leads to confusion and frustration by subordinates. Conversely, organizations set up so that each worker reports to only one supervisor provide adequate direction and accountability, which allow all workers to be more productive and efficient.

Although each member reports to one supervisor directly, every member is still responsible to the fire chief indirectly through the chain of command. The *chain of command* is the pathway of responsibility from the top of the department to the bottom, and vice versa (Figure 2.9).

With unity of command, supervisors can break down the work into specific job assignments without losing control. The fire chief can issue general orders that filter through the chain of command and are translated into specific work assignments for the various ranks down through the organizational structure.

[NFPA 1021: 2-2.1]

However, under some circumstances, violations of the unity of command principle are acceptable. During an emergency incident an order from one officer might be superseded by one from another officer. Based on the assumption that the second officer had a good reason for changing the order, the first officer should simply acknowledge the change and carry it out unless the change would put his subordinates in serious jeopardy. If the change would put his subordinates in danger, the new order should be discussed before it is implemented. Otherwise, discussing the reason for the change of orders, and the necessity for violating unity of command, can and should be postponed until the post-incident critique. An example of the need to violate unity of command might be as follows. A group of firefighters has been ordered into a burning building; however, the building has since been deemed to be in danger of imminent collapse. Therefore, anyone who sees the firefighters in or about to enter the danger zone has not only the right but the obligation to countermand the original order. However, whoever countermands the order must immediately notify the officer who issued the original order of the change.

[NFPA 1021: 2-2.2]

Another type of breach, commonly known as an "end run," occurs when a subordinate sidesteps the immediate supervisor and takes a problem directly to an officer higher in the chain of command. While there are circumstances that make it necessary for the subordinate to do this, it is generally an attempt by the subordinate to circumvent the chain of command and is usually destructive to organizational unity and cohesiveness. In most cases, the superior officer should instruct the subordinate to follow the chain of command and take the problem to his immediate supervisor. However, if the immediate supervisor is a part of the problem with which the subordinate is seeking help, the subordinate *may* be justified in going over the supervisor's head. Usually, however, sidestepping actually excludes the person who is best able to solve the problem — the immediate supervisor.

[NFPA 1021: 2-2.4]

For these reasons, it is important for all officers to make their subordinates aware of the proper method of handling problems through the chain of command. In turn, they must be willing and able to handle their subordinates' problems. To reduce the likelihood of being sidestepped in the chain of command, officers should do the following:

- Be available to listen to their subordinates' problems.
- Listen to problems sincerely, and give them due consideration.

- Take action and let the employee know that something is being done.
- If the problem cannot be solved at the officer's level of authority, the officer should take the problem to the next level in the chain of command.

One final deviation from the unity of command principle — and not a violation of it — is what is called *functional supervision*. When firefighters are assigned by their supervisor to perform duties that fall under the authority of another supervisor, the firefighters may be allowed to report to the second supervisor on matters relating to that function. For example, if company personnel are assigned to perform code enforcement inspections, it is probably more efficient for them to direct their questions to and coordinate their activities with the fire prevention supervisor *while they are performing those duties*. At all other times and for all other activities, they still report to their regular supervisor. Obviously, for this arrangement to work, both supervisors must communicate with each other and closely coordinate their activities.

Span of Control
[NFPA 1021: 2-2.1, 2-2.2]

Span of control is the number of subordinates that one individual can effectively supervise. This principle applies equally to supervising the crew of a single company or the officers of several companies under the direction of an incident commander (Figure 2.10). There is no absolute rule for determining how many subordinates that one person effectively can supervise; the number varies with the situation but is usually considered to be somewhere between three and seven. The variables that affect span of control in any given situation are:

- The ability and experience of the supervisor
- The ability and experience of the subordinates

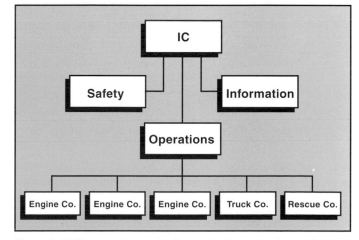

Figure 2.10 Fireground organization maintains span of control.

- The nature of the task
  - Its urgency
  - Conditions under which it must be performed
  - Its complexity
  - Rate at which it must be performed
  - Similarity/dissimilarity to tasks being performed by others
- The proximity of the subordinates to the supervisor and to each other
- The consequences of a mistake

If the tasks being performed are relatively simple and repetitive, all the workers are well-trained and are performing the same or similar tasks, then effective supervision is easier. Further, if the subordinates are working close enough to the supervisor or other coworkers that they can ask questions or get help easily, little supervision may be required. And, if mistakes by the workers are of little consequence, one person can probably supervise the maximum number of subordinates effectively.

Effective supervision is extremely difficult if the tasks being performed are very complex or the workers' level of training is minimal, the workers are performing dissimilar tasks, or the workers are widely separated from the supervisor and each other. Even if these variables are manageable, if the consequences of a worker's mistake could result in someone being injured or killed, the level of supervision required limits the number of subordinates that one person can effectively supervise to the absolute minimum.

[NFPA 1021: 2-2.3]

Examples of the span of control principle can be seen on the fireground. Proper span of control is evident when a company officer supervises the members of one engine company, a strike team leader supervises the five company officers in charge of the engines in a strike team, and a division/sector supervisor commands five strike teams and/or task forces, etc. However, the fireground can also show the effects of allowing span of control to be exceeded. On a major incident, if the incident commander fails to organize the fireground resources in a way that allows authority to be delegated appropriately, attempts to directly control all on-scene units and to make every decision at all levels, he will soon be overwhelmed by the myriad details of the operation. This can produce chaos on the fireground, a breakdown in communication and coordination, and duplication of effort by units "freelancing" at will. The result will be a confused, inefficient operation at best, and perhaps losses of life and property.

The decision to delegate authority to complete a task is often difficult; the officer may feel an obligation or commitment to guarantee that every task is done. There may be a doubt in the officer's mind that the delegated task will be completed in a manner that will meet the standards of the department. Feelings like these are natural and show that the officer is genuinely interested in doing a good job.

When delegating a task, the officer must exercise some discretion to ensure that the assigned employee is *capable of doing the job*. The officer should attempt to pick the right person for the right job.

Delegation of an assignment must be accompanied with appropriate authority and with trust that the individual will achieve the desired results using proper methods. It is difficult for anyone to accomplish a task without being given the necessary authority to complete the assignment.

Another important consideration in the delegation of authority is to make the objective clear to the individual being given the assignment. The officer should describe the task and its relationship to the overall goal or objective. In addition, the officer must make clear what resources are available and what time and safety constraints apply to the assignment.

Most administrators recognize that the span of control has limits and expect authority to be delegated. It is also realized that those accepting delegated authority will make mistakes. As a general rule, when authority is delegated and accepted earnestly, mistakes made by the subordinates should be considered as subjects for training rather than as subjects for discipline.

Division of Labor
[NFPA 1021: 2-2.6]

The division of labor concept — breaking large jobs down into smaller tasks that are assigned to specific individuals — is necessary in the fire service for several reasons: to assign responsibility, to prevent duplication of effort, and to make specific, clear-cut assignments.

To accomplish the work assignments within a fire department, the assignments are divided into groupings. These groupings include the type of task, geographical area, and time. Common divisions in a fire department include emergency services, community services, and departmental services. Within each grouping, subgroups are assigned to meet the requirements of the more specific tasks assigned to the group. A good example is the arrangement of engine and truck companies in the emergency services division. Each company is responsible for performing certain tasks that help meet the general objectives of the shift commander and the department.

Another consideration in division of labor is the number of people needed to accomplish these tasks. Fire departments typically assign teams of firefighters to each company. Each team is responsible for performing the duties assigned to that company.

For the division of labor principle to be effective, all positions within the organization must be clearly defined. Analyzing each position is the key to identifying all the skills and knowledge necessary for that job. Job analysis and job descriptions are critical to assist personnel in performing their many tasks (Figure 2.11). All personnel must know what their specific responsibilities are and understand what is expected of them.

Specialization is an important aspect of the division of labor. Tasks cannot simply be assigned at random, as few people are capable of doing all things well. When making job assignments, consideration must be given to using the best person available for the job. An effective way of handling anticipated work assignments is to train individuals to perform particular jobs (Figure 2.12).

Special training and specific jobs are used extensively in the fire service. Fire departments commonly place emergency work tasks into similar groups and assign personnel and equipment to handle these tasks. This is done by forming special units such as engine, truck, and rescue/EMS companies. Not only are several types of fire companies used for specific purposes, but personnel within a particular company may be trained for specific tasks. Hazardous materials teams are now common in many fire departments and are an example of this task orientation.

Care must be taken to provide adequate cross training so the various company members are able to perform other tasks with proficiency. One of the advantages of cross training is that it enables different fire companies to work together well because each company officer understands the capabilities, requirements, and needs of the other.

Discipline

[NFPA 1021: 3-2.1, 3-2.2]

Traditionally, discipline has been understood to mean correction or punishment. In this chapter, discipline

Figure 2.12 Some firefighters are trained to perform specialized tasks.

FIREFIGHTER—ESSENTIAL DUTIES

The following duties are considered essential for this classification: Drive and operate all fire apparatus and equipment; respond to rescue calls as part of an engine company and administer first aid; operate a variety of tools and equipment related to fire suppression, rescue, and hazardous materials emergency activities; serve as a hose operator in fire fighting situations including laying hoselines, pulling working lines, holding the nozzle to direct the stream of water on the fire, placing, raising, lowering and climbing ladders, and assisting in overhaul and salvage operations; inspect and perform routine maintenance on rescue equipment, fire apparatus, hydrants, hoses, and other support equipment; participate in continuous training in fire suppression, prevention, and inspection through both simulated and on-the-job exercises; operate engine pumping equipment; inspect commercial, residential, and other occupancies for fire hazards and compliance with fire prevention codes and ordinances; conduct fire prevention inspection and education programs; operate communication equipment; learn and study fire department rules and regulations, fire hazards and fire fighting techniques, and related subjects.

Figure 2.11 A typical firefighter job description.

refers to an organization's responsibility to provide the direction needed to satisfy the goals and objectives it has identified. In other words, *discipline* means setting the limits or boundaries for expected performance and enforcing them. This direction may come in the form of rules, regulations, policies and procedures, and standard operating procedures; but regardless of the term used, these rules must define how the department plans to operate. Furthermore, these rules must be clearly written and presented. This does not mean that giving each member a copy of the rules or placing them in each station satisfies the department's obligation to provide direction. The fire department must make a concerted effort to disseminate the information contained in the rules and regulations. Periodic formal training on this topic is critical.

The organization must share its mission statement and objectives with all of its members (Figure 2.13). This will enable all members to know what is expected of them and what must be done to work toward achieving the goals of the department. Discipline may be defined as a teaching method used to enforce the organizational limits.

Department officers must also show their commitment to the goals of the fire department by being fair and honest in the application of rules as well as abiding by the rules themselves. If the administrators are not committed to meeting the organizational goals, they cannot expect commitment from the department members. Company officers must lead by example and model the intent of the organizational goals in order to maintain the proper direction at the company level.

Fire Department Organizational Structure

Everyone has dealt with organizational structures in one way or another. From participating in recreational sports programs to living within family groups, we participate in structured activities daily. Organizational structure is important to the fire service. Teamwork and esprit de corps, quality leadership, effective discipline, and efficient operations are all important to fire service personnel, and the fire department organizational structure must accommodate these traits.

Scalar Organizational Structure
The term used to describe the common organizational structure in the fire service is "scalar." *Scalar* is defined as "having an uninterrupted series of steps" or a "chain of authority." The scalar organization is a paramilitary, pyramid type of organization with authority centralized at the top. Decisions are directed down from the top of the organizational structure through intermediate levels to the base of the structure. Information, in turn, is transmitted up from the bottom through the structure to the positions at the top.

Typically, fire departments are scalar organizations (Figure 2.14). The companies are organized in the scalar manner, the companies fit into a scalar battalion, and so on. However, operations do not always follow the rigid scalar form. In the pure form of the scalar principle of management, there is an unbroken chain — or scale — of supervisors from the top of the organization to the bottom. This chain models the flow of authority, and any action or communication taking place in the group should follow these well-defined lines of authority.

In many cases, direct communications at lower organization levels allows for quicker actions and reactions. So, within this scalar structure, certain decision-making authority is delegated to lower levels, and communication is enhanced.

The true scalar structure is well-suited for dealing with emergency situations for several reasons:

- Span of control is maintained.
- Information is centralized for decision making.
- A functional chain of command is maintained.

Line and Staff
Line and *staff* are terms that refer to the traditional organizational concept that separates fire department personnel into two distinct groups: line personnel — those who deliver emergency services, and staff — those who support the efforts of the line personnel. Typical staff functions are training, logistics, and personnel administration.

However, the traditional role of most fire departments — fighting fire — has changed over the years and today may include EMS, hazardous materials response, fire prevention, and public education. Fire departments have been forced to recruit and/or develop personnel with the specialized knowledge and skills needed to provide these services.

The addition of these new roles has caused the distinction between line and staff functions to become less definite. Company officers have traditionally reported to a battalion chief or other line supervisor during all their emergency activities and routine nonemergency activities. However, it is not uncommon today for company officers to also report to a staff officer when the company is engaged in some specialized activity (code enforcement, public education, etc.) that is under the authority of that particular staff officer. This is sometimes called *functional supervision*. While this may appear to be a

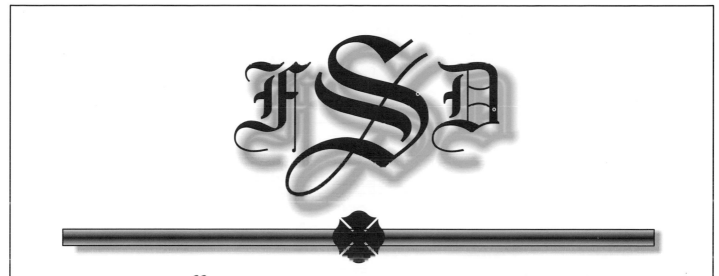

The **Stillwater Fire Department** is dedicated to providing public safety services to our citizens that result in improved quality of life and peace of mind. As a team, we will strive to minimize losses and suffering through emergency service delivery, public education, public information, and community service activities. We will provide our service and treat those we serve and each other in a manner that is honest, fair, and unbiased; honor our heritage, actively participate in our community, and serve with integrity; strive to support the individual development, personal satisfaction, and pride of all members; and endeavor to uphold the unique camaraderie and trust that is the Fire Service.

"Heritage • Service • Pride"

Figure 2.13 A typical fire department mission statement. *Courtesy of Stillwater (OK) Fire Department.*

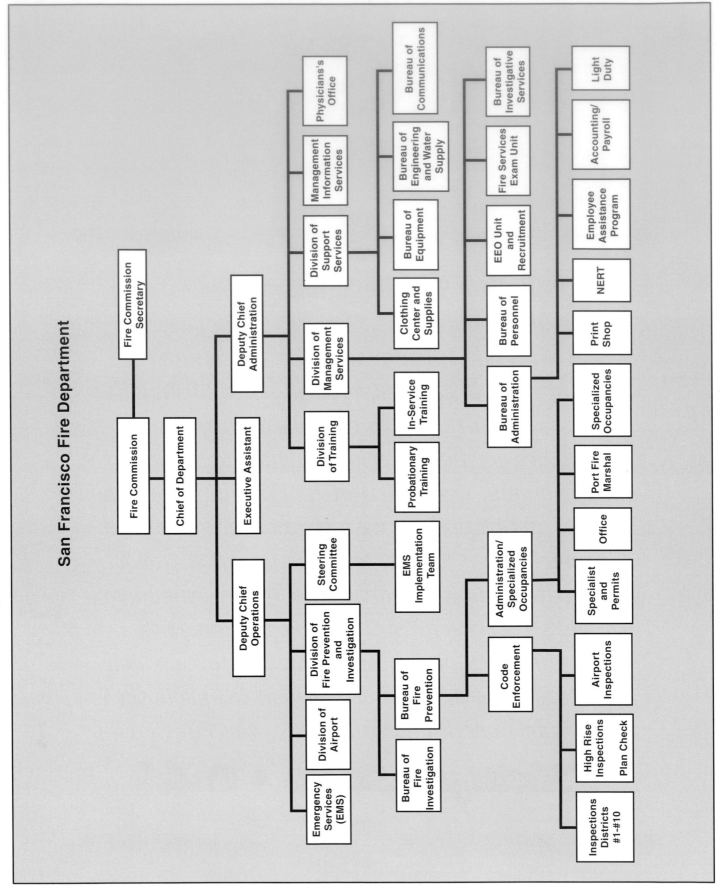

San Francisco Fire Department

Figure 2.14 Organization of a typical large metropolitan fire department. *Courtesy of Al Da Cunha San Francisco (CA) Fire Department (Ret.).*

violation of the unity of command principle discussed earlier, it really is not.

The reason that this apparent overlap of authority works is that it is an organizational decision that is agreed to and supported by all involved. Before company-level personnel are assigned to staff functions, the staff officer must coordinate with the line supervisor to whom the company is assigned. The company officers continue to report to their line supervisor except when they are performing the staff assignment — during which they report to the responsible staff officer (Figure 2.15).

Authority to Implement

Authority refers to the legal ability of an individual to make and implement decisions for which the individual is held accountable. There are two types of authority: centralized and decentralized.

The difference between centralized authority and decentralized authority is the level at which decisions are made. In a centralized authority structure decisions are made by one person at the top of the structure (Figure 2.16). Centralized authority works well in very small organizations, such as a individual fire company, but in larger organizations the leader's span of control may be exceeded unless decision-making authority is delegated. Decentralized authority allows the decisions to be made at a lower level, with the effects of the decisions reported through the structure.

Figure 2.15 Firefighters sometimes have different supervisors for different functions.

Regardless of the level at which decision-making authority is placed, accountability for the decisions is almost always centralized. The chief delegates to officers the authority to make decisions and to implement plans, but the chief is still accountable for any decisions made. As a general rule, no one in a fire department has absolute authority to avoid accounting to a higher authority (even the chief is accountable to the local governing body).

Decentralized authority is basically delegation of authority. But, delegated authority has limits. Decentralization means that authority is granted at different levels *to accomplish specific tasks.* The fire chief might give the authority to make policy changes to an assistant chief while granting authority to service equipment to the company level. The chief may also decentralize the authority to make certain decisions only in specific areas. For example, the chief may dictate what tasks are to be performed but delegate to the company officer the authority to decide when and in what order the tasks are performed.

Decentralization of authority allows for the expeditious handling of most matters. When decisions are made at lower levels in an organization, upper management personnel are freed to concentrate on more important matters. The details resulting from a decision do not have to be reported, but the effects of the decision do. For example, depending upon the size and organizational structure of the department, the chief usually *does not* need to know that the maintenance department is going to replace two pistons and six valves on Engine 7185. However, the chief *may* need to know that an engine will be out of service for an extended period for maintenance.

Ideally, decision-making authority should be delegated to the lowest organizational level possible. However, with decentralization of authority, the possibility of a duplication of efforts exists. To avoid this, department policies must define what decisions can be made and under what conditions. A review system must also be established to ensure accountability and to study the effects of decentralized decisions.

Company Organizational Structure

[NFPA 1021: 2-1.1]

In addition to knowing their department's organizational structure and understanding how they fit into it, company officers must understand how their individual companies work. While each type of company within a single department is structured the same organizationally, the makeup and personality of each individual company may be very different.

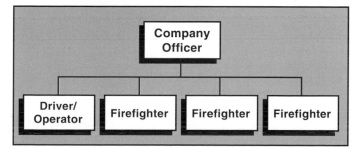

Figure 2.16 A fire company is a highly centralized organization.

Work groups (fire companies, strike teams, task forces, etc.) include individuals with many different attitudes, opinions, and backgrounds. These individuals enter this organizational structure with many expectations. They anticipate making certain contributions and also expect a number of returns from the organization. When a firefighter joins a company, he is expected to display certain specific behaviors. In turn, the firefighter anticipates certain rewards for appropriate behavior. It also follows that inappropriate or unacceptable behavior may be punished by disciplinary action or rejection of the individual by the remainder of the group. Both socially and operationally, the individual and the organization (represented by the other members of the company) have mutual expectations about each other.

Initially, individuals who join a work group go through a process of adjustment. It will take some time to learn more about what constitutes acceptable behavior and what types of results are expected and rewarded. During this period of adjustment, new members of the organization learn their roles and what is expected of them by the other members of the group and the formal leader. Just as every individual in a fire company, the company itself has a personality based on the social structure and values, needs, and objectives of the individuals comprising that company. The personality that the company projects can also impact the attitudes of the administrative personnel toward the company. It is in the company's best interest to project the most positive personality possible — and the person with the most influence over the company's personality is its company officer.

Summary

Without a valid organizational base, fire departments will not be able to fulfill their mission and achieve their goals effectively and efficiently. There are several ways in which fire departments may be organized — public, private, career, volunteer, and combination. Regardless of how they are organized, they all function with the same organizational principles — unity of command, span of control, division of labor, and discipline. These principles are important not only on the fireground but also in the daily routine. For company officers to be effective leaders, they must know and use these principles in both emergency and nonemergency situations.

Chapter 3

Company Officer's Legal Responsibilities and Liability

In our increasingly litigious society, company officers are more vulnerable than ever before to being held personally liable for their actions or inactions. The shroud of legal immunity that once protected firefighters and other public employees from liability has virtually disappeared. Therefore, it is imperative that they know what is legally required of them and know the possible consequences of failing to fulfill those requirements. But knowing what laws apply to them and how those laws are currently interpreted is an ongoing and often difficult task.

As supervisors and public employees, a great many of all company officers' day-to-day actions are dictated by a variety of laws, ordinances, and regulations. Company officers and their subordinates are subject to federal laws, state or provincial laws, local laws, as well as their departments' rules and regulations. To make matters even more difficult, these laws and regulations are not interpreted and applied uniformly in all jurisdictions. Also, the interpretations of many of these laws change over time because of court decisions.

This chapter discusses the issue of governmental immunity and the sources of laws in the United States and Canada that affect how company officers and firefighters do their jobs. Company officers in other countries must research and follow the laws and regulations that apply in their particular jurisdiction. The differences between criminal and civil laws are discussed along with tort liability and negligence. Also discussed are the U.S. and Canadian federal laws and national standards that have the most potential impact on how company officers and firefighters conduct themselves while on duty.

Governmental Immunity

Much of U.S. and Canadian law evolved from English Common Law. One of the most relevant doctrines that made this transition was that of *sovereign immunity*. Originally conceived to protect British royalty, this doctrine holds that "a sovereign is exempt from suit, not because of any formal conception or obsolete theory, but on the logical and practical ground that there can be no legal right against the authority that makes the law on which the right depends." In other words, the king can do no wrong. For centuries, this doctrine has been extended to protect any legally constituted government from liability.

In the U.S. and Canada, the doctrine of sovereign immunity had the effect of holding any federal, state, provincial, or local government immune from liability in tort (noncriminal) cases. The practical effect was that any government entity or agency, or agent thereof, was immune from liability for any action taken in an official capacity, even if negligent. For example, under sovereign immunity, a fire department and its members would be immune from liability if a fire engine ran a red light during an emergency response and collided with a vehicle that had the legal right-of-way (Figure 3.1). Even though such an act would normally be considered negligence under statutory law, the sovereign immunity doctrine would protect the department and its members from liability.

However, in 1946, the United States Government waived its immunity from liability in tort cases and allowed the litigation of such claims in federal courts. Even after the federal government's decision, most states maintained their immunity from suits for tortious injury to persons or property. But in the ensuing decades, the doctrine of sovereign immunity has been eroded through legislative modification and, in some cases, outright abolition by judicial decisions. In some states, the concept of sovereign immunity has been declared unconstitutional.

If and how immunity applies to local jurisdictions, such as counties, cities, and towns, varies because of differences in state law. In some instances, immunity is afforded to local jurisdictions on the basis that their immunity derives directly from the state. However, when a state loses its immunity, its local jurisdictions lose theirs as well. As a result, some incorporated municipalities have been held to be fully responsible for the tortious acts of their agents, just as any other corporation would be.

The concept of governmental immunity from tort claims continues to change. Several mechanisms have been established that reflect the prevailing opinion that government entities should assume some responsibility for the negligence of their agents and employees. The current status of governmental immunity laws in various states is one of the following:

- Doctrine of immunity still in force (but threatened)
- Limited liability by means of a tort claims act
  - Suits may be instituted as prescribed by statute
  - Suits brought before a special tribunal
  - Suits authorized only within prescribed limits
- Legislative claims boards
- Abandonment of immunity
  - Remedy left to the courts as if the state were a private citizen

It is important for company officers and their subordinates to realize that they — as individual employees (including volunteers) — may also be held liable. Although firefighters and other emergency responders are usually immune from liability as long as they act "within the scope of their authority," they may be held liable if they commit an act on the job that is so much at variance with their training and department policy as to constitute gross negligence. For example, if a fire engine arrives at a fire unprepared, such as without water in its tank, the department and the engine crew would probably not be immune from liability (Figure 3.2).

In such cases, plaintiffs must show that the firefighters acted with complete disregard for their training and the department's standard operating procedures. In more than one case, individual firefighters have been found liable under a punitive damages award, intended to actually punish the firefighter for such deviant behavior. In these actions, the government agency is precluded from paying the fine for the individual. Today, the continuing trend away from sovereign immunity is clear, and tort and/or negligence liability applies to governmental functions in all but a few jurisdictions.

To protect themselves and their subordinates from possible liability, company officers must learn what laws and regulations apply to their official activities and how the courts in their area have interpreted these laws (Figure 3.3). Because new laws and regulations are enacted each year, existing ones are revised or repealed, and the courts clarify the applicability and limitations of these laws through their interpretations and rulings, staying current is an ongoing responsibility of all company officers. It is an important responsibility for company officers because they and their subordinates will be held accountable for complying with existing laws, especially in the areas of environmental protection and civil rights, about which they "knew or should have known." In other words, ignorance of the law is no protection.

Figure 3.1 Firefighters *may* be protected from liability for negligence. *Courtesy of Ron Jeffers.*

Figure 3.2 A company officer is served with a notice to appear.

Figure 3.3 Company officers must know what the law requires of them.

Sources of Law

Laws come from many different sources. In general, the major sources of laws in the western world are *common law, constitutional law, statutory law, case law,* and *administrative law.*

Common Law

By definition, common law is that which is not enacted by a legislative body. Common law is based on tradition and custom within a particular country or culture. It may also be influenced by common religious beliefs. As mentioned earlier in this chapter, in the United States, Canada, and many other former British colonies, much of their federal, state, provincial, and local law is based on English Common Law. This body of law was brought to the New World before the American Revolution. Although this law was traditional or customary, much of it has become statutory law through adoption and codification by various legislatures.

Constitutional Law

In both the United States and Canada, the federal constitution is the basic law of the land. All laws enacted by Congress/Parliament, state/provincial legislatures, or local entities must be consistent with the respective federal constitution. The U.S. Supreme Court is the ultimate arbiter in matters of constitutional law in the United States. The U.S. and Canadian constitutions each create a federal governmental structure consisting of three branches — legislative, executive, and judicial (Figure 3.4). State/provincial governments mirror this structure. In general terms, the legislative branch creates laws, the executive branch implements and administers them, and the judiciary branch enforces them.

Statutory Law

Statutory laws are those that are passed by the U.S. Congress, the Canadian Parliament, state or provincial legislatures, or local entities (counties, municipalities, towns, etc.) (Figure 3.5). These laws may be revised or repealed by the body that enacted them. At the federal level, examples of statutory laws are those that created the U.S. Fire Administration (USFA), the Occupational Safety and Health Administration (OSHA), the Environmental Protection Agency (EPA), Equal Employment Opportunity Commission (EEOC), and the Internal Revenue Service (IRS). In Canada, federal agencies similar (but not identical) to those in the U.S. include Occupational Health and Safety (OH&S), Natural Resources, Atomic Energy Commission, Canadian Transportation Commission, National Energy Board, and Revenue Canada. At the state and provincial level, examples of statutory laws are tax codes, motor vehicle laws, gaming laws, hunting regulations, health and safety laws, and those governing the formation of special districts for fire protection, sanitation, recreation, etc. At the local level, examples of statutory laws are ordinances that adopt a particular edition of a building or fire code, establish speed limits on local streets and roads, require business licenses, and adopt the fire department's annual budget (Figure 3.6).

Administrative Law

Within the limits of the statutory laws that created them, government agencies such as OSHA, EPA, and state fire marshal's offices are empowered to create and enforce rules and regulations to implement the legislation for which they are responsible. These rules and regulations have the force of law. The OSHA regulations in the Code of Federal Regulations (CFR), such as 29 CFR 1910.120 (hazardous waste operations), contain the administrative laws that are intended to protect workers —

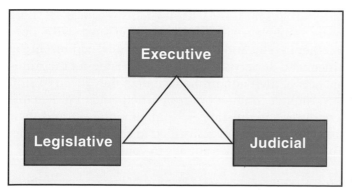

Figure 3.4 Federal and state/provincial governments have three branches.

Figure 3.5 Statutory laws result from legislative action.

Figure 3.6 Local statutory laws dictate traffic rules.

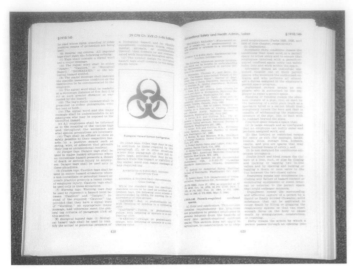

Figure 3.7 Some administrative laws are designed to protect workers.

including firefighters — in high hazard industries (Figure 3.7). Agencies such as EPA, EEOC, and others are empowered by statutory laws to create and enforce administrative laws to fulfill their mission. Obviously, as exemplified by the IRS and OSHA, the power that these enforcement agencies wield can be significant. Company officers and their subordinates are fully accountable under these administrative laws.

Case Law

This is the body of law that is the result of court decisions that affect the way a particular statutory or administrative law is interpreted and applied. Decisions by an administrative agency, such as OSHA, may be appealed to a court. The decision of the court may be appealed to a higher court — all the way to the federal Supreme Court. Once a final decision has been made by a court, the decision becomes a legal precedent that may be used to guide subsequent decisions involving the same or similar laws. However, case law varies widely from jurisdiction to jurisdiction, state to state, etc., so it is extremely important that company officers know how the statutes that directly affect their duties have been interpreted by the courts in their area. The state fire marshal's office and the jurisdiction's attorney can help in this regard.

Criminal and Civil Law

While it is possible for the same act to be a violation of both criminal and civil law, most actionable behavior is either one or the other. The difference between criminal and civil law is relatively simple. Criminal law deals with the rights and responsibilities of individuals toward society; civil law deals primarily with private rights and re-

sponsibilities. *Criminal law* is the means by which society protects itself, and its penalties are sometimes monetary (fines), loss of freedom (jail), or both (Figure 3.8). *Civil law* is the means by which individuals seek redress, usually in the form of monetary damages, from other individuals, corporations, or the government. Criminal actions (prosecutions) are brought by the government (representing the people) against an individual or group. Civil actions (suits) are usually brought by an individual against another individual or group, although there are *class action* suits on behalf of many individuals with a common complaint. Another significant difference between criminal and civil law is the standard of proof required. In criminal actions, the defendant's guilt must be proven "beyond a reasonable doubt"; in civil actions, "a balance of probabilities" or "a preponderance of the evidence" is all that is required.

Criminal Liability

Criminal laws are codified in a criminal or penal code, and everyone within the jurisdiction is subject to these laws (Figure 3.9). Typical criminal laws are those against arson, murder and mayhem, robbery, theft, embezzlement, fraud, kidnapping, extortion, drunk driving, and many other antisocial acts. These laws are intended to protect members of society from acts that would place their lives and/or property in serious jeopardy. While there are numerous federal criminal laws such as those against tax violations, civil rights violations, racketeering, drug trafficking, and a number of other offenses if state lines are crossed, most criminal laws are administered by the individual states. Acts that are defined as criminal vary from state to state; therefore, it is imperative that company officers know the laws of their state or province and how those laws have been interpreted.

Regardless of whether a law is state, provincial, or federal or how it is interpreted in a given state or province, one principle applies in all criminal cases — *an employee cannot be required by his employer to commit a crime*. Therefore, if an employee does commit a crime in the course of his duties, he must answer for it. In some cases, employers will defend employees in a civil action, but they cannot and will not in a criminal action. On the other hand, supervisors are not responsible for the criminal acts of their subordinates unless they failed to stop the criminal conduct or they participated in it. Regardless of the circumstances, company officers and their subordinates are never justified in committing a crime. This principle applies equally to volunteers.

Civil Liability

The basis for all civil law is the fact that anyone, including individuals, corporations, associations, government agencies, and even convicts in prison, has the right to sue anyone else. There need only be an unresolved issue and someone to be held accountable. Civil actions can involve any claim of loss (usually financial) and may be based on failure to perform a service or failure to exercise due caution. If a carpenter fails to perform work for which he was paid, the person who hired him can sue to recover the money paid and, perhaps, punitive damages as well.

Punitive damages are intended to *punish* the offender. If someone's car is damaged by someone else's recklessness or carelessness, the person suffering the damage can sue the other party for the cost of repairs, medical expenses if an injury resulted, rental car expenses, etc. Employees who feel that they have been sexually harassed can sue the offender for damages even if the plaintiff suffered no monetary loss. However, most civil actions against fire departments are related to tort liability.

Tort Liability

A *tort* is a civil wrong or injury. The main purpose of a tort action is to seek payment for property damaged or destroyed, personal injuries, or lost income. The following elements must exist for a valid tort action:

- The defendant must owe a legal duty to the plaintiff.
- There must be a breach of duty; that is, the defendant must have failed to perform or to properly perform that duty.
- The breach of duty must be a proximate cause of the accident or injury that resulted.
- The plaintiff must have suffered damages as a result.

The first element (duty) is relatively easy to establish in a fire-related tort because the department has jurisdiction over the fire suppression, rescue, and related activities at the fire scene. Duty is also relatively clear regarding the delivery of medical aid and in the area of emergency response to hazardous materials incidents.

The question of causation may be more difficult to establish. A *proximate cause* is one that in a naturally continuous sequence produces the injury and without which the injury would not have occurred. Therefore, *breach of duty* does not have to be the only cause; in fact, most accidents are the result of multiple factors. However, juries have been known to view the issue of proximate cause very liberally when the injuries are substantial or emotionally charged, such as when a child is badly injured. If a jury is searching for a "deep pocket" (defendants with substantial assets), it may be satisfied with a tenuous connection between cause and effect, straining the proximate cause criterion.

The fact that the plaintiff has suffered damage is often readily apparent in accident cases (Figure 3.10). As mentioned earlier, damages may be in the form of repair or replacement of property, medical expenses, or lost income. However, the dollar value of these damages may be the most contentious issue in the court proceeding.

Negligence

Negligence — breach of a legal duty — is the major issue in most tort liability cases. *Negligence* is the failure to exercise the same care that a reasonable, prudent, and careful person would under the same or similar circumstances. If the person possesses a greater amount of expertise, then his legal duty is proportionately greater. Therefore, the standard of care for which an EMT would be responsible is that which a reasonable, prudent, and careful EMT would be expected to meet and not that of a paramedic or doctor.

Figure 3.8 Violations of criminal law may result in incarceration.

Figure 3.9 Criminal laws apply to everyone.

Figure 3.10 Damage to personal property is usually apparent.

One of the key questions in negligence is the adequacy of performance. There are two ways in which one can be judged negligent: wrongful performance (misfeasance) or the omission of performance when some act should have been performed and was not (nonfeasance).

Standard of care. A critical issue in negligence liability is the care with which the company officer's responsibilities are discharged. If conduct or performance falls below a reasonable standard of care, then the responsible persons and/or organizations may be held liable for injuries and damages that resulted from such conduct. While there are factors that may limit company officers' ability to act, they have a responsibility to act in a manner that is reasonable, based on the information at hand and the resources available. When a potentially hazardous condition exists, the reasonableness of action must take into account the following factors, particularly when resources are not available to correct all such conditions:

• Gravity of harm posed by the condition

• Likelihood of harm

• Availability of a method and/or equipment to correct the situation

• Usefulness of the condition for other purposes

• Burden of removing the condition

Many items of information may be brought into court to aid in establishing the prevailing standard of care. Some of the strongest types of evidence are national consensus standards (NFPA, ANSI, etc.) and the department's own guidelines and policies. A reasonable and prudent person would be expected to follow these guidelines. Sources of information that may help to establish the standard of care include:

• Agency directives and policies

• Directives of a superior agency (legal mandates)

• Guidelines and policies of other agencies (locally accepted practices)

• Guidelines and standards developed by professional organizations (such as NFPA)

• Professional texts and manuals (such as IFSTA manuals)

• Professional journals

• Research publications

• Opinions of expert witnesses

Personal Liability

The duty owed to the public for reasonably safe care extends to all parties responsible for abating hazardous situations and delivering emergency care. This includes individual employees of public agencies and private contractors. Basically, everyone has an obligation to conduct themselves in a manner that does not cause harm or further injury to any other person. Anyone who violates this general duty of care may be liable for damages.

If a court or jury decides that an individual is liable, then a judgment of damages can be returned against the individual. Recovery of punitive or exemplary damages is one reason for suing an individual employee, especially when the public agency is prohibited from paying such damages. However, as a practical matter, government employees are not often held responsible for payment of awards. Because an individual's assets are small compared to those of the government, the "deeper pockets" are more likely to be targeted for recovery of damages. Nevertheless, being named as a defendant in a lawsuit is a serious matter.

Fireman's Rule

At the opposite end of the liability spectrum is the question of whether a property owner is liable for a firefighter's injuries suffered while fighting a fire resulting from the property owner's negligence. In most jurisdictions, the courts have held property owners immune from liability because of the so-called "Fireman's Rule." This doctrine holds that firefighters, rescuers, and other emergency responders know the risks involved and are trained to deal with those risks; therefore, they are not entitled to redress from the property owner for injury suffered as a result of performing their duty (Figure 3.11). The exception to this doctrine is if the injury was the result of a crime, such as arson, or of the property owner's gross negligence or willful and wanton disregard for the firefighter's safety. For example, if the property owner knew that his burning building contained explosives but failed to inform the firefighters of this, he would probably be held liable for any damages if firefighters were injured by a subsequent explosion.

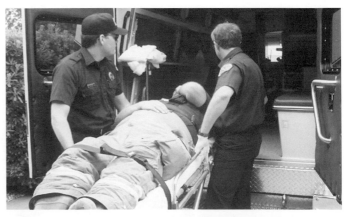

Figure 3.11 In most cases, injured firefighters may not sue the property owner for damages.

Federal Laws

As supervisors and public servants, company officers have particular interest in a number of federal laws. Because these laws are of such importance to the discharge of a company officer's duties, it is assumed that they know these laws or that they should know them, and they may be held personally liable for failing to follow any of these laws. There may also be state laws that deal with the same or similar areas, but it is beyond the scope of this manual to discuss the specific variations in state laws. Because state laws may be more or less restrictive than federal laws in a given area, company officers should learn what laws are applicable in their jurisdictions, how those laws are interpreted locally, and what those laws require of them. The federal laws that are of significance to most company officers are those that deal with protecting health and safety, the environment, and their subordinates' employment rights.

The major health and safety laws are those of the Occupational Safety and Health Administration (OSHA). The major environmental laws are those of the Environmental Protection Agency (EPA). The major laws dealing with employment rights are those in Title VII of the Civil Rights Act of 1964, the Equal Employment Opportunity Commission (EEOC), the Americans with Disabilities Act (ADA), and the Fair Labor Standards Act (FLSA).

Occupational Safety and Health Administration (OSHA)

As mentioned earlier in this chapter, the OSHA regulations for which company officers are responsible are contained in Chapter 29, "Labor," of the *Code of Federal Regulations* (Figure 3.12). This chapter contains regulations that are designed to protect the safety and health of all workers — including firefighters. Section 1910. 120 of this chapter covers training requirements and emergency response to hazardous materials incidents (Figure 3.13). Section 1910.134 covers operations that require the use of self-contained breathing apparatus (Figure 3.14). Along with NFPA 1500, *Standard on Fire Department Occupational Safety and Health Program*, this section is the basis for the "two-in/two-out rule" for interior fire attack and has wide application to many fire department activities. Section 1910.146 covers operations in confined spaces. However, a confined space may be a tank, bin, grain elevator, trench, elevator shaft, or a collapsed structure. Obviously, this section covers many of the emergency activities in which fire companies become involved. Therefore, it is extremely important that company officers be familiar with its requirements. Company officers are responsible for knowing and following all of these regulations.

Environmental Protection Agency (EPA)

The EPA regulations protecting the environment are contained in Chapter 40, "Protection of Environment," of the *Code of Federal Regulations* (Figure 3.15). These laws and regulations deal with how hazardous substances are stored and shipped. They also contain regulations designed to protect the environment by governing how contaminants are to be contained, cleaned up, and disposed of. Company officers come under these regulations whenever they must deal with releases of contaminants into the environment. Company officers and their subordinates can be held personally liable if they fail to follow these regulations during an incident. For example, if company members fail to contain a spilled

Figure 3.12 OSHA regulations are contained in the *Code of Federal Regulations*.

Figure 3.13 29 CFR 1910.120 contains training requirements for response to hazardous materials incidents.

Figure 3.14 Confined space requirements are found in 29 CFR 1910.146.

Figure 3.15 EPA rules are found in Chapter 40.

Figure 3.16 Contaminants must not be washed into sewers or storm drains.

contaminant and allow it to run into and contaminate a waterway, they can be held liable. Likewise, if they simply flush a contaminant down a sewer or storm drain, instead of containing it and disposing of it as required, they may be held liable (Figure 3.16). The point is that, for their own protection, company officers must know what is legally required of them.

Title VII

The Civil Rights Act of 1964 was the most comprehensive legislation of its type in U.S. history. From a public employment perspective, one of the most important parts of the act is Title VII. The intent of this landmark legislation was to eliminate discrimination on the basis of race, color, national origin, religion, and sex (gender). In 1967, age (40 - 70) was added to this list, and in 1978, pregnancy was added.

Title VII, Presidential Executive Orders, and court decisions based on the act, combined to place two obligations on employers — to not discriminate in employment and to eliminate the present effects of past discrimination. The first obligation was to ensure that everyone had an equal chance to be hired based on qualification. The second obligation was to take positive steps to seek out, recruit, select, develop, reward, and retain individuals who were formerly denied employment opportunities because of their race, color, national origin, religion, gender, or age. To enforce these and other antidiscrimination laws, the act created the Equal Employment Opportunity Commission (EEOC).

Equal Employment Opportunity Commission (EEOC)

The EEOC was charged with protecting the rights of all workers — especially those in what are called *protected classes*. Under EEOC regulations there are several protected classes — women, minorities, workers over age 40, and those with disabilities. It is illegal to discriminate in the recruitment, selection, promotion, or termination of anyone in one of these classes. One of the EEOC's first actions was to draft the administrative laws necessary to create and implement *affirmative action*.

Affirmative Action

This program was intended to increase the number of women and minorities hired into jobs that were formerly occupied by white males exclusively. Affirmative action does *not* mean that employment standards have to be lowered. It only requires that the standards for recruitment, selection, and promotion be *essential* for the work. Historically, there have been four primary areas of employment discrimination — disparate treatment, adverse impact, sexual harassment, and reasonable accommodation.

Disparate treatment. Also called *differential treatment*, this simply means treating an applicant or employee differently than those of another race, gender, religion, etc. Some examples of disparate treatment might be the following:

- Asking a female applicant different questions than male applicants are asked

- Denying employment to an older applicant because he *might* be harder to supervise

- Denying employment to a single mother because she *might* need time off to care for a sick child

- Denying employment to a woman because she is pregnant

- Requiring more or less of an employee than is required of those of a different race

Adverse impact. This type of discrimination occurs when an employer uses a test or other screening device that is not intended to discriminate but that adversely affects members of one of the protected classes more than other applicants or employees. Some examples of adverse impact might be:

- Requiring a high school diploma may affect older applicants because fewer of them finished high school. Doing so may also affect members of some minority groups.

- Requiring EMT, Firefighter I, or other professional certifications may affect single mothers who cannot attend these classes because of child-rearing demands.

- Using tests written in English may affect Hispanics, Asians, and other minorities.

- Minimum height and weight requirements may affect more women than men and more Hispanics and Asians than Caucasian men (Figure 3.17).

- Performance tests that involve lifting, jumping, and climbing (in excess of the actual job requirements) may affect women, older applicants, and disabled applicants (Figure 3.18).

Employers are required by EEOC regulations to use employment standards and screening devices that are directly related to performing the job successfully. Any standard or device that adversely affects a greater percentage of those in a protected class than it does other applicants or employees must be *proven* by the employer to be job-related.

Sexual harassment. One of the obvious differences between firefighters today and those of a generation ago is *gender*. Departments that employ at least one female firefighter are now the rule, rather than the exception. Title VII specifically prohibits gender-based discrimination, and the courts have ruled that on-the-job harassment is a form of discrimination.

Overt sexual harassment involves unwanted and unwelcome sexual behavior toward a worker by someone who has the power to reward or punish the worker. A stated or implied promise of a reward (promotion, salary increase, etc.) for sexual favors or a penalty (demotion, termination, etc.) for a refusal is clearly sexual harassment and is illegal under Title VII. The fact that sex between a worker and a supervisor or employer was *consensual* does not mean that it was necessarily *welcome*. If the worker consented because of an implied threat of punishment for not cooperating, it is still sexual harassment under the law. However, the harassment does not have to involve sexual intercourse. It can be any

of a number of unwanted and unwelcome acts — touching, fondling, or rubbing one's body against a subordinate's. It can even be sexually explicit language or gestures. But on-the-job behavior does not have to be sexual in nature to be considered harassment.

Supervisors (male or female) who refer to their subordinates of the opposite sex in derogatory, vulgar, and/or sexual terms are engaging in sexual harassment. For example, if a male supervisor frequently berates his female subordinates by referring to them as "bimbos" or "chicks," he is engaging in sexual harassment. Likewise, when a male worker makes a mistake, if his female supervisor rolls her eyes and throws up her hands in mock frustration and shouts, "Men!" she is also engaging in sexual harassment. But, not all sexual harassment involves supervisors and their subordinates — it sometimes involves peers.

If male workers display sexually explicit or suggestive pictures in the workplace, frequently make remarks about a female coworker's anatomy, frequently use profane language or tell "dirty" jokes, they may be engaging in sexual harassment. If male firefighters frequently berate a female firefighter's ability or frequently play practical jokes on her, they may be engaging in sexual harassment. If the female firefighter tells them that this behavior offends her and they continue it, then they *are* engaging in sexual harassment. Company officers have a responsibility to stop such behavior within their company.

Essentially, any overt or covert gender-related behavior that creates a hostile work environment is considered to be sexual harassment under Title VII and is against the law. Also, if a company officer is aware (or should have been aware) of this behavior and allows it to continue, the company officer is also engaging in sexual harassment.

Reasonable accommodation. Under the EEOC regulations, employers are required to do what is *reasonable* to accommodate their employees' differences. Among the differences that must be accommodated, if reasonably possible, are religious differences, gender-based differences, and differences based on permanent physical or mental impairment.

We are a diverse society made up of men and women of various races, religions, and nationalities. Some religions require their adherents to keep the Sabbath — that is, they cannot work from sunset on Friday until after sunset on Saturday. If it is reasonable, these individuals should be allowed to adjust their hours of work to accommodate their religious obligations. Many fire stations that were originally designed and constructed to house men only are now occupied by both male and female

Figure 3.17 Height requirements may be discriminatory.

Figure 3.18 Unrealistic screening devices are discriminatory.

firefighters. Many of these stations do not have separate toilet and shower rooms or separate dormitories, so these facilities must be shared. Some reasonable means of accommodating men and women sharing these facilities, such as reversible signs for lavatory doors saying, "Occupied/Unoccupied," or something similar must be found (Figure 3.19). Portable walls may be used to partition common dormitories into sleeping cubicles that afford a greater degree of privacy. When new stations are built or existing ones are significantly remodeled, separate facilities should be included. Under the Pregnancy Discrimination Act of 1978, female firefighters must be given the same pregnancy leave and maternity leave benefits as female workers in other professions. It is still unclear whether on-duty female firefighters must be allowed to take work breaks in order to breast-feed their babies in the fire station.

The point of the Title VII legislation is that employers should make every reasonable effort to accommodate the differences among their employees. Exactly what constitutes "reasonable" accommodation in any given situation is unclear and will remain so until the courts define it through their decisions. Years after the Civil Rights Act was passed, the reasonable accommodation requirements relating to workers with physical or mental disabilities were incorporated into a separate body of legislation, the Americans with Disabilities Act (ADA).

Americans With Disabilities Act (ADA)

The Americans with Disabilities Act of 1990 was intended to reduce or eliminate discrimination against disabled persons. The law did so by requiring "reasonable accommodation" for those with permanent disabilities. A temporary disability, such as drug or alcohol abuse or even a broken limb, does not qualify. In those businesses and government buildings where the ADA applies, reasonable accommodation means that existing barriers to access must be removed, that barriers not be included in new construction, and that auxiliary aids be provided for people with vision, speech, or hearing impairments or with any other physical or mental impairment that limits activity. However, the ADA does not apply to all businesses and groups; the federal government, Native American tribes, and private clubs are exempt. In general, the act's requirements include two major categories — *public accommodation* and *employment*.

Public Accommodation

Most retail and service businesses are considered to be public accommodations according to the act. Typical public accommodations are hotels and motels, restaurants, grocery stores, retail shops, offices, and yes, fire stations (Figure 3.20). To comply with ADA regulations, these establishments may have to provide entry/egress ramps, doorways and corridors that are wider than standard ones, lever-operated door hardware, grab rails in bathrooms, and telephones accessible to those in wheelchairs (Figure 3.21). Any business, regardless of size, that is considered to be a public accommodation must comply with the regulations — provided that compliance is not "too expensive, disruptive, or difficult, *and* if reasonable efforts have been made to comply." The primary way that company officers may become involved in the public accommodations category of ADA regulations is if they must specify the exit requirements for a public building or if they are asked to help design a new fire station or plan the remodeling of an existing one. However, company officers may be directly involved in the application of ADA regulations if they are part of the process of hiring new employees.

Figure 3.19 Gender differences must be accommodated.

Figure 3.20 Fire stations are considered *public accommodations*.

Figure 3.21 A typical ADA requirement.

Employment

Company officers are bound by ADA employment regulations and may be held personally liable for failure to comply with them. The essence of the employment category of ADA is that employers cannot discriminate against qualified applicants because of their disabilities; however, the employment regulations only apply to organizations with 15 or more full-time employees. The disabled must have equal access to employment opportunities, promotions, and fringe benefits. This may mean that a hearing-impaired applicant may have to be provided with an interpreter (signer) for the employment interview. However, ADA *does not* require that unqualified or underqualified applicants be hired. ADA regulations require that the most qualified applicant, based on education, experience, and ability, be hired.

The central question is: Can a disabled applicant perform the essential job functions with "reasonable accommodation?" Reasonable accommodation may mean changing the working environment and/or the way the job is performed — such as by providing work surfaces that are at wheelchair height and putting necessary switches and controls within reach of someone in a wheelchair. It may mean moving a job function to a ground-floor office if there is no elevator. Reasonable accommodation may also mean rewriting the job description to eliminate nonessential functions that a disabled person could not perform — but it does not require that essential parts of the job be assigned to another worker in order to accommodate a disabled one.

Company officers may become involved in the employment category of ADA in two ways — if they are tasked with redesigning a working environment to accommodate a disabled employee or if they are involved in the employment interview process. The latter is the more likely scenario and the more challenging one. During an employment interview, an applicant cannot be asked about the following:

- Whether the applicant is disabled

- The nature of the applicant's disability

- The extent of the disability

- The applicant's worker's compensation history

- The applicant's possible need to take time off for treatment

After discussing the job description and job requirements with the applicant, the interviewer can ask the applicant if he can do the job without accommodation. If the answer is "no," then the nature and extent of accommodation needed may be explored. The applicant may

Figure 3.22 Some outside training is covered by FLSA.

be required to demonstrate his ability to do the job. However, the applicant cannot be required to undergo a medical examination until after a job offer has been made — and then only if all other applicants must do the same.

Fair Labor Standards Act (FLSA)

While not part of the Civil Rights Act or Title VII, FLSA regulations are a very important body of federal law for all company officers in career departments with five or more employees. The Fair Labor Standards Act of 1938 guaranteed that workers in the private sector would be paid overtime at time and one-half if they worked more than forty hours in one week. However, FLSA did not apply to state and local public employees until a decision by the U.S. Supreme Court in 1985.

Because of the atypical work schedules of police and firefighters, Congress passed an exemption to the 40-hour rule for local public safety agencies. The FLSA workweek for police was set at 43 hours and for firefighters, 53 hours. EMS personnel are also covered by FLSA if they are an integral part of a public fire protection or police agency, but volunteer firefighters, rescue, and EMS personnel are not. Some training activities outside of the normal work schedule are covered by FLSA, and others are not (Figure 3.22). A fire department's executive and administrative personnel (management) are not covered by FLSA because they are usually not entitled to overtime pay.

While company officers are rarely involved in the administration of FLSA regulations, it is critical that they have some understanding of what the regulations require. It is also important that company officers keep accurate records of who was on duty at any given time and what their assignments were.

National Standards

There are a number of industry associations and organizations that develop and publish standards and information that directly relate to many fire service activities. While these standards and other publications do not have the force of law unless adopted by the jurisdiction's governing body, they are recognized as authoritative documents. In tort liability cases, these publications may well be used to establish the standard of care required. This means that fire departments and their personnel may be found to be liable if they failed to follow these standards — even if not adopted locally. Most of the national consensus standards that relate to fire service activities are developed by either the National Fire Protection Association (NFPA), the American National Standards Institute (ANSI), and those approved by the Standards Council of Canada (SCC).

National Fire Protection Agency (NFPA)

The majority of the national consensus standards that fire departments use are developed and published by NFPA (Figure 3.23). When the need for a standard is recognized, the association invites a number of volunteers with expertise in that field to form a committee to develop the draft of a standard. The completed draft is then made available to the public for review and comment. The public comments are reviewed by the committee, and they may or may not be incorporated into the finished document. The final version of the standard is then submitted to the NFPA general membership for adoption. Although there are hundreds of NFPA standards, some of the ones used most often by fire departments are the following:

- NFPA 1, *Fire Prevention Code*
- NFPA 49, *Hazardous Chemicals Data*
- NFPA 70, *National Electrical Code®*
- NFPA 101®, *Life Safety Code®*
- NFPA 704, *Identifications of the Hazards of Materials*
- NFPA 901, *Standard Classifications for Incident Reporting and Fire Protection Data*
- NFPA 921, *Guide for Fire and Explosion Investigations*
- NFPA 1001, *Fire Fighter Professional Qualifications*
- NFPA 1002, *Fire Department Vehicle Driver/Operator Professional Qualifications*
- NFPA 1003, *Airport Fire Fighter Professional Qualifications*

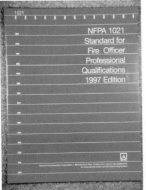

Figure 3.23 NFPA standards are important benchmarks for the fire service.

- NFPA 1021, *Fire Officer Professional Qualifications*
- NFPA 1031, *Professional Qualifications for Fire Inspector*
- NFPA 1033, *Fire Investigator Professional Qualifications*
- NFPA 1035, *Public Fire and Life Safety Educator Professional Qualifications*
- NFPA 1041, *Fire Service Instructor Professional Qualifications*
- NFPA 1051, *Wildland Fire Fighter Professional Qualifications*
- NFPA 1061, *Public Safety Telecommunicator Professional Qualifications*
- NFPA 1403, *Live Fire Training Evolutions*
- NFPA 1404, *Fire Department Self-Contained Breathing Apparatus Program*
- NFPA 1410, *Training for Initial Fire Attack*
- NFPA 1500, *Fire Department Occupational Safety and Health Program*
- NFPA 1521, *Fire Department Safety Officer*
- NFPA 1561, *Fire Department Incident Management System*
- NFPA 1581, *Fire Department Infection Control Program*
- NFPA 1582, *Medical Requirements for Fire Fighters*
- NFPA 1600, *Disaster Management*
- NFPA 1901, *Automotive Fire Apparatus*
- NFPA 1906, *Wildland Fire Apparatus*

There are many other NFPA standards that relate to specific areas within the field of fire protection. Each one is important in its own way. Company officers should familiarize themselves with the complete list of NFPA standards and study in detail those that specifically apply to their responsibilities. Most U.S. fire departments maintain a complete set of current NFPA standards. Copies of standards may be obtained by writing to the National Fire Protection Association at 1 Batterymarch Park, P.O. Box 9101, Quincy, MA 02269-9101 or by calling 1-800-344-3555.

American National Standards Institute (ANSI)

Similar to the NFPA process, the American National Standards Institute system produces voluntary consensus standards. However, the more than 11,000 ANSI standards address materials and equipment in a wide variety of fields — not just fire protection. Some of the ANSI standards that are most relevant to the fire service are:

- Z41, *Personal Protective Footwear*
- Z87.1, *Eye and Face Protection*
- Z88.2, *Respiratory Protection*
- Z89.1, *Helmets and Protective Headgear*

Obviously, there are thousands more ANSI standards, but these are the ones that are most often referenced in fire service equipment specification documents. For more information about ANSI standards, write to the American National Standards Institute at 1430 Broadway, New York, NY 10018, or call (212) 642-4900.

Standards Council of Canada (SCC)

While many Canadian fire service agencies use the NFPA professional qualifications standards for training and certification — either as written or as reference material for locally written standards — none are *law* in Canada. ANSI standards are recognized in Canada but are normally used as references in Canadian codes. For automotive fire apparatus, NFPA standards may be used, but those of Underwriters Laboratories of Canada (ULC) are used more often because ULC does testing and certification but NFPA does not. In general, standards approved by SCC are used. These standards may be developed by Canadian Standards Association (CSA), Underwriters Laboratories Incorporated (ULI), Underwriters Laboratories Canada (ULC), Canadian General Standards Board (CGSB), Bureau de Normalisation du Quebec (BNQ), Transport Canada (TC), and other agencies.

Summary

The increasing number of lawsuits against public agencies and their employees make it imperative that company officers know the laws and regulations that apply to them. They must know the federal, state/provincial, and local laws covering emergency operations, environmental protection, and civil rights. Limited immunity from tort liability may or may not exist for company officers performing their official duties, but they should not count on it. While company officers are generally not liable for the illegal actions of their subordinates, if the company officer knew or should have known about such activity — and permitted it to continue — the company officer is also culpable. Company officers need not fear doing their jobs, but they should be aware that they are accountable for anything that they do or fail to do.

This chapter provides information that will assist the reader in meeting the following job performance requirements from NFPA 1021, *Standard for Fire Officer Professional Qualifications*, 1997 edition. The colored portions indicate the topics addressed in the chapter. The numbers of the job performance requirements are also noted directly in the sections of text where they are addressed. Those in the following list that are denoted with an asterisk (*) are global in nature and are covered by reading the chapter in its entirety.

Fire Officer I

2-1.1* **General Prerequisite Knowledge**. The organizational structure of the department; departmental operating procedures for administration, emergency operations, and safety; departmental budget process; information management and record keeping; the fire prevention and building safety codes and ordinances applicable to the jurisdiction; incident management system; socioeconomic and political factors that impact the fire service; cultural diversity; methods used by supervisors to obtain cooperation within a group of subordinates; the rights of management and members; agreements in force between the organization and members; policies and procedures regarding the operation of the department as they involve supervisors and members.

An understanding of the elements of group dynamics is vital for company officers because there is a direct connection between informal group support and formal group success or failure. A company officer's role in the group becomes one of meshing the goals of the formal and informal groups. In pursuing this role, company officers influence group behavior to meet the goals of both the company and the informal group.

This chapter first defines what groups are, and then it discusses group dynamics, Maslow's Hierarchy of Needs, and Vroom's V.I.E. Theory. Also discussed are "strokes and stamp collecting" and cultural diversity as a group factor.

Groups Defined

Society is composed of a multitude of formal and informal groups, and fire departments are a reflection of the society of which they are a part. A fire company can be described as a unit or subdivision of a fire department or simply as an organized group of firefighters. For purposes of this discussion, a *group* is defined as two or more persons who interact with regard to common goals; the goals may or may not be explicitly stated.

The explicitness of the stated goals indicates the formality of the group. Formal groups usually define common goals in writing. A fire company is a formal group of firefighters who interact to meet common goals as outlined by departmental policy and its mission statement. Informal groups, on the other hand, define common goals informally. A friendship can be described as an informal group: two persons who interact with the common goal of friendship.

Within each formal group, it is common for informal subgroups to form. For instance, two coworkers in a fire company may form an informal group with the unstated goal of mutual friendship. Many potential informal subgroups exist within each formal group. These subgroups

are limited only by the common interests of the individual members of the group. Informal groups most often form around common interests such as hobbies, political interests, social interests, religious beliefs, or sports activities (Figure 4.1). Research on formal and informal groups has revealed two important facts:

* Informal subgroups form within all formal groups.

* The informal subgroup may have greater influence on the productivity and success of the formal group than does any other factor.

The point is that each informal subgroup has an effect upon the formal group, the company. The effect may be good if the members encourage each other to support the company. The effect may be negative if the individuals regard their informal group's goals as contrary to or more important than the goals of the company.

A company officer is the leader of a formal group (the company) by the authority vested in the position by the department; however, the company officer's position in any informal group and the ability to deal with the informal group are determined by group dynamics. For this reason, company officers must learn to work with the relationships within the company.

Figure 4.1 Informal groups form around common interests.

The dynamics of a group include complex social forces that act within and upon every group and that together determine group behavior. Groups have relatively static aspects such as their names (for example, Ladder Company 7), their overall functions, and perhaps a fixed number of members (Figure 4.2). But every group also has dynamic aspects — changing, interacting, and reacting. Changes in group makeup, modifications of organizational structure, and specific events all bring about group change (Figure 4.3). The directions in which groups move are determined by forces exerted from both within and outside the group. It is beyond the scope of this manual to attempt a complete explanation of group dynamics, but addressing the subject and creating an awareness of group dynamics can help company officers manage their companies — and the informal groups within them — more effectively.

Group Dynamics

The group structure of a fire company is not significantly different from the structure of any other formal or informal group. Every group, including a fire company, tends to meet the five essential elements of a group. The members of the group must:

- Have a common binding interest

- Have a vital group image

- Have a sense of continuity

- Have a shared set of values

- Have different roles within the group

The effects of these five basic elements are what make up group dynamics. A study of group dynamics involves recognizing the internal and external pressures that affect these basic elements and learning to deal with them.

Common Binding Interests

For a group to exist, the members must be drawn together by some common interest that is important to them on some level. Hobby clubs grow out of their members' shared interest in the hobby. Union members are drawn together by a need for collective strength in matters relating to their employment. Church congregations form out of common beliefs. Local governments are formed because of the common needs of the citizens for police and fire protection and other services.

The interests of individuals change and their participation in various groups may change. Some groups have interests that are binding to the individual for a lifetime, such as church membership. Other groups have interest for them only for a given period of time, such as membership in a school fraternity or sorority. Firefighters' interests may change with their personal and professional growth and with their changing goals and aspirations within the department and the fire service. Therefore, company officers should view their crew members' interests as transitory. That is, company officers must strive to not only maintain their firefighters' interest in the company and its mission but also recognize that those interests may change over time (Figure 4.4).

Vital Group Image

The members of the group must share a vital group image — that is, the members of the group must recognize the existence of their group and take pride in it. This pride contributes to group spirit and high morale.

In addition to being essential to the cohesion of the group, the group image is one of the greatest influences on the success of the group. A group tends to produce according to its image of itself. Groups that have a positive self-image tend to be higher achievers. Groups that

Figure 4.2 The company's identity is fixed.

Figure 4.3 Some aspects of the group are subject to change.

Figure 4.4 Members' interests change over time.

have low group images tend to be poor producers. A positive self-image is sometimes called *esprit de corps*. This French term refers to the common spirit existing in the members of a group that inspires enthusiasm (Figure 4.5). However, company officers must not allow this group spirit to evolve into an unhealthy rivalry with other companies. They must remind their crews that their first loyalty is to the department and not the company.

Sense of Continuity

A sense of continuity is very important to group integrity. If the members of a group have doubts about the group's continued existence, then their commitment to the group may diminish. By disturbing the members' sense of continuity, the group can be fragmented, and the members may begin to think and act more independently. The members may become very individualistic and even somewhat territorial. This is one way that management sometimes deals with what they perceive of as "problem" groups. However, company officers are concerned with how to maintain their subordinates' sense of continuity even though they are subject to being transferred to another company or even another shift or platoon. Company officers must continually remind their crews (and themselves) that they are part of a larger group — the department.

Common Values

Common values are a part of the cohesive structure of most groups. They are sometimes a composite of individual views of reality, responsibility, and integrity. The values of individual members surface as various subjects are confronted on a day-to-day basis in the normal interaction within the group structure. The values shared by a group can change as the membership of the group changes. This change usually occurs gradually and is related to group acceptance of new members' differing values. While individuals within the group have some values in common with the rest of the group, they are likely to have other values that differ. Company officers must recognize and respect these differences as long as they are not in conflict with the values of the organization.

Group values are also affected by the values of the organization (Figure 4.6). The values of the organization usually are reflected in the attitudes and actions of individuals and groups within the organization. For example, organizational values of the fire service dictate that firefighters must be trustworthy and honest. This is an organizational imperative because firefighters must sometimes enter homes and businesses when the owners or occupants are not there. Company officers must exemplify and reinforce this and other organizational values within their companies.

Roles Within the Group

Within each group, different individuals act in different roles. In formal groups, the leader is usually either assigned or elected. In informal groups, a natural or indigenous leader emerges regardless of whether any formal selection process is used. In a fire company, the company officer is the assigned leader but may not be the indigenous leader. It is obviously desirable that the company officer be the leader of both the formal and informal groups, but if this is not the case, the company officer must recognize and deal with that fact.

Roles of the Company Officer

Company officers function in various roles both on and off the job. At work, firefighters expect their company officer to fulfill the role of supervisor (Figure 4.7). At home, their roles may include that of spouse, parent, bowling team member, or church member. Most people play several roles simultaneously. For example, the fire officer is superior and subordinate at the same time: superior in rank and authority to the company members but subordinate to the next higher level of supervision or management.

Role Expectations

As mentioned earlier, a company officer's subordinates expect him to be a supervisor. Officers and firefighters alike are guided in performing their duties by what others expect of them. This is called role expectation. A company officer's perception of that role is influenced by the

Figure 4.5 *Esprit de corps* is a vital part of a fire service career.

DISTRICT VALUE STATEMENTS

We, the members of the T.F.P.D., in performing our mission, hereby make a commitment to provide:

* _Respect and support for co-workers_, as inherently deserving of the same honesty, courtesy and excellence of service we would accord any constituent.

* _Honesty, straightforwardness, and commitment to following through_, as an organization, and as individual members of the organization at all levels.

* _Leadership and guidance_ in the areas of fire protection, public education and training.

* _Cooperation and service_ of the highest quality to our constituency and members of the public who seek our advice and assistance.

* _Responsiveness and sensitivity_ to the needs of all personnel, this community and other agencies to whom we respond.

* _An effective organization actively participating_ to provide adjustments and improvements to the process necessary to fire and life safety.

* _Competence, expertise and proficiency_, continually developed within the organization to enable timely resolution of problems and increase accuracy.

* _Excellence in attention to critical detail_, an ongoing commitment to produce the best work product we can.

* _Respect and recognition for efforts_, within this organization and others.

Fire Chief   _Deputy Chief_

Battalion Chief   _Battalion Chief_

Katherine Johnson
Secretary

Figure 4.6 A clear statement of organizational values guides members' actions. _Courtesy of Tamalpais Fire District._

role expectations of the formal organization, by group members, and by the officer's own ideas of what it means to be a company officer.

It is important for company officers to realize that the ability to positively influence a group is not dependent upon being their informal leader. Generally, any member of the group can, to some extent, influence the group. Therefore, the officer must know his place within the informal group and learn to use the influence of that role. Ultimately, the company officer must strive to become the informal leader as well as the appointed leader by earning the respect of the crew members.

The most detrimental thing a company officer can do is to distance himself from the informal group. When this happens, the officer has little potential influence except from the formal authority of his office. Until a company officer has earned the respect of the group sufficiently to be seen as the informal leader, he should use the influence of the recognized indigenous leader in a positive way (Figure 4.8).

Rules and Guidelines

Each group has its own rules and guidelines. For the fire company, the rules and guidelines are departmental rules and regulations. In some cases, the informal group develops its own rules and guidelines. The informal rules can be much stronger or persuasive than the formal rules. The traditions of the group are one form of informal rules or guidelines, but these rules may be very complex. Regardless of their complexity, company officers must learn to recognize when their crew members are behaving according to these rules and guidelines. Company officers should respect these informal rules and guidelines as long as they are not in conflict with the formal rules of the organization.

For example, if the good-natured hazing that the informal rules prescribe for new members gets out of hand (in the company officer's judgment), the company officer must maintain order and discipline as mandated in the departmental rules and regulations by ordering the hazing stopped (Figure 4.9). If it does not stop, the company officer must use the coercive force of his office to discipline those who are doing it.

The Group as Individuals

In order to understand how the five basic elements of group dynamics influence the fire company, company officers must understand that the total production of the

Figure 4.8 Company officers can use the informal leaders to promote teamwork and cooperation.

Figure 4.9 Company officers must not allow inappropriate behavior within the company.

Figure 4.7 Company members expect their company officer to be a supervisor.

group is determined by the interaction of the group members on an individual basis. In other words, there is a synergistic effect within the group that produces a total that is greater than the sum of its parts. This total can be either negative or positive, depending upon the makeup of the group at the time. When company officers attempt to analyze how or why their company is behaving in a certain way, they should consider the individuals within the company and their relationships to each other. The company officers' analyses will be made easier if they understand something of the theory of basic human motivation.

Maslow's Hierarchy of Needs

People act and interact in different ways and from different motivations. Noted psychologist Abraham Maslow developed a widely accepted theory of basic motivational factors. This theory, called the *Hierarchy of Needs*, provides one explanation of why individuals behave the way they do. According to this theory, all human behavior is motivated by a drive to satisfy specific human needs.

Maslow chose the pyramid to illustrate the various needs that every person has (Figure 4.10). Satisfying these needs is a sequential and progressive process; that is, someone's most basic needs must be satisfied (by their own definition) before they can be concerned about satisfying any of the higher needs. When, by a person's own definition, their basic physiological needs have been satisfied, they can then afford to be concerned about the next higher level of needs — safety and security. People

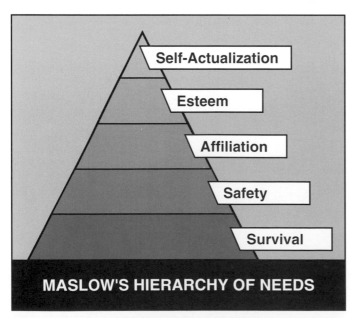

Figure 4.10 Maslow's Hierarchy of Needs explains much of human behavior.

progress upward from one level to the next until either they reach the apex (self-actualization), they acquiesce, or they die.

Basic Physiological Needs

According to Maslow, the basic physiological needs of all human beings are air, water, food, and shelter. These are our survival needs. Until people have the means to survive, they cannot and will not be concerned with anything else. In today's society, the most common way of satisfying these needs is through gainful employment. People work for money that they use to obtain the necessities. Only after these basic needs are satisfied will people even perceive the higher levels as needs. When people have what they need to survive, they will be motivated to satisfy their next level of need — safety and security.

Safety and Security

Safety and security needs are primarily those things that serve to insulate or protect people from things that might threaten their survival. Once people have found a way to provide for their basic survival, most begin to seek ways to ensure their continued survival by developing some form of safety and security. The most common form of safety and security is a savings account. Other forms of safety and security in the modern world are insurance policies, investments, workers' compensation laws, and pension or retirement systems. Many of these security devices are provided to workers as fringe benefits by their employers.

These benefit packages are almost universal in the developed countries of the world, although some are more lavish than others. In most of the industrialized world, the fulfillment of the first two levels of human needs are almost guaranteed by employment opportunities and social welfare programs. This is certainly true in the United States and Canada. For this reason, most firefighters can afford to be more concerned with satisfying higher levels of needs. The next level in the hierarchy is that of social needs.

Belonging and Social Activity

Belonging and social activity refer to those needs that people have to form relationships with others. Included is the need to belong to a group. It is at this level that the basis of informal group interactions is formed. Each member within a group uses his position in the group to satisfy his belonging and social activity needs. With the stated or implied threat of exclusion, the group is capable of exerting pressure on the individual members to conform to the group rules and guidelines.

The potential influence that the group can have upon its individual members can be used to conform to or oppose the rules and guidelines of the formal organization. If the group influences its members to be achievers, then the company officer's job is much easier. If the group tends to pressure the members to produce less than their best, the company officer will have to deal with some significant motivational problems. Company officers should remind their crew members that they belong to even larger groups, the fire department and the fire service. The extent to which company officers can influence the informal group to identify with and support the mission of the organization will determine how successful they and their subordinates will be.

Esteem and Status

Once their belonging and social activity needs have been satisfied, people will strive to meet their needs for self-esteem and status. These needs involve ego fulfillment through individual professional achievement, recognition, and the respect of one's peers. People most often seek to satisfy these needs by working for promotions, earning degrees and certificates, or doing volunteer work through churches or civic organizations (Figure 4.11). Company officers should attempt to help their subordinates develop or strengthen their self-esteem by publicly acknowledging their subordinates' achievements and by advising them on how they can achieve even more. The Strokes and Stamp Collecting section later in this chapter provides more information on this.

Figure 4.11 Recognition for achievement builds people's esteem and status.

Self-Actualization and Fulfillment

At the top of Maslow's hierarchy are the self-actualization and fulfillment needs. These needs are satisfied when people feel that they are doing what they were meant to do. When people have found their niche, their work becomes their life. They are so satisfied by and absorbed in their work that they would do it whether or not they were paid. Generally, these are the writers who *must* write, regardless of what their publishers or their readers think. They are the artists who *must* create, regardless of the public's reactions to their creations. They are the scientists or professors whose socks do not match and who get so involved in their research that they completely lose track of time, do not stop for meals, and often work through the night. And they are the firefighters who cannot *imagine* doing anything else.

Applying Maslow's Needs Model

Analyzing fire company behavior on an individual basis is somewhat easier when viewed in terms of Maslow's needs model. Of course, different individuals look to the group for the fulfillment of different needs. Unfortunately, there is no simple test that company officers can perform to help them decide which needs each individual in the company is trying to satisfy. However, the hierarchy of needs can provide some general indications.

Social Need Fulfillment

Social needs are based on a person's desire to belong and to be accepted. Using the five elements of a group as a guide, company officers can help members of the group satisfy their social needs by promoting teamwork and camaraderie within the company and pride in the department (Figure 4.12). Teamwork can be promoted by

Figure 4.12 Company officers should promote teamwork and camaraderie within the company.

sharing the workload and functioning as a team in everything from the station routine to training and emergency service delivery.

It is important that all members of the company be challenged by their work and that they get a feeling of satisfaction when the work is completed. They must be able to see that their contributions to the team effort satisfy some of their individual needs as well as those of the company and the department. Therefore, the challenge for company officers is to show the members that by satisfying the needs of the company and the department, they can satisfy their individual needs as well. One way to accomplish this is by periodically reviewing the department's mission statement with the crew and pointing out how the company contributes to the fulfillment of that mission. Posting the mission statement in all stations serves to remind individual members what they are a part of. At every opportunity, company officers should remind their subordinates that they are part of the best company in the best department in the country!

Esteem and Status Need Fulfillment

The next higher level of needs in Maslow's hierarchy is the need for esteem and status. Although often thought of as simply ego fulfillment, the need for esteem and status may be defined as an individual's attempts to influence events so that external feedback matches the individual's self-image.

Company officers can use this need in a positive way to further the interests of the company and the department by reinforcing their subordinates' self-image. If company officers can convince their crew members that to be perceived as the best firefighters in the department, they must *be* the best, then the company officers can motivate these individuals to strive for self-improvement. Motivated firefighters are more likely to take advantage of training opportunities, join professional groups, take on additional duties, and participate in other professional activities (Figure 4.13). The more they improve themselves, the better they perform. The better they perform, the better they feel about themselves. The better they feel about themselves, the more they are motivated to excel. It is a win/win process.

Vroom's V.I.E. Theory

Another behavioral psychologist, Victor Vroom, developed a theory of motivation that attempts to explain why some people are motivated and others are not — especially in culturally diverse societies. He called this the V.I.E. (valence, instrumentality, expectancy) Theory of motivation, although many people simply refer to it as

Figure 4.13 Motivated firefighters constantly strive to improve themselves.

the *expectancy* theory. In very simplified terms, it links motivation to expectations. Vroom's theory states that there are three equally important elements that combine to motivate people:

- The strength of the individual's desire to achieve some goal (valence or value)

- The availability of a means to achieve the goal (instrumentality)

- The strength of that individual's belief that he can achieve that goal (expectancy)

Because the instrumentality is represented by the job — that is a given when discussing career firefighters — the other two elements in this theory (value and expectations) are the operative ones. To the extent that these two elements exist and are strong, the person will be motivated to pursue the goal. However, if either of these elements is weak or absent, the person will not be motivated.

If firefighters see their company officers working longer hours than they do in order to complete their paperwork and other assigned duties, having to attend numerous meetings on their days off, agonizing over performance evaluations and other personnel matters, and getting few if any extra benefits, and if the difference in pay between firefighter and company officer is negligible, then the firefighters may see little benefit (low value) in seeking a promotion and would not be very motivated to pursue it. Many firefighters, company officers, and chief officers in middle management may have the experience, training, and education to qualify them to be fire chiefs. But if they see that the stresses that go along with the fire chief's job are such that the demands outweigh the rewards (low desire), they are not likely to seek an appointment as a fire chief.

Likewise, if a firefighter has a strong desire to be promoted to driver/operator or company officer, but there currently are no openings and the incumbents are all relatively young, the firefighter might see little chance (low expectation) of being promoted. He is likely to see little benefit in pursuing this goal until one of the incumbents retires or is promoted. In the same way, if a female or minority firefighter believes that there is little or no chance for promotion (low expectancy) because of real or imagined prejudice among the white male administration, they are not likely to be highly motivated. On the other hand, if members see that those who are the best prepared and most worthy get promoted, regardless of age, race, or gender (high expectancy), they are more likely to be motivated to work hard in the pursuit of their particular goals (Figure 4.14).

Vroom's theory does not apply just to motivation for promotions; it applies equally to any aspect of life — including the day-to-day activities of a fire company. Therefore, the challenge for company officers is, within the scope of their authority, to reduce or eliminate as many of those things that make their subordinates' duties unrewarding (low desire) and to increase those things that make the work rewarding (high desire). At the same time, they should also reinforce their subordinates' expectations that rewards are achievable (high expectancy). This does not mean that everyone will be promoted, but it does mean that there are other rewards such as the satisfaction of having done an outstanding job. Company officers should publicly praise those subordinates who do above-average work and encourage the others to work up to their potential.

Strokes and Stamp Collecting

In behavioral psychology, a *stroke* is anything that acknowledges a person's existence. It can be as simple as eye contact or as involved as an awards ceremony. Strokes can be either positive (rewarding) or negative (punishing).

A positive stroke is anything that makes us feel good about ourselves. It can be as little as a smile or a friendly greeting. Public praise for a job well-done is a powerfully positive stroke. Being given an important and challenging work assignment is also a positive stroke. A major positive stroke is having one's hard work, ability, and potential recognized by being promoted to a more responsible position. But not all strokes are positive.

A person's existence can also be acknowledged in a negative way. A negative stroke is anything that makes us feel less worthy or less valued. It can be silence and a lack of eye contact (the "silent treatment") or a frown. A significant negative stroke is receiving a poor performance evaluation or being chastised by a supervisor. Major negative strokes are things like being charged with a serious violation of the rules, being disciplined, or being terminated.

Nature abhors a vacuum, and people abhor being unacknowledged. As bad as some of those negative strokes sound, in the absence of any positive strokes, people will settle for a negative stroke. People want and need attention, and if they cannot get it in a positive way, they will get it in a negative way. People who have difficulty expressing their positive feelings may, under some circumstances, do something that they know will get them into trouble — just to be acknowledged. They would rather be punished than ignored. Company officers should keep this phenomenon in mind when they try to understand the behavior of their subordinates.

Another aspect of this phenomenon is what psychologists call *stamp collecting*. All strokes are converted into stamps — memories of significant emotional events. Sometimes called "gunny sacking," stamp collecting can also be positive and negative. When someone receives a number of positive strokes from the same person, he will eventually "cash them in" by doing something positive for the other person. Unfortunately, the reverse is also true. Someone who collects a number of negative stamps will eventually

Figure 4.14 The most qualified members should be promoted regardless of age, gender, race, or religion.

retaliate against the source of those stamps. It may be overtly, in the form of an altercation, or covertly by sabotaging the other person's work.

The important point for company officers to remember regarding strokes and stamp collecting is that most people tend to behave in ways for which they will receive positive strokes and tend to avoid behaviors or individuals that give them negative strokes. Company officers should take every opportunity to stroke their subordinates in a positive way. Because of the reciprocal nature of stroking and the fact that it can be contagious, positive stroking tends to strengthen group cohesiveness.

Cultural Diversity as a Group Factor

Prior to the second half of the twentieth century, the fire service throughout North America was made up almost exclusively of white males. The emphasis was on the word *exclusive*. Women and minorities were systematically excluded from membership in most fire departments. In many communities, women and minorities were not even allowed to apply for department membership. Even if they were allowed to apply for a firefighter position, the selection process was often designed to exclude them. However, because of the civil rights movement and other social and legal changes, the fire service has become a much more diverse group. While the personnel profiles of most fire departments still do not entirely reflect the populations of the communities they serve, they are closer than ever before. These changes have made the fire service much more inclusive and diverse, but they have also made the company officer's job more challenging.

Most fire service recruits today are significantly different than those of twenty or thirty years ago. In general, they have more formal education, are more computer literate, are more aware of social issues, and because they represent a broader cross section of the society as a whole, they have more diverse backgrounds and experiences. However, they generally have less work experience than their predecessors did, and most have no military experience. Company officers must recognize all these differences and wherever possible use them to strengthen their companies and more effectively pursue the goals of the organization.

Company officers (as well as department administrators who establish policy) must understand that the firefighter's job is about *performance* and not about age, race, gender, or religion. They must accept that their subordinates may not all look alike or think alike. A major challenge for company officers is not only to treat their firefighters as individuals but also to know when the subordinates must conform to organizational norms. Even though certain hairstyles, items of jewelry, figures of speech, and even certain gestures may be accepted among certain social groups, they may not be acceptable for firefighters on duty. Company officers must know and enforce departmental rules and regulations regarding acceptable hairstyle, wearing jewelry while in uniform, personal speech and conduct, and other items that may relate to appearance and also to safety.

On the other hand, company officers should take full advantage of their subordinates' individual skills, talents, and abilities. For instance, if a firefighter speaks the same language as some segment of the community, this may prove to be an asset when trying to communicate with these citizens if they speak little or no English. Firefighters from various ethnic groups can help other members of the company better understand the values and customs of those groups. This may help when designing fire and life safety messages to be presented to these groups.

Company officers will also be challenged (sometimes literally) by firefighters who enter the fire service directly out of school because these firefighters may not have learned the discipline and teamwork that others learned in the military. They may not be accustomed to following orders without asking, "Why?" They may also be a reflection of a society that encourages people to challenge authority rather than comply with orders. They may have little or no work experience and therefore may not have developed an appropriate work ethic. They may not know the importance of punctuality, reliability, and conscientiousness. Worst of all, they may not have learned to respect themselves and others. While it is not the company officer's job to teach morals and ethics, it is part of the job to see that his subordinates act morally and ethically while on duty. This means that firefighters must show courtesy to and consideration for their fellow firefighters, their superior officers, and the public. Company officers are responsible for their crew members' conduct while on duty; therefore, it is their responsibility to make sure that their firefighters know what is expected of them and to make sure that they do it.

Summary

A group is two or more people who have certain interests in common. Groups may be formal or informal. The elements of a group are a common binding interest, a vital group image, a sense of continuity, a set of common values, and the flexibility to allow different members to play different roles within the group. All groups have role expectations; in the fire service, management defines these roles. Groups also have rules and regulations. Individuals within a group have certain needs that they are trying to satisfy. Abraham Maslow identified these needs as one's basic physiological needs, safety and security needs, affiliation and social needs, esteem and status needs, and self-actualization and fulfillment needs. As each need is satisfied, the person can attempt to satisfy the next higher need. Victor Vroom theorized that people are motivated by the strength of their desire to acquire or accomplish something and by their belief that it is within their power to fulfill that desire.

While not as diverse as the society as a whole, the fire service is becoming more culturally and ethnically representative of society. With this change come both problems and benefits. Company officers must recognize their subordinates' individuality while making sure they all conform to organizational norms. The challenge for company officers is to take advantage of their subordinates' unique talents to further the goals of the organization.

This chapter provides information that will assist the reader in meeting the following job performance requirements from NFPA 1021, *Standard for Fire Officer Professional Qualifications*, 1997 edition. The colored portions indicate the topics addressed in the chapter. The numbers of the job performance requirements are also noted directly in the sections of text where they are addressed. Those in the following list that are denoted with an asterisk (*) are global in nature and are covered by reading the chapter in its entirety.

Fire Officer II

3-2.1 Initiate actions to maximize member performance and/or to correct unacceptable performance, given human resource policies and procedures, so that member and/or unit performance improves or the issue is referred to the next level of supervision.

(a)* *Prerequisite Knowledge:* Human resource policies and procedures, problem identification, organizational behavior, group dynamics, leadership styles, types of power, and interpersonal dynamics.

(b) *Prerequisite Skills:* The ability to communicate verbally and in writing, to solve problems, to increase team work, and to counsel members.

Leadership as a Group Influence

Leaders in the fire service and other professions use different types of power to influence people's behavior in order to produce intended outcomes. All these types of power are equally valid, and each is appropriate in certain situations. Most leaders use the type of power and the style of leadership that the situation demands, but some leaders attempt to use one style of leadership in all situations. This may be acceptable in stable, unchanging situations, but the situations in which company officers must function are varied and often very unstable. These situations change more dramatically, and more often, than in almost any other profession. Therefore, company officers must be capable of using a variety of leadership styles and of selecting the most appropriate style in each situation.

A good part of leadership is applied common sense, and many company officers use various styles of leadership without being aware of the names that have been attached to each style. Some company officers have learned to lead by observation — that is, they simply observed their supervisors and repeated what they saw. Unfortunately, if these officers rely solely on this form of on-the-job-training, they tend to repeat the mistakes of their supervisors and fail to use other valid techniques that their supervisors did not use.

One of the leadership challenges that company officers face is how to successfully manage a diverse workforce. Fire departments and the individual companies that make them up are staffed by personnel of both sexes, in a wide range of ages, of many races and ethnic origins, and with widely varying backgrounds and experiences. In fact, the differences among today's firefighters may outweigh the similarities. The challenge for company officers is to see each company member as an individual — with individual strengths and weaknesses — and to treat them all equally and fairly. No small challenge!

This chapter discusses the different types of power that are used in the fire service. The basic theories of leadership are discussed, along with the styles of leadership that company officers can use in various situations. Also discussed are the dimensions of leadership that company officers can use to maximize their effectiveness as leaders.

Types of Power

According to Webster, *power* is the "possession of control, authority, or influence over others." Those with power can give advice, offer rewards, or threaten subordinates with a variety of sanctions. However, leaders often do not have to actually exercise their power. Instead, the subordinate's perception of the leader's power is sufficient to produce the desired effect. According to psychologists John French and Bertram Raven, there are five types of power:

- Reward power
- Coercive power
- Identification power
- Expert power
- Legitimate power

Power itself is not inherently bad. The reasons for which power is exercised may be judged to be "good" or "bad," and the use of power can be "effective" or "ineffective." When people perceive power as something "bad," they may be thinking either that the use of power is ineffective or that the motives of those exercising the power are questionable.

Reward Power
Reward power is based on one person's perception of another's ability to grant rewards. It increases in direct proportion to the amount of rewards a person sees an-

other as controlling. Within an organization, getting a raise or bonus, being promoted to a more responsible job, or getting an expanded operating budget are all examples of the kinds of organizational rewards that workers may seek (Figure 5.1). Supervisors who have or are perceived to have this power can use it to motivate their subordinates to be more productive. Results depend on the strength of the subordinates' desire for these rewards and their perception of the supervisor's ability to provide them.

Coercive Power

Coercive power is based on the subordinates' perception of the supervisor's authority to punish. The strength of coercive power is not necessarily proportional to the authority to punish but rather to the subordinates' perception of the supervisor's authority to punish. A verbal or written reprimand for substandard work performance or suspension without pay are obvious examples of the exercise of coercive power (Figure 5.2). Withholding a promised or expected reward such as a raise or promotion is also a use of coercive power.

Identification Power

Identification power is derived from someone's desire to identify with and emulate another. Famous athletes are used to sell merchandise or deliver public service messages because of their identification power. They can influence members of the public because people want to identify with and be like the famous spokesperson. In the same way, fire service leaders (formal or informal) who are respected and well-liked can strongly influence others. Therefore, these leaders have an obligation to give sound advice and set a good example.

Expert Power

Knowledge is power, and those who have knowledge also have power. Expert power is based on one person's per-

ception that another's knowledge and expertise can help him in his endeavors. In certain situations, a formal leader will accede to a subordinate who has greater knowledge about something. For example, a hazardous materials expert may be placed in a position of authority over others of superior rank during a haz mat incident (Figure 5.3). The same may be true of any function requiring highly specialized knowledge or expertise. In any given situation, the one with the most knowledge often has the most power — even if he does not have the most authority. Company officers should know what special knowledge, skills, and abilities that their subordinates have, and they should be willing to act as a facilitator to help these subject-matter experts when the need for their expertise arises.

Legitimate Power

Legitimate power is derived from one of three sources: shared values, acceptance of a social structure, or the sanction of a legitimizing agent. Company officers may derive power from a variety of sources, depending upon their individual leadership strengths and weaknesses, but in all cases they have legitimate power because of the organizational structure of the department. Also called "position power," legitimate power is vested in company officers by the legitimizing agent — the department — in order to carry out the functions assigned to their companies (Figure 5.4). Company officers who rely on their legitimate or position power alone are not likely to be successful. They should strive to develop the ability to exercise all forms of power as each situation demands.

Figure 5.3 Specialized training and knowledge produce expert power.

Figure 5.1 Being able to promote subordinates is an example of reward power.

Figure 5.2 A verbal reprimand is an example of coercive power.

Figure 5.4 All company officers have legitimate power.

Theories of Leadership

There are as many theories of leadership as there are books on the subject. But no discussion of leadership as a group influence would be complete without a review of the more common and popular theories of leadership. This section discusses the theories in most common use in the fire service.

Theory X and Theory Y

In his book *The Human Side of Enterprise*, Dr. Douglas McGregor contrasted two attitudes toward leadership/ management, which he called Theory X and Theory Y. Each theory describes the beliefs that some supervisors have about workers, their needs, and their motivations. McGregor said that supervisors develop leadership styles based on one of these two views.

The Theory X leaders basically believe:

- The average worker is inherently lazy, dislikes work, and will avoid it whenever possible.

- Because of their inherent dislike of work, most workers must be coerced into performing adequately by threats of punishment.

- The average worker prefers to be closely supervised and shuns responsibility because of a general lack of ambition.

In contrast, the Theory Y leaders believe that:

- The average worker does not inherently dislike work — in fact, workers feel work can be as natural as play or rest.

- Workers will perform adequately with self-direction and self-control without coercion.

- Workers will support organizational objectives if they associate those objectives with their personal goals.

- The average worker learns not only to accept responsibility but, in fact, also learns to seek responsibility.

- Only a small part of the worker's intelligence, ingenuity, and imagination is ever harnessed, but with proper leadership workers will excel.

Theory X and Theory Y represent both ends of the spectrum, and few if any leaders subscribe completely to one or the other. In fact, most leaders exhibit styles that reflect both theories. In reality, a leader who is said to be a "Theory X type," probably just leans more toward that direction but still holds some Theory Y views also. The reverse is also true of "Theory Y types." Under the right conditions, both theories have application in the fire service as well as in private industry.

The X and Y theories of leadership are generally reflected in Blake's and Mouton's theory of leadership called the *Managerial Grid*, which is discussed later in this chapter. Relating the two theories, a Theory X leader would probably be most concerned with production, believing that they must constantly push their workers to perform because the workers are not self-motivated. A Theory Y leader would probably be most concerned with people and believe that, unless they are stifled by management, workers will be motivated to produce because it is human nature.

Theory Z

In the 1980s, William Ouchi coined the term "Theory Z Management." He spent years researching Japanese companies and American companies that used Japanese management styles. Japanese firms have enjoyed a high level of commitment and production from their workforce using the Theory Z management philosophy. The basic principle behind Theory Z management is that involved workers are the key to increased productivity and that each worker can perform autonomously (without supervision) because all workers are trustworthy. The basic concepts of Theory Z include the following:

- Management style that focuses on the people

- Employees remaining with the company for life

- Close relationship between work and social life

- Workers' goal to produce economic success nurtures togetherness

- Participative approach to decision making

Theory Z principles certainly have a place in the fire service. Fire service operations involve personal commitment, strategic planning and tactical teamwork, with everyone working toward a common goal. Firefighters rely on each other to handle emergency incidents safely, efficiently, and effectively (Figure 5.5). Firefighters also

Figure 5.5 Firefighters apply Theory Z concepts by counting on each other.

spend a great deal of time together resulting in the formation of a sort of family relationship. This inevitable bonding reinforces their mutual interdependence and promotes a commitment to working for the common good. Company officers should encourage this natural cohesion.

One problem that has been associated with Theory Z management is a resistance to change. In Japanese firms and American firms using this style of management, once a pattern or method has been established, it is difficult to introduce any deviation from the established pattern. Similarly, it is difficult to incorporate new innovations or equipment into the system. However, these problems can be overcome through training.

McGregor's X and Y theories fail except when applied to specific individuals. Theory Z fails if the workers do not exhibit the total unity and commitment required. One of the keys to successfully applying management theory to real situations is to remember that each theory is valid in the right situation. Company officers should know the strengths and weaknesses of each theory and be capable of applying the principles that are most appropriate in any given situation.

Managerial Grid

In their book *The Managerial Grid*, Blake and Mouton theorized that there are several basic types of leadership: bureaucratic leadership, single-issue leadership, middle-of-the-road leadership, and dual-issue leadership. Each of these types of leadership is based on the leader's concern (or lack thereof) for *people* and/or *production*.

Bureaucratic Leadership

Bureaucratic leadership is characterized by a low concern for production and low concern for people (Figure 5.6). This type of management generates just enough production to maintain the status quo. Typically, bureaucratic leadership exists in large organizations that are highly political and/or have extensive merit systems or labor contracts. However, small organizations are not exempt from this type of management.

The bureaucratic type of leadership can produce strong social ties. These ties generally evolve into a certain camaraderie that results from a mutual concern for job security. Workers may lack professional stimulation, but they have the emotional security of a widespread social network. This strong social atmosphere also acts to maintain the low levels of production. Peer pressure discourages individuals who are tempted to overachieve. Although a bureaucratic type of leadership may support the fulfillment of social needs, it frustrates workers' at-

tempts to satisfy their job-oriented self-esteem needs and higher-level needs. Self-motivated workers usually do not remain a part of such organizations for very long. If they do, they typically try to satisfy their needs outside of the organization.

Single-Issue Leadership

Single-issue leadership is characterized by an overriding concern for either production or worker needs. While single-issue leadership produces two vastly different sets of working conditions, the result is often the same: the moderately motivated workers leave for jobs that will allow them to satisfy their need for work-related self-esteem.

One form of single-issue leadership results from a high concern for production and a low concern for employee needs (Figure 5.7). This form is often associated with the Theory X perspective, attempting to arrange conditions so that the human element only minimally affects production. This form of single-issue leadership usually does not satisfy the workers' needs for self-esteem or self-actualization unless the workers can take pride in the quality of their work, no matter how menial the work may be. With the emphasis on production, it is

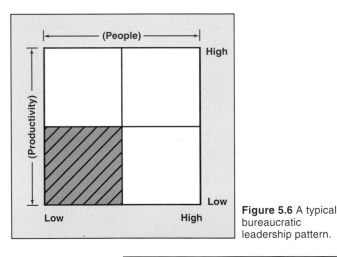

Figure 5.6 A typical bureaucratic leadership pattern.

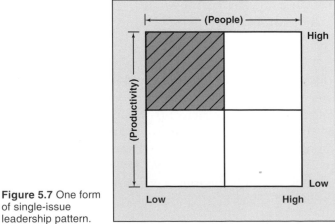

Figure 5.7 One form of single-issue leadership pattern.

unlikely that the workers' social needs will be satisfied. This type of management tends to produce high turnover rates which reinforce the manager's Theory X beliefs. This type of leadership usually breeds discontent among workers unless they recognize that the work situation (such as emergency operations) demands this leadership style and they accept it (Figure 5.8).

The second form of single-issue leadership involves a high concern for people and a low concern for production (Figure 5.9). This relationship, which produces a comfortable, friendly atmosphere for workers, is often confused with the Theory Y approach to management. If the concern to meet the needs of the workers is high, theoretically the workers will produce out of gratitude, but this does not always happen. Instead, the workers may interpret the supervisor's lack of concern for production as a personal rejection of the organization's goals. Because the manager lacks concern for production, the self-esteem needs of the workers may not be satisfied, and there will be little or no chance for self-actualization. Self-motivated workers will not remain satisfied for long in this atmosphere. Most people want to produce something of value in exchange for their wages. People tend to take pride in their work. In this form of single-issue leadership, the concern for production is low, therefore the opportunity for taking pride in one's work is low or absent.

Middle-of-the-Road Leadership

Middle-of-the-road leadership involves a moderate concern for production and a moderate concern for people (Figure 5.10). This type of leadership may seem to have advantages over the previous two; however, it may be less preferable. Production under a middle-of-the-road type may sporadically exceed the amount of concern for production because the worker can show initiative, but this will not be the usual situation. Although the middle-of-the-road type of leadership is a way for a supervisor to "get by," it is certainly not the optimum. There are times when one or the other of the single-issue leadership types may be advantageous, but the middle-of-the-road type only produces mediocrity.

Dual-Issue Leadership

Dual-issue leadership involves a high degree of concern for people *and* a high concern for production (Figure 5.11). This type of leadership offers workers the luxury of working for a leader who is concerned about their needs and is willing to allow them to produce. Under this type of leadership most of the workers' needs, including self-actualization, are attainable.

Dual-issue leadership requires worker commitment, which typically develops from the situation itself. If it does not, the leader must strive to show the workers how meeting production goals allows them to satisfy their personal goals. If this is successful, workers will usually develop a commitment. Although there is a place on the fireground for the single-issue style of leadership, in general, the dual-issue style is the most productive in nonemergency situations.

Figure 5.8 Fireground leaders exhibit single-issue characteristics.

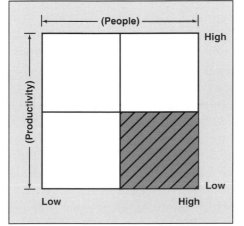

Figure 5.9 Another pattern of single-issue leadership.

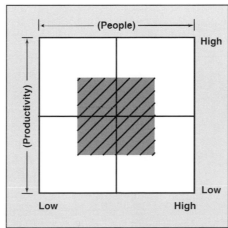

Figure 5.10 A typical middle-of-the-road leadership pattern.

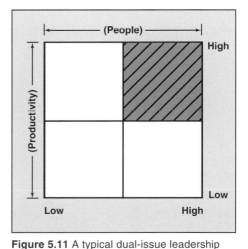

Figure 5.11 A typical dual-issue leadership pattern.

Leadership Styles

Each of the theories of leadership produces leaders who tend to exhibit a dominant style of leadership and exercise their power in different ways. In very simplified terms, there are three broad styles of leadership — autocratic leadership, democratic leadership, and laissez-faire leadership. These are general terms that incorporate a variety of specific styles, some of which have already been discussed in this chapter. Each of these basic leadership styles has strengths and weaknesses, and each has a place in the fire service.

Autocratic Leadership

Perhaps the oldest and most basic leadership style, *autocratic leadership* invests all power and authority in the leader. Autocratic leaders often hold Theory X views and those of the "scientific" manager as described by Frederick Winslow Taylor in *The Principles of Scientific Management*. In this style of leadership, the leader makes all the decisions for the group. This is the traditional style of leadership common to rigid hierarchical organizations with very centralized structures. The most extreme example of this type of organization and of autocratic leadership is the military. In the army, the sergeant yells, "Jump!" and the private asks, "How high?" The private would not think to question *why* an order should be carried out, only *how*. This sort of leadership style is absolutely necessary if the military is to function under combat conditions — the same is true of fireground operations (Figure 5.12).

Democratic Leadership

At the opposite end of the leadership spectrum from autocratic leadership, *democratic leadership* is the general term often used to describe employee-centered, participative leadership styles. In organizations that use this style of leadership, employees are not only allowed to question why an order or directive was issued, they are encouraged to do so. In fact, the employees are usually involved in the discussion that leads to the order or directive being issued. Unlike the autocratic style in which all decisions are made by the leader, in the democratic style of leadership everyone who may be affected by a decision is included in the decision-making process. This style of leadership is intended to promote a sense of ownership among those who do the work and thereby improve employee morale and productivity. This way of making and implementing decisions is a slow process that does not always lend itself to effective emergency operations.

Obviously, fire companies operate in two distinctly different modes — emergency and nonemergency. In emergency operations, there is no time to debate the relative merits of a given decision; it must simply be carried out as effectively, efficiently, and as quickly as possible. Because emergency operations are often conducted in extremely hazardous conditions, firefighters must sometimes take certain risks in order to achieve the objective. This fact places a heavy burden of responsibility on company officers and others making fireground decisions to make sure that the potential benefits justify the risks.

In their routine, day-to-day nonemergency activities, company officers have the luxury of being able to discuss various options with their crews before decisions are made. This not only allows the firefighters to contribute to the decision-making process, but it also gives them some insight into the ramifications of different options and an opportunity to practice their decision-making skills. And, because none of us is as smart as all of us, the quality of the decisions is likely to be higher if everyone is allowed to contribute.

Laissez-Faire Leadership

The third type of leadership is what might be called "leadership by exception." This style of leadership is characterized by a hands-off approach by the leader. In other words, the laissez-faire leader exercises his authority only when there is an exception to the plan that requires a decision, a change of direction, and/or additional logistical support. This style of leadership can be very effective with workers who are highly trained and experienced and who are self-motivated. The leader gives them an assignment and then allows them to complete it without interference. For example, if a company officer has a highly trained and experienced crew, he may choose to act primarily as a facilitator making sure that the firefighters have the means to do their jobs. While this style has been criticized by some because it was viewed

Figure 5.12 Fireground leaders often use an autocratic style of leadership.

as an abdication of leadership, its use is increasing as more organizations implement self-directed work teams as discussed in Chapter 6, "Elements of Supervision and Management." Many workers take great pride in how well they can perform their jobs, and they tend to prosper under this style of leadership.

The point here is that some leadership styles are appropriate in some situations but not in others. Even in the same situation, different leadership styles may be needed with different individuals. There are three factors for company officers to consider when selecting leadership styles: their own personality, the personality of the subordinate, and the situation. Company officers should develop a variety of styles that they can use in various situations. They need to be able to think and act quickly and decisively during emergencies but also be able to adapt their leadership style to one that is more appropriate when they are engaged in the company's day-to-day nonemergency activities.

Dimensions of Leadership

Company officers occupy positions that allow them to influence others. With this comes a responsibility to use their power effectively and to influence others positively. As mentioned earlier, this may require company officers to use different leadership styles with different individuals. How company officers apply their power and influence depends on their leadership ability. There are five key dimensions that determine the quality of an officer's leadership ability. An effective leader is one who can:

- Make other people feel strong and help them feel that they can influence their future and their environment.

- Build others' trust in the leader.

- Structure cooperative rather than competitive relationships.

- Resolve conflicts by confronting issues together rather than by avoiding or forcing a particular solution.

- Stimulate and promote goal-oriented thinking and behavior.

Making People Feel Strong

When people feel strong, they enjoy their work, feel personally involved, and are motivated to continue to grow in their work. Effective company officers make their subordinates feel strong — they empower them. They do this by thoughtfully evaluating each subordinate's current level of performance and their readiness for increased responsibility. Then, if the officer decides that the subordinates are ready, he can delegate certain tasks to them. If firefighters are given tasks for which they are ready,

Figure 5.13 Firefighters feel strong when their work is recognized.

even if they don't think they are, and are given the latitude and support they need to complete the assignment successfully, they will be justifiably proud of themselves and eager to take on other assignments (Figure 5.13).

Building Trust in the Leader

Effective company officers give their subordinates reasons to trust them. They build this trust by consistently demonstrating their personal and professional integrity. In this context, *integrity* can be defined as "obedience to the unenforceable." This means that they do what they believe to be right in each situation — not because it is in the rules or that they might be disciplined for not doing it — they do it because it is the right thing to do. They build trust by always speaking what they believe to be the truth, keeping their word, and being careful to never violate a confidence. A company officer's reputation is the foundation of his effectiveness as a leader — he should always protect it.

Cooperating to Achieve Common Goals

Effective company officers encourage their subordinates to cooperate with each other to achieve the company's goals and with other companies to achieve the organization's goals. While a certain amount of competition is natural and healthy, it must not be allowed to escalate into an unhealthy rivalry. If necessary, company officers must remind their subordinates that their first loyalty is to the department and not to the company or the shift. One way for the organization and everyone in it to succeed is by each company doing what they believe to be more than their share.

Confronting Conflicts

Effective company officers handle conflict by confronting it rather than avoiding it. Avoiding a problem may be less stressful in the short term, but it may allow the problem to grow, and it will be infinitely more stressful to solve a big problem than a little one. Officers should not attempt to unilaterally impose an arbitrary solution to the problem. Rather, they should discuss the problem with those involved, keeping the discussion focused on the issue or behavior and not on personalities. If those involved can agree on the nature of the problem, the solution may be simple—not necessarily easy, but simple. However, if faced with a problem that seems to be beyond their ability to solve, company officers should consult their supervisor. The supervisor may be able to see the problem from a different perspective that makes it appear less formidable or suggest a possible solution.

Differences in Those Being Lead

Just as there are different theories of leadership and different leadership styles, there are also significant differences among those being lead. Company officers must try to recognize and respect these differences while maintaining a cohesive and effective team.

Value Systems

Based on 17 years of research at one of America's leading microelectronics manufacturers, industrial psychologist Clare Graves classified workers as one of six types based on their individual value systems. The classifications that Graves developed are *achiever, involver, choice-seeker, loyalist, kinsperson,* and *loner*. Each of these classifications is typical of workers in various age groups.

Achiever

Achievers are most often workers that were born between 1965 and 1975. They are ambitious, materialistic, and have a self-oriented value system. Achievers value competition, winning, status, and rewards. They like working environments that do not arbitrarily restrict them in the pursuit of their goals. Achievers get frustrated with and may not be content to remain in static organizations or those that are slow to change. They may resent aggressive affirmative action programs if they perceive that they are being held back by the organization's preferential treatment of others.

Involver

Workers who exhibit involver values were probably born between 1946 and 1964. They value equality, harmony, activism, and a sense of community. They are skeptical of authority, and they expect to be involved in making decisions that affect them. Because of their sense of community, involvers make good volunteers.

Choice-Seeker

Workers who are choice-seekers may fall into any age group and may be some of the youngest or oldest members of the organization. Regardless of how young or old they may be, they are the products of the Information Age. They are highly individualistic and often have specialized technical expertise. Choice-seekers value privacy, information, and competence, and they care little about what others think of them. They may be highly knowledgeable computer buffs or other technical specialists such as paramedics, haz mat technicians, or rescue technicians.

Loyalist

These workers function best when there are clear rules and regulations for all to follow. Regardless of their age, loyalists share the same values as the post-World War II firefighters who were born between 1915 and 1924. They value law and order, duty, respect, and authority. Loyalists tend to be conservative and are most comfortable in the traditional hierarchical organization with one strong leader at the top.

Kinsperson

Workers who exhibit kinsperson values are attracted to volunteer organizations. This is because they value history, tradition, cooperation, and the survival of the organization. They value family and ancestry, and they have strong family ties and loyalties; however, these are also characteristics typical of gang members.

Loner

Loners are the ultimate individualists. They value individual strength and the survival of the fittest. Loners see the world in black-and-white terms. They also see it as a hostile place where only the toughest survive. Loners may have been abused children or, at the very least, the products of broken homes.

Company officers should be familiar with this way of looking at workers to help them understand one possible source of their subordinates' behaviors. This understanding may allow company officers to take the maximum advantage of each firefighter's strengths and minimize their weaknesses. It may also allow company officers to channel their subordinates' energies in constructive ways or to recognize when professional counseling should be recommended.

Gender and Leadership

With a growing number of women entering the fire service, company officers must be able to recognize and deal effectively with the differences between supervising an all-male crew and supervising a mixed or an all-female crew. The fact is that men and women work differently and communicate differently.

Men tend to work unrelentingly throughout the work day, taking few if any breaks until the work is completed. On the other hand, women tend to work at a steady pace, but with occasional short breaks. Men tend to see unscheduled tasks as interruptions that fragment their workday; women do not. Men tend to devise and attempt to hold to a rigid schedule of activities; women tend to be more flexible when scheduling activities. Men take little time for activities not directly related to their jobs; women make time for these activities. While most men identify strongly with their jobs, women tend to see themselves as complex and multifaceted. Women tend to be much more open with information; most men have difficulty sharing information.

Obviously, these are generalities that may or may not apply to any particular person — man or woman. Or they may apply in some situations but not in others. However, the point is that company officers must attempt to treat each member of their crew as an individual and must constantly strive to maximize each member's potential in pursuit of the company's and the organization's goals.

Summary

Power is the ability to influence others. The five types of power are reward power, coercive power, identification power, expert power, and legitimate power. There are also a number of different theories of leadership such as Theory X, Theory Y, Theory Z, and those identified on the managerial grid. Each theory describes the beliefs and inclinations that determine a supervisor's leadership style. In general, these different styles of leadership are classified as either autocratic leadership, democratic leadership, or laissez-faire leadership. Each style is equally valid when used in the appropriate situation. To be effective, company officers must understand the different types of power and their uses, the strengths and weaknesses of the various theories and styles of leadership, the dimensions of leadership, and the differences in those being lead.

This chapter provides information that will assist the reader in meeting the following job performance requirements from NFPA 1021, *Standard for Fire Officer Professional Qualifications*, 1997 edition. The colored portions indicate the topics addressed in the chapter. The numbers of the job performance requirements are also noted directly in the sections of text where they are addressed. Those in the following list that are denoted with an asterisk (*) are global in nature and are covered by reading the chapter in its entirety.

Fire Officer I

2-2.6* Coordinate the completion of assigned tasks and projects by members, given a list of projects and tasks and the job requirements of subordinates, so that the assignments are prioritized, a plan for the completion of each assignment is developed, and members are assigned to specific tasks and supervised during the completion of the assignments.

(a) *Prerequisite Knowledge:* Principles of supervision and basic human resource management.

(b) *Prerequisite Skills:* The ability to communicate verbally and in writing and to relate interpersonally.

Fire Officer II

3-2.1 Initiate actions to maximize member performance and/or to correct unacceptable performance, given human resource policies and procedures, so that member and/or unit performance improves or the issue is referred to the next level of supervision.

(a) *Prerequisite Knowledge:* Human resource policies and procedures, job descriptions, objectives of a member evaluation program, and common errors in evaluating.

(b) *Prerequisite Skills:* The ability to communicate verbally and in writing, to solve problems, to increase team work, and to counsel members.

Chapter 6

Elements of Supervision and Management

Company officers are in a pivotal and unique position in the labor/management dichotomy. The position is pivotal because it is the vital link between management and labor, and it can be argued that it is the single, most important position in the organizational hierarchy. As supervisors, company officers have a responsibility to represent the administration, but as members of a team (company), they must be advocates for its members. It has been said that workers (firefighters) work with tools, supervisors (company officers) work with people, and managers (chief officers) work with programs. Even though this is a gross oversimplification, it serves to identify the primary role of company officers. Yes, a company officer must sometimes use the tools of the trade to help the company achieve an assigned fireground objective. And yes, company officers must sometimes manage company-level programs. However, in most departments, the primary role of company officers is supervision.

Supervision has been defined in various ways in the many texts that have been written on the subject. A dictionary definition might be "directing with authority the work of others." The word *supervision* comes from two Latin words: *super,* meaning "over or above," and *vider,* meaning "to watch or see." Therefore, supervision is the act of watching over the work of others. So, as a supervisor, a company officer is "one who oversees the work of others." However, to be effective in this role, company officers must be far more than passive observers — they must be active participants. More than any other position in the organizational hierarchy, the company officer is the fire service equivalent of the player/coach.

This chapter discusses some of the more common theories of supervision/management. Also discussed are the responsibilities of a supervisor. Finally, supervisory skills — that is, the various skills that company officers need in order to direct and help their subordi-nates to meet the objectives assigned to the company — are discussed.

Theories of Supervision/Management

Much has been written about the theory and practice of managing programs and supervising people. Each of these many theories reflects a particular view of workers — primarily, what motivates them and what does not. The major theories in the twentieth century have been Scientific Management, Human Relations, Hygiene Theory, Theory X/Y, Management by Objectives, Leadership Continuum, and Total Quality Management.

Scientific Theory of Management

Near the beginning of the twentieth century, Frederick Winslow Taylor created what he called the Scientific Theory of Management. This theory (closely related to Theory X described decades later by McGregor) viewed workers as inherently lazy, irresponsible, and incapable of making decisions. According to this theory, workers are motivated only by the potential rewards (pay and benefits), and without close and constant supervision, they avoid work whenever possible. Taylor's way of dealing with workers was very effective, if dehumanizing.

His solution was the assembly line. He broke down each task into its smallest possible parts, creating jobs that were simple, repetitive, monotonous, and boring. Each worker would perform one small, simple job as the product passed before him. The supervisors' only jobs were to see that every worker stayed at his assigned position and that the workers never ran out of supplies. This led to some incredibly bad (though fully documented) working conditions. Because the assembly line only stopped during specified meal breaks, a worker could only leave his position on the line between these scheduled breaks if a supervisor was available and willing to replace him. If not, workers had to relieve themselves where they stood. The effects this had on working conditions in those factories and on employee morale should be obvious.

However, Taylor's theory is not all bad. In fact, there are some very positive applications in today's fire service — especially at the company level. Taylor's idea about breaking each task down into its most fundamental parts (jobs) is the same thing that a "job breakdown" does in curriculum development. The job breakdown is not only the basis for all psychomotor (manipulative) lesson plans, it serves as the basis for many of the SOPs that are used daily at the company level. For instance, a list of the steps involved in inspecting or donning an SCBA is an example of a job breakdown — which is an application of Taylor's theory.

Human Relations Theory

The Human Relations Theory of management was based on the belief that a happy worker is a productive worker. Its major proponent was Elton Mayo of Harvard. His best-known contribution to the research into worker productivity came from a study that he and his colleagues conducted at Western Electric's Hawthorne plant in Chicago during the late 1920s and 1930s. This study provided the first documented evidence to support the theory that workers are more productive when they are treated decently and given good working conditions.

The study was originally designed to test the connection between working conditions and worker productivity. A control group of product assemblers was given rest periods of various lengths, and levels of illumination in their workplace were varied at random intervals. The researchers who conducted the experiment carefully measured and recorded productivity under the plant's normal operating conditions. Then, they scheduled breaks of varying lengths and at different times during the shift. They also replaced the lightbulbs in the work area with ones that produced more light. With each change, the researchers dutifully interviewed the workers in the group and carefully checked their productivity. They found that each time they changed the break schedule or increased the lighting level, productivity increased. When they made additional changes, productivity increased even more! This process was repeated many times over several years, and with each change there was a measurable increase in worker productivity. It was only after many instances of alternately changing the group's working conditions and then carefully checking and documenting the results that the real connection was discovered.

After increasing the scheduled breaks, increasing the lighting levels, and documenting increases in productivity over many months, breaks were returned to their original length and frequency, and the original lightbulbs were reinstalled — and productivity increased again! Mayo was dumfounded until he realized what was causing the increases in productivity. He concluded that the actual working conditions were relatively unimportant. The workers were responding positively to what they perceived as management's concern for their welfare. Each time the breaks and/or lighting was changed, the workers were interviewed by one of the researchers who asked them how they liked the changes. Other researchers asked them about their work and carefully measured and documented their output. The workers felt that they and their work were valued by the company, and they responded by doing the best work of which they were capable.

For company officers, the lesson to be learned from Mayo's research is clear — show a genuine concern for the crew's welfare, and they will respond by being as creative, cooperative, and productive as they can be. A more current example of the application of Mayo's theory — and one that company officers should apply daily — is what Hewlett Packard calls "management by walking around." It simply means that managers and supervisors should not be bound to their desks. They should take every opportunity to leave their desks and walk around the workplace, observing what is and is not going on and chatting with the workers. This gives the supervisor an opportunity to see and hear what is being done, and the workers an opportunity to see and interact with their supervisor. It is a win/win strategy.

Hygiene Theory

After the hiatus in research into management and supervision caused by the Great Depression and World War II, Frederick Herzberg and his associates developed what they called the Hygiene Theory. They interviewed hundreds of working professionals about what gave them satisfaction on the job and what made them feel dissatisfied. At the time, many still believed that money was the best motivator — give workers a raise, and their morale would improve, and they would be more productive. Likewise, if they were given more time off, they would be more satisfied and more motivated to work hard. However, the research did not support these assumptions.

What Herzberg found was that if pay, time off, and similar benefits were substandard for the industry or the area, they had a much greater potential for creating *dissatisfaction* than for producing satisfaction among workers — except in the short term. Giving workers a raise, more time off, or other similar benefits temporarily improves morale, satisfaction, and productivity. But after a relatively short time, these new pay scales, vacation schedules, etc., are perceived as the norm, and their motivational value disappears. Herzberg came to refer to pay and similar benefits as *hygiene factors* because they are necessary to prevent worker dissatisfaction. He found that compensation and other benefits are of little long-term motivational value.

According to Herzberg, the things that create and sustain worker satisfaction (true motivators) are inherent in the work itself. If workers feel that what they are doing is important and that there is an opportunity for achievement, they derive considerable personal satisfaction from the job (Figure 6.1). In addition, if they receive appropriate recognition for doing the job well and are rewarded

Figure 6.1 Workers gain satisfaction from doing a good job.

with increased responsibility and opportunities for advancement, they tend to be well-satisfied and highly motivated.

Company officers can apply Herzberg's theory on a daily basis. They should take every opportunity and, if necessary, *create* opportunities to remind their subordinates of how important their work is to the citizens of the community. And, they should remind the firefighters of the importance of doing the job well — perhaps citing the Phoenix Fire Department *Customer Service* model (Chapter 9, "Community Awareness and Public Relations") as an example.

Theory X/Y

Working at the Massachusetts Institute of Technology (MIT), McGregor's research supported the conclusions that Herzberg had reached. Like Herzberg, he found that the assumptions that F. W. Taylor and others had made about the nature of working adults and what motivates them were generally not valid. While at MIT, McGregor developed his now-famous Theory X and Theory Y. For a more information about these theories, see Chapter 5, "Leadership as a Group Influence."

Company officers must be able to shift from one theory or style of management and supervision to another as the situation dictates. On the fireground, they must be able to operate within the clearly defined structure of their department's incident command/management system — a process similar to Theory X. For the company's

routine, day-to-day activities, company officers can and should use a more participative style of leadership — allowing the firefighters to participate in decisions that affect the company — a process similar to Theory Y.

Management by Objectives (MBO)

A contemporary of both Herzberg and McGregor, Peter Drucker first described the theory of Management by Objectives (MBO) in 1954. This once widely accepted theory was based on the proposition that if workers could see the "big picture" — or the goal that was to be achieved — they could more readily understand how their individual roles fit into the overall plan. This was supposed to motivate workers by showing them how important their individual contributions were to achieving organizational goals. In addition, if everyone has a specific objective to achieve, they can plan for and work toward achieving their part of the overall goal. If everyone achieves his individual objective, collectively the goals and objectives of the organization will be achieved (Figure 6.2). However, MBO is not as widely accepted in the private sector as it once was. Its critics cite two problems with it.

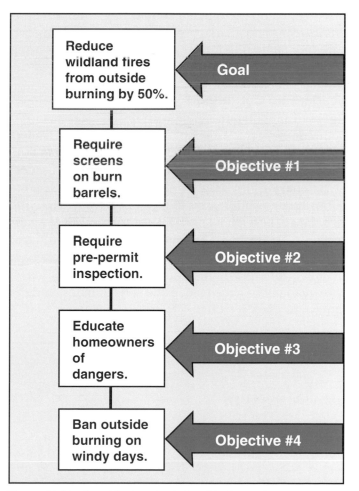

Figure 6.2 Meeting objectives leads to achieving goals.

The first problem to which critics point is the belief that MBO promotes *minimum* performance and thereby organizational mediocrity. They contend that the individual objectives, stated in terms of minimum performance or achievement, become limits. If workers are rewarded for minimum performance and are not required to perform or achieve above the specified minimum, there is little or no incentive for them to do so.

The other problem that critics cite — one that is extremely important to company officers — is the difficulty of getting workers to equate their personal goals and objectives with those of the organization. If there is a disparity between them, workers may have divided motivations. Helping their firefighters to see that achieving organizational goals and objectives benefits everyone can be one of a company officer's most challenging responsibilities.

While MBO may have lost favor in the private sector, the fire service still uses it extensively — and very effectively — in managing emergency incidents. However, it is less effective as a management tool in the day-to-day activities of a fire department or company. Whenever possible, company officers should use a more democratic or participative style of management and supervision that allows the firefighters to participate in setting the direction for the company.

Leadership Continuum

Robert Tannenbaum, along with his colleague Warren Schmidt, developed a simple diagram to depict leadership options that has become a classic in management/supervision theory. Called the "Continuum of Leadership Behavior," the diagram shows the variety of leader/subordinate relationships that can be used when trying to balance the leader's need for control against the subordinates' need for autonomy (Figure 6.3). According to Tannenbaum and Schmidt, the most appropriate behavior falls at different points along this continuum based on three variables — the leader, the subordinates, and the situation.

- **The leader**. Some leaders are more comfortable delegating authority than others. Some leaders have a greater need for control than others. Some leaders are highly motivated to develop their subordinates and give them opportunities to grow; others are not. Leaders should operate within their personal comfort zones.

- **The subordinates**. Some subordinates have a strong need for autonomy; others do not. Some are more comfortable taking risks than others. Some subordinates are eager to grow professionally and seek every opportunity to take on more responsibility; others do not. Some subordinates have prepared themselves for more responsibility; others have not. Leaders should know the individual differences among their subordinates and should factor those differences into each decision regarding delegation of authority.

- **The situation**. Because situations vary, the balance of needs for control and autonomy in different situations varies also. One of the most important situational variables is the cost of making a mistake. Emergency situations, where the cost of a mistake may be extremely high, do not lend themselves to a democratic style of leadership (Figure 6.4). On the fireground, where orders must be followed promptly and without debate, the leader may be less likely to relinquish control than in routine, day-to-day activities (Figure 6.5). The amount of control that a leader is willing to relinquish will be different in life-and-death situations than in nonemergency situations. Both the leaders and the subordinates must recognize the variables in each situation and respond appropriately.

Company officers can apply this theory in a variety of ways. On the fireground, where time is of the essence and

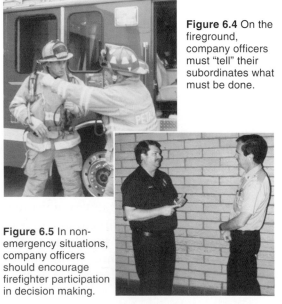

Figure 6.4 On the fireground, company officers must "tell" their subordinates what must be done.

Figure 6.5 In nonemergency situations, company officers should encourage firefighter participation in decision making.

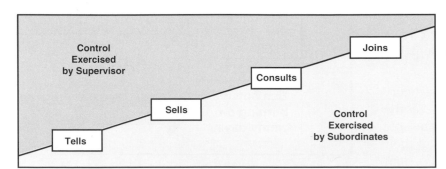

Control Exercised by Supervisor

Joins

Consults

Sells

Control Exercised by Subordinates

Tells

Figure 6.3 Leaders must choose the appropriate level of subordinate participation in decision making.

orders must be followed without question, company officers operate toward the left end of the continuum where they simply "tell" the firefighters what must be done to mitigate the emergency. In nonemergency situations, company officers may try to "sell" their subordinates on the merits of some decision that the officer had to make (perhaps because of time constraints) without consulting the firefighters. In other nonemergency situations, company officers should "consult" the firefighters to give them an opportunity to participate in decisions that affect them. Finally, whenever possible, company officers should operate toward the right end of the continuum by "joining" their subordinates in planning how to most effectively carry out their assigned tasks. The latter way of functioning is the essence of the theory of supervision/management discussed in the next section, Modern Management.

Modern Management

Although known by a variety of names — Total Quality Management (TQM), Continuous Quality Improvement (CQI), Theory Z, etc. — modern management is a very participative, and therefore democratic, style of leadership. Like McGregor's Theory Y, it is based on a belief in the value of every worker's ideas and experience, that workers want to do a good job and that they will derive great satisfaction from doing a good job. It is also based on a belief that decisions will be better if everyone has an opportunity to contribute to them. Or, as someone said, "None of us is as smart as all of us."

But modern management is also based on a relentless pursuit of *quality* — in both performance and products. The person who is most associated with this emphasis is the late Dr. W. Edwards Deming. Often cited as the architect of the post-World War II economic revival of Japanese industry, Deming is considered by many to be the father of Total Quality Management (TQM).

Total Quality Management (TQM)

Also known as *Continuous Quality Improvement (CQI)*, TQM has been adopted by many private businesses and public organizations. It is based on the following four elements:

- Customer identification and feedback
- Tracking performance with simple, statistically valid methods
- Constant and continuous improvement
- Employee participation in all processes

Customer identification and feedback. Organizations must continually monitor the needs of their customers and modify, innovate, or abandon programs or services as necessary to meet customer needs.

Tracking performance. This requires a *process orientation*, rather than a *results orientation*. TQM focuses on the process of how something gets done, not on the individual who does it. Therefore, the purpose is to monitor the performance of the process to identify changes needed to improve quality.

Constant and continuous improvement. TQM is based on a continuous effort to improve the organization's process for producing and delivering programs, services, and products. Quality service is consistently helpful, accurate, timely, and complete.

Employee participation in all processes. The most important element of a successful TQM program is changing traditional ideas about managing people. To make TQM work, it is essential for the management to value and respect all employees and their opinions, encourage employee contributions, and provide employee training and education.

As mentioned earlier, TQM was a direct outgrowth of the principles espoused by Deming in his now famous 14 points. They are as follows:

1. Create constancy of purpose toward improvement of product and service, with the aim to become competitive, to stay in business, and to provide jobs.
2. Adopt the new philosophy. We are in a new economic age. Western management must awaken to the challenge, must learn its responsibilities, and take on leadership for change.
3. Cease dependence on inspection to achieve quality. Eliminate the need for inspection on a mass basis by building quality into the product in the first place.
4. End the practice of awarding business on the basis of price tag. Instead, minimize total cost.
5. Improve constantly and forever the system of production and service, to improve quality and productivity, and thus constantly decrease costs.
6. Institute training on the job.
7. Institute leadership. The aim of leadership should be to help people and machines and gadgets to do a better job. Leadership of management is in need of overhaul, as well as leadership of production workers.
8. Drive out fear so that everyone may work effectively for the company.
9. Break down barriers between departments. People in research, design, sales, and production must work as a team, to foresee problems in production and in use that may be encountered with the product or service.

10. Eliminate slogans, exhortations, and targets for the workforce asking for zero defects and new levels of productivity. Such exhortations only create adversarial relationships, as the bulk of the causes of low quality and low productivity belong to the system and thus lie beyond the power of the workforce.

11. (a) Eliminate work standards (quotas) on the factory floor. Substitute leadership. (b) Eliminate management by objective. Eliminate management by numbers, numerical goals. Substitute leadership.

12. (a) Remove barriers that rob the hourly worker of his right to pride of workmanship. The responsibility of supervisors must be changed from sheer numbers to quality. (b) Remove barriers that rob people in management and engineering of their right to pride of workmanship. This means, *inter alia*, (among others, Ed.) abolishment of the annual or merit rating and of management by objective.

13. Institute a vigorous program of education and self-improvement.

14. Put everybody in the company to work to accomplish the transformation. The transformation is everybody's job.

Obviously, Dr. Deming had very strong opinions about management and supervision in the private sector. His success in Japan, and later in America, attests to the validity of his belief in the importance of quality. But as valid and timeless as many of Deming's points are, company officers should remember that his list of 14 points was created at a particular time in history, for a particular set of economic, industrial, and cultural circumstances, and it would not be prudent to take any one point out of context and attempt to apply it to another situation. For example, Deming strongly advocated the elimination of MBO as a management tool, but as the discussion of MBO pointed out, there are legitimate and effective applications for MBO in the fire service. The application of Deming's concepts in Japanese industry, and the working environment that resulted, eventually evolved into what came to be known as *Theory Z*.

Theory Z

As discussed in the preceding chapter, "Leadership as a Group Influence," Theory Z was the name that William G. Ouchi coined in his 1981 book by the same name. See Chapter 5 for more information about this theory. One of the concepts that evolved from Theory Z was what came to be known as *quality circles*.

Quality Circles

Quality circles were small groups of employees, usually of 5 to 15 members, who were drawn from all operational units of the plant. The group members were trained in group dynamics and communication, statistical quality control, teamwork, leadership, and other pertinent concepts. They would meet on a regular basis to discuss how to improve the quality of the services and products of the company. They would discuss ways of cutting costs and increasing productivity without sacrificing safety. In short, they would discuss anything that had to do with making the workforce more productive and the company more profitable. Since these groups enjoyed the full support of top management, their ideas and recommendations were taken very seriously and were usually implemented. Because of its successful application in Japan, the concept of quality circles was adopted by several large U.S. firms. Some of them still use quality circles, but because American workers tend to be more individualistic than Japanese workers, the concept has not worked as well in the U.S. as in Japan.

Without the organizational commitment and specific training required, the concept of quality circles has little direct application at the company level. However, the lesson for company officers is that all personnel, regardless of rank or status, have something to contribute. Company officers can elicit these ideas and suggestions by merely engaging all company personnel in formal or informal discussions — sometimes called "brainstorming sessions" — about company operations (Figure 6.6). While quality circles, per se, have not been as effective in American industry as in Japan, a similar phenomenon — *self-directed work teams* — has proven to be very effective here.

Self-Directed Work Teams

A number of the biggest and most profitable corporations in North America have embraced the concept of the self-directed work team (SDWT). In response to a changing marketplace and increasing global competition, these businesses have been forced to streamline their operations, reduce staffing levels, and do more with less. One

Figure 6.6 Brainstorming is an effective way to generate ideas.

way they have done this is by eliminating layers of management that had stifled creativity and slowed or prevented needed organizational change. They replaced these mid-level managers and supervisors with more or less autonomous teams of workers — SDWTs.

The SDWTs are tightly knit work groups with a common mission, who have been trained to perform many of the tasks formerly done by supervisors and mid-level managers. The members of these teams have been trained in management, leadership, communication, and interpersonal skills, and they have been given access to inside information about the business that they never had before. This training and information prepares them for leadership roles that sometimes pass from one team member to another on a rotating basis. Team members are also cross-trained in the production skills so that the team can still function when there are absences or when members leave the team and new members are added. In general, the SDWT concept has proven to be very successful in the private sector — so much so that some public sector organizations have begun experimenting with it.

However, it must be remembered that these corporations are creating products and delivering services that are very different from those delivered by the fire service. If, during its early formative stages, an SDWT in a private sector company makes a mistake or fails to meet its production goal, the company may lose money. On the fireground or other emergency scene, if a fire company makes a mistake it could cost someone his life. Therefore, if a fire department chooses to adopt the SDWT concept, it should be limited to nonemergency functions. In addition, like quality circles, implementing SDWTs must be done from the top down, not the other way around. While company officers and their subordinates may understand and support the concept of SDWTs, they should not attempt to implement the concept without the full knowledge and support of the department administration.

Responsibilities of a Supervisor

As mentioned earlier, company officers as supervisors are in a unique situation. This is true for more than one reason. Not only are they eligible for union membership unlike most supervisors in the private sector, but also unlike most other supervisors (except in the military), company officers not only work with their subordinates as members of a team, they also train with them, eat with them, and live with them while on duty (Figure 6.7). In some cases, they also socialize together off duty. This puts company officers in one of the most difficult leadership environments imaginable. However, company officers are first and foremost *supervisors*. As such, they share certain responsibilities with every other supervisor.

Figure 6.7 Company officers work and live with their subordinates.

According to the International City Management Association (ICMA), regardless of whether a supervisor works in the private sector or the public sector, he has five major responsibilities that are common to all supervisors:

- Getting the job done
- Keeping the work area safe and healthy
- Encouraging teamwork and cooperation
- Developing member skills
- Keeping records and making reports

Getting the Job Done

All supervisors, whether paid or volunteer, are responsible for all work that is assigned to the company and for making sure that it is done properly and on time. To accomplish this, company officers should do the following:

- Carefully plan, schedule, and coordinate work so that subordinates know what they are supposed to do and the expected results.

- Organize subordinates so that they cooperate and work together as a team.

- Delegate as much work-related authority as possible so that motivated subordinates can develop professionally. However, authority can be delegated but responsibility cannot, so company officers are still responsible for the results.

- Monitor and evaluate the quality and quantity of work being done. This can tell company officers whether the work is progressing according to plan and whether the workload is being shared equally. Monitoring also allows company officers to correct minor discrepancies before they can develop into major problems.

Keeping the Work Area Safe and Healthy

Fires and other emergencies are inherently dangerous because they are uncontrolled situations. However, if departmental SOPs are followed and a professional attitude is displayed by all personnel, many accidents can be avoided. But keeping the company safe involves far more than just following SOPs. It requires that everyone in the company, especially the company officer, be committed to working safely. This means taking appropriate risks when necessary and justified but resisting the urge to take foolhardy risks for questionable gains. Every member of the company must look out for themselves and the other members. They must also remember that they are not responsible for the emergency occurring, and it is irresponsible and unprofessional for them to put themselves at risk unnecessarily.

Because it is a company officer's first and most important duty to protect himself and the members of the company, it is also important that he act as a role model and demonstrate his commitment to safety by doing the following:

- Set a good example by following all safety rules and consistently using the appropriate safety clothing and equipment.

- Plan each job with safety in mind.

- Stress safety when teaching firefighters any new skill (Figure 6.8).

- Enforce all safety rules without exception.

Encouraging Teamwork and Cooperation

Company officers are responsible not only for the work of those they supervise but also for influencing their subor-

Figure 6.8 Safety should be stressed at every opportunity.

dinates' attitudes toward the work. In fact, it is difficult to separate the two. Employees who do good work almost always have high morale and good team spirit. They have common goals (with the team and the organization) and are willing to cooperate to reach those goals. Each feels he is making a contribution to the team and the organization. These members are satisfying their own needs while helping to meet the goals and objectives of the organization and the jurisdiction. It is the company officer's responsibility to see that his subordinates work together harmoniously and productively.

Supervising firefighters includes answering their questions and handling their complaints while maintaining order and discipline within the company. But, in addition to building cooperation within the company, it is equally important that the company officer see that company members cooperate with the other companies within the organization, the organization's management team, all other work groups in the organization, and customers outside of the organization. To do this, the company officer must communicate the organizational culture and goals downward to the company members, and identified community concerns and opportunities upward to the administration.

Developing Member Skills

While many firefighters are already highly trained and educated, there is always room for improvement. Considering the rate of technological change in our society and our profession, any company member who is not progressing is falling behind. There is little or no middle ground. The instructional skills described in Chapter 7, "Company-Level Training," are among the most critical skills for all company officers. They must take advantage of every opportunity to expand their subordinates' knowledge, skills, and abilities (Figure 6.9). In addition to training their subordinates to function safely and effectively, company officers should encourage them to grow in their jobs, accept more responsibility, and constantly strive to be the best firefighters and public servants of which they are capable. Company officers should promote and reinforce such behavior by praising their subordinates' efforts (successful or not) and by recognizing their achievements (Figure 6.10). Finally, any identified training needs that are beyond the company officer's ability and/or resources should be communicated to those responsible for department training.

Keeping Records and Making Reports

Record keeping and report writing, whether done electronically or in hard copy, are often seen as unnecessary drudgery by those who have to perform these

Figure 6.9 Company officers should always try to expand their firefighters' knowledge and skills.

Figure 6.10 Company officers should recognize their subordinates' good work.

Figure 6.11 Keeping accurate records is an important part of a company officer's job.

tasks (Figure 6.11). However, properly kept records are extremely important to the organization. When records and reports are properly and legibly prepared and submitted on time, they can help keep management informed of organizational needs. Records and reports also form the basis for a statistical record of the organization's activities, and this can be vital in the competition for scarce resources in the budget process. Thorough and accurate documentation can also be of critical importance to the successful prosecution of arson cases or to defending department members in liability suits. Finally, data from the records of various departments within the region and state/province collectively provide a basis for legislation, standards, and other initiatives.

Supervisory Skills

If company officers are to fulfill all the previously discussed responsibilities of supervisors, they need a variety of supervisory skills. Even though some skills have already been discussed in this and other chapters, they bear repeating here because of their importance to the company officer's success as a supervisor. Not necessarily in the order of importance, the supervisory skills that are absolutely necessary for any company officer are the following:

- Motivation
- Delegation
- Decision making
- Communication
- Training
- Resource management
- Time management
- Discipline
- Coaching/counseling

Motivation

As discussed in Chapter 4, "The Company as a Group," to be effective as supervisors, company officers must know what motivates and what demotivates their subordinates. In fact, because it is generally accepted that true motivation must come from within, company officers may be more effective if they concentrate on addressing organizational or situational demotivators. For example, if the firefighters have learned through past experience that finishing their assigned tasks ahead of schedule only results in their being assigned the work of others, they may be less likely to extend themselves on future assignments. Likewise, if being exceptionally productive only results in their having to do a lot of extra paperwork and record keeping later, they may be less motivated to excel.

Most firefighters — whether career or volunteer — are self-motivated. They like the job, and they like doing it well. They are eager to help those who have been temporarily rendered incapable of helping themselves. They like the feeling they get when they know they have done a good job, often done under very difficult circumstances. However, they are demotivated by what they perceive as arbitrary and unnecessary impediments to doing their real job — saving lives, reducing injuries, and protecting property. In general, firefighters are active and energetic people who want to play an active role in their jobs — the challenge for company officers is to find ways to help their firefighters channel their energies in positive directions.

One of the biggest challenges that company officers face is how to convince their subordinates that the sometimes boring, routine activities are as important as emergency responses. Company officers should seize every opportunity to point out the connection between maintenance and training activities and effective performance during emergencies. Because most of their company's on-duty time is spent in these routine activities, company officers should try to make that time as productive as possible. Some of the ways they can do that are as follows:

- Allow the firefighters to help plan how to accomplish the company's assignments.

- Within the rules of the organization, remove as many impediments to the firefighters' success as possible.

- Solicit ideas and suggestions from all members of the company.

- Reinforce positive behavior.

Delegation

One of the ways that company officers can greatly increase their effectiveness is through delegation. As mentioned earlier, authority can be delegated, but responsibility cannot. So, even if a task is delegated to a subordinate, the company officer is still responsible for the result. Properly done, delegation can increase company officers' effectiveness in two ways — it frees them from spending time performing tasks that others can do, and it helps them develop their firefighters by giving the firefighters an opportunity to expand their capabilities. However, there are things to be considered before any task is delegated:

- **What to delegate**. What are the subordinates capable of doing that would give the company officer more time to devote to those things that only he can do? Can the expectations be clearly defined in terms of quantity, quality, and time standards? Is the cost of a mistake within acceptable limits?

- **To whom to delegate**. Do any of the firefighters have the needed knowledge, skills, and abilities? If not, can they be trained? Are any of them sufficiently motivated to take on the task? If not, what will motivate them?

- **When to delegate**. Will delegating the task prevent one or more of the firefighters from completing their regular assignments? If so, is the task of a high enough priority to justify that? Will delegating this task allow the company officer to complete a task with a higher priority?

- **How to delegate**. Clearly specifying (preferably in writing) exactly what authority is being delegated and what the expectations, limitations and constraints are — quantity, quality, and time. Also specified are how progress will be monitored, evaluations communi-

cated, and how the assignment may be *undelegated* if necessary. Also to be provided are the means needed to accomplish the assignment — tools/equipment, supplies, written authority, etc.

One way of making the delegation process as effective as possible is to incorporate all the foregoing points into a written action plan. An action plan includes an achievable goal statement and a number of measurable objectives that can also serve as checkpoints to track progress toward the stated goal.

Decision Making

Company officers are faced with countless decisions every time they are on duty. Many of these decisions are relatively minor; others are not. Some decisions must be made quickly, such as on the fireground, while others allow for more thoughtful consideration. Company officers must sometimes make decisions with little more than their training, experience, and judgment to guide them. As with any skill, practice can help company officers improve their decision-making abilities. However, there are some things that company officers need to consider when faced with a difficult decision:

- Is it the company officer's decision to make? Is the issue something that may have far-reaching effects and therefore should be made at a higher level in the organization? Company officers should not pass a decision up the chain of command simply because it is difficult; however, they may want to consult with a senior officer before making a difficult decision (Figure 6.12).

- Does the company officer have enough information on which to make a rational decision? Is more information available within the time frame dictated by the situation?

Figure 6.12 When circumstances allow, company officers should seek advice before making critical decisions.

- Is there an applicable departmental SOP or local, state/provincial, or federal law? Company officers should consider the applicability of any statutory requirements.

- What are the possible consequences of a wrong decision? Is someone's life at risk? Is someone's career at risk? Is the department's public image at risk? If the risk is high, and time and circumstances allow, company officers should seek advice before making these decisions.

When all of these points have been considered, and if it is the company officer's decision to make, he should take a systematic approach to the problem. While there are many decision-making models described in the literature of supervision/management, most use the following elements:

- Define the problem.
- Identify alternative solutions.
- Evaluate the alternatives.
- Choose and implement the most promising alternative.
- Monitor the results and adjust if necessary.

As stated earlier, under emergency conditions, decisions may have to be made with less than complete information and without time to consult. In these cases, company officers must rely on their training and experience to make the best decision they can under less than ideal circumstances.

Communication

As supervisors, company officers must be able to communicate effectively. Much of their time will be spent attempting to communicate with their subordinates, their peers, the administration, and the public. As discussed in Chapter 14, "Fire Department Communications," the extent to which company officers can communicate effectively determines how successful they will be. Among the many skills required for effective communication, the most important one for supervisors is listening.

Listening is the key skill in one-to-one communication. It requires focus, energy, and a commitment to really hear what is *meant* as well as what is being said. The following list describes some things that are necessary to be an active and effective listener:

- **Share the responsibility for communication.** The listener is just as responsible for successful communication as the speaker. Communication is win/win; miscommunication is lose/lose.

- **Stop talking.** People cannot listen while they are talking.

- **One conversation at a time.** Attempting to carry on more than one conversation at a time is almost a guarantee of miscommunication.

- **Empathize with the speaker.** Attempt to understand how the speaker feels.

- **Ask questions.** Clarify and verify that you truly understand the speaker's position.

- **Do not interrupt.** Give the speaker time to say what he has to say. Then, and only then, ask questions or take issue with the speaker's position.

- **Show interest.** Look at the speaker. Facial expressions and body language can sometimes speak more clearly than words.

- **Concentrate.** Focus on the speaker's choice of words, use of expressions and gestures, and the ideas put forth.

- **Listen for what is *not* said.** Sometimes what a speaker is careful not to say is more eloquent than what he is willing to say.

- **Reserve judgment.** Do not jump to conclusions before the speaker has finished making his point. Once people *think* they know what the speaker is going to say, they stop listening and start preparing their response.

- **Control your emotions.** Anger and other emotions often make communication and real understanding impossible. Company officers should develop the ability to disagree without being disagreeable.

- **React to the message, not the messenger.** Do not judge the speaker's ideas by how he looks or acts. The speaker may have good ideas even though his appearance and demeanor reduce his credibility.

- **Separate facts from opinions.** Even though opinions and observations may have value, the facts that are being communicated are usually more important.

- **Be honest.** Do not patronize or feign interest, and do not *ever* lie — firefighters will never forget.

- **Do not personalize the issue.** Focus on the issues, not the person.

In every attempt at communication, there are always two elements — facts and feelings. It is important to deal with the feelings first. It is important to begin the communication with a simple greeting such as, "How are you?" especially if it is a telephone conversation. In face-to-face conversation, facial expressions and body language may tell the speaker that the timing is not conducive to successful communication. Telephone calls offer no such benefit, although the receiver's voice *may* reveal something about his mental and emotional state. Even though the speaker may have something important to say, if the receiver is emotionally distraught because of some personal tragedy (an illness or death in the family, etc.), he may or may not be interested in what the speaker has to say at that moment. Even on the fireground where time is of the essence, if company officers just say something like, "I know you're upset, but I need to know if everyone got out of the house," the communication between the officer and an upset homeowner whose house is on fire is likely to be better.

Training

Even though company-level training is discussed in detail in Chapter 7, it is certainly one of a company officer's most important supervisory skills, so it must be included here. It can be argued that after emergency responses, training for those responses is the company's next highest priority. In most emergency response organizations, whether fire departments, EMS providers, rescue companies, or whatever, some part of every work shift is spent in training. The firefighters in most three-platoon departments are on duty ten shifts per month. The standard for company training by the Insurance Services Office (ISO) is 20 hours per month; that means that each company should devote an average of 2 hours per shift to training. However, this guideline should be seen as a minimum, not a limit. The amount of time devoted to company-level training should be dictated by company and department needs, the training plan, and mandated requirements such as EMS recertification.

A large portion of that training is delivered by company officers. Therefore, company officers should be trained in the techniques of developing and delivering effective company-level training (Figure 6.13). They should be able to write appropriate behavioral objectives so that the training will be focused on the needs of the audience — the company members. Company officers should be trained in the four-step method of instruction and in mastery learning techniques. In addition, they should delegate the development and delivery of certain topics to motivated and qualified company members. For information about these training techniques, see Chapter 7, "Company-Level Training," and the IFSTA **Fire Service Instructor** manual.

Resource Management

It goes without saying that the most important resources in any organization are its human resources — and how to supervise and manage human resources is the main focus of this chapter. However, this section deals with the company officer's responsibilities for managing physical resources. In this context, the physical resources that company officers are required to manage are the fire station and the apparatus and equipment assigned to that station.

Even though fire stations are shared by different groups, usually three shifts or platoons, each group is responsible for the maintenance and upkeep of the facility (Figure 6.14). In some departments, one of the company officers assigned to each station is designated as the "house captain." All personnel assigned to a particular station participate in its routine, day-to-day cleaning and maintenance, but only the house captain is responsible for station repairs and major maintenance projects. In some cases, the house captain has the authority to arrange for other employees of the entity to make repairs to the station's plumbing, electrical wiring, etc., and he may or may not have the authority to employ private contractors to make major repairs. Regardless of what system is used to maintain the stations, it is imperative that it be done. Postponing needed repairs and preventive maintenance is usually false economy. What begins as a minor roof leak can eventually create the need for major structural repairs if the leak is ignored.

The same is true of the vehicles assigned to the station. If minor deficiencies are not corrected early, they can lead to expensive major repairs later — or a mechanical

Figure 6.13 Company officers should know and use effective teaching techniques.

Figure 6.14 Station maintenance is an important company function.

breakdown during an incident. In most cases, the driver/operators assigned to each vehicle are responsible for routine, daily checks of the vehicles to make sure that they are ready to respond when needed (Figure 6.15). However, it is the company officer's responsibility to make sure that these checks are made and to arrange for any deficiencies to be fixed.

It is also the company officer's responsibility to see that the equipment carried on the apparatus is maintained properly (Figure 6.16). This would include making sure that the firefighters follow the equipment manufacturer's recommendations for maintenance and care. It may also include major equipment maintenance functions such as annual fire hose tests.

While some repairs to the station, apparatus, and equipment must be made because of damage that occurs from time to time, most of the company-level resource management involves preventive maintenance. This type of recurring maintenance can be set up on a periodic schedule, and it may be possible to delegate the design of the schedule to one or more interested and qualified firefighters.

Regardless of how maintenance requests are initiated, it is important to have in place some system for tracking them. A tracking system helps to eliminate duplicate requests from officers at the same station but on different shifts. Such a system also provides a means for making sure that maintenance requests are acted upon in a timely manner.

Time Management

One of the problems that company officers share with every other supervisor is how to make the best use of the available time. Obviously, unlike any other resource, time cannot be stored — and when it is gone, it is gone forever. So the challenge for all supervisors is to make sure that they invest their time and that of their subordinates as wisely as possible. The primary time management tool available to company officers is planning, and an important part of planning is prioritizing.

One of the best ways of prioritizing assignments is to visualize a target. In the bull's-eye, only those tasks that *must be done* are listed. In the first ring, those tasks that *should be done* are listed. Finally, in the outer ring are listed those tasks that *may be done* if time permits (Figure 6.17). Once the tasks are prioritized, a timetable (milestone calendar) can be established for each task.

A milestone calendar is a graphic representation of the timetable for a particular task. If a task is estimated to take all day to complete, the company officer can set up a series of times at which progress will be checked. For example, 25 percent should be finished by 10:00 a.m., 50 percent by noon, etc. (Figure 6.18). If at any of these checkpoints the work is behind schedule, the company officer can either request a change in the deadline or request additional resources if the deadline cannot be changed.

Another device for planning and prioritizing is a time management work sheet. One of these sheets can be

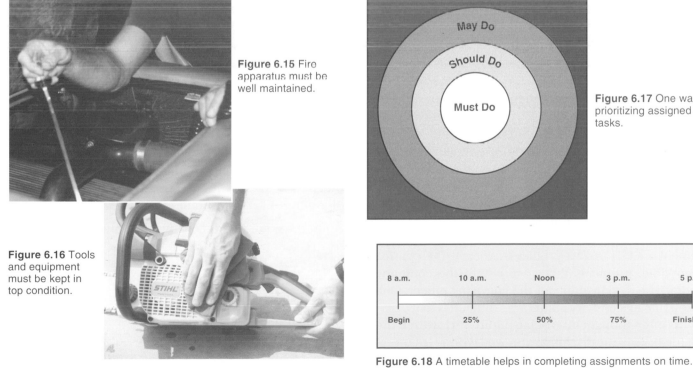

Figure 6.15 Fire apparatus must be well maintained.

Figure 6.16 Tools and equipment must be kept in top condition.

Figure 6.17 One way of prioritizing assigned tasks.

Figure 6.18 A timetable helps in completing assignments on time.

filled out for each month, and one for each work shift. While there are many different versions of such sheets, the one that follows is typical:

1. List all assigned tasks, and give each a priority (1, 2, 3; a, b, c; etc.).

2. Rearrange the list in the order of priority (highest priority first).

3. Establish a timeline for each task (deadline and checkpoints).

4. Assign those tasks that can be delegated.

5. Start on the remaining task with the highest priority.

Company officers must learn to manage not only their time but also that of their subordinates. In doing so, they must consider the effects on productivity of rest periods, meal breaks, scheduled and unscheduled days off, vacations, and holidays. The more that the firefighters can be involved in this planning, the better.

Regardless of how well-planned and prioritized the daily schedule is, it is always subject to change — especially by fires and other emergencies. While emergency calls, especially those that turn out to be needless calls, can be irritating when the company is under a deadline to complete an assignment, it is good to remember that handling emergencies is the company's primary job. By comparison, emergency calls fall into the "must-do" category of company activities. Training, code enforcement, and public education fall into the "should-do" category. Other activities, such as routine preventive maintenance, etc., fall into the "may-do" category. But emergency calls are not the only things that can disrupt a well-planned schedule for the day. Phone calls, unscheduled meetings, visitors, and citizen inquiries can all interrupt the progress on assigned tasks (Figure 6.19). However, just as with emergency calls, addressing citizen concerns is also critically important — no matter how trivial those concerns may seem at the time. Therefore, whenever possible, a certain buffer of time should be included in the timetable for each task to allow for these interruptions.

Discipline

One of a company officer's most important — and sometimes most difficult — duties is maintaining order and discipline within the company. Because it is good management practice to solve problems as near to their source as possible, problems that arise within the company become the responsibility of the company officer. One reason that disciplinary matters are difficult is that discipline is often thought of as being punitive. However, the vast majority of the discipline imposed is done to correct inappropriate behavior, not to punish. The word *disci-*

Figure 6.19 Staying focused on an assignment may sometimes be difficult.

pline comes from the root word *disciple* — a *learner*. One dictionary definition of discipline is "training that corrects." Therefore, the main purpose of discipline is to educate. Within a fire company, discipline is designed to:

- Educate and train.

- Correct inappropriate behavior.

- Provide positive motivation.

- Ensure compliance with established rules, regulations, standards, and procedures.

- Provide direction.

Types of Discipline

In general, there are two types of discipline — positive and negative. Positive discipline, sometimes called "constructive discipline," results from management establishing reasonable rules of conduct that are fairly and consistently applied. Most firefighters realize that rules are necessary if the assigned work is to be completed safely, up to standard, and on time. As long as they know what is required, most firefighters willingly conform to the rules — that is, they exercise the ultimate in positive discipline — self-discipline.

On the other hand, negative discipline involves corrective action when a firefighter disobeys or only reluctantly obeys the established rules. There are many possible reasons why firefighters may break the rules. Some, but not all, of these reasons are as follows:

- Resentment — perhaps because of wages and working conditions that are or are perceived to be substandard, bitter labor/management disputes, difficult contract negotiations, or rules being unfairly or inconsistently applied

- Boredom — perhaps because of too little work or too little interest in the work

- Ignorance — perhaps because of a lack of knowledge of the job requirements and/or the rules of conduct

- Stress — perhaps because of personal problems that affect job performance

When an established rule, regulation, or standard has been violated, the company officer is obligated to correct the inappropriate behavior. If the violation was relatively minor, the company officer should promptly do whatever the department rules require to correct the behavior — usually an informal discussion (in private) between the officer and the violator (Figure 6.20). But if the violation was serious enough — perhaps putting someone in mortal danger — in many departments the company officer is empowered to immediately suspend the violator pending an investigation. However, there are state, provincial, and federal laws designed to protect employees from arbitrary and capricious disciplinary actions.

For example, California has what are called the "Skelly Rules." In a case involving a state employee (Skelly), the California Supreme Court ruled that permanent (nonprobationary) employees have a *property interest* in their employment and that they are entitled to *due process* to protect that interest. The court held that, prior to disciplinary action being imposed, a permanent employee is entitled to "pre-removal" (predisciplinary) safeguards. At a minimum, the violator is entitled to the following:

- A written "notice of proposed action"

- The "reasons therefore"

- "A copy of the charges and the material upon which the action is based"

Figure 6.20 Disciplinary matters should be discussed in private.

- The "right to respond, either orally or in writing, to the authority initially imposing discipline"

Once these requirements have been met, the discipline may be imposed without an evidentiary hearing, unless the employee requests one. If a hearing is held, it is not intended to be an adversarial proceeding. Instead, it is intended to be informational — to minimize the risk of error in a manager's initial decision because of a lack of information. The violator, or his representative, may provide additional information and respond to the specific charges before the discipline is imposed.

Progressive Discipline

Most public entities have laws requiring some form of progressive discipline, although it may not be called by that name. In general, progressive discipline usually starts with training/education to correct the first instance of an employee failing to meet performance standards or violating the rules of conduct and then progresses to punitive measures if there are additional offenses. However, even in organizations using progressive discipline, a sufficiently serious first offense (theft, assault, gross negligence, etc.) may result in termination.

Progressive discipline usually involves three levels — preventive action, corrective action, and punitive action. However, because the action should always fit the offense, the initial action may be corrective or punitive.

Preventive action. This first step in progressive discipline involves the company officer attempting to correct the inappropriate behavior as soon as it is discovered. The idea is to prevent it from becoming a pattern or progressing to a more serious offense. Preventive action usually starts with counseling — an informal but private interview. During the interview, the company officer makes sure that the firefighter understands both the rule that was violated and the organizational necessity for the rule. The company officer should explain exactly what is expected of the firefighter in the future and what may happen if the rule is violated again. There may or may not be a written record made of this interview.

Corrective action. The second step in progressive discipline is used when a firefighter repeats a violation for which preventive action was taken or commits a different violation. It may also be used if he commits a more serious violation as a first offense. Corrective action differs from preventive action primarily in that it is always done in writing. In this step, the violator is given a letter, or one is sent by certified mail with a return receipt requested to guarantee that it is received. The letter includes the following:

- A description of what transpired in the preventive interview, if one was done

- A description of what the firefighter is or is not doing that violates department rules

- A review of department policy regarding the possible consequences if the behavior is continued or the change in behavior fails to meet department standards

- A statement informing the firefighter that a copy of the letter will be placed in his file

Punitive action. This step is used when a firefighter either continues to exhibit inappropriate behavior despite earlier corrective efforts or commits a very serious violation of department rules as a first offense. This step is intended to send a message to the violator and others that this behavior cannot and will not be tolerated. After all mandated procedural rules and safeguards have been met, the range of possible sanctions are as follows:

- Suspension
- Demotion
- Termination
- Prosecution

"Red-Hot Stove Rule"

A successful disciplinary process stands on two equally important legs. One is a comprehensive set of reasonable rules of conduct that apply equally to everyone in the organization. The other is an organizational commitment to the fair and consistent application of those rules. An extraordinarily useful device for testing these two criteria was devised by Douglas McGregor, the author of Theory X and Theory Y. McGregor's way of depicting a fair and equitable disciplinary process was through the image of a glowing potbellied stove (Figure 6.21). Understandably, it has come to be known as the "Red-Hot Stove Rule" of discipline. The image works because it contains all the elements of good discipline. If anyone is foolish enough to touch a red-hot stove:

- They had warning (the stove was glowing and emitting heat).

- They are burned immediately (no question of cause and effect).

- The result is consistent (everyone who touches it gets burned).

- The result is impersonal (if they touch it, they get burned).

However, it is sometimes difficult for company officers to remember all these things when they feel that their authority has been challenged by a subordinate's willful disregard for the department's established rules of conduct. These are times when company officers must exer-

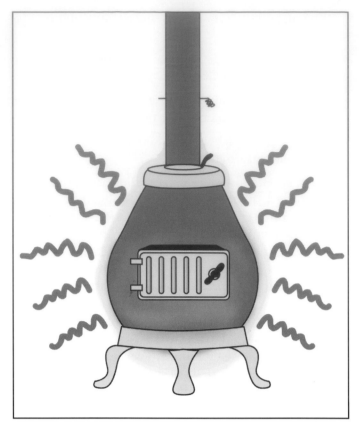

Figure 6.21 The "Red-Hot Stove Rule" is the basis for good discipline.

cise extraordinary self-control and approach the problem objectively and unemotionally. In addition, because these can be such emotionally charged issues, and because of the potential good or harm that can be done to someone's career, company officers must know their department's rules and regulations and the required disciplinary process as well as they know any emergency skill.

Coaching and Counseling

Company officers are responsible for both coaching and counseling their subordinates. While there are differences between coaching and counseling, they are sufficiently similar to be discussed in the same section. One difference is that coaching is usually done before the fact, and counseling is usually (but not always) done after the fact.

Coaching

The primary focus of coaching is helping someone achieve the required level of competence. Company officers help their subordinates develop and refine the basic skills they acquired in recruit training and help them acquire new ones. Also, because most company officers are active participants in their company's activities, they are more like players/coaches. Company officers can share their training and experience with less experienced firefighters and help those with more experience to keep their skills current. Company officers know what is required for their company to operate safely and effectively as a team at fires and other emergencies, and they must coach their firefighters to that level.

An additional benefit that is derived from the coaching process is that it affords the company officer an ideal opportunity to learn the individual strengths and weaknesses of each member of the company. This helps the company officer focus future company training and helps him make better decisions regarding delegation.

Counseling

When a firefighter is not performing up to standard — especially a firefighter who has formerly performed well — the company officer needs to find out what is causing the substandard performance. The root of the problem may be on the job, or it may be a personal problem that the firefighter cannot leave at home. In either case, identifying the source of the behavior will tell the company officer whether he should attempt to correct the behavior or whether he should refer the firefighter to a professional counselor.

If the substandard behavior appears to stem from something on the job, it is appropriate for the company officer to attempt to correct it. In most cases, substandard performance results from one or more of three root causes:

- Ignorance — the firefighter did not know what was required of him in that situation. Obviously, this can be corrected through training.

- Inability — the firefighter lacked the skills and/or physical or mental ability to perform the assigned task up to standard. This may be a training problem, or it may be the result of assigning the wrong person to the task.

- Unwillingness — the firefighter knows what is required, has the skills and ability, but for some personal reason chooses not to perform up to standard. This *will* require counseling and *may* require disciplinary action.

However, an inability to perform up to standard on the job may be the result of something unrelated to the job. A firefighter may have the requisite skills and the physical and mental ability to perform the task, but if he is absorbed in some overwhelming personal problem, he may temporarily lack the ability to focus on the job at hand. In these cases — and they are not uncommon — these firefighters are a danger to themselves and those with

whom they work. It is a company officer's responsibility to know the members of the company as individuals and to be able to recognize when they are behaving abnormally.

The company officer should confirm his observations by talking to the firefighter in private. He should describe the behavior he observed and give the firefighter an opportunity to respond. If the counseling interview confirms that the firefighter is too distracted by some personal problem to perform his duties up to standard, the company officer should refer the firefighter to whatever professional counseling services are available to department members. He should also notify the next higher level in the organization that he is relieving the firefighter from duty and request a replacement if the company's strength will be below the established minimum.

Even though professional counseling is indicated and recommended, it does not preclude the possibility of corrective discipline being appropriate also. Regardless of the underlying cause of the unacceptable behavior, the behavior must be addressed according to departmental rules and regulations.

Another form of counseling, one that does not involve a performance deficiency, is career counseling. This can be one of a company officer's most rewarding duties. Many young firefighters are appropriately ambitious and eager to improve themselves. They may dream of someday becoming a fire chief, or they may simply have a strong desire to become the best firefighter of which they are capable. Both goals are equally worthwhile. In either case, their company officer has an obligation to make them aware of what the job entails, whether as a volunteer or a career firefighter, and what opportunities exist for training and education. In departments that have professional development plans for their members, career counseling by a company officer should be noted in the member's individual plan.

Summary

As supervisors, company officers should have some knowledge of how the current supervision/management styles evolved. They also need to be aware of what their responsibilities as supervisors are. Finally, if they are to do their jobs effectively, company officers need to develop a variety of supervisory skills by self-improvement (reading books, articles, etc.), experience, departmental training, and formal education.

Chapter 7 • Job Performance Requirements

This chapter provides information that will assist the reader in meeting the following job performance requirements from NFPA 1021, *Standard for Fire Officer Professional Qualifications*, 1997 edition. The colored portions indicate the topics addressed in the chapter. The numbers of the job performance requirements are also noted directly in the sections of text where they are addressed. Those in the following list that are denoted with an asterisk (*) are global in nature and are covered by reading the chapter in its entirety.

Fire Officer I

2-2.3   Direct unit members during a training evolution, given a company training evolution and training policies and procedures, so that the evolution is performed safely, efficiently, and as directed.

(a) *Prerequisite Knowledge:* Verbal communication techniques to facilitate learning.

(b) *Prerequisite Skills:* The ability to distribute issue-guided directions to unit members during training evolutions.

Company-Level Training

[NFPA 1021: 2-2.3]

The most important duty of every firefighter is to prevent fires and other types of emergencies from occurring. However, because it is virtually impossible to prevent *all* fires and other emergencies, a firefighter's next most important duty is to prepare to safely and efficiently fight the fires that do start and to mitigate the other types of emergencies to which they respond. It is theoretically possible for a firefighter to develop the required level of proficiency through experience alone — that is, learning by doing. However, becoming technically competent solely through experience is inefficient and potentially dangerous. Emergencies occur at random intervals and vary in nature and complexity, and firefighters need to know how to safely handle these emergencies before they are confronted with them. Also, because any particular firefighter is usually not on duty every day, he could go for years without having to deal with a major fire, serious hazardous materials release, or multicasualty medical incident. To reduce the amount of time needed for a firefighter to become technically competent and to ensure that he is capable of performing all assigned duties to the level required, the preparation is most efficiently done through a structured program of education and training. In the context of this manual, *education* means the acquisition of new knowledge, skills, and abilities; *training* (sometimes called "drilling") means the review and practice necessary to maintain them over time. The emphasis of company-level education should be toward developing the firefighters' ability to safely and effectively carry out the department's policies, procedures, and protocols. While company-level training may involve some diagnostic skills testing, the emphasis should not be on catching anyone unprepared, rather it should be on identifying skill deficiencies that can be improved through practice.

This chapter discusses firefighter education and training at the company level. Included in the discussion are how education and training are most often delivered, the instructional techniques that may be used, and the types of systems through which fire departments ensure that their firefighters' skills are developed and maintained.

Education

At the company level, new information may be delivered by any of several different people depending upon the size and structure of the department and the nature of the material being presented. If the department is large enough to have a training unit, new information may be delivered by the department training officer or someone else from that unit (Figure 7.1). If the information is highly technical or specialized, such as hazardous materials or emergency medical information, it may be presented by a specialist from within or from outside the department. In other cases, the information may be delivered by the company officer.

Regardless of who presents new information to company members, the material should be presented in a

Figure 7.1 Company training may be delivered by a department training officer.

way that makes it understandable and useful to them. This means that the material should be presented by a trained instructor using a proven method of instruction, and the material should be related directly to one or more of the company members' assigned duties. In the fire service, one of the most widely used techniques for presenting new information is the *four-step method of instruction*. The steps involved in this method are *preparation*, *presentation*, *application*, and *evaluation*. This time-tested method of instruction is the most effective and efficient way of presenting new information, and it helps firefighters learn new concepts and skills to the required level in the shortest possible time. Making the new information a functional part of their routine may take practice and repetition (training), which is discussed later in this chapter.

Preparation

In this context, *preparation* means two different things. First, it refers to the company officer preparing himself to teach the class. This means starting far enough in advance to be able to thoroughly review the material, review or prepare a lesson plan, gather the needed materials and equipment, and review or prepare the necessary handout materials, exercises, and tests. It also means making sure that the material is at the appropriate level considering the firefighters' background and experience — their apperceptive base. Preparation also means having time for the company officer to rehearse the presentation, if necessary, and to properly prepare the learning environment. To be conducive to learning, the classroom should be quiet, well-lighted, and at a comfortable temperature. All materials and equipment needed for the presentation should be in place and should be tested to make sure that they function as designed (Figure 7.2).

The second use of the term *preparation* refers to the company officer preparing the firefighters to receive and assimilate the information to be presented. This can often be done by describing a situation in which the firefighters would need the information contained in the lesson. For example, if the topic is fire behavior and the company officer cites one or more case histories in which firefighters have been injured or killed by backdrafts, they can readily see how the information to be presented is important to them.

The essence of the preparation step is that both the company officer and the firefighters know the importance of the information to be presented. If either part of this step is ignored or done superficially, the rest of the presentation is likely to be less effective.

Presentation

The second step in the four-step method of instruction is the presentation of the new information to the firefighters (Figure 7.3). To be most effective, the information presented should build on other information that the firefighters already know. For example, if the new information represents a change in procedures, the existing procedures should be briefly reviewed and the reasons for the change in procedure explained. Then, when the new procedure is introduced and the training delivered, the firefighters are more likely to be receptive. On the other hand, if the new information is not directly related to something the firefighters already know, then the company officer should attempt to draw an analogy that would help the trainees put the new information into perspective. For example, if the department is about to begin providing a new service (haz mat response, etc.) that it has not done before, the instructor might draw a parallel to the introduction of some other new service in the past (emergency medical response, etc.). At the very least, the instructor should outline the need for the new service and how it will benefit the community.

Figure 7.2
Audiovisual equipment should be tested beforehand.

Figure 7.3 In the presentation step, some material may be delivered by lecture.

The presentation step may involve lecture, demonstration (with or without audiovisuals), or a combination of these techniques (Figure 7.4). However, simply showing a videotape does not qualify as an entire presentation step. Videotapes and other materials may be used to supplement the presentation but not to replace it. The essence of this step is that the firefighters be given all the information they need to meet the behavioral objective stated in the lesson plan. When this has been accomplished, they are ready for the next step — application.

Application

In the four-step method of instruction, the application step is the most important because this is where most of the learning takes place. During the application step, the firefighters are allowed to apply the new information they received in the presentation step. However, they are closely observed by the company officer as they attempt to apply the new information, and any mistakes they make are immediately corrected. They are allowed as many attempts to apply the information as the time available allows or until they can apply it correctly without assistance from the company officer.

The essence of the application step is that any lapses in instruction will be identified and any misunderstandings corrected. It is critical that the firefighters be given the opportunity to practice applying the new information until they get it right.

Evaluation

The fourth and final step in the four-step method is the evaluation. This is the test — the time when the firefighters are required to apply the new information without assistance (Figure 7.5). To be valid, the test must reflect exactly what was stated in the behavioral objective for that lesson. If the behavioral objective said that the firefighter would describe something, then that is what the test must require him to do. If it said that the firefighter would operate some new tool or device, then he must operate it according to the instructions given during the presentation step (Figure 7.6).

The essence of the evaluation step is that the firefighter demonstrate, by the means stated in the behavioral objective, that he understands the new material and can apply it effectively. However, in order for the firefighter to attain the required level of mastery of the new information, time and practice are often required. This practice is usually done within the company and under the supervision of the company officer.

Training

Company officers may, from time to time, be responsible for delivering new information to the members of their company so company officers should have basic instructor training and be able to apply the four-step method just described. In fact, they should be required to use the four-step method or mastery learning techniques whenever they deliver material for their firefighters' skill development. However, in most cases, company officers will spend the majority of their training time involved with their firefighters' skill maintenance. Rather than focusing on learning new skills, this training focuses on maintaining the skills they have already learned.

Sometimes called "drilling," skill maintenance often involves nothing more than periodically practicing

Figure 7.4 A hands-on demonstration may be necessary.

Figure 7.5 Competence is demonstrated during the evaluation step.

Figure 7.6 In a manipulative skill, competence must be demonstrated.

those skills that they do not apply frequently in the field (Figure 7.7). However, for those skills that relate directly to life safety (using self-contained breathing apparatus [SCBA], operating emergency vehicles, applying cardiopulmonary resuscitation [CPR] and defibrillation, performing technical rescues, etc.) nothing short of full mastery is acceptable. For these critical skills, another technique — *mastery learning* — is often used.

Mastery Learning

This is one of the most effective skill development and maintenance techniques, especially for the most critical skills. Like the four-step method of instruction, mastery learning has been around for many years and has proven its effectiveness. However, while mastery learning is highly effective, it is not as efficient as the four-step method because it often involves small group instruction and even one-on-one tutoring. Because it is not as efficient for group instruction as the four-step method, mastery learning techniques are normally used only with a very small group such as a fire company. In most cases, mastery learning techniques should be applied only to developing and maintaining those skills in which a mistake could cost someone his life (Figure 7.8).

Most group instructional techniques, including the four-step method, are based on the assumption that there is a direct connection between student aptitude and student achievement. According to this theory, as represented by the bell-shaped curve, a small percentage of students will only learn a little, most will learn an average amount, and another small percentage will excel (Figure 7.9). It is assumed that a student with a high mechanical aptitude will learn how to use tools faster than someone with a lower mechanical aptitude and may learn to use them better. In mastery learning theory, it is assumed that while some may learn faster than others, almost all students can learn whatever is required and to the same level of mastery, but it may take some of them longer. Experience has shown that by using mastery learning techniques, the achievement curve can reflect a more positive outcome than the aptitude curve would suggest (Figure 7.10).

Mastery learning does not require sophisticated or expensive equipment, although self-paced, interactive CD-ROM and similar study programs are helpful if they are available. Mastery learning techniques help firefighters develop mastery in two ways:

- Small-group study and practice, where two or three firefighters work together, with or without an instructor (Figure 7.11)

- Tutoring, where a firefighter (or company officer) who has mastered the knowledge or skill provides individualized help for those who are not yet at mastery level (Figure 7.12)

Mastery learning is a frequently used technique by firefighters who are preparing for promotional or certification examinations. Small-group study and practice has also been used successfully by firefighters who are working toward a college degree.

The mastery learning process is based on seven fundamental principles. They apply equally to skill develop-

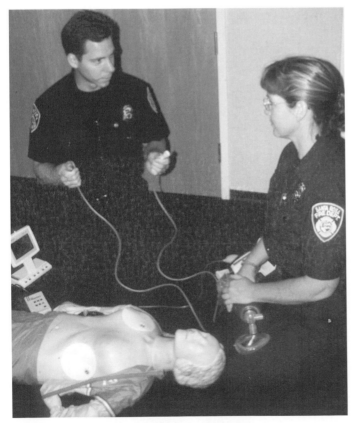

Figure 7.7 Skill maintenance requires repetition.

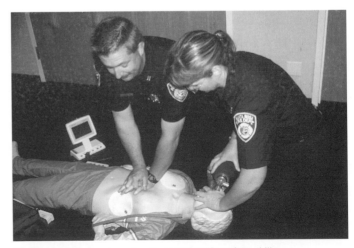

Figure 7.8 Mastery learning is used for life safety skills.

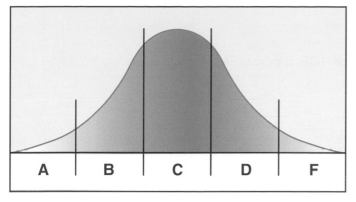

Figure 7.9 The traditional assumptions about aptitude and achievement.

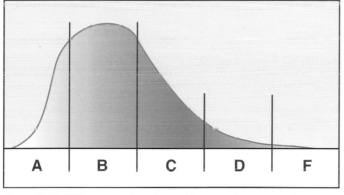

Figure 7.10 With mastery learning, achievement can exceed aptitude.

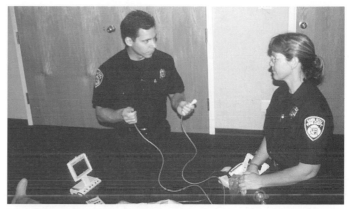

Figure 7.11 Mastery learning is used in small groups.

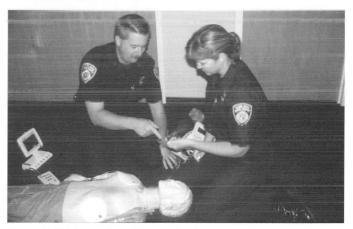

Figure 7.12 Mastery learning may involve one-on-one tutoring.

ment and skill maintenance situations, and they are very effective when used as part of a *prescriptive training* program. Prescriptive training is discussed later in this chapter. The principles upon which mastery learning is based are as follows:

1. Mastery definition
2. Small-step learning
3. Simple-to-complex sequencing
4. Reinforcement
5. Formative evaluation
6. Corrective activities
7. Summative evaluation

Mastery Definition

If firefighters are to master a skill, some means must be available to define, describe, and evaluate mastery (Figure 7.13). Mastery definition is the same as the student behavioral objective in a lesson plan or the job performance requirements (JPR) in an NFPA professional qualifications standard. These definitions must include a description of the conditions under which mastery is to be demonstrated (the "given"), how mastery is to be demonstrated (the "performance"), and what constitutes mastery (the "standard"). As discussed later in the chapter, mastery definitions are also an essential part of prescriptive training.

Small-Step Learning

Research has shown that trainees learn best when learning occurs in exceedingly small steps or units. Breaking a complex skill down into a series of small, individual steps helps the trainee avoid feeling overwhelmed by the challenge of mastering the entire skill. A step or unit can be a single concept or skill — or even a part of one. For example, in the process of donning an SCBA, a single step or unit might be how to secure the mask (facepiece) after putting it on. Through instruction and practice, each trainee must master this small step before going on to the next small step. Each trainee progresses at his own pace. Ultimately, all the steps or units involved in the entire skill must be combined in the proper sequence to demonstrate mastery.

Simple-to-Complex Sequencing

Learning efficiency is increased when the small steps involved can be taught/learned starting with the

INDIVIDUAL PERFORMANCE EVOLUTION

EVOLUTION #2 – Don SCBA

Single person – TIME: 1 min. 30 seconds

PROCEDURE:

1.   Hand touches SCBA. (Time starts.)

2.   Remove and inspect facepiece.

3.   Observe cylinder gauge. (Shout "PSI!")

4.   Turn on cylinder (at least 2 turns).

5.   Activate personal alarm device.

6.   Grasp apparatus and don according to 1191 Manual.

7.   Connect harness and adjust straps.

8.   Check regulator gauge.

9.   Don facepiece and tighten straps.

10.   Test seal on facepiece.

11.   Connect facepiece to regulator.

12.   Safety gear in place, gloves on, chin strap in place and tight. (Time stops.)

13.   Turn off cylinder and bleed off air.

14.   Replaces unit correctly with all straps fully extended.

SPECIAL EQUIPMENT NEEDS: None

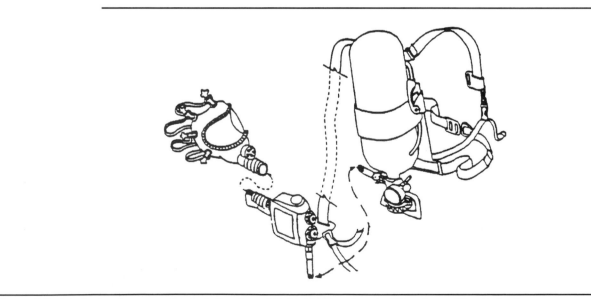

Figure 7.13 A typical performance standard. *Courtesy of California Department of Forestry and Fire Protection.*

simplest and progressing to the more complex. Sometimes called "instruction order," this involves moving from the known to the unknown, from the basic to the more advanced, and is the best way to teach or reinforce a skill. However, some skills must be taught/learned in what is called "production order" — the order in which they must be done regardless of relative complexity.

Reinforcement

People learn best when they receive frequent and immediate rewards for their efforts. Likewise, they are discouraged by failure. Trainees get positive reinforcement (reward) as they achieve mastery of each small step in a process. This positive reinforcement encourages and motivates them to progress to the next step in the process.

Formative Evaluation

The equivalent of the application step in the four-step method, formative evaluation is where progress toward mastery is checked during each small step. This is an opportunity for the trainee to demonstrate that he has learned enough about the small step to be able to master the entire skill. During formative evaluation, which is often done by the trainees themselves, performance is not graded but is merely designated as mastery or nonmastery.

Corrective Activities

Also called "remediation," corrective activities become necessary only when a trainee fails to master a small step or unit. When more instruction and/or practice are needed, the two techniques described earlier — small-group study and practice, and tutoring — are usually the most successful. This is primarily a process of trainees helping other trainees, with or without help from the instructor (Figure 7.14). In addition to their teaching/learning value, these activities are tremendous team builders.

Summative Evaluation

When the trainee is confident that he has mastered each small step in the process, it is time for the final (summative) evaluation. This is a comprehensive evaluation because all the steps in the process must be combined to demonstrate mastery of the entire skill (Figure 7.15). If required by the department, this is where grades or other classifications would be applied to the performance of each trainee.

A documented mastery learning process will also assist company officers in developing or remediating firefighters who continue to fail to master critical skills.

The mastery learning process provides a consistent skill development and skill maintenance program that can be tailored to the individual without compromising critical performance standards.

Mastery learning is a proven, highly successful mechanism for developing and maintaining the most critical skills. With all other factors being equal, a conscientiously applied mastery learning program will produce higher levels of achievement by trainees than any other teaching/learning technique used in the fire service.

Traditional Training

Traditional fire service training systems are process-based. That is, monthly training assignments specify that a certain minimum number of hours must be spent in training on certain specified topics or skills such as ladders, SCBA, or interior attack. These systems evolved in response to the ISO Grading Schedule requirement that each member receive at least 20 hours of training per month. While such systems are better than no training system at all, they often produce only marginal results. These systems tend to fail because they focus on the process, not the product. They require each member to train a certain number of hours on each assigned topic or skill, whether they need it or not, and there is no identified standard to which they must perform. The company officer dutifully leads the company members through the assigned subject matter for the required amount of time. In the training report, each hour spent discussing ladders counts as much as each hour spent raising them.

Figure 7.14 When necessary, remediation is part of the mastery learning process.

Figure 7.15 Mastery must be demonstrated on all steps during summative evaluation.

The entire training period could be spent performing the skill incorrectly, but it counts just the same. In some departments, company officers log time spent handling an attack line on a vehicle fire as "hose evolution" training. Obviously, there are quality control problems with this approach. In terms of the results produced versus the time invested, *prescriptive training* is a much better system.

Prescriptive Training

Company officers who are part of a fire department that uses prescriptive training as the primary means of ensuring that its firefighters' skills are maintained must understand and be able to function within that type of system. A *prescriptive training system* is one in which clearly defined and measurable performance standards have been developed for all the various individual skills and company evolutions deemed necessary for the department to be able to fulfill its mission. There must be standards for using SCBA, performing CPR and defibrillation, raising ladders, supporting sprinkler systems, making various types of fire attacks, operating emergency vehicles, and every other essential topic, skill, and evolution. On a periodic basis, usually monthly, the training officer prescribes a certain number of individual topics, skills, and/or company evolutions for that period. Each company member and each company as a group must demonstrate competence in each of the prescribed areas. In most cases, the company officer evaluates the skills of his company members, and the training officer and/or the company officer's supervisor evaluate the company evolutions (Figure 7.16). Any performance found to be deficient must be brought up to standard within a specified period of time. In addition, any skill deficiencies that the company officer observes in his crew's performance, sometimes called "officer determined training" (ODT), can be addressed through prescriptive training.

Prescriptive training systems are very efficient because they are performance-based systems, not process-based. This means that when the training assignments are issued, or ODT is indicated, the company officer tests the members of the company on each of the assigned or indicated topics or skills (Figure 7.17). If the firefighters can demonstrate the specified level of competence on any topic or skill, they need not spend more time on it. They can use the balance of the available time to practice any other skills in which they do not meet standard. If they demonstrate standard competency in all the assigned areas and if the company officer has not observed any deficiencies, they can be assigned other important duties instead of just "going through the motions" to meet an arbitrary time requirement.

Summary

Making sure that the members of their company are sufficiently trained to perform their duties safely and effectively is one of the most important responsibilities of all company officers. There are some proven methods for company officers to use when delivering skill development or skill maintenance training — the four-step method of instruction and mastery learning techniques. When used in a conscientiously applied program of prescriptive training, these methods and techniques will help company officers fulfill this critical responsibility.

Figure 7.16 Company performance is evaluated by a training officer.

Figure 7.17 Individual performance is evaluated by the company officer.

Section III • Community and Government Relations

This chapter provides information that will assist the reader in meeting the following job performance requirements from NFPA 1021, *Standard for Fire Officer Professional Qualifications*, 1997 edition. The colored portions indicate the topics addressed in the chapter. The numbers of the job performance requirements are also noted directly in the sections of text where they are addressed. Those in the following list that are denoted with an asterisk (*) are global in nature and are covered by reading the chapter in its entirety.

Fire Officer II

3-1.1*   **General Prerequisite Knowledge**. The organization of local government; the law-making process at the local, state/provincial, and federal level; functions of other bureaus, divisions, agencies and organizations; and their roles and responsibilities that relate to the fire service.

Government Structure

Clearly, company officers play an important role in helping their fire department to be an effective part of its local community and in working with other government and nongovernment agencies. A key to this ability is an understanding of how governments operate and a familiarity with other agencies that are involved directly or indirectly in the fire protection process. This chapter discusses the types of local, state/provincial, and federal governments and their impact on fire protection agencies. Also discussed are many of the private and professional organizations with which fire service personnel interact.

Local Government

The following paragraphs address local government at several levels:

- City
- Township
- County
- District

These terms are not standard across North America, and their precise meaning varies greatly from one region to another. This section gives an overview of typical governmental structures at the local level. All firefighters — and especially those interested in becoming company officers — should acquaint themselves with the organizational structure of the government bodies that oversee their jurisdiction and other jurisdictions with whom they must work.

Municipal (City) Government

In most of the United States and Canada, communities either have no formal government system or use designated officials to conduct those affairs that are of common interest to the residents of the community. The officials are generally elected by the eligible voters in the community, though some officials may be hired. In communities with formal governments, the three most common structures are:

- Council-mayor government
- Council-manager government
- Commission government

These three forms of government differ primarily in how the actual administration of municipal operations occurs, as explained in the following paragraphs. However, they also share certain characteristics. The chief common characteristic is the use of an elected body — the council or commission — to represent the citizens in conducting the business of the community. These council members or commissioners may be elected at large or as representatives of specific sections of the municipality. In an at-large election, candidates can reside in any part of the city, with all eligible voters being able to vote for one or more candidates. The at-large system is intended to free the legislators from undue influence by any particular constituency or neighborhood group. This system is most common in smaller towns, whereas larger communities tend to be divided into districts, wards, or precincts (Figure 8.1). These subdivisions are generally intended to consist of approximately equal numbers of citizens, who elect one or more council persons or com-

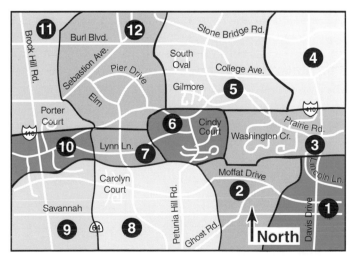

Figure 8.1 Some jurisdictions are divided into wards or precincts.

missioners to represent them. The use of political subdivisions is an attempt to ensure that each area of the city and each segment of the population receives equal representation. Most cities use either an at-large or ward form of representation, though a few have both at-large and ward council members or commissioners.

Fire department officials must work with and advise local governments. Elected officials tend to seek visible connections to programs and departments that are well thought of by the public. Therefore, every fire department should make an effort to publicize its programs and successful operations so that the public is aware of the benefits they reap from the department. Skillful politicians recognize the value of such publicity and will seek to associate themselves with beneficial contributions to the city's welfare, which in turn leads to greater support of fire protection agencies.

Council-Mayor Government

The council-mayor form of city government generally consists of one official elected at large, the mayor, and a group of representatives who normally serve districts, wards, or precincts, though some city councils are elected at large. This type of government may further be classified as a weak- or strong-mayor form. Under the weak-mayor concept, the council actually administers the business of the city while the mayor serves primarily as a figurehead and often has another full-time job or business. In some weak-mayor systems, the mayor does not even have a vote in matters placed before the council and frequently serves only as an ambassador of the city to welcome distinguished visitors and to serve in ceremonies. Other weak-mayor systems allow the mayor to vote in the event of a tie in a council vote or in all proceedings with the mayor's vote carrying no more weight than that of any other council member.

A mayor in strong-mayor systems is generally the official head of the city's government and often serves in a full-time capacity. Such mayors tend to set policy for the conduct of the community's business and often have substantial influence over council proceedings and actions, frequently serving as the head of the council and voting on all matters before the council. Strong mayoral systems commonly assign the mayor a great deal of authority in the hiring or appointing of other city officials, and the mayor often serves as the supervisor of department heads, including the fire chief or fire commissioner.

The council-mayor form with a strong mayor is perhaps the most common form of city government in Canada, where the elected head may be referred to as a mayor, reeve, warden, or overseer. Sometimes council members are given specific functional roles similar to the commissioner concept and may be referred to as controllers, aldermen (alderpersons), or councilors.

Whether working with a strong- or weak-mayor system, the fire chief must be able to deal effectively with the mayor and the council. Under both systems, the mayor is the chief representative of the city and should be invited to all official fire department functions and ceremonies, especially those public ceremonies related to fire protection and prevention awareness. Similarly, council members should be invited to events that take place in their wards or districts. The fire chief and other officers will be required to work with the council and mayor to determine the department's structure and organization and to ensure that city operations and ordinances support effective fire protection. Therefore, department officers should become familiar with the functioning of the council-mayor system as implemented within their city and to understand the personalities of the persons who serve in those positions.

Council-Manager Government

As cities have continued to grow in area and population, their governing bodies have begun to recognize two key concepts: (1) It is often desirable to maintain a separation between the political planning of the city and its day-to-day administration, and (2) proper municipal administration requires formal training. Consequently, many metropolitan areas have adopted a council-manager form of government. Under this concept, the voters elect representatives to serve on the city council. The city may also have an elected mayor comparable to a weak mayor within the council-mayor system in that the mayor is basically a figurehead who may or may not vote on council issues. However, the key characteristic of this approach is that the council hires a professional public administrator to manage the daily affairs of the city. The manager reports to the council and advises them on various matters but usually does not get to vote on council agenda items. The manager's principal duty is to see that the council's policies are carried out in an efficient manner and within budget.

Under this system, fire department officers have two different facets of government with which to deal. Involving elected officials in events that will enhance their public standing is still helpful in building a good relationship with the mayor and council members. However, the department's actual supervisor is more likely to be the city manager (Figure 8.2). Often the fire chief reports directly to the city manager or to a bureau head who works for the city manager. The bureau head may have a

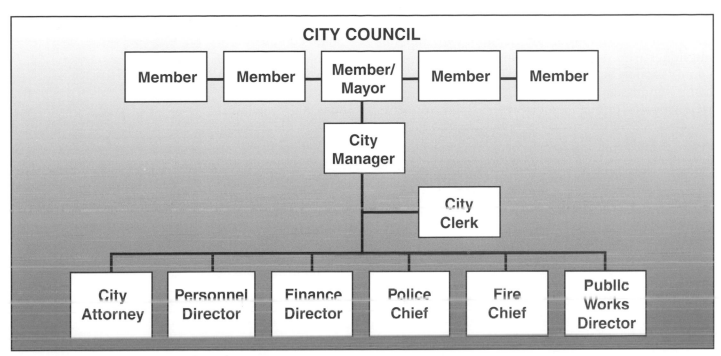

Figure 8.2 A typical council-manager form of government.

title such as Director of Public Safety or something similar. Either way, the role of fire officials under this form of government may emphasize the business side of running the fire department with less emphasis on public relations. The city manager expects the fire department to operate efficiently and to be able to provide evidence of its efficiency. The department's relationship with the city manager will depend largely on matters of professionalism, budget performance, public liability, and resource management. The city manager is likely to require formal presentations and reports covering the status of fire department operations and extensive documentation of planning.

The city manager often views the fire chief as one of several department heads who must look beyond their individual concerns to see the greater perspective of what is in the best overall interest of the city and who must work together as a team. Consequently, the chief and other fire department officers may serve on committees that address cross-departmental issues. For example, the city manager may allocate a portion of the city budget to public safety and task the department heads to determine and agree to a distribution of those funds among their various departments. A committee of fire department officers may work with representatives of other departments to formulate a list to be considered for next year's budget addressing major equipment expenditures for the entire city.

Commission Government

A commission is similar to a council system and may or may not have a mayor. The current trend is away from commission forms, but many older cities and some other political divisions still use this approach. Commissions tend to be three- to five-member boards elected at large within the community. The unique aspect of this system is that responsibility for the various functional operations of the city are generally divided among the commissioners. For example, a city may have a three-person commission, with one commissioner responsible for finances, a second responsible for maintenance of the infrastructure, and the third for services. Thus, the first commissioner would oversee the budget, tax collections, and related matters, while the second would see that the streets, sewer system, city buildings, water system, and other physical structures were maintained and expanded as necessary. The third commissioner in this example would be responsible for the police and fire departments, refuse collection, health department, and social services. Consequently, under this concept, each commissioner is like a city manager for a portion of the community's operations, but they are also elected officials like council members. Because they are generally less trained than a city manager and often have other full-time jobs, commissioners usually rely more directly on the fire chief and other department heads for the day-to-day operation and planning for their departments.

Commissioners serve as advocates on behalf of those functions under their supervision. So, one key to success for a department head is to create a good working relationship and good communications with the commissioner who oversees that department. Then the commissioner can adequately justify requests to the rest of the commission. The fire chief and other officers must work with and through their assigned commissioner to be effective. However, they cannot afford to give the appearance of ignoring other commissioners. This is a consideration because many commissioner systems allow the senior commissioner to determine the responsibilities of the commission, which means that oversight of the department may transfer from one commissioner to another.

Township Government

Township governments are generally commission-type bodies; however, a common term for the commission is *board of trustees*. Responsibilities for operation of the township are divided among the trustees. Thus, many of the guidelines for the relationship between the fire department and the trustees are the same as that discussed for commission forms of city government. One distinction between boards of trustees and commissions that is often valid is that terms of office are sometimes less rigid among trustees. The commissioners in most city commissions serve for a prescribed period of time — usually two, four, or six years. Position elections are generally offset so that only one or two posts are filled during any given election. This helps to maintain continuity within the governing body. There is a tendency for more variation in the election intervals of trustees. Some boards use offset election periods while others open all positions during periodic elections. Frequently, each position on the board is designated as a "seat" or "place," and candidates file for a specific seat and run against only the persons who file for the same seat. Senior trustees may not face opposition when seeking re-election and often serve until they resign.

County/Parish Government

County and parish governments were originally formed in order to de-centralize state and provincial governments. Before modern transportation, and even today in some remote areas, traveling to the state capital to conduct business was difficult. Consequently, county and parish offices tended to reflect the state-level organization. However, increasing urban populations and a decline in agriculture have meant that the nature of counties as a political unit has changed. Some cities have grown to occupy entire counties, and land that once had been farms has given way to houses, multifamily dwellings, shopping centers, and manufacturing plants (Fig-

ure 8.3). As a result, many counties have adopted a municipal form of government rather than reflect the state or provincial organization. Thus, the three most prevalent forms of county and parish government today parallel the common forms of municipal government:

Figure 8.3 Some cities occupy the entire county.

* County commission
* County commission-manager
* County commission-executive

County Commission

The commission form of government continues to be the most common form of county and parish government. This form takes one of two prevalent structures: (1) Commissioners or supervisors are elected at large and assume responsibility for a specific set of operational functions, or (2) the county is divided into districts, and commissioners are responsible for the operation of their represented districts and jointly are responsible for overall operations. In actual practice, most routine matters within a district or in an assigned area are handled by the responsible commissioner, while county-wide matters and larger issues are decided by the whole commission. For county fire departments and for fire districts that are supervised by county or parish commissions, the guidelines for working with the commission are similar to those given for city commissions. The commissioners are elected officials who wish to have a good public image and who require effective communications and information from the fire protection agencies within their districts.

County Commission-Manager

Equivalent to the council-manager form of city government, the commission-manager or commission-administrator concept in county and parish government is motivated by the perceived need to provide separation between county politics and administration of county business. It consists of an elected commission, who hires an administrator to manage the affairs of the county and implement the policies of the commission. In a few instances, the manager is also an elected official. As with the city level of government, fire protection agency officials must strike a workable balance between communicating with and promoting the elected commissioners while providing the manager with solid evidence of efficient planning and operation.

County Commission-Executive

The strong-mayor form of the council-mayor concept of city government is largely duplicated at the county or parish level by the commission-executive structure, with the commission being equivalent to the council and the executive or chief executive representing the strong mayor. Under this concept, there are essentially two branches of government: the commission as the legislative branch and the executive as the executive branch. The commissioners generally represent a district within the county or parish and enact policies and ordinances; the executive is elected at large and prepares the budget, oversees the department heads (and often appoints them), and sees to the day-to-day operation of the county. The county executive often has a staff, which may include a professional administrator. The executive generally conducts commission meetings. Fire chiefs and other department heads must recognize that they are working with elected officials and that both the commissioners and the executive are likely to expect some degree of loyalty and involvement with the department heads.

Fire Districts

As mentioned earlier, some fire departments are established to provide service to areas known as fire districts. In many instances, such districts are governmental bodies empowered by their state or province to implement and enforce regulations and to raise and administer revenues. Such districts are legal entities that can enter into contracts and agreements with other government bodies and corporations, impose taxes and fees, borrow money, and own property. Most fire districts operate under an elected board of directors. Occasionally, when a fire district overlaps the jurisdictions of several local governments, the board will be an appointed body with one or more representatives from each of the encompassed government entities.

In most cases, the state or province will designate one of its existing agencies to oversee and coordinate the actions of fire districts. This level of support may simply consist of informal training and networking for the districts, or it may go to the extent of setting standards for the districts and verifying their compliance with those standards.

Several factors have increased the popularity of fire districts, especially in rural areas. Virtually all levels of government face a scarcity of funds that can be partially offset through cooperative efforts, such as the pooled resources of fire districts. The effective operations of other types of districts — including school, hospital, and water districts — have set precedents for expansion of the concept. Recent federal regulations such as the Superfund Amendments and Reauthorization Act (SARA) of 1986 have placed more responsibility for emergency preparedness and response at the local level and have emphasized the need for interagency cooperation. Such cooperation frequently leads to closer planning and the elimination of duplicated services among fire protection agencies. Consolidating numerous small fire protection agencies into larger, more efficient fire districts is often the next logical step because it reduces or eliminates costly duplication.

Impact of Local Governments on Fire Protection Agencies

The operation of local government impacts fire protection agencies in two primary ways. First, governing bodies make decisions that directly relate to the operations of such agencies, such as allocating funds, approving or disapproving purchase and staffing requests, implementing ordinances related to fire protection and other emergency services, and reviewing and approving agreements with other fire protection agencies and governments. Second, local governments oversee other agencies with whom the fire department must work, which can affect department policies, procedures, responsibilities, resource requirements, and other factors.

Lawmaking Process of Local Governments

The actual process of enacting laws varies from one form of local government to another, but it is essential that company officers understand the process. Such understanding is a requirement of NFPA 1021, *Standard for Fire Officer Professional Qualifications*. A fire protection agency's effectiveness in accomplishing its mission can be directly affected by how well its officers and firefighters understand the legislative process at all levels of government and how involved they are in trying to influence that process.

At the local level, legislation is enacted by the council, commission, or board that has jurisdiction over the territory and matter being regulated. In terms of fire protection issues, the local government will generally consider any information presented by the department; therefore, it is imperative that the department be aware of the potential ramifications of such legislation and take an active role in advising the governing body. But company officers should also be aware of impending legislation that may not appear on the surface to have a direct impact on fire department operations. For example, the local government may be considering zoning changes that would interrupt emergency response and evacuation routes or that would allow construction of a high-risk facility beyond the reasonable response of existing resources. Expansion of the city water system may not include consideration of hydrant requirements, or the pending contract with the city's fuel supplier may not contain provisions for diesel fuel being available at all hours of the day or night. Thus, company officers should not only be familiar with the lawmaking process but should also actively monitor it and be involved in the process as both a professional and a citizen (Figure 8.4).

Agencies of Local Governments

In addition to the fire protection agency, a local government is likely to include one or more of the agencies discussed in the following paragraphs.

Law Enforcement

Local police and sheriff's departments work with fire departments in the shared responsibility of protecting the public. These agencies may even share the same department head or supervisor. Law enforcement agencies support fire protection efforts through crowd and traffic control, with large-scale evacuations, and by providing protection to firefighters during civil unrest (Figure 8.5).

Building Department

In most localities, the building department is responsible for ensuring that building codes, including fire codes, are enforced during construction and renovation. This is

the first step in the fire prevention process and precedes the fire inspection program. The building department can also be a useful resource to fire protection personnel by assisting with the emergency planning process. The building department frequently maintains files of building floor plans that indicate structural layout, locations of entrances and exits, fire suppression systems, and other features that can assist with the emergency response (Figure 8.6).

Water Department

The need for a good working relationship between the fire department and water department is fairly obvious. During the water service planning phase, the two agencies must ensure that hydrant locations, pressure, pumping and storage capacities, and other factors support fire protection requirements (Figure 8.7). This coordination must continue during the day-to-day operations of the two agencies. Then the fire department is informed of any planned or unexpected interruptions in water service, and the water department is informed of any unusual usage requirements of the fire department (because of a major fire or a water-intensive exercise, for example). Local water departments often have responsibility for the sewer and storm drain systems within a community. These systems are particularly important to fire departments tasked with the control and cleanup of hazardous material spills.

Figure 8.7 Fighting major fires would be very difficult without support from the local water department.

Figure 8.6 The building department can help by requiring built-in fire protection.

Figure 8.4 Company officers should follow local events carefully.

Figure 8.5 Law enforcement personnel can be very helpful at emergency incidents.

Zoning Commission

The zoning commission coordinates use of land within the community and determines the types of structures that can be located within a given area, such as single-family housing, multiple-family housing, business, agricultural, light industrial, and heavy industrial. The use of land affects its fire prevention and protection requirements and, thus, fire department planning. The zoning commission is often involved in the selection and allocation of sites for fire stations and support buildings such as training centers and maintenance facilities.

Street Department

Local street departments not only maintain roads and highways, but they also keep the fire department informed of planned repairs that will result in road closures or detours, and other traffic problems that might affect emergency responses (Figure 8.8). They often involve the fire department in the planning of fire lanes, bridges, intersections, entrances and exits for facilities, and other factors that may affect the operation and maneuverability of response apparatus. The street department can further assist the fire department through the use of automatic traffic signal control devices that assist with a prompt response. Finally, the street department usually has a role in hazardous material incidents on public thoroughfares.

Judicial System

Local courts must render decisions in cases of arson, insurance fraud, failure to comply with fire codes, and others that may require testimony by fire service personnel. Emergency incidents frequently are the scenes of crimes and other events that require adjudication and that also may involve the presence in court of firefighters. One segment of the fire protection effort that often works closely with the courts is the fire marshal. Fire marshals may obtain inspection warrants to compel businesses to allow firefighters to inspect their premises or obtain court orders to force compliance with code requirements or to cease operation.

Office of Emergency Preparedness

Most communities have an agency that is responsible for preparing for and responding to disasters. This office may be part of the fire department or may be a separate agency, such as the office of emergency preparedness or civil defense (Figure 8.9). Such emergencies are likely to require response by fire, rescue, and emergency medical personnel. The fire department works with this agency to define the department's role and responsibilities during large-scale disasters. In some jurisdictions, the head of

Figure 8.8 The street department must keep the fire department informed about street closures.

Figure 8.9 The agency responsible for response to large-scale disasters can greatly assist local fire departments.

the emergency preparedness agency may be empowered to command law enforcement, fire, rescue, and EMS operations when a major emergency is declared.

Civic Groups

Although civic groups such as the Chamber of Commerce, fraternal organizations, service clubs, local businesses, and others are not government agencies, they can do a lot to assist fire protection agencies in promoting fire safety. These groups allow the fire department to provide fire education to members and assist the department in publicizing and hosting classes, demonstrations, and other efforts designed to promote public awareness of fire and related safety issues.

State and Provincial Governments

Although fire protection is largely a local issue, fire protection agencies are affected by state and provincial legislation and must sometimes work with agencies of the state and provincial governments. For these reasons, company officers should be familiar with the structure and operation of this level of government.

State Governments

In the United States, state governments are generally modeled after the structure of the federal government with three functional branches: legislative, executive, and judicial. The legislative branch is responsible for enacting laws Members of the legislative branch are elected to represent their counties, parishes, or districts. All states except Nebraska have bicameral legislatures (consisting of two houses); Nebraska's legislature is unicameral (one house).

The head of the state's executive branch is called the *governor*. A governor serves as the head of state and is granted certain powers and responsibilities that vary from state to state. Generally, these powers include the right to veto or approve legislation, call the legislature into session, serve as commander of the state's militia and law enforcement agencies, and perform similar duties.

The judicial branch is responsible for interpreting state constitutions and overseeing the state's court system.

While the legislature may pass laws affecting fire protection and the judicial branch may involve the presence of firefighters before the bench, the greatest interaction between fire departments and the state government is through the administrative offices and agencies that serve under the governor. These are described in more detail later in this chapter.

Provincial and Territorial Governments

Canada is divided into ten provinces and two territories. Though both provinces and territories have governments, the powers of the territorial governments are more limited than those of the provinces. Provincial governments consist of three branches that include a unicameral legislative assembly (or National Assembly in Quebec), an executive branch headed by a premier, and a court system. Each province also has a lieutenant governor appointed by Canada's governor general; however, the position is largely honorary and carries no real legal authority. The duties of each branch are similar to those of the corresponding sections of U.S. state governments.

The political head of the Yukon Territory is the leader of the majority party, who carries the title of government leader. In the Northwest Territories, a commissioner appointed by the federal government provides political leadership. Each territory has a legislative assembly and a court structure similar to the provincial systems.

In Canada, much of the provincial and territorial influence over fire protection agencies is through interaction with the agencies described in the following section.

Agencies of State and Provincial Governments

Because the structure and function of agencies vary greatly among the states and provinces, company offic-

ers must make an effort to become familiar with the exact agencies and their responsibilities that are active in their political subdivision. The following list contains brief summaries of some of the more common agencies that influence fire protection in the United States and Canada. Remember that not all the agencies listed are to be found in all states and provinces and that in some areas agencies not listed may be of even more importance than those included here. Note, too, that agencies with the same or similar names may have different responsibilities and objectives in different jurisdictions. Not all the organizations described are government-sponsored, but each supports or affects the implementation of fire protection within the states and provinces.

Fire Marshal

Most states and provinces maintain a fire marshal's office. In as many as 47 of the states, the fire marshal serves as the principal authority on fire protection. Under some government structures, the fire marshal's office is an independent agency, while in others the position is part of another department, such as the state police. The responsibilities of the fire marshal vary greatly from state to state and province to province. However, a key responsibility under most state and provincial governments is to advise the legislature or assembly on fire-related legislation and to oversee the fire prevention program. In cases of fire involving state or provincial property, the fire marshal generally conducts cause and origin investigations. The fire marshal commonly serves on panels and committees tasked with state and provincial planning for hazardous materials control and disaster preparedness.

Fire Training Programs

Many states and provinces deliver fire training programs through their fire marshal's office, colleges and universities, or vocational training systems. Training is provided at the institution's facilities or, in some cases, at local fire department facilities. These programs often provide technical advice and planning assistance to local fire protection agencies.

Fire Commission

A few states and provinces have established commissions to conduct fire service training and certification programs. Most receive funding from the legislature or assembly to support operation of the commission. The agency is headed by a commissioner or director who oversees the commission's operations and influences its objectives.

Fire Chiefs Association

Many states and provinces have fire chief associations in which fire chiefs meet to consider common problems and objectives. Although not a governmental agency, most of the associations formally or informally lobby for legislation and remain available to the legislative and executive branches of the state or provincial government for advice on pending legislation.

Firefighters Association

Another nongovernmental agency operating on behalf of fire protection at the state and provincial level is the firefighters association. These associations generally work to influence legislative action, establish benefits for firefighters, implement fire protection awareness and training programs, and promote other efforts to improve public safety and the working conditions of firefighters.

State or Provincial Police

Fire departments often have to respond to fires and other emergencies outside the jurisdiction of their local police force. In such cases, state or provincial police often serve in the law enforcement role to provide traffic and crowd control, conduct large-scale evacuations, and protect firefighters during civil unrest (Figure 8.10). State and provincial police may also assist with arson investigations and other legal matters that cross jurisdictional boundaries. As stated earlier, in some states, the state fire marshal's office is under the jurisdiction of the state police.

Highway Department or Turnpike Authority

Roadway planning, maintenance, and control at the state or provincial level generally fall to the highway department or turnpike authority. Consequently, these agencies have a role in providing fire departments with usable thoroughfares to support emergency responses and to accommodate the required apparatus. Similarly, these agencies need to keep local fire officials informed of highway closures, detours, and repair work that might impede a response. The highway department and turnpike authority usually participate in state- or provincial-level disaster and hazardous materials incident planning, with local offices participating at the city and county level.

Environmental Protection Agency

Many states and provinces have established agencies to oversee environmental protection. In addition to serving in inspection, enforcement, and training roles, personnel from these agencies often assist in the development of response plans and frequently deploy to incident sites to support local response efforts.

Health Department

When a fire involves a medical facility, food vendor, place of lodging, or public building, the health department frequently inspects the facility after the incident to evaluate its suitability for continued service. The agency may request information or assistance from local fire protection agencies that responded to the emergency.

Forestry Department

Local fire departments often establish mutual aid agreements with the state or provincial forestry department and the logging industry (Figure 8.11). Under these agreements, the local fire department may assist in fighting fires that involve forest or other public lands. In reciprocation, the forestry department may make resources such as personnel and heavy equipment available to local fire departments, especially to assist in suppressing rural fires.

Figure 8.10 State or provincial police work closely with local agencies.

Figure 8.11 State fire fighting agencies assist local jurisdictions through mutual aid agreements.

Office of Emergency Preparedness or Civil Defense

Because local fire departments may have to respond to large-scale disasters or other emergency situations, they must be able to work with higher-level agencies, such as the office of emergency preparedness or civil defense, that also are involved in the planning or actual response. Further, such agencies may provide personnel, management, equipment, and other support to local resources for smaller emergencies (Figure 8.12).

Special Task Forces

Members of the legislative and executive branch and special interest groups, such as the insurance commission, may request support from local fire protection agencies to conduct task force studies that address special problems or situations. Generally, it is in the best interests of the fire department to support such requests when possible. The individuals and the department are likely to benefit from the exposure and visibility to other agencies and organizations, as well as have the chance to provide accurate information that can help ensure favorable actions with regard to department operations.

Other State and Provincial Agencies

Company officers should become familiar with the responsibilities, organization, and operations of other state and provincial agencies that may have some impact on local responses. For example, if a jurisdiction includes or is near a state or provincial park, interaction with the park and recreation department is important. If the jurisdiction includes navigable waterways, coordination with higher-level agencies responsible for such systems is vital. Local departments should exert an effort to identify these and other special needs within or near their jurisdiction and to ensure that coordination with these other agencies is addressed in planning and operating procedures as necessary.

Figure 8.12 The emergency preparedness agency can provide resources to local jurisdictions.

Federal Government

The federal governments of Canada and the United States have acknowledged their roles in providing for the public safety through the establishment of agencies and the passage of legislation to protect their citizens in emergencies and to reduce the risk of life-threatening incidents. These agencies operate within the structure of the government through the support of public funds and under the direction of elected or appointed officials. The legislation has been introduced and approved under the lawmaking processes of the respective nations.

Structure of the United States Federal Government

The federal government of the United States consists of three branches: the legislative branch represented by Congress, the executive branch represented by the President and Cabinet, and the judicial branch represented by the Supreme Court and the lower federal courts. While all three branches are involved in most aspects of running the government, basically Congress passes laws that are approved and enforced by the executive branch. Through legal actions, the Supreme Court rules on whether federal, state, and local laws are within the framework of the Constitution.

The President is the nation's chief executive and has the following principal duties:

- Enforces federal laws
- Appoints high-ranking federal officials, ambassadors, and representatives to international organizations
- Commands the armed forces
- Conducts foreign affairs
- Recommends laws to Congress
- Approves or vetoes laws passed by Congress
- Serves as the ceremonial head of the nation

The President is elected by the people through the electoral college to serve a four-year term. The Constitution allows the President to serve no more than two elected terms, plus up to two years of another President's unfinished term.

The President oversees a number of offices and agencies that make up the Executive Office, the Cabinet, and independent agencies. The Executive Office consists of 12 offices and councils, such as the National Security Council, Council on Environmental Quality, Office of Science and Technology Policy, as well as the White House Office staff and Office of the Vice President. The President has authority to expand or reduce the numbers and staffing of these offices.

The President's Cabinet consists of the heads of the 14 departments within the executive branch, such as Defense, Treasury, Health and Human Services, Commerce, and Energy. These department heads are referred to as *Secretaries* or, in the case of the Justice Department, *Attorney General*. Most of the cabinet members are assisted by one deputy or undersecretary and two or more assistant secretaries. All these positions are presidential appointments that normally last only during the terms of the president who appoints them. Most of the departmental work is done in field offices for the various bureaus, divisions, branches, sections, and units into which departments are divided. Staff members below the assistant secretary level are members of the civil service.

Legislation enacted by Congress often requires some means of implementation, such as obtaining funding for the space program. To carry out the requirements of various legislative acts, numerous agencies have been created, such as for the regulation of interstate commerce. These agencies exist as part of the executive branch, and the President appoints the administrators or directors who manage them. However, the Senate must approve the appointees and, if they are removed from office, the President must inform the Senate of the reason for their removal.

The legislative branch includes Congress and eight administrative agencies. Congress consists of two houses — the Senate and the House of Representatives. Two senators are elected from each state, and each serves a six-year term. In addition to enacting legislation, the Senate approves certain presidential appointments, ratifies treaties, and holds impeachment trials to remove federally elected officials from office. The House of Representatives includes a certain number of representatives from each state based on the population of the state, and each representative serves a two-year term. The larger the population of a state, the more representatives it sends to Congress so that the states with the smallest populations have one representative while California, which is the most populous state, has more than 50 representatives. The exclusive powers of the House include bringing charges of impeachment against officials and introducing legislation to fund the government's operations through taxation. Congress's administrative agencies include the Government Printing Office, General Accounting Office, Library of Congress, Congressional Budget Office, and four others.

The judicial branch is headed by the nation's highest court, the Supreme Court. It also includes nearly 100 district courts and 13 courts of appeal or circuit courts. Cases involving federal laws or issues of constitutionality are tried in district courts and can be appealed to circuit courts and, from there, to the Supreme Court. Federal judges are appointed by the President with approval of the Senate and serve for life or until they resign.

Lawmaking Process of the United States Federal Government

Congressional sessions in the United States last for two years. During that time, thousands of potential laws are introduced in the form of bills. A *bill* is the written description of the legislation that is presented to Congress. All bills must be sponsored by a member of Congress, though most are actually written by Congressional staff specialists called *legislative counsels* or by lawyers representing special-interest groups. The idea for a bill may come from the public, press, a special-interest group, Congress, the President, or another part of the government. However, any bills dealing with taxes and spending must originate in the House of Representatives. The sponsor of the bill gives it to the house clerk, who reads the title of the bill publicly so that it will appear in the Congressional Record. The bill then goes to the Government Printing Office for duplication and distribution. Congress maintains committees that have responsibility for various segments of government operations. The bill is assigned to a House Committee for review by the Speaker of the House and to a Senate Committee for review by the Senate Majority Leader. The committee studies the bill and often calls experts, as well as other interested persons or groups, to testify about the bill. The committee may send the bill on to the rest of the originating house, revise it and release it to the house, or "table it" — that is, take no action.

Released bills are placed on the Congressional calendar for debate and vote by the members of the originating house. On the specified date, the bill is read aloud. Members are then allowed to express their opinions about the bill and to debate its perceived merits and flaws. Members can propose amendments to the bill. These proceedings continue until there is no more discussion or for as long as the House Rules Committee permits or, in the Senate, until the members vote to limit debate. The members then vote on the bill, with a simple majority of voting members being required for approval of most bills.

The approved bill is passed on to the other house of Congress, where a sponsor introduces the bill by being recognized by the presiding officer and announcing it to the other members. The presiding officer assigns it to a committee. As in the originating house, the bill is then subject to study and, if approved by the committee, debate by the members in the legislative chamber. If the bill is approved by the second house, it goes to a conference committee, which includes representatives of both houses of Congress. Their task is to work out the differences between the Senate and House versions of the bill and to prepare a final draft approved by the committee. The revised version of the bill is submitted to both houses for another vote.

Once both houses approve the bill, the Government Printing Office prints the final version, and the bill is enrolled as an act. The clerk of the house that originated the bill certifies it and obtains the signatures of the presiding officers of both houses.

Congress sends the act to the President, who has ten days (excluding Sundays) to review the document. During this time, one of four following actions take place. The President can approve the act by signing and dating it and marking it as approved. The act then becomes law. The President can veto the act by returning it to Congress with an explanation as to why it was rejected. If an act is vetoed by the President, Congress can override the veto with a yes vote of two-thirds of the members present. The act then becomes law without the approval of the President. If Congress fails to override the veto, the act is dead and must begin again as a bill if it is to be reconsidered. Finally, the President can choose to take no action on the act. Chief executives sometimes choose this method to show their disagreement with parts of the legislation. If the President fails to approve or veto the act within the allotted time, it will become law without the chief executive's signature if Congress is still in session at the end of the 10 days. However, if Congress submits legislation to the President with fewer than 10 days remaining in the session and the President refuses to sign it, the proposed law is effectively disapproved in an action called a *pocket veto*.

Once a law is approved, responsible departments and agencies are then required to implement the law within their interpretation of the legislation and the guidelines set forth in the act. Any citizen or group can use the judicial system to challenge legislation that has been passed by Congress and enacted as law. A case that requires the court to rule on the constitutionality of the law must be brought. The case can proceed through appeals all the way to the Supreme Court, which can take one of three actions:

- Choose not to hear the case, which in effect declares the challenge invalid without actually ruling on constitutionality

- Hear the case and find in favor of the law

- Hear the case and determine that all or some of the law is not consistent with the Constitution

In the event that a law (including state and local laws) is overturned by the Supreme Court, the law is no longer enforceable, and legislative bodies which have approved the law or similar laws must address the issue through other laws.

U.S. Federal Agencies Involved in Fire Protection

In 1974, Congress passed the Federal Fire Prevention and Control Act (15 U.S.C. 2201) to provide improved training, assistance, coordination, and standards for fire protection. The act also established the United States Fire Administration. This legislation marked the federal government's first extensive regulatory efforts in the field of fire protection. Over the years, this involvement has intensified as a result of a growing awareness of modern threats to public safety, the increased use and transport of flammable and hazardous materials, continuing developments in fire suppression technology, improved communications, and a growing trend toward interorganizational cooperation among both government and private agencies.

Firefighters play a substantial role on both sides of these efforts. They must comply with and often enforce the laws and regulations, and they frequently benefit from the improved training and operating procedures that develop through such cooperation. Firefighters also contribute to defining these agencies and their operations by testifying before Congress and serving on committees as individuals and as representatives of professional organizations.

Federal Emergency Management Agency (FEMA)

FEMA is an executive agency that serves as a single point of contact within the federal government for emergency management activities. Its role is that of a supporting partner to organizations within and outside the fire service that are involved in emergency management. FEMA's organizational structure reflects the functions of emergency management: preparedness, response, mitigation, and recovery (Figure 8.13). In addition to these emergency management functions, the agency also supports risk-reduction and loss-prevention programs. From its headquarters and ten regional offices, FEMA oversees the operations of the U.S. Fire Administration, Federal Insurance Administration, and Urban Search and Rescue (US&R) task forces located throughout the country.

United States Fire Administration (USFA). Headquartered in Emmitsburg, Maryland, the USFA administers an extensive fire data and analysis program and provides

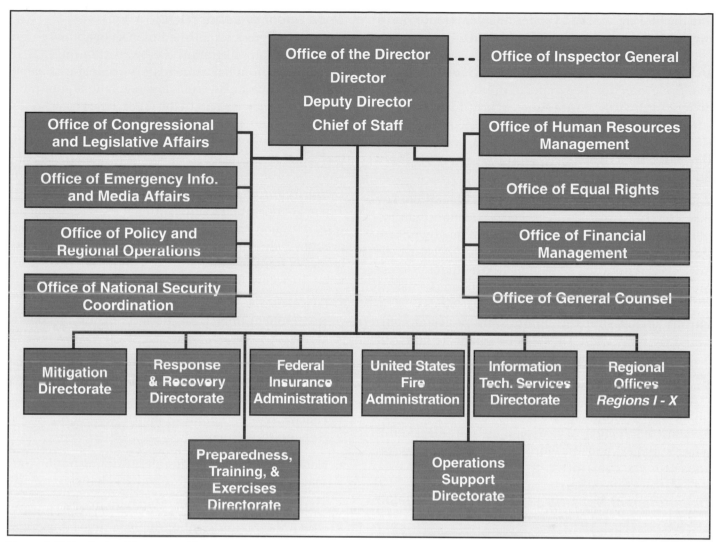

Figure 8.13 The Federal Emergency Management Agency.

overall fire policy and coordination. USFA acts as the lead agency in federal fire prevention and arson control programs, along with state and local fire service and law enforcement agencies (Figure 8.14). In conjunction with the National Institute for Occupational Safety and Health (NIOSH), the USFA administers a program concerned with firefighter health and safety. The USFA Administrator reports to the Director of the Federal Emergency Management Agency (FEMA).

National Fire Academy (NFA). The NFA is part of the National Emergency Training Center (NETC), colocated with the USFA in Emmitsburg, Maryland. The NFA provides training programs ranging from fire service management to the hazard mitigation of various materials and from arson investigation techniques to fire code application by architects and local building officials. Some fire-related training is also provided by the NETC's Emergency Management Institute (EMI) (Figure 8.15). The EMI's main focus, however, is on the training of civil defense forces which include the fire services. The NFA

Figure 8.14 The U.S. Fire Administration headquarters located in Emmitsburg, MD.

Figure 8.15 The Emergency Management Institute (EMI) is located at the National Fire Academy.

and the EMI are headed by superintendents reporting to the FEMA Associate Director for Training.

U.S. Department of Agriculture (USDA)

The fire protection programs of the U.S. Department of Agriculture (USDA) are aimed at fire prevention and education in rural areas and are carried out by the USDA Forest Service, more commonly known as the U.S. Forest Service (USFS), and the Farmers' Home Administration.

Known to millions through its familiar symbol Smokey Bear, the USFS provides fire protection to more than 200 million acres of forests, grasslands, and nearby private lands (National Forest System) (Figure 8.16). It also conducts research and develops improved methods in forest fire management (Forest Fire and Atmospheric Research) and provides technical and financial assistance to state forestry organizations to improve fire protection efficiency on nonfederal wildlands (Cooperative Fire Protection). Research is also conducted on wood and wood-based products.

The Farmers' Home Administration makes loans to public bodies and nonprofit corporations in rural areas for the construction of fire stations, the provision of water supplies, and the purchase of fire suppression apparatus and equipment.

Department of Housing and Urban Development (HUD)

The Manufactured Housing and Construction Standards Division of the Department of Housing and Urban Development (HUD) promulgates and enforces rules regarding the safety and durability of manufactured housing, including fire safety standards. These rules are for consumer protection and to determine eligibility for HUD loans and mortgage insurance policies.

Department of the Interior (DOI)

The Bureau of Land Management (BLM) within the DOI provides protection against wildfires on 545 million acres of public land and services and supports the Interagency Fire Center in Boise, Idaho (Figure 8.17). The Center provides logistic support for the U.S. Forest Service; the U.S. Department of Commerce's National Oceanic and Atmospheric Administration (NOAA); Bureau of Land Management; Bureau of Indian Affairs; National Park Service (NPS); and the Fish and Wildlife Service. The NPS also provides presuppression and suppression services and administers a fire safety program to protect national park visitors, employees, resources, and facilities.

Department of Labor (DOL)

In 1970, Congress established the Occupational Safety and Health Administration (OSHA) within the DOL to develop and promulgate mandatory occupational safety and health standards — rules and regulations applicable at the workplace. As part of the enforcement of its rules, OSHA conducts investigations and inspections, and it cites and penalizes companies for violations of the standards.

Department of Transportation (DOT)

Ten major operational units within the DOT investigate, research, analyze, and provide for the safety of vehicles, avenues, the environment, passengers, and cargoes in all modes of transportation. All these functions heavily involve fire safety. The organizational units are:

- Five divisions of the U.S. Coast Guard (ports, marine environment, merchant marine, marine fire safety, and safety programs)

- Three divisions within the Federal Aviation Administration (airports, special programs, and aircraft safety and airport technology)

- Federal Highway Administration (interstate highways)

- Federal Railroad Administration

- National Highway Traffic Safety Administration (on-road vehicle safety hazards and accidents)

- Maritime Administration (Merchant marine)

- Urban Mass Transportation Administration (buses and subways)

Figure 8.16 Smokey Bear symbolizes the U.S. Forest Service.

Figure 8.17 The National Interagency Fire Center located in Boise, ID.

- Materials Transportation Bureau (hazardous materials)
- Transportation Safety Institute (safety and security management, training)
- Transportation Systems Center (applied research)

Related to but independent from the DOT, the National Transportation Safety Board investigates and makes recommendations with respect to traffic accidents, including vehicular fire incidents.

Department of the Treasury

Through its network of agents across the United States, the Bureau of Alcohol, Tobacco, and Firearms (BATF) conducts a vigorous arson investigation program, including training and technical assistance to state and local law enforcement and fire authorities. The BATF's firearms and explosives programs protect interstate and foreign commerce from interference and disruption by reducing hazards to persons and property stemming from the insecure storage of explosives.

Consumer Product Safety Commission (CPSC)

The CPSC's Fire and Thermal Burn Program encompasses the investigation of injury patterns, data collection, research, and the promulgation and enforcement of mandatory standards with respect to consumer products.

Other U.S. Federal Agencies

Federal agencies, such as the Nuclear Regulatory Commission, U.S. Coast Guard, and Federal Aviation Administration, can play important roles in fire protection and emergency response procedures and planning. For example, while most jurisdictions will have little or no contact with the Nuclear Regulatory Commission (NRC), interaction with the NRC may be a normal part of a department's operations if its jurisdiction includes a nuclear power plant. Company officers must acquaint themselves with those federal agencies that may become involved in incidents that are likely to occur within the jurisdiction and in neighboring jurisdictions.

Structure of the Canadian Federal Government

The Canadian federal government is modeled after the national structures of both the United States and Great Britain. Canada is a federation of self-governing provinces and territories, much as the United States is a federation of self-governing states with a federal government consisting of three branches. Canada's legislature is called Parliament and consists of two houses: the House of Commons and the Senate. The judicial branch includes a Supreme Court, Canadian Federal Court, and lower courts. The most apparent differences in the structures of the U.S. and Canadian federal governments show up in the executive branch. Although Canada is an independent nation, it recognizes the sovereign of Great Britain as its official head of state. Thus, the king or queen of Great Britain presides in the same role over Canada, although no real powers are granted to the monarch. The British sovereign is officially represented in Canada by an appointed official termed the Governor General. However, the true chief executive of the Canadian government is the Prime Minister. The Prime Minister is assisted by a cabinet of approximately 40 ministers for various functional areas of the government.

The Senate is the upper house of Parliament. Technically, its 104 members are appointed by the Governor General, but the Governor General simply acts on the recommendations of the Prime Minister. The Senate cannot introduce legislation that involves spending money and has limited powers in approving constitutional amendments.

Members of the House of Commons are elected by voters of provincial districts called *constituencies*; however, a candidate need not live in the constituency or even in the province to run for office. Although members of the House are elected to five-year terms, elections are frequently held before the end of that term. This is because under Canadian law if the House of Commons fails to pass government-sponsored legislation, the Prime Minister must resign or ask the Governor General to call for a general election in which the people will elect a new House of Commons. While most members of the House seek re-election and often win, in theory the entire membership of the House could be replaced in a general election well before the expiration of their five-year term.

The Prime Minister is not directly elected to that position. Instead, the Prime Minister is a member of the House of Commons. Canada normally has three to four major political parties, and the Prime Minister is a member of the party that holds the majority membership of the House. Although officially appointed by the Governor General, the Prime Minister is in reality named by the majority party and serves in that role only as long as his party maintains a majority. Should the Prime Minister's party fail to hold a majority, the Prime Minister must resign or request the Governor General to call for a new general election. However, the Prime Minister may at any time ask the Governor General to dissolve the House of Commons and hold a new general election.

The Cabinet ministers are also members of the House of Commons or, rarely, the Senate. They are appointed by the Governor General upon the recommendation of the Prime Minister. Because of the likelihood that the Cabinet will be overturned in a general election, each also works under a deputy minister, who is a civil servant and the actual permanent head of the ministry.

Canada's Supreme Court adjudicates appeals in both criminal and civil suits. The Federal Court of Canada has two divisions, one for trials and one for appeals. It hears all cases involving the federal government — for or against. Judges, justices, and associate or puisne judges are appointed by the Prime Minister or by the Governor General in Council, which is the Governor General working with the advice and consent of the Cabinet.

A major difference in the philosophies of the two federal governments regards the limits of powers in the states and provinces. The United States has a relatively strong investment of powers in the governments of the states. Under the U. S. Constitution, states have all rights not specifically withheld by the Constitution. The only way that the U.S. federal government can overturn a state law is through the Supreme Court ruling that the law violates the Constitution.

Canada, however, grew into its independence during the years following the Civil War in the U.S. This conflict raised doubts in Canada about allowing the provinces too much independence; thus, the Canadian Constitution allows Parliament to overturn any law enacted by a province or territory. Canada also is more restrictive in the powers granted to its provinces, originally allowing them to legislate only 16 areas of government, such as education and health.

Lawmaking Process of the Canadian Federal Government

The Canadian Parliament recognizes two types of bills: public bills that affect the general population and private bills that affect individuals or small groups. Although any bill that does not involve spending may originate in either house, in actual practice virtually all bills are first introduced in the House of Commons and follow the steps described in this section.

All public bills begin the lawmaking process when a Cabinet minister requests that a bill be published in the Notice Paper. If the bill involves taxes or spending, a minister must still sponsor the legislation but only at the request of the Governor General in Council. After this notice, the minister requests permission in Parliament to introduce the bill through a first reading. Upon approval of the request, the bill is read for the first time without discussion. This is followed by a second reading during which members may debate the bill's principal objec-

tives but not the details of the legislation. At the end of the debate, the House votes on the bill. If the bill passes, the presiding officer forwards it to an appropriate committee.

The committee discusses the bill and returns it to the House with a written evaluation of the bill, its impact, suggested changes, and other information. The House may accept the committee report or return it to the committee for revision. Once the House accepts the committee report, the bill is debated on the floor. Amendments may be proposed and voted upon until such time as the presiding officer determines that the bill should be put to a vote. At this time, there is a third reading with some limited debate allowed and the proposal of additional amendments permitted.

If the bill receives the approval of the House, it goes to the Senate. There it undergoes a process similar to its introduction and review in the House. The Senate can take only limited actions on bills dealing with taxes and spending, but Senate committees can offer amendments to *reduce* spending or make amendments on other types of bills. When the bill goes to the floor of the Senate for its third reading, one of three actions can be taken. If the House version is approved without amendment, the bill goes to the Governor General. If the Senate votes the bill down, it must be resubmitted for a first reading and the process repeated. While the Senate cannot defeat a spending bill, it can delay passage of the bill for up to 180 days in this manner. Finally, the Senate may pass the bill with amendments. In this case, the bill is returned to the House for review of the Senate amendments.

If the bill is returned to the House, members review and vote on the Senate amendments. If they do not accept the amended bill, the House convenes a joint committee meeting with representatives of the Senate to work out compromises. The final version of the compromise legislation goes through three readings and a vote in each house. However, if the committee is unable to agree to compromises, the legislation is dead.

Legislation approved by Parliament goes to the Governor General for signature, who signs the bill into law. The legislation becomes effective immediately or at a time determined by the Cabinet.

Canadian Agencies Involved in Fire Protection

Numerous Canadian federal agencies have some form of interaction with the fire service. The following sections highlight these agencies and the relationship they have with the fire service.

Department of Labour

The Canadian Department of Labour through its Labour Relations Board works to prevent and settle labor disputes, including those that may involve unionized firefighters and the services on which firefighters depend. Additionally, the Canadian Centre for Occupational Health and Safety is administered within this department. The Centre oversees regulations intended to protect workers, including firefighters, in the workplace. Because these regulations also affect the use and storage of dangerous goods (hazardous materials) in the work place, Centre actions can influence how fire protection agencies respond to emergencies within such facilities.

Department of Public Works

Responsible for the construction and maintenance of public thoroughfares, bridges, and public buildings, the Department of Public Works and its field offices must work closely with fire protection agencies to ensure that their structures promote effective emergency response and fire safety. The Department must keep fire protection agencies informed of road closures, detours, and other situations that may prevent an effective and timely response. Canada's waterways and harbors also fall under the purview of the Public Works Department so that specific coordination may be required for the fire protection of watercraft and marine facilities within a jurisdiction.

Office of the Comptroller General

The Comptroller General oversees all federal spending in Canada. The Office is also responsible for government-sponsored economic development and regulatory affairs. Thus, fire protection agencies are affected by both the level of financial support provided to relevant programs and by specific regulatory actions taken by the Office.

Department of Consumer and Corporate Affairs

The Department of Consumer and Corporate Affairs through its Standards Council is responsible for much of the regulation of consumer welfare and safety. Though many of these standards are related to food and drug products, some of the regulations deal with product safety issues that can prevent injuries and reduce deaths in emergency situations, such as flame resistance and vehicle safety, and with similar standards.

Department of Finance

The Department of Finance prepares the federal budget and proposes it to Parliament. The Department of Insurance also resides within the finance ministry.

Department of Transport

The Department of Transport oversees virtually all transportation and communications within Canada. Because many transportation systems within Canada are government-owned, the Department's responsibilities include maintenance and operation of the national railway company, St. Lawrence Seaway Authority, Canadian Aviation Safety Board, and the Northern Pipeline Agency. The Department is involved in the regulation of hazardous materials transport on land, in the air, and on water.

Ministry of State for Science and Technology

Coordination of federally funded research falls to the Ministry of State for Science and Technology. Such research supports fire protection efforts for improved operating procedures, fire-retardant and suppression materials, apparatus development, construction methods, and first-aid techniques that can aid the objectives of firefighters.

Department of the Environment

The Department of the Environment plays a role in hazardous material incident response planning and the use of chemicals and methods in fire suppression. The Department also has responsibility for maintaining certain public and historical sites within Canada and, thus, must coordinate fire protection planning with local agencies.

Department of the Solicitor General

One of the primary responsibilities of the Solicitor General's Office is to run the federal prison system. However, a major division of the Department is the Royal Canadian Mounted Police, which works closely with fire departments and other law enforcement agencies throughout the nation and frequently assists with emergency responses.

Department of Agriculture

The primary fire protection concerns that are within the purview of the Department of Agriculture are the offices for forestry and mines. These offices are responsible for the maintenance of government-owned forests and mining operations and for the regulation of commercial timber and mining operations. Thus, the Department is able to work with local fire protection agencies to establish mutual aid agreements and to assist in response planning.

Other Canadian Federal Agencies

Many of the other departments have lesser roles in influencing fire protection operations in Canada. However, within a particular province or district, the importance of any given agency may be more pronounced, and fire officers need to become familiar with the need for coordination with particular agencies within their department jurisdiction.

Private and Professional Organizations

There are a large number of private and professional organizations with which company officers should be familiar. Each of these organizations has a specific role in the fire service, and the company officer should understand what those roles are and when they can be of assistance.

Congressional Fire Services Caucus

With more than 300 dedicated members, the Congressional Fire Services Caucus is the largest congressional caucus on Capitol Hill. Providing a bipartisan representation, the members of the caucus are drawn together by a mutual concern for the safety of our citizens and a respect for those who respond to fires and other emergencies.

Congressional Fire Services Institute

The Congressional Fire Services Institute is a nonpartisan, nonprofit organization dedicated to the task of educating the members of both houses of Congress on issues of importance to the emergency services. Because of its nonpartisan nature and the expertise of its members, the Institute is often consulted by members of Congress who need objective information about the emergency services and related issues.

International Fire Service Accreditation Congress (IFSAC)

IFSAC is an accreditation system operated by member organizations. Its purpose is to accredit entities that provide certification of fire service personnel, utilizing professional qualification standards at the state, province, or territory level. IFSAC accredits training organizations in numerous states, provinces, and foreign nations. Within IFSAC there are two separate and distinct assemblies, each with its own board of governors. The Degree Assembly accredits qualifying programs at degree-granting institutions such as community colleges and four-year institutions. The Certificate Assembly accredits training entities that certify those successfully completing specified training courses according to recognized standards.

International Fire Service Training Association (IFSTA)

IFSTA is an educational alliance formed in 1934 to develop training materials for the fire service. Committees meet each July (and at other times as needed) to review existing or proposed manuals. All validated manuals are published by the Fire Protection Publications division of Oklahoma State University (Figure 8.18). IFSTA's objectives are:

- To develop training materials and visual aids for publication
- To add new techniques and developments
- To delete obsolete and outmoded methods
- To validate training material for publication
- To provide materials for students and instructors to assist in certification
- To upgrade the fire service through training

IFSTA publications are used in all the U.S. states and Canadian provinces. A number of federal government agencies and several foreign countries have adopted the IFSTA publications as their official training manuals (Figure 8.19).

International Municipal Signal Association (IMSA)

IMSA was organized in 1896 as an educational, nonprofit organization dedicated to conveying knowledge, technical information, and guidance to its membership. Its

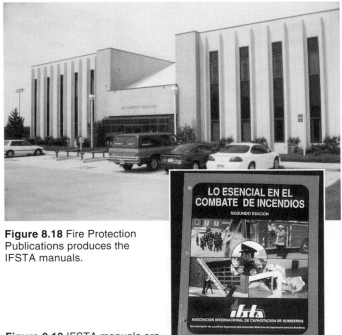

Figure 8.18 Fire Protection Publications produces the IFSTA manuals.

Figure 8.19 IFSTA manuals are translated into other languages.

current membership of more than 3,000 consists of municipal signal and communication department heads and their first assistants (Figure 8.20). The range of communications covered includes traffic control, fire alarms, and police alarms. There are sixteen sections of IMSA based on geographical areas in the United States and Canada, and a Sustaining

Figure 8.20 IMSA members play a vital role in emergency management.

Section to serve the regional needs of its members. The *IMSA Signal Magazine* is the Association's bimonthly publication.

International Society of Fire Service Instructors (ISFSI)

Organized in 1960, the International Society of Fire Service Instructors is composed of people responsible for training firefighters, fire officers, and rescue and emergency medical personnel. Its goal is to develop uniform professional standards for fire service instructors, to assist in the development of fire service instructors through better training and educational opportunities, to provide the means for continual upgrading of such instructors through in-service training, and to actively promote the role of the fire service instructor in the total fire service organization. It has members in all fifty states and ten foreign countries.

National Board on Fire Service Professional Qualifications (NBFSPQ)

The National Board on Fire Service Professional Qualifications (NBFSPQ) was created to improve life safety and fire protection through a national system of fire service professional qualifications certification and accreditation. The NBFSPQ supports the development of NFPA standards (NFPA 1000 series) on certification and accreditation, the utilization of such standards, a National Registry of Fire Service Professional Qualifications Certification, and the NFPA Fire Service Professional Qualification Standards. Accreditation of certifying organizations is carried out by the National Professional Qualifications Board (NPQB) under the direction of the Board of the Directors of the NBFSPQ. The Board of Directors receives advice from an advisory council made up of representatives of those organizations utilizing the system. The Board of Directors represent the organizations

appointed August 2, 1989, by the former Joint Council of National Fire Service Organizations to a select committee for determining the future for a national fire service certification accreditation program. The work of the select committee in establishing the NBFSPQ constituted the last activity of the former Joint Council.

National Volunteer Fire Council (NVFC)

The NVFC was organized in 1976 as an organization of various state volunteer firefighters associations and of individual volunteer firefighters. Its purpose is to represent and pursue the interests of volunteer firefighters and volunteer fire departments throughout the United States. Among its objectives are to provide a forum for the formulation of unified positions concerning developments nationally affecting volunteers and to support fire prevention education in the lower grades of school systems.

International Association of Arson Investigators (IAAI)

The International Association of Arson Investigators was formed at Purdue University, West Lafayette, Indiana, in 1949, when insurance industry, fire service, and law enforcement personnel from the United States and Canada met to discuss the growing arson prob-

Figure 8.21 IAAI members have the technical expertise needed to investigate fires.

lem and the need for training and education in fire investigation (Figure 8.21). The Association has the following objectives:

- To unite for mutual benefit those public officials and private persons engaged in the control of arson and kindred crime

- To provide for exchange of technical information and developments

- To cooperate with other law enforcement agencies and associations to further fire prevention and the suppression of crime

- To encourage high professional standards of conduct among arson investigators

- To continually strive to eliminate all factors that interfere with administration of crime suppression

Active membership in the IAAI is open to any representative (21 years of age or older) of government or of a governmental agency and to any representative of a business or industrial concern who is actively engaged in some phase of the suppression of arson and whose qualifications meet the requirements of the Membership Committee of the Association. Associate membership is open to persons not qualified for active membership after determination of their qualification by the Membership Committee. The IAAI publishes a quarterly bulletin, *The Fire and Arson Investigator*, and conducts an annual meeting in conjunction with a conference on arson, normally as part of a state arson seminar. Various committees are organized to assist the Association in its attack on the arson problem, such as the Fire Marshal Advisory Committee, the Fraud Fires and Organized Crime Committee, the Insurance Advisory Committee, the Legislative Committee, the Photography Committee, the Police Advisory Committee, the Riots and Civil Disorders Committee, and the Technical Advisory and Training Committee.

International Association of Black Professional Fire Fighters (IABPFF)

The IABPFF was organized in 1970 with the following goals:

- To create a liaison among black firefighters across the nation

- To compile information concerning injustices that exist in the working conditions in the fire service and to implement action to correct them

- To collect and evaluate data on all deleterious conditions where minorities exist

- To see that competent blacks are recruited and employed as firefighters where they reside

- To promote interracial progress throughout the fire service

- To aid in motivating African-Americans to seek advancement to elevated ranks (Figure 8.22)

Figure 8.22 The IABPFF promotes the interests of African-American firefighters.

The organization is a Life Member of the National Association for the Advancement of Colored People.

International Association of Fire Chiefs (IAFC)

The IAFC was organized in 1873 to further the professional advancement of the fire service and to ensure and maintain greater protection of life and property from fire. Its purposes are fulfilled by:

- Conducting research and studies of major problems affecting the fire service at community, state, provincial, regional, national, and international levels

- Developing and implementing an active program vital to the continued well-being of the fire service

- Serving as the recognized organization for the exchange of ideas, information, knowledge, and experience in areas affecting the safety of life and property from fire

- Encouraging and developing public education in fire prevention to preserve human life and material resources

- Promoting educational programs in the best interests of the fire service.

Active membership includes the following classifications: chief of department and all chief officers of regularly organized public, governmental, or industrial fire departments; state and provincial fire marshals; fire commissioners and/or fire directors who devote full time to administration and fire fighting operations. Associate membership includes fire commissioners and/or fire directors not responsible for administration or for fire fighting operations; directors of public safety; public officials; officers and members of fire departments; individuals interested in the protection of life and property from fire; and officers of recognized fire prevention organizations. Sustaining membership includes individuals and/or concerns engaged in the manufacture or sale of emergency apparatus or equipment and/or individuals or concerns otherwise interested in the field of fire protection. Other membership categories are active life members, associate life members, and honorary life members.

The IAFC also has more than twenty committees, or interest groups, that function for the organization including the Metropolitan Committee (chiefs of the major cities) who serve the Association in the special areas of their concern. These committees include arson, communications, emergency medical services, fire prevention, hazardous materials, health and safety, industrial and federal fire departments, professional development, urban search and rescue, and volunteers. The IAFC holds an annual conference with a major technical and educational exhibition each year and offers a series of publications on fire service matters to all interested persons. It has a membership of more than 10,000 and a headquarters staff of approximately 15.

Metropolitan Committee of the IAFC

The Metropolitan Committee of the International Association of Fire Chiefs, also commonly known as the *Metro Chiefs*, was organized in 1965. The membership of the Metropolitan Committee is limited to active fire chiefs of cities or jurisdictions having a population of more than 200,000 or a minimum of 400 career members and who are current members of the International Association of Fire Chiefs. The mission of the Metropolitan Committee is to assist the International Association of Fire Chiefs in developing and propagating policy relating to major fire departments.

Emergency Medical Services (EMS)

Almost 90 percent of all fire protection agencies in the United States provide some level of emergency medical service. This service may be first responder, emergency medical technician-basic (EMT-B), or paramedic. A growing number of these agencies provide cardiac defibrillation as well. The IAFC established an EMS section to assist local fire chiefs with the challenges presented by this very worthwhile community service.

International Association of Fire Fighters (IAFF)

Organized in 1918, the IAFF has approximately 175,000 members in the United States and Canada. The IAFF is affiliated with the American Federation of Labor and Congress of Industrial Organizations in the United States and the Canadian Labor Congress (AFL-CIO/CLC). Any person who is engaged as a permanent and paid employee of a fire department is eligible for active membership through the chartered local, state, or provincial associations and joint councils. Conventions of the Association are biannual. The IAFF headquarters provides a variety of services to the membership including technical assistance.

National Registry of Emergency Medical Technicians (NREMT)

NREMT registers emergency medical services providers across the United States. It is a private not-for-profit agency. The NREMT Board of Directors is comprised of members from national EMS organizations or who have expertise in the field. Established in 1970, the NREMT has tested more than 750,000 emergency medical technicians.

Underwriters Laboratories Inc.

Underwriters Laboratories Inc. (UL) in the U.S. and Underwriters' Laboratories of Canada (ULC) are not-for-profit corporations having as their sole objective the promotion of public safety through the conduct of "scientific investigation, study, experiments, and tests, to determine the relation of various materials, devices, products, equipment, constructions, methods, and systems to hazards appurtenant thereto or to the use thereof affecting life and property and to ascertain, define, and publish standards, classifications, and specifications for materials, devices, products, equipment, constructions, methods, and systems affecting such hazards, and other information tending to reduce or prevent bodily injury, loss of life, and property damage from such hazards." Formed separately by the same founder, these two organizations have now joined (Figure 8.23). An independent public service corporation, UL/ULC has no capital stock or shareholders, and exists solely for the service it renders in the field of fire, crime, and casualty prevention.

Factory Mutual Research Corporation (FMRC)

The research function of Factory Mutual Research Corporation (FMRC) is to conduct research and development in the field of property loss control (Figure 8.24). This activity serves the needs of the Factory Mutual System and is available to other entities, such as government agencies, trade associations, and individual businesses, through contracts.

The scope of the research ranges from basic investigation into the nature of fire to the development of standards for direct use by industry in establishing practices designed to minimize loss. Although such standards are intended primarily for Factory Mutual System members, they are recognized and widely used by others. Between the extremes of basic research and standards, major effort is made in the area of applied research. This activity includes studies, surveys, operations research, experi-

Figure 8.23 The UL and ULC are now one organization. *Courtesy of Underwriters Laboratories Inc.*

Figure 8.24 Factory Mutual is a well-established research and testing agency. *Courtesy of Factory Mutual.*

mentation, laboratory-scale testing, and full-scale testing to evaluate hazards and protection of storage, manufacturing operations, and construction arrangements.

Building and Fire Research Laboratory (BFRL)

Formerly the National Bureau of Standards' Center for Fire Research, the Building and Fire Research Laboratory (BFRL) of the National Institute of Standards and Technology (NIST) is located in the NIST complex at Gaithersburg, Maryland. The laboratory conducts research designed to improve codes and standards. This work is done by developing improved or new test methods and by using large-scale tests to validate the test method developments. Work is also conducted on acquiring knowledge of the properties of materials and their performance in fire conditions. The laboratories also create mathematical models to predict performance of materials under fire conditions.

Society of Fire Protection Engineers (SFPE)

Organized in 1950, the Society of Fire Protection Engineers is the professional society for engineers involved in the multifaceted field of fire protection engineering (Figure 8.25). The purposes of the Society are to advance the art and science of fire protection engineering and its allied fields, to maintain a high ethical standing among its members, and to foster fire protection engineering education. Its worldwide members include engineers in private practice, in industry, and in local, regional, and national government, as well as technical members of the insurance industry. Forty chapters of the Society are located in the United States, Canada, Europe, and Australia.

Figure 8.25 The SFPE represents fire protection professionals. *Courtesy of Society of Fire Protection Engineers.*

Membership in the Society is open to those possessing engineering or physical science qualifications coupled with experience in the field and to those in associated professional fields.

The Society serves as an international clearinghouse for fire protection engineering state-of-the-art advances and information. It publishes the *SFPE Bulletin*, a newsletter with regular features; the *Journal of Fire Protection Engineering*; and a series of "Technology Reports" covering technical developments of interest to the engineering community. It also publishes occasional special reports.

Summary

Fire departments do not exist in a vacuum. They are an integral part of the local community and of the state or province in which they are located. They must interact with other local, regional, and national organizations — both public and private. In order to do the best job possible for the citizens of the community, company officers need to be aware of the governmental structure of which their agency is a part, and of the myriad other organizations that may be able to assist in the delivery of services at the local level.

This chapter provides information that will assist the reader in meeting the following job performance requirements from NFPA 1021, *Standard for Fire Officer Professional Qualifications*, 1997 edition. The colored portions indicate the topics addressed in the chapter. The numbers of the job performance requirements are also noted directly in the sections of text where they are addressed. Those in the following list that are denoted with an asterisk (*) are global in nature and are covered by reading the chapter in its entirety.

Fire Officer I

2-3.1   Initiate action to a citizen's concern, given policies and procedures, so that the concern is answered or referred to the appropriate individual for action and all policies and procedures are complied with.

(a) Prerequisite Knowledge: Interpersonal relationships and verbal and nonverbal communication.

(b) Prerequisite Skills: Familiarity with public relations and the ability to communicate verbally.

2-3.2   Respond to a public inquiry, given the policies and procedures, so that the inquiry is answered accurately, courteously, and in accordance with applicable policies and procedures.

(a) Prerequisite Knowledge: Written and verbal communication techniques.

(b) Prerequisite Skills: The ability to relate interpersonally and to respond to public inquiries.

Community Awareness and Public Relations

Most fire departments and their personnel are highly regarded by the members of their community, but they should not take this for granted. Every fire department or other emergency service organization must be aware of its public image and of the importance of maintaining a positive one. How the community perceives its fire department and the level of service provided by its members is of vital importance to the operation of the department. A strong, positive public image can result in a higher level of funding for the department. Likewise, a negative public image can result in a budget that restricts the department's ability to fulfill its charge.

But funding is only one of many ways in which the department's success can be directly or indirectly affected by the community's perception of it. If some factions within the community think of the department as being part of "the establishment" and not as part of the community, then they may have little or no interest in cooperating with the department's fire prevention efforts. They may even be motivated to engage in vandalism and other criminal activity such as stealing fire equipment from neighborhood buildings, disabling built-in fire equipment, or even committing arson. On the other hand, if the department and its personnel are thought of as being an integral part of the community, members of the public can be effective advocates for fire safety at the neighborhood level.

While the public's perception of the fire department is influenced by what they see and hear from the various news media, the primary source of their image of the department is their day-to-day contact with department personnel at fires, medical aid calls, rescues, inspections, public education presentations, and times when the citizens make inquiries or lodge complaints. Because most of this day-to-day public contact is with company-level personnel from the nearest fire station, the company officer is in an ideal position to influence the outcome of these contacts and therefore to influence the public's perception of the department.

This chapter discusses community awareness and public relations, including both group presentations and media programs. Also discussed are handling citizen concerns and public inquiries.

Community Awareness

Because much of the department's public image is directly related to how the members of the community perceive the department, it is imperative that department personnel at all levels know the various factions that make up the local community. These factions may be divided along socio-economic, racial, ethnic, religious, age, or gender lines — or a combination of them (Figure 9.1). The extent to which department personnel know each of these groups and their unique interests, as well as the interests they may share with other community groups, determines how well the department is able to serve the individual members of those groups — the department's external customers/employers.

Figure 9.1 Department personnel must know the makeup of their community.

It is important for department personnel at all levels, but especially at the company level where the majority of public contact takes place, to make a conscious effort to get to know the people in their response district (their primary customers) and the community as a whole (their employers). Department personnel can eventually get to know their primary customers solely through contact during routine nonemergency activities and during emergency calls, but this unmethodical approach is very inefficient and may even produce some very negative results in the process. For example, if department personnel are unaware of the customs of certain religious or ethnic groups, they may inadvertently offend members of these groups by doing something that is perfectly normal in our society as a whole but unacceptable within the particular culture involved. Seemingly minor and inconsequential incidents of this nature may have far-reaching effects on the department's image with that particular group.

Just as firefighters are able to fight fires more effectively and more safely in occupancies with which they are familiar (due to pre-incident planning), they are more likely to be able to deliver a higher level of service if they are familiar with the needs and peculiarities of those they are serving. Therefore, in order to better understand the various factions within the community as a whole and the immediate response district in particular, it is important for the company officer to actively seek opportunities to interact with these groups whenever possible (Figure 9.2).

Public Relations

Although they are closely related, in the context of NFPA 1021 and this manual, there is a difference between community awareness and public relations from the fire department's standpoint. In the former, department personnel strive to become knowledgeable about the various factions within the community in order to serve them better. In the latter, they strive to acquaint the community with the department's mission and, of course, to show the department and its operations in the best possible light. In a very real sense, public relations is the process of marketing the department to the community.

While there are other ways to enhance the department's public image, the means most often used by fire departments is *public education*. As described in more detail in Chapter 10, "Public Education Program Development and Implementation," public education is one of the most cost-effective activities of any emergency service organization. In terms of public relations, it is an ideal way for the department to enhance its public image while providing a valuable public service. Actively seeking opportunities to interact with the community in this way can generate a tremendous amount of goodwill for the department. Two of the most effective means of enhancing the department's image through public education are *group presentations* and *media programs*.

Group Presentations

As mentioned earlier, every opportunity to deliver a fire safety message to a community group is also a good way to get to know that group and to develop a positive relationship with them. This is where the line between community awareness and public relations blurs; however, as long as the outcome is positive, the distinction is unimportant.

Civic groups, service clubs, and other organizations within the community are usually looking for speakers to address their meetings, and these engagements can provide the department with numerous opportunities to make fire safety presentations. From the community awareness standpoint, it is important that these presentations be made by the local fire company. This provides them with an opportunity to interact directly with people from the local neighborhood. From the public relations standpoint, it may be more important that these presentations be made by public education specialists within the department in order to maintain consistency in the message and its delivery in all neighborhoods throughout the community. If company officers are trained to deliver effective fire safety messages in this way, the number of available speakers within the department is greatly increased. Regardless of how and by whom these presentations are made, it is most important that every opportunity to make such presentations be taken.

Media Programs

Live and/or prerecorded fire and life safety messages delivered by fire department personnel through the vari-

Figure 9.2 Company officers should get to know the people they serve.

Figure 9.3 Many ways of serving the community are available.

Figure 9.4 Citizen complaints should be received in a friendly and professional way.

ous media can be a very effective way to increase public awareness while enhancing the department's public image. As a condition of their operating licenses, broadcast media are required to set aside a certain amount of their broadcast time for public service messages. Many fire departments across North America have taken advantage of these opportunities. Very often, company officers are given the opportunity to research, develop, and deliver these messages. In one community in northern California, a company officer hosts a weekly fire and life safety program on the local public service channel (Figure 9.3). Other fire departments are involved in similar programs that benefit both the public and the department.

Newspapers and other print media also provide opportunities for the department to educate the public about fire and life safety and thereby enhance the department's public image. Service clubs and other civic organizations often provide space in their newsletters for public safety pieces. Restaurants may allow the department to use their paper place mats for public service messages.

While it is important to target high-risk periods, such as the 1st of July in Canada, the 4th of July in the U.S., and Fire Prevention Week, it is also recommended that the department carry on a year-round program of public education activities. This continually draws positive attention to the department. If company officers maintain a close relationship with the various groups that comprise their response district, they can often recognize opportunities for public education efforts that might otherwise go unnoticed.

Handling Citizen Concerns

[NFPA 1021 2-3.1]

The term *citizen concerns* often translates into citizen *complaints*. That is, they have a concern/complaint with something the department, district, or city has done — or

not done, as the case may be. The issue may involve something directly under the control of the department, such as burning regulations or weed abatement. These issues are appropriate for department personnel, usually the company officer, to deal with. But the issue may also involve something over which the fire department has no jurisdiction — parking regulations, for example. These concerns may be brought to the fire department simply because department personnel wear uniforms and badges that are similar to those worn by the police. Or, it may be that the nearest fire station is the closest government facility to the citizen's residence. Regardless of how or why a citizen complains to the local fire station, the company officer must be prepared to deal with the concern in a friendly, courteous, and professional manner (Figure 9.4). Even if the citizen is angry or upset, the company officer must remain calm and in control — allowing the citizen to voice the concern/complaint in his own way. If the citizen is so irate that he is verbally abusive or threatens to resort to physical violence, the company officer should call for police assistance.

One of the first skills required of the company officer when dealing with irate citizens is effective listening. He must develop the ability to hear what the citizen means, even when the citizen is unable to articulate the concern clearly. This may require an extraordinary degree of familiarity with the idioms used by the people of the neighborhood (community awareness) or the ability to read the citizen's body language — or both. Very often, just allowing the citizen to voice the complaint will cause him to calm down and be able to look at the issue more rationally. The essential point is that the company officer must try to understand the true nature of the complaint so that he can begin to do something about it.

Once the real issue has been identified, it is up to the company officer to either resolve it or refer the citizen to the appropriate person or office. If it is within the company officer's means and authority to satisfy the citizen's concern/complaint, he should do so. Even if the concern is outside the company officer's purview, he should take a personal interest in seeing that the concern/complaint is resolved to the citizen's satisfaction and as soon as possible. This may require the company officer to speak on behalf of the citizen with whoever is empowered to deal with the citizen's issue (Figure 9.5). Unless the concern/complaint is voiced during an emergency operation, the citizen's concern becomes one of the company officer's most important responsibilities at that moment and until it is resolved.

In order to refer the citizen to the appropriate person, it is necessary for the company officer to be thoroughly familiar with the departmental and jurisdictional rules and regulations that apply and with the full range of services that are available to the citizens. He must know what is and is not possible under existing regulations and what avenues are or are not open to the citizen who has a problem. The company officer's duty is to use every legal and ethical means within his authority to satisfy the citizen's concern. To the extent required by department policy, the company officer must also document the complaint and its disposition (Figure 9.6). Such documentation may prove to be invaluable should the issue progress to litigation.

In reality, handling citizen concerns/complaints is the essence of customer service in the public sector. As such, how these concerns/complaints are resolved determines to a great extent how the public views its fire department. Because fire departments in general are committed to providing the highest level of service and because of the relationship between customer service and the department's public image, it is critically important that all such issues be resolved as reasonably and as

quickly as possible. While company officers are bound by department policy in such matters, department policy makers might do well to follow the customer service policy of one major U.S. retail chain when setting policy for the department. This firm's policy dictates that when employees receive a customer complaint, they are to do four things:

1. Apologize to the customer for being inconvenienced.

2. Identify the nature of the complaint.

3. Ask the customer how they would like the complaint resolved.

4. Do it.

If the employee perceives the customer's requested resolution as unreasonable, he is not allowed to refuse the request but must refer the customer to the next higher level within the organization. This process continues until the customer is satisfied or until the highest level of local management is reached. In this firm's system, only the store manager is empowered to refuse to comply with a customer's request for complaint resolution. While this policy may not be reasonable for public agencies, those who set policy for these agencies should attempt to comply with the spirit of this approach.

One class of citizen complaints is different from most, if not all, of the others — those that involve an act or omission by a member of the department. Because of the sensitivity of these issues in terms of the department's image, the concern for the rights of all involved, and the possibility of litigation, these cases must be handled with extreme care. The company officer receiving the complaint must know and follow department policy to the letter, but in most cases, policy will require him to begin the process of formalizing the complaint by starting to document it. He should attempt to elicit as much pertinent information as possible from the complainant regarding the alleged incident. When this has been done, the company officer should reassure the citizen that the complaint will be fully investigated and that he will be informed of the results of the investigation. The company officer should then forward the complaint through channels to the appropriate individual or office.

The company officer who received the original complaint may or may not be involved in the investigation of it. In either case, he should make it a personal responsibility to see that the complainant is informed (by the appropriate member of the department) of the results when the investigation has been completed. If the company officer is tasked with contacting the complainant, he must be careful to not divulge any information that may be considered to be privileged or confidential. Be-

Figure 9.5 Company officers should actively pursue solutions to citizen complaints that they receive.

Figure 9.6 Company officers should fully document every complaint that they receive.

fore contacting the complainant, the company officer should consult with his supervisor and/or the personnel department to clarify what information can and cannot be made public.

Handling Public Inquiries

[NFPA 1021 2-3.2]

While sometimes similar to handling citizen concerns, handling public inquiries is usually less strident and confrontational. However, citizen concerns/complaints often begin with a seemingly straightforward inquiry. It is only when the citizen gets the anticipated response that he reveals the true nature of the visit. But, in most cases, citizen inquiries are just that — genuine requests for information or clarification.

Just as in handling concerns/complaints, company officers must develop the ability to hear what the citizens mean as well as what they ask. Citizens are often not familiar with legal or regulatory language, and they simply need to know whether and how some particular regulation applies to them (Figure 9.7). Once again, this requires that company officers be able to understand the true nature of the question and know what remedies are available under the circumstances. He must know what forms are required and be willing and able to assist the citizen in filling them out (Figure 9.8). Obviously, many of these functions can and should be delegated to the members of the company, but the responsibility for the result remains with the company officer.

Figure 9.7 Citizens may need help understanding code requirements.

Figure 9.8 Citizens may need help in completing required forms.

The Phoenix (AZ) Fire Department has developed a customer service philosophy that might serve as a model for other fire departments and emergency response organizations. The following list is excerpted (with permission) from *Essentials of Fire Department Customer Service*, by Alan Brunacini.

1. *Our essential mission and number one priority is to deliver the best possible service to our customers.*

   While changes in technology, the current environment, our service delivery menu, and organizational complexity have created huge differences in our business, the most important element has not changed — the relationship and feeling between the customer who has a problem and the firefighter who responds to solve that problem. The two become intensely involved in a very special experience that defines essentially why we exist as a service. If we screw up that intense relationship (for any reason), both the firefighter and the customer can be in big trouble. The most profound evidence of our existence to the customer is that we show up when they are having a bad day and call us for help. Based on that reality, being a firefighter involves making a promise to the customer that we will respond to their call and do our very best. If we become so modern, so distracted, or so overcome with our own qualifications and importance that we lose sight of that promise and can't get that vision back, we should make an adjustment in our fire service vocation/avocation and go sell aluminum siding to people who live in brick houses.

2. *Always be nice — treat everyone with respect, kindness, patience, and consideration.*

   This human-to-human process begins with the initial call to request assistance. As Fire Department operational participants concerned with the long term impact and effect of service to the customers within our community, we are absolutely compelled to examine the most consistently important and memorable part of the service delivery experience to the customer — being NICE. When we receive feedback, observe, review, critique, listen, and examine being nice within a fire department service delivery context, it involves the basic behaviors of respect, kindness, patience, and consideration.

   Nice isn't some blue sky, smiley-face program — it is a combination of both a definitive set of high level technical service delivery activities combined with another definitive set of ways we humanely deliver that service. While it may be just another day at the office for us, it's a pretty special day for the people we serve.

3. *Always attempt to execute a standard problem-solving outcome: quick/effective/skillful/safe/caring/managed.*

Customers trust us as pros to manage the system and expect that we will provide the correct combination of system pieces required for effective operation. They also expect that we have the capability (and inclination) to put all the pieces together in a way that solves their problem when they call us for help. Our current vision for effective service delivery involves coordinated teams of well-trained, managed, and motivated firefighters. These teams utilize the resources of the response system to deliver service in a way that delights(!) the customer.

Consistently excellent fire department service is the result of an explicit, long-term, planned, acted out, and refined organizational approach. The smart money will always bet on the future of any organization after watching how they regularly and consistently connect with their internal and external customers.

4. *Regard everyone as a customer.*

It's pretty easy to develop tunnel vision when we deliver service because we are inclined to be highly preoccupied with and focused on the direct customer and their environment. While we should always give the customer our undivided attention (another item in this essay), we should realize that we are always on stage and that we are typically exposed to a lot of people.

A progressive change in our mentality (and approach) involves regarding everyone we encounter, both directly and indirectly, as a person who is our customer. This expanded customer consideration includes the person who receives our service directly and anyone who knows and is closely connected to that customer like family, neighbors, friends, or associates. This group generally has an intense interest, emotional connection, and personal concern for the welfare of the person receiving direct service and the effect and outcome of the emergency event. These people are very much an integral part of the incident, and we should treat them in a positive way and include them in our customer service incident action plan (respect, kindness, consideration, patience).

Family members are a very special group that many times require more attention than the main incident problem or customer. Family members become intensely involved, interested, and emotionally connected when a loved one is injured, sick, or threatened in any way. Situations that involve children or elderly relatives particularly require increased sensitivity on the part of our members. Many times the actual incident problem is very straightforward and solvable, but the reaction and involvement of family members requires another "treatment" focus and approach. Officers should include family members in their initial evaluation and develop an incident action plan for dealing with the entire family.

The way we handle family members (either good or bad) creates a lasting memory and feeling.

NOTE: In addition to the very valid points that Chief Brunacini made in this section, making prior arrangements to have members of the clergy available to counsel family members is also a good idea.

5. *Consider how you and what you are doing looks to others.*

As previously stated (over and over) every part of our system is firefighter driven and directed. This includes how we look to the customers — as individuals and as an organization.

This impression is created and maintained by the direct and indirect impression and feeling the customers develop in response to the appearance, performance, and behavior of our members. Simply, we create a human customer reaction in response to how our human firefighters look and what we are doing (human/human).

Our image must be planned and managed at the point and moment the customer impression is created. We never get that opportunity back — the deodorant ad says "you never get a second chance to make a first impression" (they ought to know).

The firefighter in control of that customer impression becomes, in effect, our department image maker. This creates the very practical reality that the really high impact of our customer contact system is the human part. This quickly shows that our firefighters are directly in control of the customer service delivery experience. It also shows that fire department managers have no real capability (and hopefully no inclination) to guard the customers from the firefighters.

6. *Don't disqualify the customer with your qualifications.*

Firefighters today are trained and equipped to deliver a very high level and very broad range of emergency services. Our members come on duty prepared to use a full range of their technical skills and abilities. However, our customers sometimes call us for problems that our members do not define as serious or critical. In the vast majority of cases, whatever the customer called us for is an emergency to them — regardless of how we redefine their situation. If the problem is minor, there is a temptation for our members to define the event as a "snivel" call — a big time problem occurs when our members act out that "snivel" definition.

If our firefighters, who are typically more qualified (actually, a lot more) than ever before, develop a judgment that some of our customers are less qualified than ever before (because their problem did not come up to the firefighters' training/skill level or definition of a "righteous" call), our firefighters disqualify those people as customers and begin to treat them in a callous, indifferent, sometimes rude, and disrespectful manner. If this occurs frequently enough over a period of time, our reputation goes from being heroes to being jerks...as we lose customer support, acceptance, and affection, our organization begins to decline.

7. *Basic organizational behavior must become customer-centered.*

We must recognize that basic fire department customer service delivery on the business end involves three major players: workers, bosses, and customers. The customers are those who receive service or are in some way connected to the event. Workers are firefighters who operate on the task level. They do the skilled manual labor that directly solves the customer's problem. Bosses are first level supervisor company officers who personally and directly manage and lead the service delivery event. These three players are intensely connected operationally and come together right where service is delivered. While there are a lot of other people and places required to create the READY, GET SET, only workers and their bosses can do the GO part of the organizational service delivery operation.

An absolutely essential fire department customer service player is the company officer boss. They are typically Captain and Lieutenant types who do first level supervision as an integral (inside) part of the service delivery team — right where and when the service delivery event occurs. They don't need to make a phone call to get permission, check a form or a computer screen, deal with a middleman (or woman), or look up in the ops manual to determine what is going on. They can directly see, touch, feel, hear, smell, and sense the activity, progress, and outcome of service delivery as it is actually occurring.

Company officers operate inside the basic fire department service delivery team — the fire company. They are the only bosses with continuous access and control of the fire company peer process (the most powerful organizational influence). Their presence and effect are so consistently powerful because they are with the vast majority of a fire department's human resources all the time.

8. *We must continually improve our customer service performance.*

We should approach the future with a great deal of optimism. Our history reflects we can do about anything that is required to reach our objective — we practice this in the street (where we should really keep score) every day. We do this basically because of the dedication, brains, fortitude, and good nature of our firefighters. Sometimes, the American fire service beats itself up by a self-characterization of being backward, inbred, and resisting change. This is baloney — while firefighters are naturally skeptical, not easily impressed, and don't change just for the sake of change, we are not going to hell in a hand basket or a 1500 GPM pumper. Our customers will love us for the next 200 years for the same reasons they have for the last 200. We are there when they need us, we care about them, we get the job done, and they can trust us (WOW!).

What we are about now is making a good thing even better, gently overpowering and bringing along the negative people and stuff in our business, and always redirecting ourselves in a positive direction.

While everything is not perfect and never will be, I'm sure happy we didn't seek employment in the savings & loan business, the U.S. Senate, or as a television evangelist. We must continually improve our approach to the management of change to prepare us for what is next. We must recognize that customer change must drive effective fire service change in the future.

Summary

Much of the fire department's ability to fulfill its mission depends upon how the members of the community view the department and its personnel. From support in the governing body for departmental budget requests, to cooperation from the citizens with fire prevention and similar programs, the department depends on its positive public image. Much of the goodwill (or lack thereof) that maintains the department's public image is generated through day-to-day interactions between department personnel and the citizens. Very often these interactions take the form of citizen concerns being expressed to department personnel or of citizen requests for information from the personnel. How these concerns and/or inquiries are handled can make a lasting impression on the citizens involved, so it is imperative that all such interactions be dealt with in a very friendly, professional, and expeditious manner.

This chapter provides information that will assist the reader in meeting the following job performance requirements from NFPA 1021, *Standard for Fire Officer Professional Qualifications*, 1997 edition. The colored portions indicate the topics addressed in the chapter. The numbers of the job performance requirements are also noted directly in the sections of text where they are addressed. Those in the following list that are denoted with an asterisk (*) are global in nature and are covered by reading the chapter in its entirety.

Fire Officer II

3-3.1* Deliver a public education program, given the target audience and topic, so that the intended message is conveyed clearly.

(a) *Prerequisite Knowledge:* Contents of the fire department's public education program as it relates to the target audience.

(b) *Prerequisite Skill:* The ability to communicate in writing.

Public Education Program Development and Implementation

Another component of a fire department's overall fire and injury prevention effort is the fire and life safety education program, often called simply *public education*. The purpose of a fire and life safety education program is to inform members of the community about the fire and life safety hazards they face and what they can do to mitigate those hazards — that is, to help them change their behavior in a way that results in fewer fires, injuries, and property losses within the community. But, instead of attempting to educate the entire community as a whole, it is more practical and more effective to divide the community into smaller, more manageable groups. These groups may include preschoolers, school children, homeowners, apartment tenants, those with disabilities, public and private employees, medical and nursing facility personnel, church groups, service clubs, and civic organizations. The programs used to educate these groups may focus on home fire escape planning, baby-sitting safety, cooking accidents, clothing fires, juvenile firesetting, scald prevention, first aid for burns, home fire safety inspections, smoke detectors, fire extinguishers, and residential sprinkler systems. The programs should reflect the community or communities they are designed to serve. For example, if the community is adjacent to wildland areas or incorporates developments in the wildland/urban interface, the programs should include information about fire safe roofing, defensible space, and similar topics. If there are ethnic enclaves in the community, fire and life safety materials may need to be printed in each group's native language.

Regardless of how large or small a fire and life safety education program is, it must be well-planned and conscientiously delivered if it is to accomplish its purpose. Such programs must be based on specific, measurable goals and objectives and be focused on specifically identified groups. For example, a goal of reducing fires and burn injuries to residents of boarding homes for the aged

by 50 percent might translate into one program intended to educate the residents of these facilities and another program for their staffs.

This chapter addresses company-level participation in the planning, development, and delivery of fire and life safety programs. The primary emphasis is on the five-step planning process — identification, selection, design, implementation, and evaluation.

Company-Level Participation

When properly trained in the concepts of fire and life safety education, company officers can be valuable assets to the fire department as well as to the community they serve. Company officers can play important roles in the development and delivery of fire and life safety education. In fire departments that are not large enough to have a full-time fire and life safety educator on staff, company officers and their subordinates can use on-duty time to develop and deliver these programs. An additional benefit that can result from fire companies delivering fire and life safety programs within their respective response districts is that a bond of goodwill between the fire department and the community can be developed or reinforced.

As mentioned earlier, company officers and their subordinates may be asked to participate in the planning and development of the department's fire and life safety education program (Figure 10.1). Because of their close contact with the community, company-level personnel can provide input that is very useful in developing program goals and objectives that target the most pressing needs within the community and in focusing the delivery on the most appropriate group or groups. Especially if company-level personnel will be assigned to deliver the program, then they should be allowed to participate in its development. Regardless of who is assigned to develop

Figure 10.1 Company-level personnel may be involved in developing fire and life safety programs.

Figure 10.2 Incident data may help identify fire and life safety problem areas.

the program, he should follow a structured and organized plan. Such a plan is outlined in the IFSTA **Fire and Life Safety Educator** manual. It is called the *five-step planning process.*

The Five-Step Planning Process

Providing a systematic planning and action process, it is composed of the following steps:

- **Identification** of major fire and life safety problems
- **Selection** of the most cost-effective objectives for the education program
- **Design** of the program itself
- **Implementation** of the program plan
- **Evaluation** of the program to determine impact

These steps — or similar steps with different names — are not limited to public fire and life safety education planning; they are also well-recognized in other safety education disciplines. In the five-step planning process, each step consists of several fact-finding activities and a decision. The fact-finding activities involve answering a series of questions about the local jurisdiction. A suggested "to do" list is included for each activity.

Experienced users of the five-step planning process advise "first-timers" to be flexible with the "to do" list. This list identifies the sorts of tasks that will have to be done, but it is not a hard-and-fast checklist. The five-step method can be used for planning any of the various types of fire and life safety education programs. However, for the purposes of this discussion, the examples focus on fire and burn prevention themes.

Identification

Identifying the most significant local fire and life safety problems and concerns is the objective of the identification step (Figure 10.2). The following are some of the questions asked during the identification process:

- **What are the major fire and burn hazards?**
  - Research records on the causes of fires and burn injuries.
  - Identify the most frequent causes of fires and burn injuries.
  - Identify any patterns of local fires and burn injuries.

- **Where are the high-risk locations?**
  - Identify neighborhoods or building occupancy types with high fire and burn injury risks.
  - Identify why the risks are above average.
  - Plan to concentrate resources in these high-risk locations.

- **When are the high-risk times?**
  - Identify times of day, week, or year with the highest incidence of fire loss or burn injuries.
  - Identify types of fires occurring at these times.
  - Plan to concentrate fire safety messages at these times.

- **Who are the high-risk victims?**
  - Identify groups with high fire death and injury rates.
  - Identify why they have an above-average fire and injury rate.
  - Involve these groups in the fire education planning effort.

- **What is the high-risk behavior?**
  - Identify which behaviors — acts or omissions — cause fires and burn injuries.
  - Identify how the behaviors can be changed.
  - Teach the people exactly what to do and what not to do.

Hazard and Risk

In everyday conversation, the terms *hazard* and *risk* are often used interchangeably. Technically, however, hazards and risks describe two different things. The term *hazard* usually refers to the source of a risk. A *risk*, on the other hand, is the likelihood of suffering harm from a hazard. Risk can also be thought of as the potential for failure or loss. In other words, *risk* is the exposure to the hazard, and a *hazard* is a condition, substance, or device that can directly cause an injury or loss.

Examples of fire-related hazards include ignition sources (such as smoking materials or faulty electrical wiring) or behaviors (such as children playing with matches or persons overloading electrical outlets).

Fire-related risk is often expressed as the number of incidents, injuries, or deaths per capita (for each unit of the population) (Figure 10.3). Depending upon the source of information, the per capita unit may be one person, a thousand people, or a million. To avoid comparing apples to oranges, public fire and life safety education planners must be clear as to what per capita means in each statistical table or report.

Education programs — no matter how good they are — cannot change hazards that are substances or devices. For example, education simply cannot change the temperature of a cigarette lighter or the flammability of gasoline. (NOTE: Technology may change substances or devices.) Education can, however, influence some people to change some conditions or behaviors, such as smoking in bed. Other conditions — age or disability, for example — are unchangeable. In those cases, the educa-

tor must develop programs to reduce the risk, the exposure to the hazard. For example, a program to teach nursing home caregivers to supervise residents' smoking helps reduce the risk (likelihood of suffering harm from a hazard, potential for failure or loss, or exposure to a hazard) even though the hazards (sources of risk or the condition, substance, or device) are unchanged.

Gradually, during the identification step, a picture or scenario of a community's biggest fire and life safety problems will begin to emerge. In some cases, answers to two or three of the questions may combine to form a scenario (such as "inoperable smoke detectors in single-family homes" or "burn injuries from scalds to residents of the Pine Meadow Retirement Apartments"). In other cases, a single issue (juvenile firesetting, for example) will emerge as "the" problem (Figure 10.4).

Identifying which fire and life safety problems to address is the critical first step in developing a targeted public education program. The answers lead to a decision: *What is the major fire or life safety problem to be reduced through education?*

Selection

The objective of the selection step is to choose the most cost-effective or achievable objectives for the public education program. Being aware of the scope and limitations of available resources is important if planners are to be realistic about what an education program can accomplish. As a result, the questions in the selection step focus on resources (Figure 10.5). In many ways, the selection step comes close to a primer on finding new resources — funding, materials, and talented people — for public fire and life safety education.

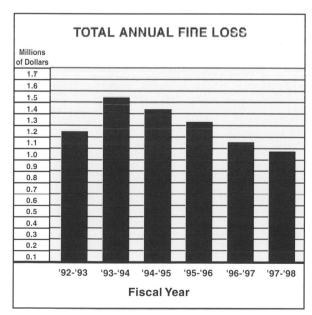

Figure 10.3 The number of fires per capita is an example of fire risk.

Figure 10.4 The program goal must be identified.

Figure 10.5 The goal helps identify the needed resources.

Following are some of the questions and sample tasks considered in the selection step of planning:

- **Who are your potential audiences?**
  - Refer to the high-risk victims listed in the identification step.
  - Identify those who influence the high-risk victims.
  - Select the audience on which the educator will have the greatest potential impact.

- **What are the potential costs and benefits of various training options?**
  - List alternative program objectives.
  - Identify what will be needed to achieve program objectives.
  - Review existing programs, and determine the advantages of purchasing educational materials versus making your own.
  - Determine cost of the needed fire education materials.
  - Estimate loss-reduction impact of each program objective. (How much loss reduction can realistically be expected?)

- **What resources are available within the community?**
  - Identify influential people in the community.
  - Identify those who speak the native language of the target group.
  - Identify signers for the hearing impaired.
  - List all local media, service clubs, and civic organizations.
  - Make personal contact with key people and groups.
  - Ask local businesses and organizations what materials, equipment, or personnel they could contribute to your program.
  - Choose the most effective approach within limits of local resources.

By the end of the selection step, program planners will be able to reach a crucial decision — *the specific objectives of the education program*. The objectives should be clear, measurable, and attainable. In addition, answers to the questions in the selection step will be used to complete the design, implementation, and evaluation steps. For example, information about major fire hazards and high-risk locations, times, victims, and behaviors will be very helpful when it is time to answer design step questions such as *"What is the primary message?"* In much the same way, insight about high-risk victims and potential audiences is critically important in deciding on the best formats, times, and places for education messages. The selection and design steps are so closely related that it is sometimes difficult to distinguish one from the other. That is normal. The important thing is to make sure that the program design is based on specific objectives selected to address a specific local problem.

Design

The design step is the bridge between planning a fire education program and actually implementing it in the field. The objective of the design step is to develop the most effective means of communicating (delivering) the program's message to the identified audience (Figure 10.6). In other words, this is the time when the fire educator decides what to say and how to say it, based on the message, audience, and available resources.

Following are some of the questions asked during the design step of planning:

- **What is the content of the fire and life safety education message?**
  - Direct messages toward specific hazards.
  - Appeal to positive motives.
  - Show the context of the problem and desired behavior.

- **What is the best format for the message?**
  - Match format to message.
  - Match format to audience.
  - Match format to resources.

- **What is the best time and place to deliver the message?**
  - Determine when the target audience will be most receptive to fire and life safety messages.
  - Schedule (both time and place) messages for maximum effect.

Figure 10.6 The medium must fit the audience.

After answering these questions, program planners are ready to actually design a program package and determine how to produce the program materials. Presenting the design concept and materials to a sample audience is a good "reality check" at this point. The decision at the end of the design step is *to approve or revise the education program package.*

Focusing on the Target Audience

Because the company officer is most often the presenter of the fire and life safety education program, he should help determine which parts of the education program are best suited for each audience. For example, it would be inappropriate to present the same program to a service club or other civic group as would be presented to a kindergarten or preschool class. Depending on the makeup and diversity of the group, the company officer must tailor the education program to suit the attention span and educational level (apperceptive base) of the intended audience (Figure 10.7). Therefore, the fire and life safety program must be flexible enough to reach diverse audiences.

High-risk groups are often the target audience for public fire and life safety education programs; however, looking beyond the high-risk group may lead the educator to the best target audience. On a community level, residents of a neighborhood with an unusually high incidence of home fires would be a very logical target audience for such programs. In other cases, however, some "outside" group may have so much influence or control over the high-risk group that the outside group becomes the target audience. For example, to effect a reduction in the number of smoking-related fires and resulting burn injuries among the residents of retirement homes within the community, it would be more effective to target the retirement home staff, rather than the residents, because the staff controls when and where the residents can smoke (Figure 10.8).

Likewise, preschool children are a high-risk group, and many lifelong attitudes and behaviors are formed during the preschool years. Based on these factors, preschool children could certainly be a major target audience for fire and life safety education. But preschoolers have only limited control over their own environment; they do not control the nature and quantity of combustible litter that is allowed to accumulate in their surroundings, the availability of matches and cigarette lighters, or the temperature setting of the family water heater. Their mental, emotional, and physical development may limit the actions they can take to save themselves from harm. For these reasons, *other* groups may be the target audience for programs to reduce the risk of fire-related injury to very young children. Parents, grandparents, older siblings, baby-sitters, and day-care staff are examples of other target audiences that may be even more effective than having preschool children as the target audience (Figure 10.9).

In the same way, educators may need to look beyond the noninstitutionalized aged and infirm as a high-risk group to find the most appropriate target audience. Young and middle-aged adults (who may care for their elderly parents), elder-care centers, directors of local senior citizen's programs, physicians, and workers in retirement or nursing homes are examples of other possible target audiences.

Implementation

The implementation step is where the day-to-day job of public fire and life safety education happens. Most company officers will spend more of their time implementing (delivering) these programs than in developing them (Figure 10.10). Planning the implementation step includes answering the following questions and identifying the associated tasks:

Figure 10.7 The program must be tailored to the audience.

Figure 10.8 Targeting the staff may be more effective than targeting the residents.

Figure 10.9 Targeting parents may be more effective than targeting their children.

Figure 10.10 Company-level personnel may be the primary deliverers of the message.

- **How will the target audience participate and cooperate in implementing the program?**

  — Involve target groups in implementing programs.

  — Tell target audiences what to expect.

  — Reinforce messages through endorsement by local opinion leaders.

- **How will fire educators be trained and scheduled?**

  — Organize fire service personnel and volunteers from outside the fire service.

  — Match community contacts with target audiences.

  — Train people for their education job.

- **How will materials be produced and distributed?**

  — Assign production responsibilities.

  — Produce or purchase materials.

  — Distribute materials to fire and life safety educators.

To make sure that the education program that looked so good "on paper" actually works, the educator will need to observe day-to-day program implementation. In this way, the company officer will be guided to the ultimate implementation decision: *monitoring and making ongoing adjustments and refinements to the program as needed during its implementation.*

Delivering the Program to the Target Audience

The actual teaching of a class is what the implementation step is all about. The presentation is the actual transfer of facts and ideas — making the subject come alive. The presentation should follow the lesson plan: explaining information, using supplemental training aids, and demonstrating methods and techniques (Figure 10.11). Company officers should use the most effective teaching methods — and materials — for each specific audience.

Communication Skills

Effective fire and life safety educators must be effective communicators. As with any other skill, effective communication requires understanding the process and practicing the techniques. Communication is actually much more complicated than it appears. Communication techniques are tools to prevent breakdowns, and knowing how to avoid breakdowns will make the company officer a more effective communicator.

Effective communication requires more than the ability to speak before a group or to write clearly. It has been described as both a *process* that explains how people interact with each other and as a *cycle* of interchanged information. In this context, *communication* is defined as the ongoing process that educators and their audiences use to complete the exchange of information and attitudes about fire and life safety.

This process involves a *sender* (the person who initiates the communication), a *message* (that which is intended to be communicated), a *medium* (the way that the message is delivered), a *receiver* (the intended recipient of the message), *feedback* (the way in which communication is verified), and an environment (the location where and conditions under which a message is sent). For a sender to be successful, he must be aware of and consider the effect of all of these elements.

The sender must be aware of his relationship to the receiver — supervisor/subordinate, expert/layman, authority figure/private citizen — as well as the environment. A company officer's credibility and authority may vary depending upon the circumstances under which he is trying to communicate. To a subordinate, a company officer may represent an authority figure or a fellow team member, depending upon the circumstances in which communication is attempted. To a private citizen, a company officer in uniform certainly represents an authority figure and may be perceived as an expert in matters relating to fire and life safety. Depending upon the circumstances (environment), the citizen's reaction (feedback) to a company officer's statement (message/medium) may vary widely. At a fire or other emergency, a citizen may acknowledge the receipt and understanding of an order to evacuate an area by quickly following it without question. At a public education presentation, citizens may be more likely to ask questions for clarification and/or to verify their understanding of what a company officer says.

At the same time, a company officer may vary the message and the medium, depending upon the circumstances. During an emergency, he may use a very direct and authoritarian manner of speaking in order to convey urgency. But during a public education presentation, he may use a more relaxed sort of delivery that invites interaction with the audience (Figure 10.12). Each approach is appropriate for the environment in which it is used.

Evaluation

This is the "bottom line" of public fire and life safety education. It is the point for measuring the impact of education programs and modifying them as needed. The techniques used to measure impact may vary from obtaining immediate feedback from program attendees, to monitoring long-term statistical trends. The former is valuable for its freshness and immediacy, but it lacks the objective validity of the latter. Most company officers are more likely to be involved in obtaining immediate feedback from their audiences than in the collection and analysis of statistical data. Regardless of how feedback is obtained, it *must* be heeded.

While positive feedback may be very gratifying, negative feedback may be more valuable. With positive feedback, there is the possibility that those responding are simply being polite and condescending. On the other hand, negative feedback indicates that something is wrong with the program — either the message or the delivery — or both! Conscientious fire and life safety educators must be willing to accept this sort of criticism constructively and review and adjust the program as needed.

Immediate Feedback

Immediate feedback can be obtained by simply asking open ended overhead questions and gauging the responses from the audience. Little or no response generated from questions may indicate that the intended message has not been communicated to the audience or that those who know the answers are simply reluctant to respond. In either case, the fire and life safety educator must recognize that work is needed on the design and/or delivery of the program.

Another method of obtaining immediate feedback is by asking the members of the audience to fill out an evaluation form at the end of the program. Some people like the anonymity of this device and are more likely to respond honestly than if they were asked for an oral response. Others dislike this task and will either decline to do it or simply complete the form in a cursory fashion.

A similar device that works well with some audiences, but not as well with others, is the pretest/posttest approach. At the beginning of the program, the audience is asked to take a short quiz (usually true/false) to test their knowledge of the topic to be presented. Then, after the presentation, they are asked to take a similar quiz but with the items worded slightly different than in the first quiz (Figure 10.13). Most people will score higher after the presentation than they did before it, and this gives them a feeling of accomplishment and satisfaction. As with the written evaluation, however, some people resent being asked to take these tests, so this technique should be used selectively. This approach works better with school children, who are accustomed to taking tests, than with adults, who may experience some test anxiety.

Regardless of how immediate feedback is sought, the greatest response from the audience is most likely to be generated if the educator has been careful to establish a rapport with them (Figure 10.14). The time and effort spent making the audience comfortable with the pro-

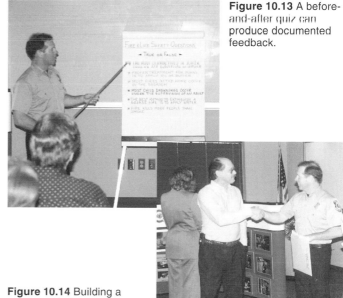

Figure 10.13 A before-and-after quiz can produce documented feedback.

Figure 10.11 The message must be demonstrated as well as explained.

Figure 10.12 Audience participation should be encouraged.

Figure 10.14 Building a rapport with the audience can produce feedback.

gram and with the presenters will more than justify itself in the quality and quantity of audience participation and feedback. With younger audiences, humor and games are often effective vehicles for involving them in the program (Figure 10.15). With older audiences, a more didactic approach that increases their awareness of the problem and suggests some solutions may be more appropriate (Figure 10.16). With some adult audiences, it may be necessary to show them pictures of fires and burn victims to get their attention. However, this very direct approach can be too psychologically traumatic for some, so it *must* be used with discretion.

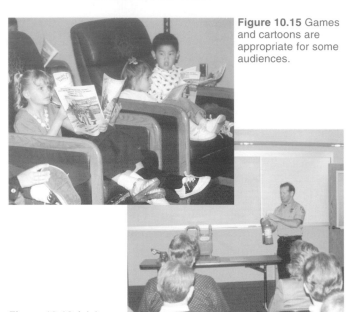

Figure 10.15 Games and cartoons are appropriate for some audiences.

Figure 10.16 Adults may respond to an informational approach.

Long-Term Feedback

The other approach to evaluating program effectiveness is to simply monitor the results over time. Even though most company officers' only involvement in the collection and analysis of fire and life safety data is limited to contributing data through their individual incident re-

ports, they should understand that the validity of the data is directly related to the accuracy and completeness of their reports.

As with any other educational program, the point of the department's fire and life safety education program is to change people's behavior. If the program has succeeded in giving people better tools with which to function and the motivation to use them, it should result in a positive change in the data on fire and life safety within the community. Regardless of what the audiences *thought* of the program, if it resulted in fewer fires, injuries, or property losses, then it obviously succeeded. On the other hand, if there is little or no positive change in the data, it probably means that the program was less than successful. Either way, this is the most meaningful and reliable evaluation possible.

The obvious disadvantage to using this approach is the amount of time needed to see results — positive or negative. This delay in obtaining feedback may result in an ineffective program being delivered many times to a variety of audiences. An enormous amount of time and effort can be invested in a program that produces only marginal results. Therefore, while long-term statistical data may produce the most reliable evaluation of program effectiveness, it is also the least useful as a basis for making day-to-day adjustments to the program.

Summary

Fire departments can significantly reduce the number of fires, and the resulting deaths, injuries, and property losses through the delivery of carefully designed public education programs. If these departments use the five-step planning process to focus their public education efforts on specific groups, and with specific and measurable goals, public education can be a very cost-effective activity. Company officers may be involved in the design and development of these programs, and will almost certainly be involved in their delivery.

Section IV • Administration

This chapter provides information that will assist the reader in meeting the following job performance requirements from NFPA 1021, *Standard for Fire Officer Professional Qualifications*, 1997 edition. The colored portions indicate the topics addressed in the chapter. The numbers of the job performance requirements are also noted directly in the sections of text where they are addressed. Those in the following list that are denoted with an asterisk (*) are global in nature and are covered by reading the chapter in its entirety.

Fire Officer I

2-1.1*   **General Prerequisite Knowledge**. The organizational structure of the department; departmental operating procedures for administration, emergency operations, and safety; departmental budget process; information management and record keeping; the fire prevention and building safety codes and ordinances applicable to the jurisdiction; incident management system; socioeconomic and political factors that impact the fire service; cultural diversity; methods used by supervisors to obtain cooperation within a group of subordinates; the rights of management and members; agreements in force between the organization and members; policies and procedures regarding the operation of the department as they involve supervisors and members.

Labor Relations

Labor relations is a general term for the contractual arrangements between a department's administration (management) and its rank-and-file members (labor). The contracts that exist between management and labor in the fire service vary widely. In some, the contract is merely implied because there is no formal written contract between the parties. In most others, a written contract specifies the rights and responsibilities of both groups.

Some of these contracts are nothing more than the bylaws of an association established at the time of its formation. These bylaws may remain in effect with little or no change for decades. Other contracts are memorandums of understanding (MOU) between an entity (city, town, state/province) and the union that represents the rank-and-file members of the department. These contracts are the result of sometimes intense negotiations between the union and management, and they are usually valid for a specified period of time after which they must be renegotiated.

In many departments, company officers are in a very difficult position because of the labor/management dichotomy. Because they are supervisors, their subordinates may view them as representing management. But because they are often members of the union or association that represents the firefighters, they may be viewed by management as being pro-labor. Therefore, it is extremely important for company officers to be aware of the rights and responsibilities of both groups.

This chapter discusses the history of labor relations in general and in the fire service in particular. Also discussed are some of the more typical agreements between firefighters and their departments and the rights that are granted to each under these agreements. Finally, conflict resolution and job actions are discussed along with more conciliatory and productive ways of dealing with labor/ management issues.

History of Labor Relations

In the early years of the twentieth century, workers who joined a union took a significant risk. At that time, employers had the legal right to fire any worker whom they believed might be engaging in union activities — and they did not hesitate to do so. In fact, many employers required job applicants to sign a pledge that they would not join a union. If they broke their pledge, they were fired. Prior to 1932, these *yellow-dog contracts*, as they were called by the unions, were upheld and enforced by the courts.

The New Deal era, created during the first term of President Franklin D. Roosevelt, introduced a period of significant change in national labor relations that would last well beyond the New Deal itself. Over the following three decades, several key pieces of legislation were enacted that greatly expanded the rights of workers and curtailed the power of employers. The most prominent of these laws were the Norris-La Guardia Act of 1932, the National Industrial Recovery Act of 1933, the Wagner-Connery Act of 1935, the Fair Labor Standards Act of 1938, the Taft-Hartley Act of 1947, and the Landrum-Griffin Act of 1959. Together with some antitrust legislation, these laws formed the basis for labor relations as we know them today.

Norris-La Guardia Act

The Norris-La Guardia Act made yellow-dog contracts unenforceable by any U.S. court. In doing so, it established the legal principle that an employee cannot be forced into a contract by the employer in order to obtain or keep a job. In addition to making yellow-dog contracts unenforceable, the act made it almost impossible to get an injunction to prevent a strike. Prior to the act, employers could get an injunction not only against strikes but also against picketing as well.

Even with the passage of the Norris-La Guardia Act, employers could still threaten and fire workers for engaging in union activity. But with the act in force, unions had the right to strike, picket, and boycott without interference from the courts.

National Industrial Recovery Act (NIRA)

In an attempt to revitalize a U.S. economy that was then four years into the Great Depression, President Roosevelt persuaded Congress to pass the National Industrial Recovery Act (NIRA) in 1933. NIRA guaranteed unions the right to collective bargaining. Roosevelt wanted this legislation in order to keep wages up and thus maintain workers' purchasing power. The Act was also a windfall for organized labor, and workers joined both the American Federation of Labor (AFL) and the new Congress of Industrial Organizations (CIO) in large numbers. However, in 1935, the Supreme Court ruled that the NIRA was unconstitutional and struck it down.

Wagner-Connery Act

Following the Supreme Court's decision on NIRA, Senator Robert Wagner (NY) immediately introduced the Wagner-Connery Act, which was quickly passed by Congress. Commonly known simply as the "Wagner Act," it included the following provisions:

- Allowed workers to decide, by a majority vote, who was to represent them in the bargaining process

- Established the National Labor Relations Board (NLRB)

- Defined unfair labor practices and gave the NLRB the power to hold hearings, investigate such practices, and issue decisions and orders concerning them

- Prohibited management from interfering with or coercing employees who tried to organize

- Required management to bargain with a recognized union although management was not obligated to agree to any of the union's demands

- Outlawed yellow-dog contracts entirely (**NOTE**: The Norris-La Guardia Act had only made them unenforceable.)

In 1936, a strike by the United Auto Workers (UAW) brought the Wagner Act before the Supreme Court, where it was upheld. The Wagner Act was an attempt to restrain management and to equalize the power of both management and labor. However, the Act did not impose penalties for any violations, nor did it provide the NLRB with any real power to enforce its decisions or orders. The Act did not become effective until it went before the courts. For example, the NLRB decided that a group of employees had been fired in violation of the Wagner Act — but it was not until the courts agreed that the employees were reinstated with back pay.

During the late 1930s and early 1940s, union membership grew under the protection of the Wagner Act and favorable court decisions. However, shortly after World War II, a series of major strikes threatened the transition of the economy from war production back to a peacetime orientation. These strikes made it apparent that with government protection and favorable court decisions, unions had grown substantially stronger than their management counterparts. In an attempt to restore some balance, Congress passed the Taft-Hartley Act of 1947, over President Truman's veto.

Fair Labor Standards Act (FLSA)

The Fair Labor Standards Act was passed in 1938 to guarantee that workers in the private sector would receive overtime pay at one and one-half times their normal rate of pay for work beyond 40 hours in one week. However, the act did not apply to state and local public employees until a U.S. Supreme Court decision in 1985. The effect of the act is primarily related to how firefighters and other emergency workers are classified and compensated. See Chapter 3, "The Company Officer's Legal Responsibilities and Liability" for a more detailed discussion of this legislation.

Taft-Hartley Act

The Taft-Hartley Act provided specific penalties for NLRB violations, including fines and imprisonment. In addition, Taft-Hartley modified the Wagner Act in the following ways:

- **Union representation.** The act gave workers the right to choose not to join a union, thus outlawing the closed shop. It limited representation election (which were held to determine whether a union — and which union — should represent the employees) to one per year. The act also gave employers the right to express their "views, arguments, or opinions" about union membership, as long as "such expression contains no threat of reprisal or force, or promise of benefit."

- **Unfair labor practices.** The act protects employees from being pressured by unions to join. Employees are also protected from having to pay exorbitant union dues or initiation fees. Employees who refuse to join a union are protected against possible union reprisals. Taft-Hartley requires unions to "bargain in good faith" as the Wagner Act had previously required employers to do.

- **Bargaining procedures.** When negotiations for the renewal of a labor contract fail to produce a new agreement, Taft-Hartley provides for a 60-day cooling-off period in which the existing contract remains in effect. Negotiations for contract renewal normally start 60 days before a contract expires. If an impasse is reached after 30 days of negotiating, the Federal Mediation and Conciliation Service must be notified of the dispute.

- **Regulation of unions' internal affairs.** Rules regarding union membership requirements, dues, initiation fees, elections, etc., must be made available to the government as well as to the membership.

- **Strikes during a national emergency.** If a strike would affect a key industry or put the health and safety of the nation in jeopardy, the President can invoke Taft-Hartley to keep workers on the job while trying to settle the dispute.

Landrum-Griffin Act

Following the merger of the AFL and CIO in 1955, widespread corruption was found in older union locals. As a reaction to these revelations, Congress passed the Landrum-Griffin Act of 1959. The act included the following:

- A union members' bill of rights intended to ensure that unions are run in a democratic manner

- A requirement that labor unions disclose the assets of the union and the names and assets of every union officer and employee to the government annually and, in addition, a requirement that employers are to report any financial relationship they have with a union or union representative

- A set of guidelines that established minimum requirement for the election, responsibilities, and duties of all union officers and officials

- Amendment of portions of Taft-Hartley concerning secondary boycotts, union security, and the rights of some workers to strike; also imposed further restrictions on the rights of unions to picket for recognition

Public-Sector Unions

Despite the fact that private-sector unions had prospered in the years immediately before, during, and immediately after World War II, membership in public-employee unions lagged far behind. In the mid-1950s, fewer than 1 million government employees were members of unions. However, in January 1962, President Kennedy issued an order that gave federal employees the right to bargain collectively for the first time. Then in 1969, President Nixon further expanded the rights of public-employee unions by establishing a Federal Labor Relations Council similar to the NLRB for unions in the private sector. The result of these executive orders, along with a changing social climate, was that public-employee unions grew to more than 4 million members by 1970. Some also grew more militant.

Even though public employee strikes were illegal, in the late 1960s several major cities experienced strikes by public employees including sanitation workers, teachers, police, and firefighters. In 1968, the International Association of Fire Fighters (IAFF) rescinded its 50-year-old rule prohibiting strikes by its affiliated locals. In 1970, employees of the U.S. Postal Service went on strike. Even though the strike was illegal and the postmaster general was forbidden by law to negotiate with the strikers, he did so anyway. The final result was that the strikers were reinstated without penalty and even received raises. In addition, Congress recognized the union as the bargaining agent for the postal employees. This proved that even the federal government was no longer immune from strikes.

In 1981, the members of the Professional Air Traffic Controllers Organization (PATCO) went on strike over a variety of issues. This action severely hampered commercial flight operations at U.S. airports. When they failed to return to work as ordered, President Reagan fired all striking members and decertified the union. This action clarified the Reagan administration's view of labor relations. In response, employers stiffened their resolve against what they perceived as the growing militancy of public-employee unions, and they increased their efforts to pass right-to-work laws.

It should be clear that the history of labor relations in North America has been anything but stable. Sometimes amicable, sometimes bitterly hostile, labor and management have continued to coexist because each one needs the other. The major firefighter unions are no exception.

Firefighter Unions

Some full-time career firefighters are represented by the International Brotherhood of Teamsters and others by the American Federation of State, County, and Municipal Employees (AFSCME). However, most career firefighters belong to locals affiliated with the International Association of Fire Fighters (IAFF), which is affiliated with the AFL-CIO.

International Association of Fire Fighters (IAFF)

The IAFF differs from most private-sector unions in the relationship of its national and international levels to the individual locals. In private-sector unions, the parent organization exercises considerable control over the operation of each local. In the IAFF, its international officers help organize locals and, when invited to do so, help resolve local labor disputes. They also strive to improve pay, pensions, working conditions, and firefighter health and safety while allowing the locals considerable autonomy. Unlike most private-sector unions, the IAFF also allows supervisors (company officers) to be members of the union, and they are included in the bargaining unit. IAFF locals are organized democratically — that is, the members vote to select their officers, decide initial positions to be taken in collective bargaining, and ratify contracts.

Contracts and Agreements

Contracts and agreements result from negotiations (sometimes called meet-and-confer) between union representatives and those of the jurisdiction. These documents may vary from one entity to the next, but they generally contain the following elements:

- **Constitutional clauses.** Examples of such clauses are a preamble and statement of purpose; definitions; the term (period of time) that the agreement covers; re-opening conditions and procedures; and amendments.

- **Union security.** These clauses usually describe the bargaining unit that the agreement covers and list the steps by which a union is recognized as an employee representative.

- **Management rights and prerogatives.** These clauses confirm that management has the right to decide matters not specifically covered in the agreement.

- **Grievance procedures.** These clauses describe how employee grievances may be filed and also include a statement of nonreprisal for filing a grievance.

- **Conditions of employment.** These clauses describe the wages, hours, and working conditions. Included are fringe benefits; holidays, vacations, and leaves; apprenticeships and training; hiring and firing; safety; and strikes and lockouts.

- **Disciplinary procedures.** These clauses describe the steps involved in rendering discipline. Included are the procedures for reprimands, suspensions, reductions in pay, demotions, and terminations.

These are some of the typical contract elements; there may be others depending upon local conditions, past practices, internal and external politics, and other variables. Many of the items included in these contracts are dictated by local, state, or federal law. However, the elements to be included and the specific language used are subject to the collective bargaining process.

Collective Bargaining

Collective bargaining is the general term for what is most commonly referred to as "negotiations" or, in some cases, "the meet-and-confer" process. As the term implies, there is bargaining involved — a process of give-and-take (Figure 11.1). Each side attempts to make the best deal possible for those that they represent, but both sides also have a legitimate interest in reaching an equitable and workable agreement. Unresolved labor disputes, regardless of whether they lead to a strike or other job action, usually have a detrimental effect on morale and productivity and may create such ill will between management and labor that it can take years to overcome. This sort of lose-lose scenario should be avoided whenever possible. One of the best ways of avoiding this result is to have skilled negotiators representing both sides.

In most cases, each side uses a team of representatives rather than a single negotiator. This allows each team to come to the table with a broader range of experience and expertise than would be possible with a single representative. There is no "ideal" composition for these teams, but some of the more typical teams are the *management team* and the *labor team*.

Management Team

The team that represents the entity, regardless of whether it is a district, city, county, etc., is usually lead by a high-ranking member of management. This is usually not the most senior member (mayor, city manager, board chairman) but is someone who is empowered to speak for the entity. In many cases, the vice mayor or assistant manager will head the team. The personnel officer, finance officer, and/or the legal officer (attorney) may also lead or be part of the team. Some entities include the department head (fire chief); others do not.

Labor Team

The team representing labor is usually composed of a select group of union members and may or may not

Figure 11.1 Collective bargaining requires good-faith negotiation by both sides.

include the union president. In some cases, the union team will be lead by a professional negotiator hired by the union. In other cases, the team will merely consult with a negotiator outside the bargaining process (Figure 11.2). In any case, the team must be able to speak for the membership, although any agreement reached will have to be ratified by a vote of the membership.

Contract Issues

As mentioned earlier in the discussion of contracts and agreements, there are many possible issues to be negotiated. However, some of these issues are more critical than others. Among the most critical are wages, working conditions, and job security.

Wages

While many strikes, slowdowns, sick-outs, and other job actions have been initiated over wage issues, research has consistently shown that salary is not the main concern of most employees — union or nonunion. Firefighters organize for a variety of reasons other than wages and other monetary issues. Prominent among these other issues are being kept informed about management policies and decisions that affect them and having some voice in such decisions before they are made and/or implemented. There are other nonmonetary reasons that firefighters organize; however, as indicated in Maslow's Hierarchy of Needs, unless and until a person's basic survival needs are satisfied (by that person's definition), salary (needed to satisfy survival needs) will be his overriding concern. In most cases, whether a firefighter does or does not receive a salary increase is not really a matter of survival — but it feels that way. In reality, a salary increase is more likely to merely have some effect on the firefighter's standard of living and that of his family. However, there are other issues related to salary that are of considerable importance to firefighters.

One significant issue related to salary is fairness. Firefighters know what others within and outside the department are being paid. They know what their chief officers are paid. They know what law enforcement personnel within the jurisdiction are paid. They know what firefighters in other nearby fire departments are paid. And they also know what firefighters in the state, province, or area of the country are paid. If their salary is just slightly below what they perceive as the norm, they may be disgruntled but resigned. On the other hand, if the salaries of those in management are above average and the salaries of firefighters are below average, then the firefighters are likely to feel that this is unfair, and salary

may be their primary issue during negotiations (Figure 11.3). Closely related to, but different from, fairness is the issue of self-worth.

Firefighters and other workers often equate how much they are being paid to how much they and their contributions are valued by the organization. Just as in the issue of fairness, how much firefighters are actually paid is not as important as how it compares to what others are paid. If firefighters are paid at or above the average of firefighter salaries in the area, they are more likely to feel valued by the department. However, if their salary is significantly below the others, considerable resentment and discontent can be generated. The firefighters will not only feel that this is unfair, but they also will see the disparity as evidence that their contributions to the department and the community are underappreciated.

Working Conditions

This area is always important to firefighters, but it may or may not be their highest negotiating priority. As with salary, the priority that firefighters put on working conditions issues is relative to their perception of salary equity and the conditions under which others work. If they perceive that their salaries are out of line, that is likely to be the primary issue. If not, then working conditions may be. Working conditions are also viewed by firefighters in terms of fairness and self-worth. While there are a number of items that can be important working conditions issues, one of the consistently most important issues is that of hours worked.

There are two primary issues related to work hours the number of hours worked per week and the schedule on which those hours are worked. Line firefighters in most departments in North America work an average of 56 hours per week, although some work less and others more. If firefighters work more than a 56-hour week, they are likely to put a high priority on reducing their work-

Figure 11.2 Some unions rely on professional assistance outside the bargaining process.

Figure 11.3 Compensation is often the union's highest negotiating priority.

week. How those hours are worked is the other primary issue related to the workweek. The result of dividing a 168-hour week by 56 is 3. Therefore, most departments that work a 56-hour week divide their workforce into three equal groups. Each group, whether called a crew, platoon, or shift, is on duty one-third of the time. They are usually designated as A-shift, B-shift, and C-shift, etc.

Within the 56-hour week there are several different ways to arrange the schedule. While firefighters on less than a 56-hour week often work a 10-hour day shift or a 14-hour night shift, most firefighters on a 56-hour week work 24-hour shifts. In some departments, the shifts are arranged in a 3-day cycle of one-on and two-off. In others, a more complicated schedule is used. One of the most popular is a 9-day cycle in which any given shift works 3 of the 9 days and has 6 days off. For example, A-shift works Monday, Wednesday, and Friday of a given week, with Tuesday and Thursday off. When they have finished their Friday shift (normally on Saturday morning, but shifts are started and ended at different times in different departments), A-shift would be off Saturday, Sunday, Monday, and Tuesday. They would begin their next 9-day cycle on Wednesday. The other two shifts work the same 9-day cycle. Although a particular shift may work more or fewer than 56 hours in a particular week, each works an *average* of 56 hours per week over the year (Figure 11.4).

There are advantages and disadvantages to every work schedule, and it is impossible to satisfy everyone's likes and dislikes with any single schedule. But to maintain stability and continuity in the operation of the department, once a schedule has been implemented, it should not be changed unless there is some compelling reason to do so. However, both the number of hours worked per week and how those hours are scheduled can be significant issues during negotiations.

There are other issues relating to working conditions that must be resolved from time to time. Among these are issues related to shift trades, overtime, use of sick leave and vacations, grievance procedures, and discipline. The last two items relate directly to the other major issue about which firefighters are often concerned — job security.

Job Security

One of the reasons that some people are attracted to public employment in general and the fire service in particular, is the perception of a high level of job security. In fact, many in the private sector willingly trade their higher income potential for the greater job security offered in the public sector. However, in recent years, the once common assumption of lifetime employment in a fire department has proven to be false. Fire departments and other essential services are usually among the last to be cut in a fiscal crisis, but they are not totally immune to cutbacks and layoffs.

When layoffs or reductions in force are unavoidable, unions usually insist that the cuts be made on the basis of seniority — last hired, first fired (Figure 11.5). On the other hand, management usually wants to make the cuts on a cost/benefit basis, without regard to seniority. In fact, it may be to the department's advantage to target more senior members who are at the top of their salary range but who are also eligible to retire. If they can induce

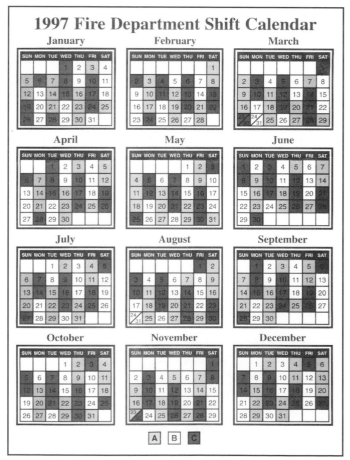

Figure 11.4 A commonly used work schedule.

Figure 11.5 Unions favor using seniority as the basis for reductions in force.

some of these individuals to retire (perhaps retire early), they can greatly reduce the budget for salaries without having to lay off anyone. If a sufficient number of these high-salaried workers retire and if their positions are left unfilled, the savings can be significant. But, in general, management wants to be able to retain those that they perceive as contributing the most while costing the least, regardless of seniority.

Even in the absence of a fiscal crisis there can still be job security issues. As mentioned earlier, one of the reasons that firefighters and other workers organize is to be able to voice their opinions and concerns without fear of reprisal by vindictive supervisors or employers. No matter how well written a fire department's grievance procedure is, if the firefighters are afraid to use it, the procedure will be ineffective.

Conflict Resolution

Conflicts about how a labor contract is to be interpreted or how it is to be implemented are inevitable. Every organization experiences these difficulties from time to time. They may arise during negotiations for contract renewal or at some point during the term of the contract. How these conflicts are resolved will depend upon the maturity and experience of those involved and on the amount of goodwill between them. One of the best ways of resolving labor contract conflicts is by maintaining open lines of communication.

Conflict Communication

A large part of the collective bargaining process is communication. Representatives on both sides should try to ensure that the true meaning of the messages they send is what is received. If not, misunderstandings occur and the process can break down. Sometimes, representatives of one side know what they want to convey, but a different message is received. This sometimes happens because people are individuals with different experiences, attitudes, values, beliefs, biases, and assumptions. Both the sender and the receiver respond to the same words differently, and this sometimes prevents the intended message from being received and understood. Even if the sender is capable of sending a clear message, the receiver may be defensive or preoccupied. The receiver may have biases or mental stereotypes that get in the way of understanding. However, careful and conscientious negotiators can reduce these communications difficulties by using the following:

- **Precise communication.** This simply means taking the time to think before speaking. Negotiators should try to find just the right words and phrases and just the

right voice inflection, facial expression, and body language to make sure that the message sent is the one that was intended.

- **Awareness of the audience.** The sender should consider how the audience will respond to certain words and phrases because of how their backgrounds and experiences, likes and dislikes, and biases and stereotypes will affect their perceptions of what is said. Without being deceptive or dishonest, the sender can choose words that are less inflammatory than others but that mean the same thing.

- **Two-way dialogue.** This means that a conscientious sender will follow the message with appropriate questions to see whether the message was received and understood as intended. If it was not, the message can be rephrased to make it clearer to the audience.

Taking the time to carefully consider how to send and respond to messages during a labor conflict can greatly reduce the chances of misunderstanding and will perhaps even resolve the dispute. In any case, as long as open lines of communication can be maintained, there is hope for resolving any conflict. However, in some cases, despite the best efforts of honest and sincere representatives on both sides, communications do break down, and the conflict continues unresolved. This means that another form of conflict resolution must be used. The three most widely used forms of conflict resolution are mediation, arbitration, and fact-finding.

Mediation

Mediation, also called third-party mediation, involves hiring a neutral third party to meet separately with both sides in a conflict to identify the real issues and concerns that have caused the impasse. The mediator can clear up misconceptions that one side holds about the positions of the other and perhaps get negotiations started again. Mediators often use information from other labor disputes around the country to move one or both sides away from unrealistic and untenable positions. They can also help both sides gain access to high-ranking officials who can perhaps find a way to settle the conflict. Considering how costly strikes can be, hiring a mediator to resolve a conflict can be money well spent.

Arbitration

Arbitration is sometimes required by local or state law and is usually binding on both sides. The process can use a single arbitrator or a panel of three, usually chosen by both sides from a list supplied by a professional organization, such as the American Arbitration Association. Arbitrators hear evidence from both sides in the dispute, conduct independent research, and decide on a binding solution (Figure 11.6). Sometimes, neither management nor labor particularly likes the procedure because it takes the final decision out of their control. Many fire departments are beginning to favor binding arbitration over the possibility of facing a strike and the damage that can do to the department's public image.

There are different forms of arbitration available. In one form, each side proposes its best offer on each issue to be resolved. The arbitrator chooses one of the offers on each issue without compromise. The procedure theoretically forces each side to make reasonable proposals on each issue. In other forms, the arbitrator must decide between each side's list of proposals in total. The arbitrator is not free to decide on an issue-by-issue basis — one side's entire list of proposals must be accepted. Because it is an all-or-nothing process, this forces each side to propose its most reasonable package.

Fact-Finding

Fact-finding is similar to arbitration. Arbitrators look at the facts and develop a list of suggested solutions, but their suggestions are not binding. In some cases, the procedure can identify facts that persuade the governing body to make concessions in return for a settlement. However, some feel that neither management nor labor is forced to make a serious effort to propose its best offers. The procedure never actually resolves a dispute, and the suggestions might not satisfy either party. Nevertheless, fact-finding is one of the most commonly used ways to resolve conflicts in the public safety sector.

In the absence of effective communication between mature people of good will, some labor conflicts seem to defy resolution. If mediation, arbitration, and fact-finding are either not used or are not successful, the situation may deteriorate into some form of job action.

Job Actions

The most widely known job action is a strike — but there are others. Especially in the public safety sector where strikes were illegal, workers invented other ways of applying pressure on management in order to achieve their goals. Some of these other types of job actions are slowdowns, sick-outs, and selective duty.

Slowdowns

When contract or grievance negotiations bog down or begin to go in a direction counter to the interests of the firefighters, but are not yet bad enough to warrant a strike, firefighters may choose to express their displeasure by means of a work slowdown. There are different ways for firefighters to reduce their productivity, but one of the most common is called *work-to-rule*.

Figure 11.6 Arbitrators hear evidence from both sides.

Rather than performing their duties in the normal way in which they make hundreds of small daily decisions about the reasonable application of the countless rules that apply to their jobs, firefighters follow each and every rule to the letter. And they follow each rule in a deliberately slow and extraordinarily careful manner. The many safety checks that are part of the daily preparation for emergency calls can consume the entire workday if done "by the book." While not the most effective tactic available to them, a coordinated work-to-rule campaign can get the attention of management — and management should pay attention to it.

Work-to-rule is often used in departments that have a history of retaliating against anyone participating in a job action. It is difficult to discipline a firefighter for doing exactly what the work rules specify.

Sick-Outs

If a slowdown has not produced the desired effect, firefighters may resort to another tactic called a *sick-out*. Sometimes called the "blue flu," this tactic involves an organized campaign of a certain minimum number of firefighters calling in sick each day. This forces the department to either hire other firefighters on overtime to replace the missing ones, allow some units to operate with less than their normal complement of personnel, or close some stations and consolidate the crews within the remaining units. Like slowdowns, this tactic is designed to get management's attention.

Unlike work-to-rule, a sick-out is a clearly illegal activity because it involves firefighters defrauding the jurisdiction. In effect, firefighters who call in sick when they are not, are committing perjury. Obviously, this tactic could involve serious risk for those who participate.

Selective Duty

This unusual tactic is what might be called a "semi-strike." While the firefighters report for duty as scheduled, once on duty they refuse to do anything but respond to emergency calls. After they check their emergency clothing and equipment to make sure everything is ready if needed, the firefighters sit down, play cards, watch TV, or do anything other than their normal routine duties. This tactic can put a lot of pressure on company officers — unless they are part of the job action also. The point of this tactic is to get management's attention without angering the public by reducing the level of emergency response as in a full strike.

Strikes

These drastic job actions result from a complete breakdown of the negotiations process. The reasons that the process breaks down are many and varied. Strikes are seldom caused entirely by either management or labor; they are almost always the result of both sides being inflexible, unreasonable, and often immature. Even though strikes by public safety employees are illegal in most jurisdictions, rarely is anyone prosecuted for leading or participating in a strike. One of the conditions for settling these strikes is an agreement by management not to retaliate against those who participated and by the union not to retaliate against firefighters who refused to participate.

Strikes by firefighters and other public safety employees are the ultimate lose/lose scenario. Firefighter strikes impose a hardship on the public, and the public tends to hold both sides responsible for failing to provide the level of services to which their taxes entitle them (Figure 11.7). The public image of both the union and the department — that may have taken years to create — can be destroyed in a single day. Union officers may also be sued for damages that result from fires and other emergencies to which the striking firefighters refused to respond. Obviously, strikes should be avoided if at all possible.

Historically, there have been numerous firefighter strikes in the United States. Between 1975 and 1980, there were strikes by members of four major metropolitan fire departments — San Francisco (1975), Memphis (1978), Kansas City (1979), and Chicago (1980). None of these actions achieved the aims of the unions, and in fact, all suffered substantial losses. Because of the ineffectiveness of these actions, and the loss of public support that resulted, many firefighter union locals have adopted more conciliatory means of achieving their ends. Some progressive locals have joined with equally progressive department administrations to form labor/management teams that function in a process called *relationship-by-objectives*.

Relationship-by-Objectives (RBO)

The RBO program is designed to improve relationships between labor and management. It concentrates on the process by which labor and management may work cooperatively. It is not intended to change the labor/management relationship structure. In other words, it does not replace the negotiation process between the entity and the union. Nor does it change anyone's responsibilities — the fire chief still manages the day-to-day activities of the fire department, and the union president manages the activities of the union. The RBO program is intended to guide the participants in the following:

- Identification of viewpoints, conflicts, and concerns that hinder a productive labor/management relationship
- Formation of an objective-based plan designed to resolve problems and to build a mutually beneficial working relationship

An optional objective of the program is the:

- Development of skills that will enable participants to work together to address labor/management concerns

The program leads participants through the steps necessary to identify problems and solutions and to develop an action plan to be executed when they return to the workplace. Through a series of presentations and activities, participants identify problems, conflicts, and concerns; openly discuss sensitive subjects; work together to propose actions to improve the relationship; and create an objective-based and time-specific plan to implement these actions.

To make this or any similar program work, both labor and management must want it to work   and they must be willing to do whatever it takes to make that happen. For the program to be successful, the participants on both sides must trust and respect each other's personal and professional integrity. Assistance with learning and applying the RBO program is available free to any interested department from the Federal Mediation and Conciliation Service, 2100 K Street NW, Washington, DC 20427, (202) 606-8091.

Figure 11.7 Firefighter strikes often infuriate members of the public.

RBO is a proven program in the field of labor relations. However, it is not the only successful labor relations model in use. The Mesa (AZ) Fire Department (MFD) uses a different labor/management system that produces excellent results.

MFD Model

Like RBO, the MFD model is based on mutual respect between the representatives of both labor and management. The MFD model encourages interaction and involvement among labor and management leaders within the department in the process of jointly developing action plans designed to define and establish the desired relationship for the future. The following points (used by permission) not only describe the MFD labor/management philosophy, but also serve as a general description of any healthy labor/management relationship.

1. Labor and Management understand the types of work they do well together and use the roles of Labor and Management creatively and/or traditionally to achieve the goals of the organization. Results are not accomplished at the expense of each other.

2. Labor and Management leaders put the good of the organization as a whole above the good of either Labor or Management…or the individual leaders of each group. The formal contract is a very important component of the Labor/Management process, but it does not drive the relationship.

3. The leadership of Labor and Management keep their word by doing the things that they say they are going to do.

4. The leaders of Labor and Management meet on a pre-scheduled basis to conduct joint planning and problem-solving utilizing Action Plans that are co-developed and monitored for progress.

5. Labor and Management leaders realize that there will be disagreements on certain issues. The leadership is able to proceed with issues on which there is agreement while continuing to communicate on areas where disagreement exists.

6. Labor and Management leaders value the importance of maintaining open, productive relationships. The Labor/Management relationship would not be sacrificed by either party's leadership to achieve a single outcome on a specific issue.

7. Labor and Management leadership are committed to (and focus on) the importance of providing the highest quality of service or product possible to the external customers.

8. Labor and Management leadership are committed to (and focus on) the importance of providing the best support possible to the organization's members…the internal customers.

9. When the organization is struggling, Labor and Management leaders work together to survive the difficult period and find opportunities for improvement as a result of the event or situation.

10. Management leaders share the authority for decision-making and creating the vision and policies of the organization. Labor leaders accept responsibility for decisions that are jointly made and positively represent their involvement within the decision-making process.

11. The energy of the Labor/Management effort within the organization is driven towards collectively solving problems and planning for the future.

12. Labor and Management leaders understand and accept their roles within the organization and respect each others' professionalism and integrity internally and externally.

13. Labor and Management leaders meet regularly (and as a special need arises) to communicate and coordinate efforts for a variety of needs and issues within the organization.

14. Labor and Management leaders cooperatively participate on committees or teams assigned to address issues within the Labor/Management process…and the scope of each assigned group is well defined in an effort to address general cultural, policy, or specific procedural processes.

15. Labor and Management leaders are pro-active in addressing issues that typically lead to grievances. Complaints by members are communicated and processed within the organization.

16. Labor and Management leaders focus their efforts on planning and problem-solving, while also discussing culture, policy, and defining procedures. It is understood by both parties that the Labor leaders manage the day-to-day operations of the Union or employee group, and Management manages the day-to-day operations of the organization…and that each conducts business within the scope of the policies and procedures that have been jointly developed.

In the cooperative labor/management environment that results from conscientiously applying these principles, labor and management leaders play their roles in a way that is function-based, not ego-based, and their energies are directed toward what is best for the organization as a whole. The focus of the leadership is on the quality of services or products delivered externally and on the needs and support of the members of the organization internally. Power, control, and influence are infused throughout the organization. Management shares its authority for decision-making, and labor accepts responsibility for its role in the decision-making process. Leaders develop the ability to agree to disagree on some issues while continuing to work on other unrelated issues. Smart risk-taking is encouraged and managed. Grievances are rare.

In both the RBO program and the MFD model, there is an emphasis on a shared responsibility for decision-making, conflict resolution, and direction-setting. This does *not* mean comanagement — each group maintains its own identity and responsibilities — but it does mean

Figure 11.8 To build a healthy labor/management relationship, one side must make the first move.

that there is a commitment by the leaders of both labor and management to work together for the greater good. However, working together in this way requires a mutual respect and trust — a new concept for some. To replace the old adversarial relationship between labor and management with this new type of cooperative working relationship requires that one of the leaders — the fire chief or the union president — have the courage and foresight to take the calculated risk of making the first move (Figure 11.8).

Summary

Company officers are in a unique situation compared to supervisors in most private sector unions which exclude supervisors from membership. Because company officers represent management as supervisors but are also eligible for union membership, they must often walk a very fine line. This position makes it imperative that they know what contracts and agreements are in effect between the department and its rank-and-file members and what each faction's rights and responsibilities are under those agreements. Company officers should also have some knowledge of labor relations in general and about firefighter unions in particular. They should have some knowledge of typical contract issues and of the various means available for resolving those issues. Company officers should also be prepared to be active participants in any initiative directed toward building a cooperative relationship between labor and management in their department.

Chapter 12 • Job Performance Requirements

This chapter provides information that will assist the reader in meeting the following job performance requirements from NFPA 1021, *Standard for Fire Officer Professional Qualifications*, 1997 edition. The colored portions indicate the topics addressed in the chapter. The numbers of the job performance requirements are also noted directly in the sections of text where they are addressed. Those in the following list that are denoted with an asterisk (*) are global in nature and are covered by reading the chapter in its entirety.

3-4.2*   Prepare a budget request, given a need and budget forms, so that the request is in the proper format and is supported with data.

(a) *Prerequisite Knowledge:* Policies and procedures and the revenue sources and budget process.

(b) *Prerequisite Skill:* The ability to communicate in writing.

Budgeting

Every fire service agency, from the smallest volunteer company to the largest fire department, must have a budget with which to operate. The revenues that fund the department's budget may come from a variety of sources. In the case of a volunteer company, the revenues may come from fund-raising events such as bake sales, pancake breakfasts, benefit dances or golf tournaments, and/or private and corporate donations. In most other fire departments, funding comes from tax revenues, fees for service, government subsidies and grants, and similar sources.

Budgets are of interest to a variety of people within the jurisdiction. Citizens and citizen groups are interested because of their legitimate concern for how their taxes are spent. Business groups are interested because businesses pay the majority of the taxes that fund the budget. Members of the governing body use the budget to implement the decisions they make on behalf of both groups. Administrators use the budget to carry out the policies and priorities set by the governing body, and company officers use the budget to keep their companies operating from day to day.

The budget of any public entity is a legal document. Once approved, those who are empowered under the law to administer the budget are bound by it. Because it is unlawful to make a gift of public funds, these funds may be spent only for those goods and services specifically approved in the budget. However, some discretion is allowed in transferring funds to cover unexpected contingencies. But, more than just a means to control the expenditure of public funds, a fire department's budget is a *plan* that identifies what the department intends to accomplish during the coming fiscal year. Company officers must know what is in their department's budget as well as what has been allocated for the operation of their station or companies. In most fire departments, company officers play an important role in the development and administration of the departmental budget. Company officers can also play an important role by communicating budget decisions to their subordinates and explaining how these decisions address the company's needs and impact the company's operations.

This chapter discusses the types of budgets used by most public entities, including fire departments. Also discussed are the types of operating budgets and the process of creating and implementing a departmental budget.

Types of Budgets

In general, there are two types of budgets used by public entities — *capital* budgets and *operating* budgets. Even though these budgets include very different items and serve very different purposes, they are often combined into one budget document. Company officers are often involved in planning and preparing both types of budgets.

Capital Budgets

Capital budgets cover major purchases — items that cost more than a certain specified amount of money and are expected to last more than one year, usually three or more years. Fire apparatus and equipment, fire hose, fire stations, and training facilities are typical capital items (Figure 12.1). Many public entities have multiyear capital improvement plans (CIPs) for these and other major investments. A typical CIP may include a multiyear plan for resurfacing the streets within the jurisdiction or building a new city hall. Where a CIP exists, each year's capital budget represents that year's portion of the expenditures included in the CIP.

Company officers in many fire departments are tasked with identifying the need for fire-related capital items and for developing the justifications to support these budget requests. The needs analysis may focus upon the age and/or condition of the existing item if the request is for a replacement or on the operational need if the request is for an additional item (Figure 12.2). For example, if there is a need to replace an aging fire engine with a more modern one, the limitations of the existing unit must be described in very objective terms, as well as what a new unit will do that the old one cannot. Also, the costs and benefits of refurbishing the old unit must be compared to the price of purchasing a newer one. The price of purchasing a new unit can be reduced by the resale value of the old unit, unless the old unit is to be kept and used as a reserve (Figure 12.3).

If the request is for an additional unit, the same sort of justification must be developed. A new engine may be needed to service a newly annexed or recently developed area, or new/additional hazards such as those associated with a retirement complex or a processing plant. Servicing the new area may increase the number of emergency calls and/or increase response distances, which affect average response time. New or additional high-risk occupancies or processes may also increase the need for specialized/additional equipment. Or, acquiring an additional engine may be one part of a strategy for lowering the jurisdiction's ISO rating and thereby reducing the citizens' fire insurance costs.

The same is true of fire stations and other department facilities. A fire station may be old and in need of major repairs, or it may be poorly located because the area surrounding it did not develop as expected. The station may be too small for the number of apparatus and personnel that are now assigned to it (Figure 12.4). Just as in the apparatus example, the costs and benefits of remodeling the station must be weighed against building a bigger, more modern facility. In some cases, development around an older fire station may have increased the property values enough that the station now occupies extremely valuable real estate. The current market value of the station property may be more than enough to build a new station in a less expensive but more strategic location (Figure 12.5).

Helping to prepare budget requests for capital items that will increase the department's operational capability can be some of the most challenging and rewarding assignments for company officers. While company officers are usually not directly involved in expending the funds in the capital budget, they can still contribute to the capital budget by helping to develop the department's long-range plans such as seeking accreditation or developing a new training center. However, company officers

Figure 12.1 Fire apparatus are capital budget items.

Figure 12.2 The need for capital expenditures must be justified.

Figure 12.3 The cost of new fire apparatus may be reduced by selling the replaced unit.

Figure 12.4 As a department grows, some older fire stations may no longer be adequate.

Figure 12.5 The land on which an older fire station sits may be more valuable than the station.

may be directly involved in expending funds from the other major type of budget — the department's operating budget.

Operating Budgets

Unlike the capital budget that is used to pay for one-time, long-term purchases, the department's operating budget is used to pay for the recurring expenses of the day-to-day operation of the department. The largest, single item in the operating budget of most career fire departments is the cost of personnel — salaries and benefits. In many fire departments, personnel costs, sometimes called *personal services,* represent as much as 90 percent of their operating budgets. In some others, the percentage is even higher! However, operating budgets also pay for the station utilities, office supplies, fuel for the apparatus, cleaning supplies, and countless other items needed to function on a daily basis (Figure 12.6).

Company officers are usually responsible for preparing budget requests to obtain the items needed to operate their particular station or company, excluding personal services. This usually involves the relatively simple process of updating the requests from previous years to reflect today's needs. Unless there has been an increase in the number of personnel in the company or a significant increase in company activities (emergency or nonemergency), these requests change little from year to year. In most departments, all the company officers assigned to a particular station work together to produce a single budget request for that station. To help them in this process, company officers should maintain a budget file that serves as a collection point for funding ideas that emerge throughout the year. Reviewing this file reduces the likelihood of needed items being overlooked during the budget process. The requests from the individual stations are then combined to form a single budget request for the department. It is important for all officers to participate in this process both to share the workload and to reduce the chances that something is overlooked. Once the budget is approved, it may be difficult to pay for anything that was not requested.

In the process of preparing the station's budget request, company officers should use the proper forms, and these should be typed or neatly and legibly completed (Figure 12.7). They should supply all the required information (specifications, descriptions, catalog numbers, etc.), and except where specifically allowed, they should not reference previous budgets or other documents. In other words, an entry such as "Same as last year" is unacceptable.

An important point relating to preparing budget requests is that the requests should *not* be inflated. A common ploy is to inflate all requests on the assumption that none will receive full funding — therefore, if ten widgets are needed, fifteen are requested. This is a dishonest and counterproductive practice. This places the person who must explain and defend the requests (usually the fire chief) in a very awkward and vulnerable position. Also, if requests for operating funds are inflated, then the amount of money available for the capital budget may be reduced. To help the taxpayers and their elected representatives make informed decisions about how tax revenues are spent, company officers have a responsibility to make every budget request as accurate and realistic as possible.

For most company officers, their involvement in capital budgets is more limited and less direct than their involvement in their departments' operating budgets. Therefore, the balance of this chapter focuses on operating budgets.

Types of Operating Budgets

There is a variety of different types of operating budgets used by fire departments, both public and private, career and volunteer. Some jurisdictions use a combination of more than one type of budget. To function effectively in the budget process, company officers must know what type of budget their department uses. The most commonly used types of operating budgets are *line-item, program, performance,* and *zero-base budgets.*

Line-Item Budgets

Many public entities use the line-item budget because those reviewing it easily can see where the

Figure 12.6 Operating budgets also fund daily operating needs.

Figure 12.7 Budget requests should be typed or neatly written.

money goes. Designed to help prevent overspending, this budgetary system provides strong central control. Line-item budgets organize departmental expenditures into various categories. The two main categories are *personal services* and *other expenses*. As mentioned earlier, personal services is, by far, the biggest category.

Personal Services

This category includes the regular salaries of all personnel, as well as overtime pay, salaries of part-time employees, and special pay for serving out of classification. Also included in this category are employee benefits such as vacation, sick leave, pension contributions, life insurance, and workers' compensation insurance. Considering that fringe benefits cost some entities an amount equal to 50 percent of base salary, it is easy to see why the personal services category represents such a high percentage of the budget.

Other Expenses

In this category, funds are allocated for each of a variety of goods and services. Contract services for the maintenance of apparatus and facilities fall into this category. Also included are contracts with fuel suppliers, laundry services, and other vendors. This category includes funds for paying the monthly utility bills for the stations, buying pens, paper, paper clips, cleanser, exam gloves, and other supplies (Figure 12.8). Considering the variety of activities in which most fire companies engage, it is also easy to see how extensive the list of items in this category can be.

Figure 12.8 Daily supplies and materials are funded by the operating budget.

Program Budgets

These budgets are often a form of line-item budget that uses different categories than the classic line-item budget uses. Program budgets, as the name implies, are categorized by program or activity. In a fire department, each program — fire suppression, fire prevention, EMS, fire administration — is a separate category in the budget (Figure 12.9). The line item for each program shows how much of the overall budget is allocated to that program — how much overtime is related to public education, etc.

Performance Budgets

Similar to program budgets, performance budgets are also categorized by function or activity. However, these budgets fund each activity based on projected performance. For example, the budget for fire prevention is based upon conducting a specified number of inspections in various types of occupancies. Also included in a performance budget is a breakdown of the cost of each unit of performance — per inspection, per plan review, per EMS call, per fire call, etc. (Figure 12.10). Obviously, this can be a very complicated and labor-intensive budget to use.

Zero-Base Budgets

Organized similar to program budgets, zero-base budgets (ZBB) subject each and every function to scrutiny every year. In ZBB, there is no assumption that because a program or activity was funded last year, it will automatically be funded this year or to the same level. Every program must be justified every year. Even those programs that are obviously needed year after year must be scrutinized each year in terms of their funding levels (Figure 12.11). The department head may be asked to provide the cost/benefit data on each of three levels of funding for each program in the department. For example, the chief may be asked to provide the cost/benefit data on maintaining average response times of 4 minutes, 6 minutes, and 8 minutes. Or, he may be asked to provide the data on maintaining the fire prevention bureau at its current level of funding, cutting it 10 percent and cutting it 20 percent. Obviously, producing the data necessary for each program or activity to be evaluated at various levels of funding can be an enormous amount of work.

The Budget Process

As mentioned earlier, company officers usually collaborate with their peers when developing the budget requests for their station. However, the more that each one knows about the budget process and the better they are able to draft their proposals, then the more likely the requests are to be supported by the chief and approved by the governing body. In general, there are five steps in the budget process — *planning, preparation, internal review, external review*, and *implementation*.

Planning

Even though everyone responsible for budget preparation should keep records and make notes throughout the year, three to five months before the end of the fiscal year, the budget process begins in earnest. At this point, the entity should have a fairly clear picture of estimated revenues, based upon tax projections, expected grants and subsidies from the state, provincial, or federal governments, expected fees for services, and other sources.

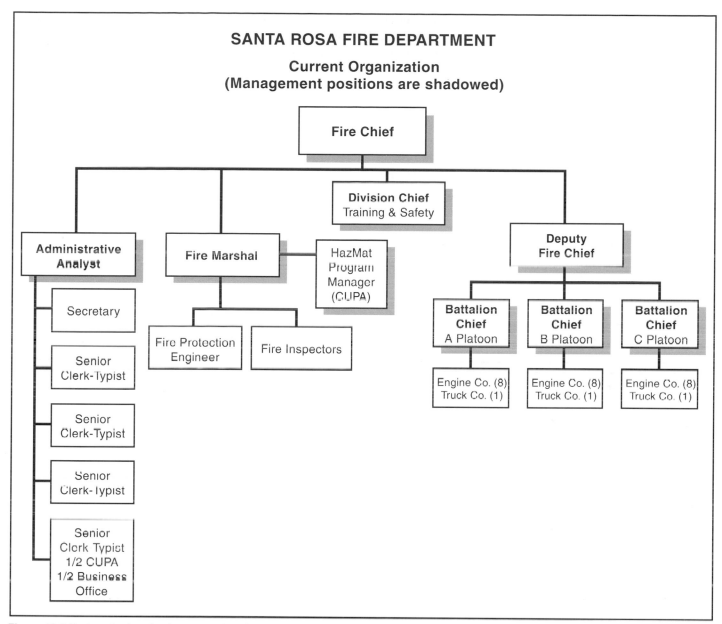

SANTA ROSA FIRE DEPARTMENT

Current Organization
(Management positions are shadowed)

```
                              Fire Chief
                                  |
          _____|_____
          |                       |                        |
          |               Division Chief                   |
          |               Training & Safety                |
          |                                                 |
  Administrative      Fire Marshal    HazMat           Deputy
    Analyst                           Program          Fire Chief
     |                   |            Manager              |
     |                   |            (CUPA)       _____|_____
  Secretary        _____|_____                  |        |       |
     |             |           |              Battalion Battalion Battalion
  Senior      Fire Protection  Fire            Chief    Chief    Chief
 Clerk-Typist   Engineer     Inspectors       A Platoon B Platoon C Platoon
     |                                             |        |        |
  Senior                                      Engine Co.(8) Engine Co.(8) Engine Co.(8)
 Clerk-Typist                                 Truck Co.(1) Truck Co.(1) Truck Co.(1)
     |
  Senior
 Clerk-Typist
     |
  Senior
 Clerk Typist
 1/2 CUPA
 1/2 Business
   Office
```

Figure 12.9 Each major function is a separate category in a program budget. *Courtesy of Santa Rosa (CA) Fire Department.*

Figure 12.10 Performance budgets break down the cost of each service delivery.

Figure 12.11 Each division must justify its existence annually in a zero-base budget system.

The only involvement by company officers at this stage, if any, is limited to preparing estimates of the fees to be generated by the services provided by the department.

Preparation

Estimated revenues from all sources are translated into preliminary budget priorities by the governing body. At this time, the chief may be informed of the general fiscal conditions and what parameters to work within during departmental budget planning and preparation. He may be told to submit the same budget as last year, adjusted for inflation. Or, he may be told to submit a budget that reflects an across-the-board cut of some specified percentage. In any case, those responsible for preparing the department's budget request must begin their work.

At this point, the chief and his staff must decide what services the department can and should provide during the upcoming year and at what levels. In most cases, the departmental budget request reflects the same services and service levels as the previous year. However, there may be a need to add a new service (haz mat response, EMS, technical rescue, etc.) because of a change in the response district that adds a new class of hazard or significantly increases an existing hazard. There may also be a need to delete or reduce an existing service. The need to delete or reduce a service that the department has historically provided (refilling citizens' fire extinguishers, providing medical transportation, etc.) may result from someone opening a business that provides these services. In some jurisdictions it is considered unfair competition for the local government to provide a service that is available in the private sector (Figure 12.12). However, there is a growing trend in some areas for public agencies to compete with the private sector if service levels will be improved and/or delivered at a lower cost.

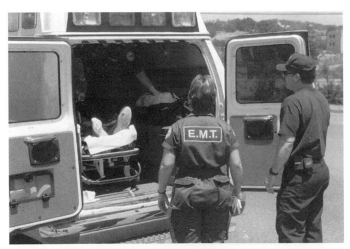

Figure 12.12 Public emergency services may be in direct competition with private providers.

The decisions regarding services and service levels must be translated into concrete program proposals, and a funding request must be developed for each program. Each program must be described in terms of personnel needs, equipment needs, material needs, and other costs. Company officers are likely to be heavily involved in the process of describing these programs and of developing the funding request for each one. In this process, they should use whatever budget request forms that the entity provides. Typically, these forms are constructed in a way that helps company officers and other budget preparers to supply all the needed information and justification. Using these forms conscientiously helps the entire process flow more smoothly and increases the chances of the budget request being approved.

All requests should be kept as simple as possible. The simplest, most direct language should be used. In the narrative description of the services and their funding requirements, the language should be such that anyone can understand it — no acronyms or fire service jargon. Those who ultimately decide to approve or disapprove these requests may have little or no knowledge of fire service terms. If a request is to be disapproved or reduced, it should be done on the merits of the program — not because the request could not be understood.

In addition, funding requests for capital items should be separated from those for operating expenses. As mentioned earlier, capital items are those that are expected to last for more than one year. Even though these two categories must be separated, they are usually submitted as part of the same document. Once all this data is compiled and translated into specific requests for specific programs and activities, the first draft of the departmental budget request is finished. Because this request will be thoroughly scrutinized along with the requests from every other department in the organization, its chances for approval are increased if the document is as correct as it can be. Therefore, before it is submitted for external review (by the governing body), prudent administrators insist that each departmental budget request go through a diligent internal review first.

Internal Review

In this context, *internal* refers to the organization as a whole, not just the fire department. Therefore, the fire department's budget request is thoroughly reviewed by the organization's administrator (or the administrator's staff) and the chief. The chief may be asked to explain and justify each request. If he cannot do so to the administrator's satisfaction, the administrator may reduce or eliminate a specific request. Or, the chief may be asked to provide additional justification. He may also be asked whether some service can be provided with fewer personnel or whether there are other economies that can be realized by providing the service differently. For example, should the department charge a fee for this service? The point of this process is to refine the department's budget request even further and to increase the chances of its being approved with little or no change.

After a thorough internal review, the department's budget is incorporated into the combined budget request for the entire organization. This document is then submitted to the governing body for an external review.

External Review

This is the final review that the budget request document receives. The governing body schedules one or more public hearings so that the citizens of the jurisdiction can have input into the decisions on the budget. The budget may be sent back to the administrator to be reworked in light of citizen concerns. The governing body then considers both revenues and expenditures and may adjust either or both to balance the budget and meet the needs of the citizens. When the concerns of the citizens have been addressed and the budget is in balance, the governing body approves the budget, and it becomes law.

Once the budget has been approved, the administrator, department heads, and supervisors (company officers) now have the funds with which to turn the vision reflected in the budget into reality. They must use their administrative and managerial skills to implement the budget.

Implementation

Once the budget is adopted, the fire chief and the rest of the department personnel must use the budgeted funds to implement the programs and activities that provide the services approved by the governing body. In addition to important fiscal details, the approved and adopted budget represents a plan for the department's operation for the coming year. Many fire chiefs take this opportunity to meet with all or most of the department personnel to review the budget and explain what it will mean to the department's operation. In departments too large to make a mass meeting practical, a written or videotaped budget message from the chief may serve the same purpose. Regardless of how it is done, the importance of sending this message cannot be overemphasized.

The budget tells those who must function within its limitations whether new personnel can be hired, whether staff cuts will be necessary, whether vacant positions can be filled, and whether new equipment can be purchased. In addition, the budget requests that were approved or disapproved may say something about how the governing body perceives the job being done by the department — or they may simply reflect fiscal reality. The budget message should include any specific praise or criticism by the governing body of the department's operation. While the praise may be gratifying, the criticism may be more valuable. If the criticism is viewed objectively, it can serve as a way to focus future priorities and performance within the department.

Grants and Gifts

Many fire departments supplement their general budgets with grants and gifts. These are either private or corporate donations, or subventions from the state/provincial government to those departments to meet specific needs. For example, in Virginia, a portion of all fire insurance premiums paid is returned to local fire departments to pay for training and training-related materials. In many communities, service clubs and other civic organizations have donated funds to purchase a hydraulic rescue tool or a semi-automatic defibrillator. It is important that funds donated for capital purchases be used for that purpose only — and not for operating expenses. It is also important that company officers be able to identify the services and/or pieces of equipment provided by donated funds.

Summary

All fire departments — even volunteer companies — must have some sort of budget with which to operate. Apparatus and equipment must be obtained somehow. Even if most of the resources are donated, there are the costs of equipping and maintaining them. There are costs of insurance and other mandated programs. Most fire departments use one of the recognized budgetary systems to provide funds for the purchase of capital items such as apparatus, equipment, and facilities and for the day-to-day operation of the department. Company officers can play important roles in both the preparation and implementation of the department's budget, and in communicating the budget decisions to the members of their companies.

Chapter 13 • Job Performance Requirements

This chapter provides information that will assist the reader in meeting the following job performance requirements from NFPA 1021, *Standard for Fire Officer Professional Qualifications*, 1997 edition. The colored portions indicate the topics addressed in the chapter. The numbers of the job performance requirements are also noted directly in the sections of text where they are addressed. Those in the following list that are denoted with an asterisk (*) are global in nature and are covered by reading the chapter in its entirety.

Fire Officer I

2-4.2*   Execute routine unit-level administrative functions, given forms and record management systems, so that the reports and logs are complete and files are maintained in accordance with policies and procedures.

(a) *Prerequisite Knowledge:* Administrative policies and procedures and records management.

(b) *Prerequisite Skills:* The ability to communicate verbally and in writing.

Information Management

A large part of most company officers' on-duty time is spent writing reports and keeping records. In many fire departments and volunteer companies, reports may be written in longhand or typed, and logs and records may be handwritten. However, in a growing number of other fire departments, reports are done on word processors, and records are kept in electronic databases. Many company officers regularly use the Internet as an information resource when preparing reports for their departments. The proliferation of personal computers in the fire service during the last decade has forced many company officers to learn new skills, but it has also freed them from much of the drudgery associated with writing reports and keeping records by hand. However, company officers need to remember that electronic mail (E-mail) is not a secure medium, so confidential or privileged information should not be transmitted this way. Company officers are responsible for knowing and following department rules and regulations regarding the use of electronic and other forms of official communication for personal messages ("junk mail") and for seeing that their subordinates do likewise.

This chapter discusses the various forms of routine nonemergency communication that company officers use in the course of their duties. Discussed are written communications, including report writing such as incident reports and personnel reports and also letter writing. Record keeping, including maintenance reports, activity records, and personnel records are also covered. Finally, electronic data storage and retrieval are discussed.

Written Communications

There are many types of written communication that company officers may have to complete while performing their duties. Obviously, much of the written communications produced by company officers is read by others within the department. Their written communications also may be read by those outside the department but within the organization or by those outside the organization. Regardless of who the intended readers are, the majority of company officers' written communications are either reports or letters. Both of these are detailed in the following sections.

Report Writing

Reports are required to document most company activities such as training, emergency responses, fire prevention activities, fire investigations, and injuries to civilians and firefighters. Chief officers cannot, and should not, individually supervise these company-level activities; however, to ensure that these activities are being performed in accordance with the overall goals of the department and the organization, chief officers must rely on the reports and records submitted by the company officers within the department (Figure 13.1). The reports that company officers submit perform two functions: They keep the administration informed of the accomplishments, problems, and daily operations of the company, and they provide data on which the administration

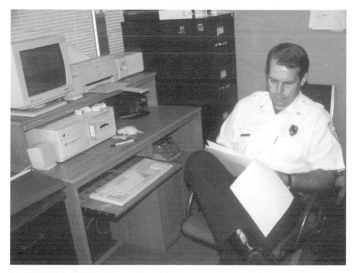

Figure 13.1 Chief officers depend on company-level reports to keep them informed.

can base decisions concerning the operations of the department as a whole. Many of the reports become part of a larger report or database on which the administration bases short- and long-term planning decisions.

Company officers' responsibilities clearly include writing well-organized and informative reports (Figure 13.2). Company officers should remember that any report they produce is a reflection on the company and on themselves. They should also remember that the vast majority of the reports they write are public records and as such may be read by people outside the department. These reports may even be used as evidence in court.

The majority of the reports submitted by company officers only require filling out standard departmental forms and various logbooks. Reports are designed to provide factual and useful information to the department, so these reports should be neat in appearance and legible to the reader. This often requires that the report be typewritten or printed by a computer. However, the content of the report is even more important than its appearance. Information within the report should be structured in a manner that is logical, easily understood, and not confusing.

Producing a well-written report requires the use of complete sentences, correct grammar and syntax, the most appropriate words, and correct punctuation. These basic requirements apply to any type of report, but they are a challenge for some company officers. Some reports submitted by company officers contain all the necessary information, but because of poor grammar, incomplete sentences, or incorrect punctuation, the intended meaning of the reports is unclear. Company officers can reduce these writing problems by developing their writing skills through training and practice and by having a second person proofread their reports before they are submitted.

Misspelled words reflect poorly on the writer and may cause the reader to question the accuracy and credibility of the report. Any doubt about the spelling of a particular word should be settled by consulting a dictionary — or using a computer's spell checker (Figure 13.3). Run-on or partial sentences make it difficult to understand the writer's meaning; it is generally good writing practice to use short, clear sentences. Many good, easy-to-use style manuals are available for verifying correct word usage and punctuation.

Unfortunately, many reports are submitted with misspelled words, little or no punctuation, and inappropriate grammar and syntax. Unnecessary words or words that are vague or ambiguous because they have more than one meaning should not be used. Company officers

Figure 13.2 Writing reports and keeping records are part of a company officer's job.

Figure 13.3 Company officers should consult a dictionary whenever they are in doubt.

should use words that clearly convey the meaning intended and should avoid words that force the reader to speculate about what is actually meant. Taking the time to prepare a well-written report includes allowing time for proofreading to identify common writing mistakes. After the report is grammatically correct and proper use of words and appropriate punctuation have been ensured, the report should be made as neat in appearance as possible.

Using these basic report-writing guidelines helps company officers present themselves and their company in a positive and professional manner. Because a company officer's duties include oral and written reports, it is important that they develop the ability to communicate clearly and effectively. It is beyond the scope of this manual to teach professional business communications; therefore, it is recommended that all company officers take advantage of every opportunity for training in effective report writing. This type of training is available at local community colleges and through televised courses for those in remote locations.

Incident Reports

Most fire departments report their fire-related activity on either the National Fire Incident Reporting System (NFIRS) or their state's version of it (Figure 13.4). For simplicity and standardization, many departments use the NFIRS form to report all emergency responses, regardless of their nature. In those departments, fires, EMS calls, and rescues are all reported on the same form.

A — NFIRS-1 Basic

FDID ☆	State ☆	Incident Date ☆ (MM DD YYYY)	Station	Incident Number ☆	Exposure ☆

☐ Delete ☐ Change ☐ No Activity

NFIRS - 1 Basic

B — Location ☆

☐ Check this box to indicate that the address for this incident is provided on the Wildland Fire Module in Section B "Alternative Location Specification."

Census Tract ☐

☐ Intersection
☐ Block address
☐ In front of
☐ Rear of
☐ Adjacent to
☐ Directions

Number/Milepost   Prefix   Street or Highway   Street Type   Suffix

Apt./Suite/Room   City   State   Zip Code

Cross street or directions, as applicable

C — Incident Type ☆

Incident Type

D — Aid Given or Received ☆

1 ☐ Mutual aid received
2 ☐ Automatic aid recv.
3 ☐ Mutual aid given
4 ☐ Automatic aid given
5 ☐ Other aid given
N ☐ None

Their FDID   Their State
Their Incident Number

E₁ — Dates & Times

Midnight is 0000

Check boxes if dates are the same as Alarm Date.

	Month	Day	Year	Hour	Min
Alarm ☆ — ALARM always required					
☐ Arrival ☆ — ARRIVAL required, unless canceled or did not arrive					
☐ Controlled — CONTROLLED optional, except for wildland fires					
☐ Last Unit Cleared — LAST UNIT CLEARED, required except for wildland fires					

E₂ — Shifts & Alarms

Local Option

Shift or platoon   Alarms   District

E₃ — Special Studies

Local Option

Special Study ID#   Special Study Value

F — Actions Taken ☆

Primary Action Taken (1)

Additional Action Taken (2)

Additional Action Taken (3)

G₁ — Resources ☆

☐ Check this box and skip this section if an Apparatus or Personnel form is used.

	Apparatus	Personnel
Suppression		
EMS		
Other		

☐ Check box if resource counts include aid given resources.

G₂ — Estimated Dollar Losses & Values

LOSSES: Required for all fires if known. Optional for non fires.   None

Property	$	☐
Contents	$	☐

PRE-INCIDENT VALUE: Optional

Property	$	☐
Contents	$	☐

Completed Modules

☐ Fire-2
☐ Structure-3
☐ Civilian Fire Cas.-4
☐ Fire Serv. Casualty-5
☐ EMS-6
☐ HazMat-7
☐ Wildland Fire-8
☐ Apparatus-9
☐ Personnel-10
☐ Arson-11

H₁ — Casualties ☐ None

	Deaths	Injuries
Fire Service		
Civilian		

H₂ — Detector

Required for confined fires if the occupants were alerted

☐ Detector alerted occupants

H₃ — Hazardous Materials Release

N ☐ None
1 ☐ Natural gas: slow leak, no evacuation or hazmat actions
2 ☐ Propane gas: <21 lb. tank (as in home BBQ grill)
3 ☐ Gasoline: vehicle fuel tank or portable container
4 ☐ Kerosene: fuel burning equipment or portable storage
5 ☐ Diesel fuel/fuel oil: vehicle fuel tank or portable storage
6 ☐ Household solvents: home/office spill, cleanup only
7 ☐ Motor oil: from engine or portable container
8 ☐ Paint: from paint cans totaling <55 gallons
0 ☐ Other: Special HazMat actions required or spill > 55 gal., Please complete the HazMat form

I — Mixed Use Property

NN ☐ Not mixed
10 ☐ Assembly Use
20 ☐ Education use
33 ☐ Medical use
40 ☐ Residential use
51 ☐ Row of stores
53 ☐ Enclosed mall
58 ☐ Business & residential
59 ☐ Office use
60 ☐ Industrial use
63 ☐ Military use
65 ☐ Farm use
00 ☐ Other mixed use

J — Property Use ☆

Structures

131 ☐ Church, place of worship
161 ☐ Restaurant or cafeteria
162 ☐ Bar/tavern or nightclub
213 ☐ Elementary school or kindergart.
215 ☐ High school or junior high
241 ☐ College, adult ed.
311 ☐ Care facility for the aged
331 ☐ Hospital

341 ☐ Clinic, clinic type infirmary
342 ☐ Doctor/dentist office
361 ☐ Prison or jail, not juvenile
419 ☐ 1- or 2- family dwelling
429 ☐ Multi-family dwelling
439 ☐ Rooming/boarding house
449 ☐ Commercial hotel or motel
459 ☐ Residential, board and care
464 ☐ Dormitory/barracks
519 ☐ Food and beverage sales

539 ☐ Household goods, sales, repairs
579 ☐ Motor vehicle/boat sales/repairs
571 ☐ Gas or service station
599 ☐ Business office
615 ☐ Electric generating plant
629 ☐ Laboratory/science lab
700 ☐ Manufacturing plant
819 ☐ Livestock/poultry storage (barn)
882 ☐ Non-residential parking garage
891 ☐ Warehouse

Outside

124 ☐ Playground or park
655 ☐ Crops or orchard
669 ☐ Forest (timberland)
807 ☐ Outdoor storage area
919 ☐ Dump or sanitary landfill
931 ☐ Open land or field

936 ☐ Vacant lot
938 ☐ Graded/cared for plot of land
946 ☐ Lake, river, stream
951 ☐ Railroad right of way
960 ☐ Other street
961 ☐ Highway/divided highway
962 ☐ Residential street/driveway

981 ☐ Construction site
984 ☐ Industrial plant yard

Look up and enter a Property Use code only if you have NOT checked a Property Use box: Property Use

NFIRS-1 Revision 6/9/98

Figure 13.4 The NFIRS report form.

K1 Person/Entity Involved

Local Option

Business name (if applicable)

Area Code   Phone Number

☐ Check this box if same address as incident location. Then skip the three duplicate address lines.

Mr., Ms., Mrs.   First Name   MI   Last Name   Suffix

Number   Prefix   Street or Highway   Street Type   Suffix

Post Office Box   Apt./Suite/Room   City

State   Zip Code

☐ **More people involved? Check this box and attach Supplemental Forms (NFIRS-1S) as necessary.**

K2 Owner

☐ Same as person involved? Then check this box and skip the rest of this section.

Local Option

Business name (if applicable)

Area Code   Phone Number

☐ Check this box if same address as incident location. Then skip the three duplicate address lines.

Mr., Ms., Mrs.   First Name   MI   Last Name   Suffix

Number   Prefix   Street or Highway   Street Type   Suffix

Post Office Box   Apt./Suite/Room   City

State   Zip Code

L Remarks:

Local Option

Fire Module Required?

Check the box that applies and then complete the additional Fire mod. based on Incident Type as follows:

☐ **Buildings 111**	**Complete Fire & Structure**
☐ **Special structure 112**	**Complete Fire Mod. & the I block on Structure Module**
☐ **Confined 113-118**	**Complete Basic Module**
☐ **Mobile Property 120-123**	**Complete Fire Module**
☐ **Vehicle 130-138**	**Complete Fire Module**
☐ **Vegetation 140-143**	**Complete Fire or Wildland**
☐ **Special outside fire 161-164**	**Complete Fire Module**

ITEMS WITH A ☆ MUST **ALWAYS** BE COMPLETED!

☐ **More remarks? Check this box and attach Supplemental Forms(NFIRS-1S) as necessary.**

M Authorization

Officer in charge ID   Signature   Position or rank   Assignment   Month   Day   Year

Check box if same as Officer in charge. ➡ ☐

Member making report ID   Signature   Position or rank   Assignment   Month   Day   Year

Figure 13.4 Continued.

Regardless of what form is used for incident reports, company officers should keep in mind that these reports are open public records and may be used in future litigation. Therefore, completeness, simplicity, and accuracy are important.

Company officers' responsibility for incident reporting varies with their role in a particular incident. In some incidents, a company officer is the incident commander and is therefore responsible for compiling a consolidated report that documents the activities of all units involved in the incident. In other incidents, a company officer is in a subordinate role under the direction of a chief officer. In that case, the company officer is responsible for reporting only his company's activities.

Regardless of who is responsible for the incident report, it should be consistent with the National Fire Incident Reporting System (NFIRS) and contain all essential information:

- Location/address
- Date
- Time
- Number of personnel responding
- Number and type of apparatus responding
- Persons responsible for the property
- Incident type
- Type of property involved
- Level and area of origin
- Cause and spread factors if the incident was a fire
- Information about the structure if one was involved
- Information about the presence and effectiveness of built-in fire protection systems
- Damage and loss information

In addition, the narrative description should include a description of the overall operation including special factors involved, reasons for special or unusual actions (deviations from departmental SOPs), and recommendations for any follow-up required. In most cases, a diagram will help clarify the situation being reported, and one should be included in the report (Figure 13.5).

If the incident involved any casualties, a report should be filed on each one. Department policies and procedures must be followed regarding what to include in casualty reports, but most reports of this type include the following:

- Name of injured/deceased
- Home address

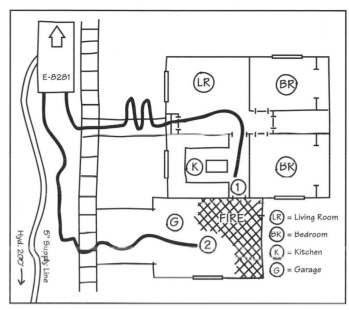

Figure 13.5 Diagrams make incident reports clearer.

- Age
- Gender
- Firefighter or civilian
- Notification of next of kin
- Notification of parent/guardian/spouse

In addition, a description of the injury, the mechanism of injury, and the medical aid given are usually included. If patients were transported to a medical facility, how they were transported, by whom, and to what facility should also be listed. All injuries sustained by firefighters must be reported, no matter how minor they seem at the time. Complications from such injuries can occur in the future, and failure to report an injury can affect the firefighter's eligibility for workers' compensation.

If a company officer was not in charge of the entire incident but was in charge of only one of several companies involved, the company officer must prepare a company report — sometimes called a "run report." The specific information required in a run report varies from department to department, but in general, the report should include the following:

- Company number
- Names of the personnel who responded as part of the company
- Apparatus and equipment used on the incident by the company
- Amount of water used by the company
- Any equipment lost or broken
- Narrative description of what the company did

Narratives. A detailed narrative should be a part of every incident report. In the narrative portion of the report, the writer should attempt to paint a verbal picture of the company's activities from the time of its dispatch until it returned to quarters or to another assignment. In general, company officers should use the following guidelines when preparing the narrative portion of their reports:

- Organize the narrative in the chronological sequence of events.

- Avoid using fire service jargon, acronyms, or technical terminology that some readers may not understand.

- Be thorough. Gather information from all company members before writing the report, and clarify any apparently conflicting information. Identify the pertinent positive and negative conditions.

- Include only known facts. Do not include speculation.

Emergency Medical Service (EMS) Reports. The typical EMS report is a combination of an incident report, which is open to the public by law, and a patient care report that is privileged information that the public is not allowed to see. For this reason, some EMS providers use separate reports to satisfy these two needs.

The *EMS response report*, which is open to the public, provides information about the response, its location, who responded, the general nature of the incident (auto accident, medical, etc.), how many patients were involved, and information about patient transport to a medical facility. Cross-referenced to that report is a *patient care report* that provides the very specific privileged patient information, such as the nature of the medical problem (fracture, diabetes, overdose, etc.), mechanism of injury, vital signs, patient's medical history, medications used, allergies, and treatment (Figure 13.6).

Personnel Reports

Company officers are also typically required to prepare and submit reports on the personnel in the company. These reports take a variety of forms, but the two most common are *performance evaluations* and *work improvement plans*.

Performance evaluations. There are more than a dozen different ways to evaluate and quantify a member's work performance, and each uses a different form in the evaluation process. Some of these evaluation systems use a numerical rating scale; others rate performance on a descriptive scale from unsatisfactory to outstanding. Company officers should be trained in the theory and application of the particular evaluation system used by their department.

In general, performance evaluations serve three purposes — to inform the member and the administration of how well the member is performing his assigned duties, to form the basis for a work improvement plan if the member's work is substandard, and to document the member's work history in case termination for nonperformance becomes necessary.

Most performance evaluation systems require a formal review of each member's work performance on an annual basis, with one or more informal progress evaluations at intervals between the annual reviews. In the formal review, both the quantity and quality of the member's work performance are evaluated according to whatever standard is used in the department's system. This review is intended to identify both the member's strengths and accomplishments and any performance that needs to be improved. It is also an opportunity for the member and the company officer to jointly establish one or more work-related goals toward which the member can strive in the coming year. If the member's work performance is found to be substandard, a work improvement plan may be in order.

Work improvement plans. These plans are used when some or all of a member's work performance is significantly below standard or when the performance of a critical skill is below standard to any degree (Figure 13.7). A *work improvement plan* is a form of contract between the member and the supervisor that identifies specific performance improvements that must be made by specific dates. Identified in the plan are specific training/retraining that the department will provide, as well as ongoing monitoring procedures and periodic testing that will be used to evaluate the member's progress.

Regardless of which type of report is needed, the company officer responsible for the report should use whatever form the department has adopted and should complete all parts of the form. If a printed form is used, it should be filled out in ink of a color that contrasts with the print on the form (Figure 13.8). This makes check marks easier to see and therefore less likely to be overlooked. If a narrative is required as part of the report, it should typed or legibly written.

Letter Writing

There are several types of letters that company officers may be expected to write in the course of their duties. Company officers must sometimes write letters to people inside and outside the department and the organization. The most common types of letters that company officers write are memoranda and business letters.

A — NFIRS - 4 Civilian Fire Casualty

| FDID ☆ | State ☆ | MM DD YYYY Incident Date ☆ | Station | Incident Number ☆ | Exposure ☆ | ☐ Delete ☐ Change |

B — Injured Person

☆ 1 ☐ Male   2 ☐ Female

First Name _____ MI _____ Last Name _____ Suffix _____

C — Casualty Number ☆

Casualty Number _____

D — Age or Date of Birth ☆

Age _____ ☐ Months (for infants)

OR

Date of Birth
Month _____ Day _____ Year _____

E₁ — Race

1 ☐ White
2 ☐ Black
3 ☐ Am. Indian, Eskimo
4 ☐ Asian
5 ☐ Multi-racial
U ☐ Undetermined

E₂ — Ethnicity

1 ☐ Hispanic

F — Affiliation

1 ☐ Civilian
2 ☐ EMS, not fire department
3 ☐ Police
0 ☐ Other

G — Date & Time of Injury

Midnight is 0000.

Date of injury
Month _____ Day _____ Year _____

Time of injury
Hour _____ Minutes _____

H — Severity ☆

1 ☐ Minor
2 ☐ Moderate
3 ☐ Severe
4 ☐ Life threatening
5 ☐ Death

I — Cause of Injury

1 ☐ Exposed to fire products including flame heat, smoke, & gas
2 ☐ Exposed to toxic fumes other than smoke
3 ☐ Jumped in escape attempt
4 ☐ Fell, slipped, or tripped
5 ☐ Caught or trapped
6 ☐ Structural collapse
7 ☐ Struck by/or contact with object
8 ☐ Overexertion
9 ☐ Multiple causes
0 ☐ Other
U ☐ Undetermined

J — Human Factors Contributing to Injury

☐ None

Check all applicable boxes

1 ☐ Asleep
2 ☐ Unconscious
3 ☐ Possibly impaired by alcohol
4 ☐ Possibly impaired by other drug
5 ☐ Possibly mentally disabled
6 ☐ Physically disabled
7 ☐ Physically restrained
8 ☐ Unattended person

K — Factors Contributing to Injury

☐ None   Enter up to three contributing factors

Contributing factor (1) _____

Contributing factor (2) _____

Contributing factor (3) _____

L — Activity When Injured

1 ☐ Escaping
2 ☐ Rescue attempt
3 ☐ Fire control
4 ☐ Return to fire before control
5 ☐ Return to fire after control
6 ☐ Sleeping
7 ☐ Unable to act
8 ☐ Irrational act
0 ☐ Other
U ☐ Undetermined

M₁ — Location at Time of Incident

1 ☐ In area of origin and not involved
2 ☐ Not in area of origin & not involved
3 ☐ Not in area of origin, but involved
4 ☐ In area of origin and involved
U ☐ Undetermined

M₂ — General Location at Time of Injury

Check ONE box. If undetermined, leave blank and skip to Section N.

1 ☐ In area of fire origin → Skip to Section N
2 ☐ In building, but not in area
3 ☐ Outside, but not in area → Skip to Section M₅

M₃ — Story at Start of Incident

Complete ONLY if injury occurred INSIDE

Story at START of incident _____ ☐ below grade

M₄ — Story Where Injury Occurred

Story where injury occurred, if different from M₃ _____ ☐ below grade

M₅ — Specific Location at Time of Injury

Complete ONLY if casualty NOT in area of origin

Specific location at time of injury _____

N — Primary Apparent Symptom

01 ☐ Smoke only, asphyxiation
11 ☐ Burns & smoke inhalation
12 ☐ Burns only
21 ☐ Cut, laceration
33 ☐ Strain or sprain
96 ☐ Shock
98 ☐ Pain only

Look up a code only if the symptom is NOT found above

Primary apparent symptom _____

O — Primary Area of Body Injured

1 ☐ Head
2 ☐ Neck & shoulder
3 ☐ Thorax
4 ☐ Abdomen
5 ☐ Spine
6 ☐ Upper extremities
7 ☐ Lower extremities
8 ☐ Internal
9 ☐ Multiple body parts

P — Disposition

☐ Transported to emergency care facility

Remarks   Local option
_____
_____
_____
_____

NFIRS-4 Revision 6/9/98

Figure 13.6 A typical patient medical report form.

PERFORMANCE IMPROVEMENT PLAN

Employee's Name   Date _____

1. **Description of Performance/Incident:**

2. **Measurable Improvement Goals:**

3. **Training/Direction Recommended/Required (Specify):**

4. **Improvement Time Frame:**

5. **Consequences:**

6. **Employee Input / Rebuttal:** (Optional)

X _____   X _____   _____
   I acknowledge the PIP   **I disagree with the PIP**   **Date**

X _____   X _____   _____
   Supervisor   **Witness (*if necessary*)**   **Date**

A print out or photo-copy of this completed form should be made for (1) the employee, (2) the immediate supervisor, and (3) Human Resources.

Figure 13.7 A work improvement plan is a form of contract. *Courtesy of Tualatin Valley Fire and Rescue (OR).*

	BASIC CASUALTY REPORT								Form 902G

BASIC CASUALTY REPORT
Fill in this Report in Your Own Words _____Stillwater_____ Fire Department ☐ Revised Report   Form 902G

GA — FD ID: *6005* | Incident No.: *1781* | Idex No.: | Casualty No.: *01* | Injury Occurred: Mo. *06* Day *10* Year *98* | Time: *0215*

GB — Casualty Name (Last, First, MI): *Stevens, George M.* | Injury Reported: Mo. *06* Day *10* Year *98* | Time: *0230*

GC — Affiliation: *Firefighter* | D.O.B.: *08.15.40* | Age: *5|7* | Sex ☒ Male ☐ Female | Race: *W* | *1* | National Origin ☐ Hispanic?

GD — Home Address: *1818 Ramsey St.* | City: *Stillwater* | State: *OK* | Zip: *74075* | Telephone No.: *(405) 043-9101*

GE — Case Severity: *Minor* | *1* | Primary Apparent Symptom: *Foreign body* | *2|7* | Primary Part of Body: *Eye* | *1|2*

GF — Secondary Apparent Symptom: *N/A* | | | Secondary Part of Body: *N/A* | |

GG — Casualty Type by Situation Found: *Building Fire Injury* | *3|1* | Final Disposition of Casualty: *Memorial Hospital by AMR* | *2*

GH — Familiarity with Incident Area | Condition of Person Prior to Incident | Activity at Time of Injury

COMPLETE ON ALL CASUALTIES

Figure 13.8 Forms should be completed in ink of a contrasting color.

Memoranda

Usually shortened to just "memos," memoranda are a form of letter that is usually reserved for internal communication only — that is, within the department or the organization. Their format usually includes the following headings: *Date, To, From,* and *Subject* (Figure 13.9). Memos are sometimes used to document a face-to-face conversation or telephone call. They are also used for the following purposes:

• To transmit the same information to several locations or individuals

• To provide a written record of decisions, requests, or policies

• To provide specific information concerning questions or requests in a somewhat informal manner

Although some departments have specific forms that are used instead of memoranda for certain specific applications, memos are often used to request permission, order supplies, request repairs, etc. If a memo is used to request something of a high-priority nature, such as the repair of a piece of first-line apparatus, it should be followed up with a phone call to the responsible individual or office so that immediate action can be initiated (Figure 13.10). Otherwise, a memo might languish unnoticed in someone's in-basket for some time before it is read and action is taken.

As with any other official document, memos and other forms should be completed fully. Every line or box on the form should be marked. If the information requested on a particular line or in a particular box does not apply, it should be marked "N/A" (not applicable) rather than being left blank (Figure 13.11). If a line or box is simply left blank, the recipient has no way of knowing whether the line or box was left blank because it did not apply or whether it was overlooked by the person who filled out the form. If E-mail is used as a form of memo, the same degree of care should be used in composing the text of the message as is done with hard copy memos.

Business Letters

As mentioned earlier, official written communications reflect on both the officer who wrote them and on the department. A poorly written letter gives the reader a negative impression of both the writer and the organization represented. Letters are an effective communications medium if they are written correctly and in a manner appropriate for the intended reader and the subject being discussed. All business letters should be on department letterhead and be grammatically correct, properly punctuated, and written in clear, straightforward language. In a business letter, the company officer who wrote it represents the department; therefore, all correspondence should be professional and in accordance with department rules, SOPs, and policies. There are a number of different styles used for writing business letters, and each department should adopt and train their personnel in the use of one of them for their official business correspondence. In the absence of an officially adopted style guide, company officers should use one of the nationally recognized style manu-

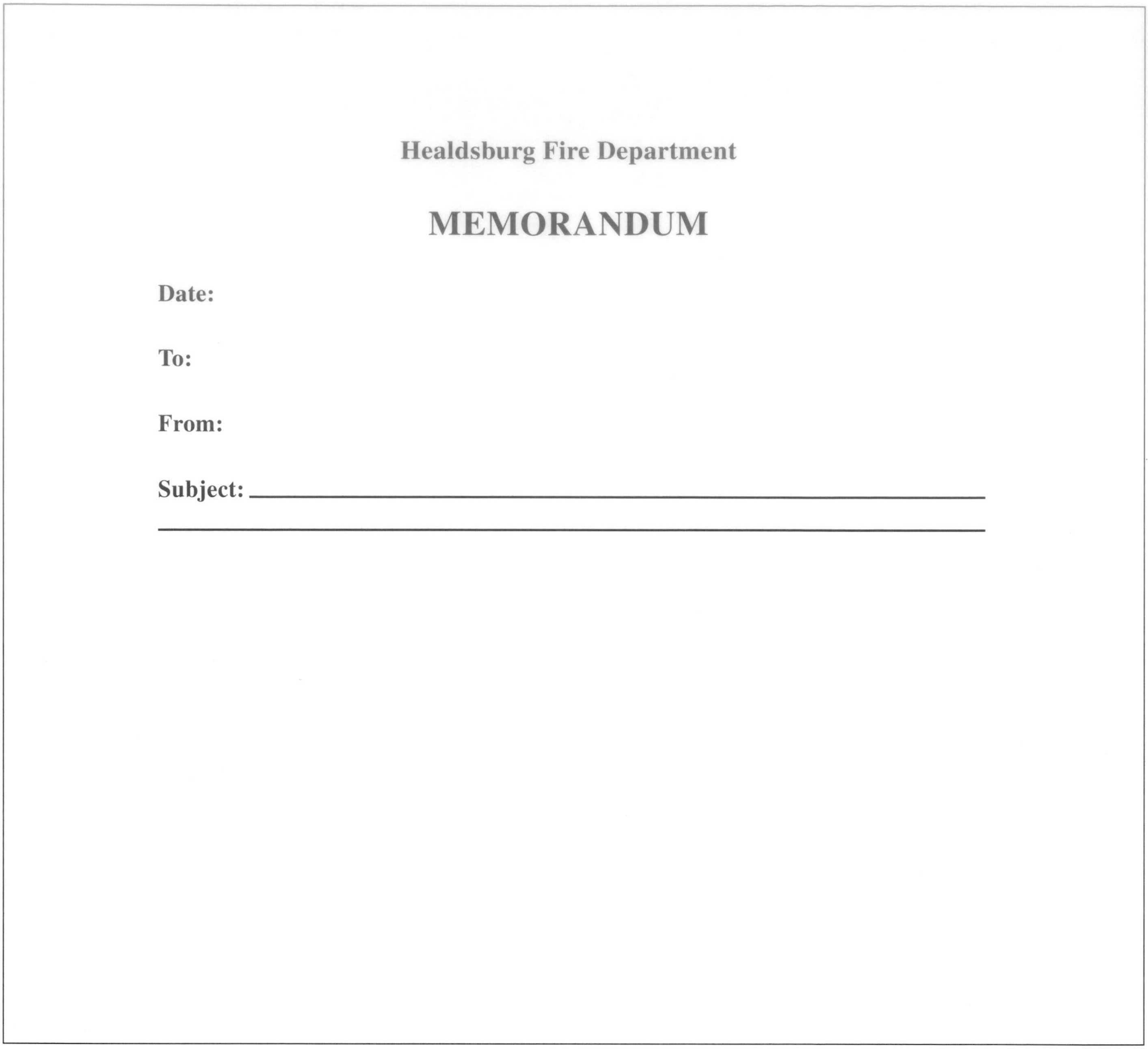

Healdsburg Fire Department

MEMORANDUM

Date:

To:

From:

Subject: _____

_____

Figure 13.9 A typical memo form.

Figure 13.10 Company officers should follow up on repair requests.

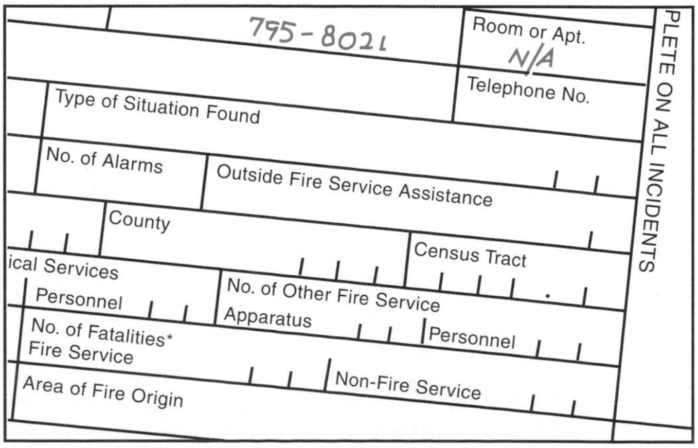

		795-8021	Room or Apt. N/A	
	Type of Situation Found		Telephone No.	
	No. of Alarms	Outside Fire Service Assistance		
	County		Census Tract	
ical Services				
Personnel	No. of Other Fire Service	Apparatus		
No. of Fatalities* Fire Service			Personnel	
Area of Fire Origin	Non-Fire Service			

PLETE ON ALL INCIDENTS

Figure 13.11 Forms should be filled out completely.

als available in any public library (Figure 13.12). Just as with report writing, it is beyond the scope of this manual to teach the mechanics of business correspondence, and company officers are encouraged to develop their letter-writing skills through a combination of training and practice.

Figure 13.12 One of several good style manuals.

Record Keeping

There are a host of different types of records kept by fire departments — many of them are kept at the company level. There are records kept on department facilities, vehicles, and major pieces of equipment. There are records kept on department functions and activities. And, there are records kept on department personnel. Therefore, the three main categories of record-keeping at the company level are *maintenance, activity,* and *personnel records.*

Maintenance Records

Fire departments keep maintenance records of their stations and other facilities, as well as of their vehicles and certain pieces of equipment. Maintenance records are usually kept in two distinct but closely related categories — *preventive maintenance* and *corrective maintenance.*

Preventive Maintenance

As the name implies, preventive maintenance is done to prevent damage from occurring and to extend the useful life of an item by reducing wear. The roofs of the stations are inspected periodically, and any wear or damage is repaired in order to prevent costly water damage within the structure. The exterior siding is inspected and maintained for the same reason. The oil is changed in the fire apparatus' engines, and the chassis are lubricated to reduce the likelihood of breakdowns that could be disastrous if they were to occur during an emergency. The same is true of gasoline-driven generators and other equipment. Fire hose is inspected and tested annually to prevent it from failing during a fire. The wooden handles of tools are inspected and treated with oil to keep them smooth and prevent dehydration. These are but a few of the countless examples of preventive maintenance that take place at the company level.

Unlike corrective maintenance (repairs), which can be needed at any time, preventive maintenance is usually performed according to a schedule (Figure 13.13).

Experience and the manufacturers' recommendations combine to form the basis for this schedule of periodic inspection and maintenance. Frequent inspection and cleaning often reveal incipient problems that are relatively easy and inexpensive to correct in their early stages. Left unnoticed and uncorrected, many minor problems can develop into major breakdowns and require expensive repairs.

The need for preventive maintenance is clear, and the basis for it is record keeping. Conscientiously applying a preventive maintenance schedule by inspecting the items under the company's control (and carefully recording the results) is one of many important reasons for keeping records at the company level (Figure 13.14).

Corrective Maintenance

There are few items in a fire station or under a company's control that are not vitally important. Apparatus, tools and equipment, SCBA, EMS and rescue gear, and other pieces of emergency equipment must be maintained in a state of readiness (Figure 13.15). When any of these items are damaged or cease to function, they must be repaired or replaced as soon as possible. Deciding when or if to replace an item is often based on its maintenance record. A record showing that the item is relatively new and up-to-date would probably indicate that the item should be repaired. On the other hand, a record showing that the item is old and out of date and that it has a history of increasingly frequent failures or breakdowns may indicate the need to replace the item with something newer and more reliable. In either case, the maintenance record is a critically important part of the decision-making process.

Activity Records

Most fire companies are extremely busy with both emergency and nonemergency activity. They sometimes work day and night — around the clock. Just as in maintenance, some of the company's activities are schedule-driven, others occur at random intervals. Company members inspect and test the apparatus and their personal protective equipment when they come on duty and record the findings on the various sheets and forms provided (Figure 13.16). They inspect and clean the station and the equipment; these findings are recorded in the daily log. Company members attend classes or participate in drills or exercises, and these activities are recorded on the appropriate training forms. They conduct pre-incident surveys or fire prevention inspections, and that is recorded (Figure 13.17). Also recorded are any emergency calls to which the company responds.

FIRE APPARATUS INSPECTION AND MAINTENANCE SCHEDULE 1998

M - MONTHLY
Q - QUARTERLY
SA - SEMI-ANNUAL
A - ANNUAL

JANUARY	FEBRUARY	MARCH	APRIL	MAY	JUNE	JULY	AUGUST	SEPTEMBER	OCTOBER	NOVEMBER	DECEMBER
A-SHIFT	A-SHIFT	A-SHIFT	A-SHIFT	A-SHIFT	A-SHIFT	A-SHIFT	A-SHIFT	A-SHIFT	A-SHIFT	A-SHIFT	A-SHIFT
3201-M	3201-Q	3201-M	3210-M	3201-SA	3201-M	3201-M	3201-Q	3201-M	3201-M	3201-A	3201-M
3206-A	3206-	3206-	3206-	3206-	3206-	3206-A	3206-	3206-	3206-	3206-	3206-
3214-M	3214-M	3214-A	3214-M	3214-M	3214-M	3214-Q	3214-M	3214-SA	3214-M	3214-M	3214-Q
3218-M	3218-SA	3218-M	3218-M	3218-Q	3218-M	3218-M	3218-A	3218-M	3218-M	3218-Q	3218-M
3217-M	3217-SA	3217-M	3217-M	3217-Q	3217-M	3217-M	3217-A	3217-M	3217-M	3217-Q	3217-M
3241-M	3241-M	3241-M	3241-A	3241-M	3241-M	3241-Q	3241-M	3241-M	3241-SA	3241-M	3241-M
3245-Q	3245-M	3245-M	3245-A	3245-M	3245-M	3245-Q	3245-M	3245-M	3245-SA	3245-M	3245-M
3246-M	3246-Q	3246-M	3246-M	3246-A	3246-M	3246-M	3246-Q	3246-M	3246-M	3246-SA	3246-M
B-SHIFT	B-SHIFT	B-SHIFT	B-SHIFT	B-SHIFT	B-SHIFT	B-SHIFT	B-SHIFT	B-SHIFT	B-SHIFT	B-SHIFT	B-SHIFT
3202-M	3202-A	3202-M	3202-M	3202-Q	3202-M	3202-M	3202-A	3202-M	3202-M	3202-Q	3202-M
3203-M	3203-M	3203-Q	3203-M	3203-M	3203-A	3203-M	3203-M	3203-Q	3203-M	3203-M	3203-SA
3207-A	3207-	3207-	3207-	3207-	3207-	3207-A	3207-	3207-	3207-	3207-	3207-
3215-M	3215-A	3215-M	3215-M	3215-Q	3215-M	3215-M	3215-SA	3215-M	3215-M	3215-Q	3215-M
3219-M	3219-Q	3219-M	3219-M	3219-SA	3219-M	3219-M	3219-Q	3219-M	3219-M	3219-A	3219-M
3231-Q	3231-M	3231-M	3231-A	3231-M	3231-M	3231-Q	3231-M	3231-M	3231-SA	3231-M	3231-M
3234-M	3242-M	3242-M	3242-A	3242-M	3242-M	3242-M	3242-Q	3242-M	3242-SA	3242-M	3242-M
3270-M	3270-Q	3270-M	3270-M	3270-M	3270-M	3270-M	3270-M	3270-SA	3270-M	3270-M	3270-Q
C-SHIFT	C-SHIFT	C-SHIFT	C-SHIFT	C-SHIFT	C-SHIFT	C-SHIFT	C-SHIFT	C-SHIFT	C-SHIFT	C-SHIFT	C-SHIFT
3204-A	3204-	3204-	3204-	3204	3204-	3204-A	3204-	3204-	3204-	3204-	3204-
3205-A	3205-	3205-	3205-	3205-	3205-	3205-A	3205-	3205-	3205-	3205-	3205-
3208-A	3208-	3208-	3208-	3208-	3208-	3208-A	3208-	3208-	3208-	3208-	3208-
3209-A	3209-	3209-	3209-	3209-	3209-	3209-A	3209-	3209-	3209-	3209-	3209-
3210-M	3210-M	3210-Q	3210-M	3210-M	3210-A	3210-M	3210-M	3210-Q	3210-M	3210-M	3210-SA
3213-M	3213-A	3213-M	3213-M	3213-Q	3213-M	3213-M	3213-SA	3213-M	3213-M	3213-Q	3213-M
3216-SA	3216-M	3216-M	3216-Q	3216-M	3216-M	3216-A	3216-M	3216-M	3216-Q	3216-M	3216-M
3240-M	3240-M	3240-M	3240-A	3240-M	3240-M	3240-Q	3240-M	3240-M	3240-SA	3240-M	3240-M
3247-M	3247-M	3247-Q	3247-A	3247-M	3247-M	3247-M	3247-M	3247-Q	3247-SA	3247-M	3247-M

Figure 13.13 Preventive maintenance is schedule-driven. *Courtesy of Fairfield (CA) Fire Department.*

Figure 13.14 Inspection results should be recorded.

Figure 13.16 Daily checks should be recorded.

Figure 13.15 Emergency tools and equipment must be maintained in a state of readiness.

Figure 13.17 Company inspection activities should also be recorded.

Daily Logs

In addition to filling out activity-specific forms, most companies record their daily activities on some form of daily log. While some departments keep their daily logs electronically, others still maintain a handwritten hard copy. Similar to a ship's log, the daily log at each station is the official record of what the company members did during their work shift. While the layout of these logs varies from department to department, most contain the same items of information. The heading of a typical daily log sheet contains the following:

- Department name
- Date
- Company or unit designator
- Roster of personnel on duty

On the face of the sheet below the heading, there are usually a number of lines for recording the emergency calls on which the company responded. Each line may have a space for the times (time of alarm and time of return), the address or location of the call, and the type of call (fire, EMS, rescue, needless call, false alarm, etc.) (Figure 13.18).

The reverse side of the sheet may have nothing but lines from top to bottom (Figure 13.19). These lines are for entering the routine, nonemergency activities of the company and its members during the shift. Such routine activities as checking the apparatus and equipment and cleaning the station are entered. Any emergency apparatus or equipment found to be damaged or otherwise not ready for service — such as the water or fuel tank on a pumper left empty or SCBA cylinders depleted — should be logged. Such occurrences should also be discussed between the responsible station officers as well. Also entered are activities such as company training, conducting code enforcement inspections, making public education presentations, and testing hose. Names of visitors to the station are also logged, along with any tours of the station by the public. Some of the most important entries are those documenting any accidents or injuries involving company personnel. These entries may be important evidence in workers' compensation claims.

Because the daily log is a legal document, the company officer is usually required to sign and date the form on the line immediately below the last entry. In this way, the company officer attests that all of the foregoing is a true and complete record of the company's activities during that shift. If some item was inadvertently left out, it may be added below the officer's signature, but the person making the addendum must also sign and date the form as the company officer did — even if the same company officer makes the addendum.

Personnel Records

Other than attendance records (daily roster of personnel) and similar documents, personnel records are generally confidential. Therefore, company officers must be careful to protect that confidentiality by keeping the company personnel records under lock and key. Because work on these records can be interrupted at any time by an emergency call, company officers should be ready to quickly lock these records in a drawer or filing cabinet if an alarm sounds. They must never be left on a desktop or anywhere that might allow someone else to see them while the company officer is away from his desk.

In most cases, company officers will keep either or both of the two types of personnel records described earlier in this chapter — performance evaluations and work improvement plans — for each member of the company. Each of these instruments has its own format, and company officers should be trained in how to use these forms.

Electronic Data Storage/Retrieval

Many fire departments are using some form of electronic data storage and retrieval system to keep records of all types. They are also using computer based word processors for writing reports and other documents. Obviously, the company officers in these departments must learn to use whatever system that their department has purchased.

The variety of hardware and software available for electronically storing and retrieving data is almost overwhelming. However, company officers are only responsible for learning to use the system adopted by their department. Even though this can still be a daunting task for some, it is one that company officers must undertake if they are to stay current and be able to function at maximum efficiency (Figure 13.20). In terms of hardware, they must learn to manipulate the components that are required to make any computer function. In terms of software, they must learn to use programs designed for the particular operating system adopted by their department or organization. Among the many operating systems available, the most common are the Apple Macintosh®, Microsoft Windows®/DOS, UNIX®, and several different systems from IBM®. There are countless software programs available for these systems, and many of them are quite similar.

Most of these operating systems are used to operate large mainframe computers. A mainframe computer may

SHIFT LOG
CITY OF SANTA ROSA
FIRE DEPARTMENT

PLATOON		BATTALION CHIEF			DATE	
DUTY CHIEF			ON-CALL INSPECTOR			
COMPANY			COMPANY			

TITLE	NAME	TIME	TITLE	NAME	TIME
OFFICER			OFFICER		
DRIVER			DRIVER		
F.F.			F.F.		
F.F.			F.F.		
SAED OPER			SAED OPER		

TIME	RUN	COMPANY	LOCATION	TYPE

Figure 13.18 A typical daily log form. *Courtesy of Santa Rosa (CA) Fire Department.*

	Roll call and assignments given
	Daily apparatus checks and emergency equipment checks
	Daily exercise period
	Firehouse cleaned as needed
	Water use amount
	Utilities notified

TIME	

Figure 13.19 The reverse side of a typical daily log form. *Courtesy of Santa Rosa (CA) Fire Department.*

Figure 13.20 Company officers must become proficient with their department's information systems.

be as large as a minivan, and it is used to receive and store the data from many individual terminals throughout a corporation or government agency. However, most computers are small, desktop units commonly referred to as *personal computers*. Most personal computers run on one of two operating systems — Macintosh or the IBM-compatible Windows. Even though not technically correct, most personal computers and computer terminals are referred to as either "Macs" (Macintosh) or "PCs" (IBM-PC or IBM-compatible clones). A *clone* is a computer from another manufacturer who has been licensed by the original manufacturer to produce hardware that looks and functions like the original products, but with a different label.

Hardware

Regardless of which type of computer the department uses, the hardware that company officers must master is virtually the same. If the computers in the stations are stand-alone units — that is, they function independently and are not interconnected on a *local area network* (LAN) — each one has a *central processing unit* (CPU). Although it is easy to think of the monitor as the computer, it is the CPU that does all the work. On networked systems, each station will have what is sometimes called a *dumb terminal* that is connected to a mainframe computer at some central data processing location — but it looks very similar to the stand-alone unit. In either case, in order to use the computer or terminal, a monitor is required. To issue commands to the CPU, a keyboard is needed — and in many cases, a *mouse* is also used.

To make the computer even more functional, one or more peripherals are needed. *Peripherals* are ancillary devices connected to but not part of the computer. Typical peripherals are printers, modems, scanners, zip drives, and other similar devices. These devices allow the computer to print, transmit, reproduce, or store the data it

processes. However, all of this hardware is of little value without the software to harness the computer's awesome power.

Software

This is the universal term for the coded programs that make computers perform useful work. There are programs for storing, retrieving, and manipulating all sorts of data. Some of the most useful for company-level record keeping are called *spreadsheets* (Figure 13.21). These programs are very well suited for budgeting, scheduling, tracking, forecasting, and other numbers-related activities. Once installed, spreadsheets automatically perform certain mathematical functions whenever new data are entered. A new entry is automatically added to the previous total, and all other mathematical/statistical relationships are adjusted to reflect the new data. Spreadsheet programs are available for keeping training records, hose records, preventive maintenance records, inspection records, and the records of many other fire department functions — often, all in one package.

However, some of the most useful software for company officers are *word processing* programs. These programs allow company officers to use a computer as they would a typewriter, but word processors have many features not found on even the most sophisticated typewriters. Word processors make composing, manipulating, and editing text so effortless that there is no longer any excuse for company officers turning in reports that are not well-organized, correctly punctuated, and free of spelling errors (Figure 13.22).

Figure 13.21 Spreadsheets are used for record keeping.

Figure 13.22 A popular word processing program.

There are several times as many PCs in use as there are Macs because the IBM system was developed primarily for business applications; the Mac was developed primarily as a user-friendly personal computer. However, the major difference between PCs and Macs is how well they function in different applications. In many ways, PCs and Macs are equally functional because the Windows environment uses the same *graphical user interface* (GUI) as Macintosh, so they both look and work like a Mac. Both systems are well-designed for word processing. While PCs and their clones are more adept at the massive numerical manipulation required for business applications, Macs are clearly superior for creating complex computer graphics.

The point of this discussion is not to endorse any particular computer or operating system — each has its strengths and weaknesses. The point is to acquaint company officers with the types of hardware and software available to help them manage the growing amount of information for which they are responsible. Company officers must learn to use whatever system their department has. Additionally, if their department is considering the purchase of one or more computers, company officers should be ready to provide intelligent input into the system selection should they be asked.

The Internet

The Internet is a worldwide network of computers that was set up in 1969 to allow universities and other research institutions to quickly and easily share information with the U.S. military and defense contractors. Internet access is now available to the general public, and millions of computer users access it daily. The Internet is not a computer destination; it is a means by which individual computer users can communicate with others around the world. Users can send and receive electronic mail (E-mail) messages, transfer data files, access thousands of special-interest groups (including fire-service-related groups), various "newsgroups" or "bulletin boards," and even download software programs. There are countless groups, organizations, and individuals that can be accessed through the Internet. When company officers have questions relating to a particular topic, they can visit various web sites that can either provide the information needed or direct them to other sites on the web. There are groups of fire apparatus and equipment manufacturers. There are groups involved in EMS, rescue, and other disciplines. There are general fire service groups where individuals can ask questions of the entire group, and anyone in the group can respond to the question — it is an electronic open forum.

To access the Internet, users must have a computer with a modem. They must have the appropriate software — called a *web browser* — to connect to the World Wide Web (WWW). They must also subscribe to one of the Internet access providers, such as America OnLine® (AOL), CompuServe®, or Prodigy®. Apart from the access provider's monthly subscription fee, access to the Internet is free — there are no hourly charges or per-message fees.

The key to using the Internet efficiently is for company officers to know what they want from the web and know how to get it. To achieve this level of proficiency, they must have access to the Internet, and they must learn as much as possible from printed information, from the Internet itself, from other Internet users, and by logging on and exploring for themselves. Like any other tool, if the Internet is used properly, it can be of tremendous benefit to company officers.

Summary

Because of the amount of time that most company officers spend writing reports and keeping records and because of the importance of those reports and records for their departments, it is imperative that company officers perform this task well. Many of the reports that company officers write will be read by people outside of the department — perhaps by lawyers in court — so the reports should be as concise and well-written as possible. The way these reports look and how clearly they convey information reflect on both the officers who wrote them and on their departments. Likewise, the data contained in the records that company officers keep may be critically important to the department in the budget process and in countless other ways. They may form the basis for decisions regarding future staffing levels, equipment purchases, and other important considerations.

This chapter provides information that will assist the reader in meeting the following job performance requirements from NFPA 1021, *Standard for Fire Officer Professional Qualifications*, 1997 edition. The colored portions indicate the topics addressed in the chapter. The numbers of the job performance requirements are also noted directly in the sections of text where they are addressed. Those in the following list that are denoted with an asterisk (*) are global in nature and are covered by reading the chapter in its entirety.

Fire Officer I

2-1.2*   **General Prerequisite Skills**. The ability to communicate verbally and in writing, to write reports, and to operate in the incident management system.

2-2.1   Assign tasks or responsibilities to unit members, given an assignment at an emergency operation, so that the instructions are complete, clear, and concise; safety considerations are addressed; and the desired outcomes are conveyed.

(a) *Prerequisite Knowledge:* Verbal communications during emergency situations, techniques used to make assignments under stressful situations, methods of confirming understanding.

(b) *Prerequisite Skills:* The ability to condense instructions for frequently assigned unit tasks based upon training and standard operating procedures.

2-2.2   Assign tasks or responsibilities to unit members, given an assignment under nonemergency conditions at a station or other work location, so that the instructions are complete, clear, and concise; safety considerations are addressed; and the desired outcomes are conveyed.

(a) *Prerequisite Knowledge:* Verbal communications under nonemergency situations, techniques used to make assignments under routine situations, methods of confirming understanding.

(b) *Prerequisite Skills:* The ability to issue instructions for frequently assigned unit tasks based upon department policy.

Fire Officer II

3-4.3   Prepare a news release, given an event or topic, so that the information is accurate and formatted correctly.

(a) *Prerequisite Knowledge:* Policies and procedures and the format used for news releases.

(b) *Prerequisite Skills:* The ability to communicate verbally and in writing.

3-4.4*   Prepare a concise report for transmittal to a supervisor, given fire department record(s) and a specific request for details such as trends, variances, or other related topics.

(a) *Prerequisite Knowledge:* The data processing system.

(b) *Prerequisite Skills:* The ability to communicate in writing and to interpret data.

telephonic or radio communication lacks the visual aspect of face-to-face communication, company officers should use language that is easily understood and subject to as few interpretations as possible.

Company officers must always consider the possibility of a language barrier or misinterpretation of terminology. The best way to keep this from happening is to use simple, direct words in a brief, uncomplicated message. This is particularly important during emergencies when excitement, activity, and noise levels are high. Both the medium and the message are key factors that company officers should consider when communicating with others.

The medium in the communication process includes nonverbal communication commonly called *body language.* With oral communication, the receiver often "hears" what is not said more clearly than the spoken words. Our gestures, facial expressions, stance, and even how we dress sometimes speak louder than our voice. What is communicated nonverbally may not be what we had in mind, but it is usually a large part of how the message is received and interpreted.

Another important medium used for communicating information is through written words, graphic displays, or commonly accepted symbols. In this form of communication, the receiver must visually identify the message, interpret the meaning, and respond or provide feedback that the message was understood. Examples of written forms of communication in the fire service are as follows:

- Letters or other correspondence (with paper or electronically)

- Standard operating procedures (SOPs)

- Symbols used in pre-incident planning

- Training aids (graphics, charts, and photos)

Each example of written communication must convey the information that the sender wants the receiver to understand and must be in a form that is appropriate for the message.

Listening and Hearing

As supervisors, company officers spend much of their time writing or speaking, but communication includes listening and hearing. The topic discussed here is not how to get others to hear them, but how company officers hear others. Listening to others takes up a good part of our time every day. However, research has shown that the average person takes in only a fraction of what they hear. Fortunately, effective listening can be learned. Good listening skills pay off in greater efficiency and personal satisfaction (Figure 14.3). First, people must realize that listening is an active process.

Some people merely listen, but they do not hear. Hearing and understanding a message requires active listening. Active listeners maintain eye contact with the speaker and exhibit alert facial expressions and posture. Questions and comments from the listener show interest and give the speaker cues about misunderstandings and the need to clarify or expand on certain points. This lets the speaker know that the message is being received.

Understanding the speaker's words is as important as hearing their sounds. Words have different meanings for different people, so the listener must try to understand the speaker's intent. Listening with understanding involves interpreting word meanings; that is, listening with understanding involves empathy. *Empathy* is the ability to put oneself in another's place, and being able to empathize is an essential skill for the company officer. Empathy means that the receiver understands the sender's feelings and motives. However, empathy does not necessarily translate into *sympathy*. The receiver can understand the sender's feelings on a particular issue but not necessarily agree with the sender's position. Company officers must be aware that a listener's silence may be interpreted by the speaker as acquiescence or agreement when that is not necessarily true.

Bias or prejudice can be a barrier to communication. We may not like someone for any number of reasons, and we may therefore listen to him without really hearing. Company officers should guard against this very human tendency and make a conscious effort to really hear what the speaker is saying. It is most important that they understand what everyone — not just those whom they like — says to them.

Boredom can make people listen without really hearing. If the subject does not interest them or if the speaker is dull, their minds may drift to other thoughts. Bored listeners may, because of politeness or some other reason, attempt to hide their disinterest by responding to

Figure 14.3 Effective communication reduces friction and improves morale.

what is being said with nods of agreement or an occasional "Oh" or "Hmmm." This ploy is a waste of the speaker's time and effort as well as the listener's.

A good listening environment is also important. An absence of loud ambient noise, a comfortable temperature, and the expectation in both sender and receiver that the message will be important enough to merit attention make for a good listening environment. Company officers must constantly be aware of the listening environment or risk not being heard and not hearing others.

Listening is an extremely important skill for company officers when dealing with their subordinates. When a subordinate indicates a need to "talk about" something, the company officer should either talk privately with the firefighter or schedule a time to talk if the request comes at a time that is not conducive to a private conversation. One of the highest compliments a firefighter can pay the supervisor is "I can talk to the captain. He listens and really hears me."

Formal Communications

In this context, formal communications consist of written policies and procedures, standard operating procedures, orders and directives, and fireground orders. These communications are essential to the successful discharge of the department's responsibilities to the citizens of the community.

Written Policies and Procedures

Policies and procedures are examples of "standing" or "repeat-use" plans designed to deal with the recurring problems of an organization. Communicating these plans in writing helps ensure that organizational objectives will be met throughout all divisions of the department.

A *policy* is a guide to decision making within an organization. Policies originate with top management in the department and are disseminated to lower echelons for implementation. These policies not only aid in decision making, but they also define the boundaries within which the administration expects company officers to act.

Some policies arise from appeal to management for guidance in making decisions about exceptional cases. For instance, a fire officer who does not know how a certain case should be handled might refer the matter to a superior. Appeal is made upward until someone in the hierarchy is reached who has the authority to make the decision. The decision maker may write a policy for handling similar cases in the future. Or, as is often the case, a

company officer makes a decision in order to dispose of a problem, and this decision serves as a precedent which evolves into department policy.

Unwritten policies, sometimes called *organizational norms* or *past practice*, are a result of tradition within the organization. Such policies are implied in the routine activities of the organization. Implied policies develop where no clear policy exists. This is especially true in organizations where policies are not written or if written policies are out-of-date.

Unwritten policies can come to have as much force as if they were written. Employee organizations may also desire to use unwritten past practice as a tool to mold written standards or to establish a precedent for settling grievances. It can be seen how deeply rooted tradition is when a department tries to change from traditional implied policies to newer written ones.

Policy is sometimes imposed upon fire departments by federal, state, and local governments. Equal employment opportunity practices are imposed by the federal government and the Fair Labor Standards Act and the Americans with Disabilities Act. Many state governments are now adopting federal standards for the control of hazardous materials. Local codes and ordinances also impact fire department operations.

Policies must be put in writing to make the administration's intent clear. Written policies give department members a reference point for decision making. Collectively, these written policies form the department policy manual. Written policies promote more uniform, consistent practices throughout the organization and more predictable outcomes in the field.

The company officer's duty regarding policies is to understand and apply them fairly, consistently, and with discretion. Correct interpretation and application of department policy may require consultation (through the chain of command) with the administration. Formal instruction on department policies and their interpretation are necessary for all department members. Company officers must explain departmental policies and procedures to subordinates and new employees as part of their indoctrination. In addition, whenever company officers learn of a new law or regulation from any level of government, they have an obligation to inform their superiors about it. This allows the department administration to determine whether new departmental policies and procedures are needed in order to comply with the new legislation.

A *procedure* is a written communication closely related to policies. While a policy is a guide for thinking or decision making, a procedure is a detailed plan of action.

A procedure details in writing the steps to be followed in carrying out organizational policy for some specific, recurring problem or situation. For instance, most organizations with personnel departments require those seeking employment to first apply at the personnel office. This procedure for processing new applicants then directs the personnel department (and they, in turn, direct the applicant) through the successive steps that must be followed in the application process.

Standard Operating Procedures

Most fire departments provide their personnel with specific, detailed information about how specific situations should be handled. A number of different names are used for these documents — *general operating guidelines, general operating procedures* — but the most common term used is *standard operating procedure* (SOP). Development and use of the SOPs allow an organization to make the best use of its human resources. Having a consistent point of reference helps all members of the organization perform to a measurable standard. Misunderstandings about techniques, responsibilities, and procedures are reduced by having the specific SOP on a subject to reference. Emergency response and operations at incidents require clear, decisive action on the part of incident commanders, company officers, and firefighters. Standard operating procedures provide the direction on which specific actions are based. SOPs are the basis for much of the company-level skills training, such as initial fire attack, supporting automatic sprinkler systems, coordinated fire attack, fireground search and rescue, and others.

Orders and Directives

[NFPA 1021 2-2.1, 2-2.2]

Orders are based upon the authority delegated to the officer to implement departmental policies and procedures; directives are not. Both orders and directives are needed to carry out departmental functions. They may be either written or verbal. Because an *order* is based upon a policy or procedure, compliance is mandatory. Because a *directive* is not based on a policy or procedure, it is more in the nature of a request. In both routine and emergency situations, company officers may issue many orders, directives, and requests (Figure 14.4). However, on the fireground, they are all considered to be orders because of the seriousness of the situation.

Issuing orders on the fireground is an important supervisory duty for company officers. If an order is understood and carried out, the work gets done. Besides getting things accomplished, orders aid in training and developing cooperation. Properly given orders result in the need

Figure 14.4 Company officers must give clear and concise orders on the fireground.

for less supervision in the future as members learn what is expected of them. It is important that company officers control their emotions when issuing orders on the fireground. Detection of any anxiety, uneasiness, or excitement in their company officer can affect the emotional stability and performance of the firefighters. Fireground orders must be issued calmly and must be clear, concise, and complete.

Another important supervisory duty of company officers involves issuing and enforcing unpopular orders. The administration sometimes establishes policies and procedures that may adversely affect the firefighters, and it usually falls to the company officers to issue and enforce these orders. As mentioned in Chapter 1, "Assuming the Role of Company Officer," if company officers are to do their jobs, they must be willing to subordinate their personal feelings and support the administration's position.

This support by company officers must not be half-hearted or obviously forced — it must be genuine or at least appear so. One of the best ways that company officers can develop this kind of support for an unpopular order is to find out why the order was issued. Since fire chiefs and the other chief officers do not issue orders frivolously, they must have had good reasons for issuing the controversial order. Company officers should make every effort to find out what those reasons were. With that information, company officers can explain the necessity for the order and answer any questions that their subordinates might have about the new order.

Face-to-Face Communications

Face-to-face, oral communications are generally the most effective means of conveying information. This is because the sender and receiver are speaking directly with each other. It would seem that this method would eliminate misunderstandings, but this is not the case. The reason misunderstandings occur is that people interpret messages differently.

People sometimes give little thought to what they are saying. This is unfortunate because both the content of the message and the manner in which it is delivered influence the listener's understanding. They also lead the listener to form judgments of the speaker's competence and character. This is very important to the company officer because it is important that the message influences firefighters in a positive manner and leaves them with the impression that the officer is indeed competent to lead them.

As simple as face-to-face communication may appear to be, there are several problems that hinder effective transfer of messages:

- Officer-firefighter relationships
- Selective listening
- Semantics
- Emotional context
- Physical barriers
- Cultural differences

Firefighter-Officer Relationships

When firefighters are assigned to a new or different company, they may need help in learning the personality and culture of the new group. The company officer should open a clear line of communication from the beginning of the relationship to smooth the transition for the new member. A one-on-one conversation between the officer and the new member is a good way to open a dialogue and start to build a positive relationship. A good second step might be to have that same type of open discussion with other members of the company. Step three could be to have the members share expectations with the new member.

Selective Listening

Selective listening is self-explanatory. Even when people appear to listen, they may hear only what they want to hear. This is a common problem and something nearly everyone does. There are two major reasons for selective listening. One, there is too much to hear so the listener only hears what he can understand. Two, the listener does not like what is being said and so hears only the parts of the message with which he agrees.

Semantics

Many English words have more than one meaning. What matters in communication is not the dictionary definition but the way the listener interprets the words used by the speaker. People interpret words differently depending on the context in which the words are used and on many other factors such the age, gender, race, nationality, and personal background and experiences of the listener. These factors can present a major communications barrier. Company officers must keep this in mind when dealing with the public. Officers should use nontechnical terms that the public can understand. Company officers should also realize that new firefighters may not understand the language of seasoned firefighters. If the officer speaks to the new firefighters in words that are familiar to them, misunderstanding will be minimized.

Emotional Context

Company officers must sometimes function in highly stressful situations. In order to hear and be heard under these conditions, they must control their own emotions and try to calm those with whom they are trying to communicate. The emotional state of an individual greatly influences his communications abilities. A speaker who is angry may send a message that is not well thought out. Likewise, a listener who is angry is more likely to misunderstand a message. In both cases, communication can be difficult and frustrating (Figure 14.5).

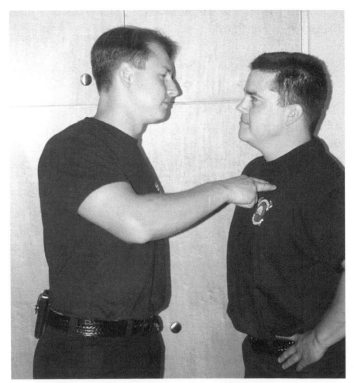

Figure 14.5 Anger makes communication difficult.

Physical Barriers

Physical barriers add to the other communications problems on the fireground. If radio contact cannot be made, shouting may be necessary. Another problem can be the high noise level on the fireground. These two factors result in difficulties in speaking and hearing clearly. Although not possible in all situations, officers should try to be face-to-face with the people with whom they are trying to communicate.

To ensure that messages are received and understood, the speakers should communicate as effectively as possible. Not everyone has excellent communication skills. All people have the ability to say what they mean and mean what they say, but they may not be able to say it clearly. To ensure that what is said is received correctly, the speaker should keep in mind these basic rules of effective spoken messages:

- Be adaptive to the audience (children, professionals, non-English speakers).
- Have a specific purpose (to inform, to persuade).
- Be brief (get to the point).
- Be focused (stick to the point).
- Be clear (specify meanings).

Cultural Differences

Both within their companies and among the citizens of the community, company officers must be able to communicate with people of different ages, races, and genders (Figure 14.6). The fire service is no longer the white male enclave that it once was. More than ever, it reflects the society as a whole. As mentioned earlier in this chapter, it may be useful for company officers with firefighters of different races or genders, or both, to meet with them individually and collectively to talk about how to communicate effectively with each other and with the public at large (Figure 14.7).

Communicating With Victims

When communicating with victims, company officers must be especially adaptive to this particular audience. Victims are often so overwhelmed by their traumatic experience that the communication between them and the officer is extremely difficult. Officers should make every effort to reduce distractions and talk on the victim's level.

Young juvenile victims may be much more difficult to communicate with if they have not yet developed language skills. Lack of language skills and fear are two of the biggest barriers to communication with children. An additional communications barrier with young children is that they may have been taught not to talk to strangers — even those in uniform. Company officers should talk with these young victims in as calm an environment as possible. One technique that is very helpful in communicating with children is to kneel down to their level (Figure 14.8). Children feel much less threatened by someone on their level than by what appears to be a giant firefighter towering over them.

Public Speaking

Another communications challenge that company officers frequently encounter is the opportunity to speak in public. Speaking in front of a group is a problem for a great many people who experience "stage fright." Officers will feel more confident when speaking before a group if they are thoroughly prepared. Impromptu speaking engagements can be difficult for even the most seasoned

Figure 14.6 Communicating with citizens in a diverse community may be a challenge.

Figure 14.7 Talking together is a good way of learning to communicate with each other.

Figure 14.8 Communicating with children may take patience.

public speakers. Company officers should prepare for their speaking engagements and know their material; they should not try to "wing it." With an outline to work from and a solid knowledge of the material, even the most shy person can become comfortable and even proud of his achievements in this area.

Presentations

Formal presentations must be carefully planned, rehearsed, and refined. Again, company officers should know their material, practice it until they are comfortable with it, and then practice it some more.

In addition to the dialogue portion of their presentation, company officers may be communicating through many other modes. These include:

• Visual aids

• Handout materials

• Body language

• Tone and inflection of voice

• Appearance

They should choose colorful visual aids that clarify and reinforce the spoken presentation. Any lettering on overhead transparencies must be large enough to be read from anywhere in the room. Audiovisual equipment should be set up and tested well in advance of the presentation (Figure 14.9). Extra projector lamps, extension cords, and other supplies should be available for contingencies.

Handout materials should have a professional look and be carefully assembled. If the audience has to fumble through a mess of disorganized or illegible written material, the effectiveness of the presentation will suffer and create a negative image of the presenter.

Speakers should use good posture and avoid annoying habits, such as rubbing their nose, scratching their ear, and rattling keys or change in their pockets. They should not lean on the lectern; aside from making them look lazy, they may find that the lectern does not support their weight!

Finally, they should project their voice so that the most remote audience members can hear clearly. They should use a public address system if they feel strained by speaking loudly enough to be heard. They should shift their attention to all parts of the room to avoid focusing on someone who looks like they are interested; the other audience members will notice this and lose interest in the presentation. For more information on speaking techniques, see the IFSTA **Fire Service Instructor** manual.

Media Relations

Another public speaking opportunity with which company officers sometimes have to cope is speaking with the media (Figure 14.10). The occasion may be planned and prearranged, or it could be a spur-of-the-moment interview on the incident scene. In any case, the company officer must be prepared for this possibility and represent the department well as a spokesperson.

Speaking with or being interviewed by the media can be a challenge. The media can be either a friend or an enemy. Company officers should work with the media, be honest and forthright, and follow their departmental policies and procedures. Some departments have a designated information officer (PIO) assigned to answer media questions on large incidents. If the department has a PIO on scene, company officers should politely direct questions and interview requests to the PIO. If there is no PIO assigned or available, company officers should follow departmental policies and procedures when being interviewed. The following guidelines will be helpful to company officers who are assigned to give an interview:

• There is no such thing as "off the record." Anything said to a reporter can be quoted. Do not be misled by the friendly reporter who says "Just between us…"

• Beware when asked leading questions. Sometimes reporters will use this tactic to get the answer they want. Listen to the questions carefully and thoughtfully and answer "yes" or "that's correct" only if the facts in the questions are 100 percent accurate and no inaccurate conclusions have been drawn.

• Avoid getting into disagreements or becoming defensive with reporters. Defensiveness may suggest that information is being withheld, even if it is not.

Figure 14.9 Audiovisual equipment should be checked beforehand.

Figure 14.10 Company officers may be interviewed by reporters.

- Do not be led into answering questions beyond your area of expertise. Refer such questions to those who have the necessary information, or offer to find the answer — and always follow through.

- Avoid using esoteric fire service terminology. If a technical term must be used, explain its meaning at the time it is used.

- Honesty is the best policy. Be as frank and open as possible without divulging confidential information about victims' identities, possible fire cause, etc.

- Do not answer "What if…" questions. Do not answer hypothetical questions, explaining that you are not prepared to speculate.

- Listen for false or misleading information in reporters' questions. If a question contains false information, politely discount the misinformation and provide accurate information.

- Beware of the forced-choice question. If either way of answering the question would be inaccurate, then answer with a separate, factual response. Be tactful, but refute the false information.

- Do not volunteer information, especially if it is speculative. For example, to prematurely suggest to the media that a fire is possibly of electrical origin could have an adverse affect if an arson case is later developed from that fire.

- Be prepared. Rehearse your interview technique, and try to improve delivery.

NOTE: For more information on this topic, see ICS 220-2, *Information Officer Checklist*.

News and Press Releases
[NFPA 1021 3-1.3]

Fire departments that do not have a full-time PIO may task company officers with preparing press or news releases. However, publishers usually will not print a prepared statement verbatim. They may use a few direct quotes, but they will edit the piece and make it fit their particular editorial style. In this editorial process, the information in the original release may be distorted. In most cases, reporters prefer to gather the facts relating to the incident and write the story themselves. When supplying the facts relating to an incident, company officers are in fact being interviewed, and they should use the guidelines just discussed in the "Media Relations" section.

If a reporter should ask for a prepared news or press release on a particular event or topic, it can be submitted in outline form — leaving it to the reporter to flesh out — or it can be submitted in narrative form as though it were

a script. Regardless of which form is used, the content should be limited to the facts of the event or topic and should be as simple and straightforward as possible. In preparing the piece, the following guidelines should be used:

- Summarize the piece in the first sentence by answering the questions Who? What? When? Where? and Why? This does not necessarily have to be in that order.

- Use the inverted pyramid style of organization by putting the most important facts first and the least important ones last.

- Limit sentence length to no more than 20 words.

- Write no more than four or five lines per paragraph; one-sentence paragraphs are acceptable.

- Use the active voice ("Fire Chief Jones announced..." instead of "It was announced by Fire Chief Jones...").

- Write clearly and concisely; avoid flowery language and technical or esoteric terms (use "hazardous materials" instead of "haz mat" and "National Fire Protection Association" instead of "NFPA").

- Be sure that all direct quotes and paraphrased statements are properly attributed.

For more information on the preparation of news and press releases, see the IFSTA **Fire and Life Safety Educator** manual.

Informal Communications: The Grapevine

All fire departments have an official system of communications through the chain of command. Official organizational information is transmitted through this system. In addition to this formal system, almost every department has an equally active informal system of communication. This informal system is most often called *the grapevine*. The grapevine is a social communications network that transmits the organization's social news and, often, unofficial versions of official information.

In general, the grapevine system is a communications system; however, it is not a preferred method of transmitting official communications. In some instances, official news traveling through the grapevine can have extremely detrimental effects upon the morale and operations of a department. The basic flaws in the grapevine system that make it unacceptable from the department's point of view are:

- There is no method of ensuring that inaccurate or false information can be distinguished from official information. A rumor has the same validity as official information.

- There is no way to ensure that complete information is transmitted. Often, in cases of disputes, only the information supporting the speaker's point of view is presented, or if presented, the facts are out of context.

- There is no way to ensure information is not slanted because of personal bias of the speaker.

- There is no method to allow for clarification of information or correction of misinformation through the system.

- There is no method to prevent confidential disclosures that can embarrass either the department or individual members.

Most company officers and other department officials make an effort to limit departmental business being passed through the grapevine. Others simply pretend that it does not exist, and that allows the adverse effects of the grapevine to flourish because these individuals are completely excluded from the grapevine and have no way of knowing what information/misinformation is being transmitted. To minimize the effects of the grapevine, company officers should recognize its existence and counteract misinformation with factual information at every opportunity.

The single most effective method of minimizing the effects of the grapevine is for the administration to provide an adequate flow of official information. Rumors develop and grow when the members of the organization have only the grapevine to rely on for information. One good method of providing a regular flow of official information is by posting a daily or weekly information bulletin in every station (Figure 14.11).

Information that tends to require the closest attention to prevent grapevine distortion is information about the following:

- Promotions

- Hirings and firings

- Layoffs, transfers, or shift changes

- Disciplinary actions

- Equipment purchases

- Accidents or injuries

- Personal information about coworkers

Some of these areas are privileged information under the law, and no one representing the department is allowed to discuss them with anyone who is not directly involved. However, in those areas about which the department is allowed to disseminate information, the department should do so as soon as is practical after a decision is made. For most decisions, a memorandum to all stations is usually adequate (Figure 14.12).

Figure 14.11 Official information should be posted for all to see.

Figure 14.12 Official decisions should be announced as soon as possible.

Summary

Communication involves much more than mere "talking." For communication to be effective, a message must be sent and understood. Communication is a process that involves the sender, the message, the medium, the receiver, and feedback from the receiver. Listening is also an important part of effective communication. To receive the message with the meaning intended, the listener must take an active role and be alert.

There are two types of communication — informal and formal. The grapevine is an informal communications network that can be used to receive information but should never be used to transmit it. Formal communication may take many forms. Written policies and procedures are plans for dealing with recurring problems. Fireground orders are different from routine directives. Due to the danger involved, company officers must be able to issue fireground orders that are clear, concise, and complete. Fireground communication involves both "face-to-face" communications and radio communications. Company officers must also know how and when to use various types of written communications.

This chapter provides information that will assist the reader in meeting the following job performance requirements from NFPA 1021, *Standard for Fire Officer Professional Qualifications*, 1997 edition. The colored portions indicate the topics addressed in the chapter. The numbers of the job performance requirements are also noted directly in the sections of text where they are addressed. Those in the following list that are denoted with an asterisk (*) are global in nature and are covered by reading the chapter in its entirety.

Fire Officer II

3-5*   This duty involves conducting inspections to identify hazards and address violations and conducting fire investigations to determine origin and perliminary cause, according to the following job performance requirements.

3-5.1*   Describe the procedures for conducting fire inspections, given any of the following occupancies:

(a) Assembly

(b) Educational

(c) Health care

(d) Detention and correctional

(e) Residential

(f) Mercantile

(g) Business

(h) Industrial

(i) Storage

(j) Unusual structures

(k) Mixed occupancies

so that all hazards, including hazardous materials, are identified, appropriate forms are completed, and appropriate action is initiated.

Fire and Life Safety Inspections

The most important duty of every firefighter is to prevent fires and other emergencies from occurring because that is the most cost-effective way of protecting life and property. A fire that does not occur cannot harm the citizens or their property, nor can it put firefighters in jeopardy. While preventing all emergencies is virtually impossible, that should still be the goal toward which every fire department strives. Even when fire departments fall short of reaching that goal, if department personnel make a conscientious effort, then they are likely to measurably reduce the loss of life and property within the jurisdiction. One of the most effective ways of preventing fires and other emergencies is through the adoption and enforcement of appropriate ordinances, codes, and standards to reasonably regulate the activities of the citizens of the jurisdiction. The enforcement of these regulations is often done at the company level through a conscientiously applied inspection program.

This chapter discusses the authority under which fire department personnel enter and inspect private property, some of the more common codes and standards, the responsibilities of company-level fire inspection teams, and the mechanics of preparing for and conducting inspections. Also discussed are the various considerations involved in inspecting different types of occupancies, conducting exit drills, and inspecting and testing various types of built-in fire detection and protection systems.

Authority

In general, unless an emergency is in progress on the property, firefighters cannot enter private property without being invited in by the owner or occupant. Under common law and most statutory law, the existence of an unfriendly fire or other emergency constitutes implied permission to enter. Exceptions to this fundamental rule of law are in the cases of military firefighters on base and of members of industrial fire brigades on company property. In these cases, all property is under the ownership or

control of the parent organization, and tacit permission for its firefighters to enter has been granted by that organization. For the rest of the fire service, the right to enter private property for the purpose of conducting inspections must be granted by the occupant or by local ordinance. The local governing body (city or borough council, county board of supervisors, etc.) must adopt an ordinance that authorizes the fire chief (and his agents) to enter private property within the jurisdiction, at any reasonable hour, to conduct fire and life safety inspections. This ordinance should contain a section that specifically authorizes department personnel to enter and that provides for the issuance of an inspection warrant if the occupant refuses to allow inspection teams to enter. If the ordinance number is not printed on the department's inspection form, all company members should memorize the number. So, if their right to enter is questioned by a property owner, then they can cite the number.

Ordinances, Codes, and Standards

In most cases, the local jurisdiction adopts one or more ordinances delegating authority to the fire chief for protecting the public from fires and certain other hazards. Through these ordinances, it usually adopts certain regional or national codes and standards by reference. For example, rather than write its own fire code, the governing body may choose to adopt the current edition of the *Uniform Fire Code*™ (UFC), published by the International Fire Code Institute. In adopting a particular edition of the UFC, the governing body also may choose to amend it to make it more applicable to local conditions. So the ordinance would make that specific edition of the UFC, as amended, the law within the jurisdiction. That edition of the UFC would continue to be applicable within the jurisdiction, even after a more recent edition was published, unless the governing body chose to formally adopt the newer edition in the same way it adopted the first one.

Likewise, the local governing body may choose also to adopt other codes and standards on the recommendation of the fire chief or other local officials. Some of the more common of these standards are the *National Electrical Code* (NEC), which is published by NFPA, the *Uniform Building Code* (UBC) or any one of several other regional building codes, and NFPA 101®, *Life Safety Code*® (Figure 15.1). It is these and similar codes and standards, as amended by the local governing body, that fire company members attempt to enforce when they inspect local businesses. Obviously, in the role of "player/coach," the company officer must be thoroughly familiar with the codes and standards adopted locally.

Company-Level Inspection Responsibilities

When company officers and their crews inspect local buildings, they carry with them certain responsibilities. Chief among these is a responsibility to act on known violations and to ensure that fire and life safety hazards are mitigated. To do this, fire inspection teams must be thoroughly prepared for the inspection and must be conscientious while conducting it.

While private citizens have the right to ignore hazardous conditions they may see, on-duty firefighters have no such right. In fact, firefighters have a *duty to act*. When the local jurisdiction adopts one of the national codes, the fire department's responsibility to inspect all buildings (other than private residences) within the jurisdiction is identified clearly in the code. While the exact terminology may differ among codes, each of these model codes specifies that the fire chief is responsible for ensuring that these buildings are inspected. Except for certain high-hazard occupancies, the actual inspections are usually delegated through the fire marshal or fire prevention officer to personnel at the company level.

Company-level personnel are responsible for conducting these inspections as often as required by the code. Most codes require each building to be inspected at least once each year. Certain high-hazard occupancies, such as places of public assembly, may require more frequent inspection. In many departments, the company officer has the responsibility to see that these inspections are made.

When conducting fire and life safety inspections, company officers and their crews are responsible for identifying anything on the premises that might cause a fire or contribute to its spread or that might impede the occupants' egress from the building if there is an emergency. Any of these conditions is a violation of one or more sections of the applicable code. It is the inspection team's responsibility to identify the specific code section that

applies and to see that the building owner or occupant takes appropriate and timely action to bring the occupancy into compliance with the code — in other words, to eliminate the hazardous condition.

In some cases, violations must be corrected immediately. For example, if access to an exit door is obstructed or the door is found to be locked, this clear life safety hazard must be corrected before the inspection team leaves the premises (Figure 15.2). These are types of hazards that the occupant can eliminate immediately. However, some violations may require more time to correct. For example, if a fire alarm system is inoperative or a required exit door has been blocked during renovation, the occupant must be given a reasonable amount of time in which to comply. Other violations may be of less immediate concern and the occupant incapable of complying with the code immediately. For example, if one or more of the fire extinguishers in the building appear to be operative but are due for annual service, the inspector should allow the occupant a reasonable amount of time (perhaps a couple of weeks) in which to arrange for a fire extinguisher service company to come and service their extinguishers. The amount of time allowed for correcting any particular violation varies depending upon the nature of the violation and the department policy.

When an occupant has been notified of the existence of a violation and the required corrective action explained, he also should be notified (in writing) of when to expect a follow-up inspection to see that the violation has been corrected (Figure 15.3). It is the company officer's responsibility to see that the follow-up inspection is made on the specified date. If the follow-up inspection reveals that the hazard has been eliminated, the code enforcement inspection process has served its purpose and is virtually over. All that remains is to thank the occupant

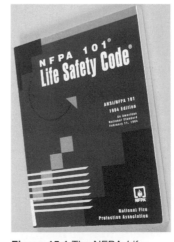

Figure 15.1 The NFPA *Life Safety Code*®.

Figure 15.2 Serious life safety hazards must be corrected immediately.

for his cooperation and to complete the necessary paperwork (Figure 15.4). However, if nothing has been done to correct the violation or if a halfhearted attempt was made, but the hazard still exists, then the inspection team must follow departmental guidelines regarding how to get compliance with the code. A number of possible avenues are available. These range from making another attempt to convince the occupant of the necessity for compliance and scheduling a second follow-up inspection, to forwarding the problem to the fire prevention bureau, and to issuing the responsible party a citation. In extreme cases, the inspection team may be empowered to force the business to cease operation or vacate the occupancy until compliance with the code is obtained. Whether to take this action depends on the situation and department policy. The company officer is responsible for knowing department policy and applying it appropriately.

Preparing for Inspections

A major factor in the success of any inspection is preparation. While all fire and life safety inspections have certain characteristics in common, each class of occupancy has some characteristics that make it different from all other classes, and within each class there are differences among individual occupancies. The extent to which company-level personnel prepare themselves to inspect a particular occupancy often determines the quality of the results of the inspection (Figure 15.5).

The purpose of any fire and life safety inspection is to leave the occupancy safer than before the inspection and the occupants more knowledgeable about protecting themselves and their property from fires. With this in mind, when a fire company is assigned a particular occupancy to inspect, it should begin to prepare for the inspection by gathering information. The information needed may come from a variety of sources and varies with the type of occupancy and the company members' levels of expertise.

Except for information about completely new occupancies, one of the best sources of useful information about a particular occupancy is the record of previous inspections there. This record provides background information about the building's ownership and occupancy and includes other critical information such as phone numbers and emergency contacts. The record also shows the types of activities that are conducted within the facility, as well as any previous code violations and their nature. Information about previous inspections may reveal patterns of compliance or noncompliance that can indicate the owner's level of commitment to fire and life safety — or lack thereof. For example, if there are fewer and less serious violations found each time the building is inspected, it probably means that management is making a conscientious attempt to comply with the code. On the other hand, a record showing the same number and types of violations every time the occupancy is inspected may indicate that the ownership and management do not take safety issues very seriously. At the very least, the record indicates a need for more public education with the ownership and management of the business.

A good source of general fire and life safety information is the *NFPA Inspection Manual* (Figure 15.6). This handy, pocket-sized book provides general information

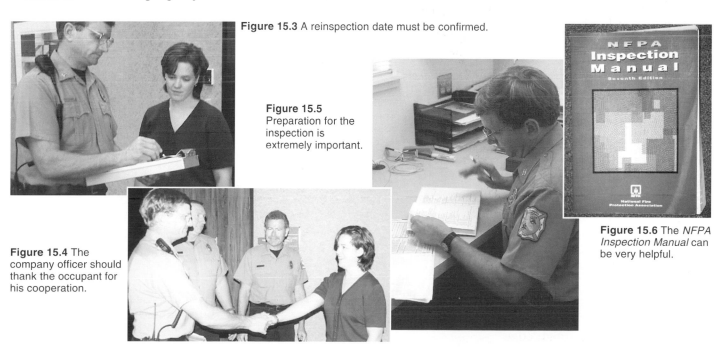

Figure 15.3 A reinspection date must be confirmed.

Figure 15.5 Preparation for the inspection is extremely important.

Figure 15.4 The company officer should thank the occupant for his cooperation.

Figure 15.6 The *NFPA Inspection Manual* can be very helpful.

about a large variety of processes, equipment, and systems found in many businesses. It covers general housekeeping, building construction and finishes, electrical wiring and devices, HVAC systems, welding and cutting, and the hazards associated with a variety of materials such as flammable and combustible liquids, plastics, and combustible dusts. It also contains information about a variety of fire extinguishing systems. These are but a few of the dozens of topics discussed in this book. However, for the requirements related to any particular type of occupancy, a more specific source is needed.

The most specific and most authoritative source of information about any particular class or type of occupancy is the code or codes adopted by the local governing body. For example, if the *Uniform Fire Code™* has been adopted, in addition to general fire and life safety requirements that apply to all occupancies, it specifies in great detail exactly what is required for various processes in many different types of occupancies. Some of the occupancy types covered by this code are places of assembly, bowling alleys, repair garages, lumberyards and woodworking plants, tire-rebuilding plants, tents and temporary membrane structures, automobile wrecking yards, shopping malls, and dry-cleaning establishments. Some of the processes covered are the application of flammable finishes, fruit-ripening, fumigation, welding and cutting, manufacture of organic coatings, and semiconductor fabrication. Some of the special equipment covered are oil-burning equipment, industrial baking and drying ovens, and mechanical refrigeration. Some of the special subjects covered are compressed gases, cryogenic fluids, flammable dusts and other explosive materials, fireworks and pyrotechnic materials, flammable and combustible liquids, and hazardous materials. Company officers and their crews should consult the *NFPA Inspection Manual*, the locally adopted codes, and any other sources needed to become familiar with the requirements for the type of occupancy they have been assigned to inspect.

When company members have familiarized themselves with what to expect in the type of occupancy assigned and with the inspection history of that specific occupancy, they are ready to gather the equipment needed to conduct the inspection. In general, the items needed are as follows:

- Working flashlight
- 50-foot (15 m) measuring tape
- Clipboard
- Inspection form
- Graph paper and a straightedge
- Pen, pencil, and eraser
- Camera with flash

In addition, each member needs coveralls if they may have to enter attics or other crawl spaces (Figure 15.7). For some occupancies, pressure gauges and/or other specialized equipment may be needed (Figure 15.8). If the members have thoroughly researched the occupancy to be inspected, the types of equipment needed should be obvious.

Once all this preparation has been done, the inspection is ready to be scheduled. Some departments require that company officers call each business in advance to make an appointment for an inspection; others do not. Some departments require a systematic scheduling of inspections by geographical area to ensure the public that the inspection process is consistent and not selective. There are good and valid reasons for each way of doing business. Company officers must know department policy and follow it.

Before the company leaves the station to conduct an inspection, all company members must be briefed thoroughly on what is expected of them during the inspection. They should present a businesslike appearance — in other words, they should be well-groomed, and their uniforms should be clean and crisp. They should be reminded that anytime they are in public, for any purpose, they should strive to make the best possible impression on business owners and other members of the public. A large part of the success of the inspection de-

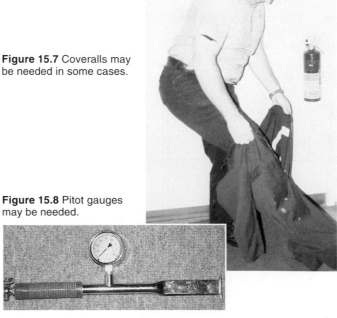

Figure 15.7 Coveralls may be needed in some cases.

Figure 15.8 Pitot gauges may be needed.

pends on how the business owner and the employees of the business perceive the firefighters conducting the inspection.

Conducting Inspections

When the company arrives at the business to be inspected, it should drive around the facility, or the block in which it is located, to observe the surrounding area. Company members should make note of, and perhaps photograph, the hydrants, potential exposures, overhead obstructions, business name and address as displayed on the front of the building, and anything else that might impede or improve their ability to locate and fight a fire in that particular business. They should park their apparatus in a way that does not interfere with employees or customers and that allows the company to respond quickly if called during the inspection. Most departments require that one member of the company remain with the apparatus during the inspection. This allows the apparatus to be moved if necessary and provides some security for the apparatus and the tools and equipment carried on it.

The inspection team members should enter the business through the main entrance and go directly to the main office (Figure 15.9). They should contact the person responsible for the safety and security of the building or facility. In small businesses, this may mean dealing directly with the business owner; in larger firms, a manager or maintenance supervisor may be the designated representative. The company officer should introduce himself and the members of the company. He should then state the reason for the visit — to conduct a fire and life safety inspection as required by the code. He should explain the purposes of the inspection, how it is conducted, and the possible outcomes.

Before starting the inspection tour, the representative should be asked to review the background data listed in the inspection record (address, ownership of the building, ownership of the business, both business and emergency phone numbers, etc.) to make sure it is still current (Figure 15.10). In the case of a new business, this data should be compiled at this time.

At the beginning of the inspection, the representative should be asked to either accompany the inspection team throughout the tour or designate someone else to do so. Having a representative of the business with the team is very important to the success of the inspection. The representative can answer any questions that the team might have, can open locked doors, etc. It should be made clear to the representative that the team is interested in more than just the fire extinguishers. *The inspection team's primary concern is the means of egress. All other factors involved in the process are secondary to the occupants' ability to leave the premises in an emergency.* It also should be explained to the representative that the team must be able to inspect every room, space, or compartment by direct, visual observation (Figure 15.11). If company members would have to don special clothing to avoid contaminating "clean rooms" or other environmentally controlled areas, then they should do so. If the business is concerned about the security of trade secrets being compromised during the inspection, some rea-

Figure 15.9 The inspection team should use the main entrance.

Figure 15.10 Background information should be verified.

Figure 15.11 The team must have access to all spaces.

sonable accommodation must be made that allows the team to inspect the sensitive room or area. If this requires that company members sign an agreement to not reveal what they have seen, then they should do so (Figure 15.12). It is not uncommon for private firms doing business under contract with the federal government to require each member of the inspection team to complete a personal data form before being allowed to enter the premises.

There is no set pattern for conducting fire inspections. However, whatever pattern is chosen must be systematic and thorough. Some businesses are so small that inspecting their premises is relatively simple and takes only a few minutes (Figure 15.13). Others are quite large and complex, often occupying more than one building, and they take several hours to inspect (Figure 15.14). Even though the team has surveyed the exterior of the building and its surroundings in general, it may choose to start the formal inspection from the outside. This allows them to measure the building, make notes or take pictures of salient features such as sprinkler connections or of potentially dangerous construction features such as unsupported canopies or other overhangs (Figure 15.15). It also allows them to evaluate how accessible the building is to fire apparatus.

From the inside, the team may choose to start at the lowest level and systematically work its way to the roof, or vice versa (Figure 15.16). Some feel that starting from the roof gives the team another opportunity to see the entire building or facility from a different vantage point and that doing this sometimes may be useful; others disagree. Regardless of where the tour is started, the most important thing is to ensure that it be done in a way that results in each and every compartment within the building or facility being inspected. The floor plan should be checked against the previous one to see whether any major remodeling has been done or additions have been made to the building. If no floor plan exists, one should be drawn during the inspection tour. The representative accompanying the team should be asked to open any doors that are found to be locked.

General Inspection Categories

In all occupancies, regardless of size or classification, there are certain general fire and life safety items that must be inspected. Many departments have these common violations listed on their inspection form so that the inspection team need only check the appropriate box to indicate a violation of that section of the code (Figure 15.17). These items fall into the following categories:

- Access and egress
- Storage

Figure 15.12 Team members may have to sign confidentiality forms.

Figure 15.13 Some occupancies can be inspected in minutes.

Figure 15.14 Some occupancies may take several hours to inspect.

Figure 15.15 Starting the inspection from outside may reveal special features.

Figure 15.16 Some prefer to begin the inspection on the roof.

1	☐	NO HAZARDS NOTED THIS DATE		
		FIRE EQUIPMENT & SYSTEMS		
2	☐	T19-567 (b)	Provide "2A 10BC" Fire Extinguisher	
3	☐	T19-563.2 (a)	Fire Extinguisher to be Accessible and Visible	
4	☐	T19-563.7	Mount Extinguisher on wall 3'-5' from floor	
5	☐	T19-575.1	Provide Yearly Service of Extinguisher	
6	☐	T19-904 (a) 3	Auto-Sprinklers maintained operable/Quarterly Inspection	
7	☐	T19-904 (a) 4	Auto-Sprinklers Certification due every 5 Years	
8	☐	T19-904 (a) 5	Fixed Extinguishing System—Maintenance/Service	
9	☐	HSC13113.7	Provide approved Smoke Detectors in each Dwelling unit	
10	☐	NFPA13-4-2.5.1	Provide 18" clearance below sprinklers	
11	☐	1001.5.1	Fire Alarm Systems/Maintenance and Testing	
12	☐	1001.5	Fire Alarm Extinguishing Equipment Maintenance	
13	☐	1003.1.1	Fire Sprinkler System Required	
14	☐	1006.2.1	Fixed Extinguishing System—Protection of Kitchen Grease	
15	☐	1006.2.7	Fixed Extinguishing System—40BC Extinguisher Required	
16	☐	1006.2.8.3	Fixed Extinguishing System—Remove Grease Buildup	
17	☐	1006.2.5.2	Fixed Extinguishing System—Semi-Annual Service Req'd	
		ELECTRICAL		
18	☐	8504	Abatement of Electrical Hazards	
19	☐	8506.1	Extension Cords—Prohibited Use	
20	☐	8507	Multiplug Adapters—Prohibited Use	
21	☐	8509.2	Electrical Panels Access—Minimum of 30" Clearance	
22	☐	NFPA 70-110.22	Mark Electrical Panels Legibly	
		EXITS		
23	☐	1203	Obstructing the Width of Exits	
24	☐	1207.1	Maintain Egress Doors, Exits Shall be Openable	
25	☐	1207.3	Exits Openable W/O Key/Special Knowledge	
26	☐	1207.4	Exit Doors—Panic Hardware Comply UBC	
27	☐	1211.1	Provide Exit Illumination—Emergency Lighting	
28	☐	1212.1	Exit Signs—Indicate Direction of Exit	
29	☐	1212.3	Exit Sign Graphics—Min. 6" Letters	
30	☐	1212.4	Exit Signs—Illumination Requirements	
		BUILDING & STORAGE REQUIREMENTS		
31	☐	901.4.4	Address Numbers Required	
32	☐	902.4	Key Box Required/Access	
33	☐	1112.1	Restore Required F.R. Construction	
34	☐	1112.2.1	Fire Assembly— Fire Doors/Dampers/Maint req'd.	
35	☐	1112.2.2	Obstruct Operation of Fire Door/Assembly	
36	☐	1103.2.1	Accumulation of Comb. Wast Material on Lots	
37	☐	1103.2.1.3	Comb. Rubbish/Oily Rags Approved Container(s)	
38	☐	1103.2.2	Dumpsters prohibited within 5' of Comb. Wall	
39	☐	1103.3.2.4	Storage Prohibited in Mech./Elect. Rooms	
40	☐	1107.1	Heat Appliance Clearance to Combustible—Meet UMC	
41	☐	1210.3	Stairway—Storage Beneath Prohibited unless FR	
42	☐	7401.6.4	Compressed Gas Cylinders—Securing	
43	☐	7902.5.9	Storage Cabinets—Flammable Liquids	
44	☐	SRCC 8001.3.3	Haz Material—Update HMMP/HMIS	
45	☐	8001.7	Visible Hazard ID Req'd—NFPA 704 Placard	
46	☐	8003.1.7.1	Provide Secondary Containment of Haz. Mat.	

PERMITS REQUIRED

47	☐	Candles/Open Flame	52	☐	Hazardous Materials
48	☐	Dry Cleaning	53	☐	High Piled Combustible Storage
49	☐	Dust Producing Operation	54	☐	Liquified Petroleum Storage
50	☐	Flammable & Combustible	55	☐	Places of Assembly
		Liquids (Roseland)	56	☐	Spraying & Dipping
51	☐	Garage/Repair	57	☐	Care Facility or Day Care

Figure 15.17 A typical violations list. *Courtesy of Santa Rosa (CA) Fire Department.*

- Housekeeping
- Processes
- Waste management
- Fire protection

Housekeeping

Accumulations of litter in the workplace can be hazardous in several ways. Trash and litter can obscure or block access to the means of egress. Even though trash and litter rarely start a fire (except in the case of spontaneous combustion), they can conceal other things that can start fires. Trash and litter often provide additional fuel to any fire that does start.

Access and Egress

This is the most important category to be inspected. It includes such things as whether the business name is on the front of the building and whether address numbers are clearly visible from the street (Figure 15.18). These can be critical items when emergency responders are attempting to locate the business at night, in bad weather, and in a hurry. It also includes whether fire apparatus can get close enough to the building to reach it with aerial devices and preconnected attack lines or whether the lines would have to be extended (Figure 15.19).

Also included in this category is the most important single item to be inspected — the means of egress from the building. If all occupants have a way of getting out in the event of an emergency, it is possible for the other parts of the fire and life safety system to fail without

Figure 15.18 The occupancy should be easily identified.

Figure 15.19 Some buildings have poor access for fire apparatus.

anyone being injured or killed. Even if the building burns to the ground, the building and the business almost certainly are insured and can be rebuilt; someone killed in a fire or other emergency cannot be brought back to life.

According to NFPA 101®, *means of egress* is defined as "a continuous and unobstructed way of exit travel from any point in a building or structure to a public way consisting of three separate and distinct parts: (a) the exit access, (b) the exit, and (c) the exit discharge." Additionally, to be compliant with CABO/ANSI A117.1, *American National Standard for Accessible and Usable Buildings and Facilities*, the code also requires an *accessible means of egress* that is defined as "a path of travel, usable by a person with a severe mobility impairment, that leads to a public way or an area of refuge." A *public way* is defined as "any street, alley, or other similar parcel of land essentially open to the outside air, deeded, dedicated, or otherwise permanently appropriated to the public for public use and having a clear width and height of not less than 10 feet (3 m)." An *area of refuge* is defined as "(a) a floor in a building when such building is protected throughout by an approved, supervised automatic sprinkler system..., and (b) a space, in a path of travel leading to a public way, that is protected from the effect of fire, either by means of separation from other spaces in the same building or by virtue of location, thereby permitting a delay in egress travel from any level." All new and existing buildings must comply with these requirements.

When found during an inspection, any obstruction such as furniture, filing cabinets, or storage that reduces the original width of an exit passageway must be removed immediately (Figure 15.20). Making sure that every exit is well-lighted, clearly marked, unobstructed, unlocked, and functions as designed is also part of the inspection process. Exit doors must remain unlocked from the inside whenever the building is occupied, and they must be openable from the inside with a single motion that does not require a key or any special knowledge. Depending upon the occupant load served, exit doors may be required to swing open in the direction of exit travel and be equipped with panic hardware (Figure 15.21).

Processes

There are countless ways in which industrial processes can start fires or contribute to their spread. Because there are so many ways, requirements for each of the various classes of occupancies have been developed and are included in the various codes. The hazards specific to each of the major occupancy classifications are discussed later in this chapter. It is critically important that company officers and their crews thoroughly research the code requirements applicable to the occupancies they are assigned to inspect.

Storage

Storage may consist of raw materials from which the company's products are made, boxes containing the finished products, or both. In either case, flammable materials, such as cardboard boxes, must be kept separate from sources of ignition. This may include prohibiting smoking and/or welding and cutting operations in certain areas (Figure 15.22). Storage also must not interfere with automatic sprinklers or other built-in fire protection devices or systems.

Waste Management

Besides being potential environmental hazards, accumulations of flammable or combustible waste can be a significant fire and life safety hazard. Just as with flammable storage, these materials must be kept separate from sources of ignition. With flammable wastes, this

most often means proper containment — everything from putting oily rags into approved, self-closing containers to putting flammable trash in metal containers in sprinklered enclosures (Figure 15.23).

Fire Protection

This item is based on the assumption that the other parts of the system may not always be successful in preventing fires. Fire protection includes everything from the employees knowing how to recognize and report a fire, to their knowing the capabilities and limitations of various types of portable fire extinguishers and how to use them safely, to built-in fire detection and alarm systems, and to automatic sprinklers and other built-in fire suppression systems. Company-level personnel must be sufficiently knowledgeable to answer employee questions related to fire prevention and protection. They also must be able to assist plant safety and security personnel in these areas when asked (Figure 15.24). Company-level personnel also must be capable of inspecting and, if required, test-

Figure 15.20 Exit obstructions must be removed immediately.

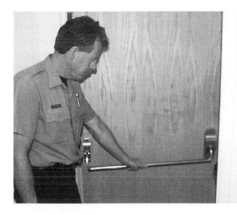

Figure 15.22 Smoking and open flames may be prohibited in certain areas.

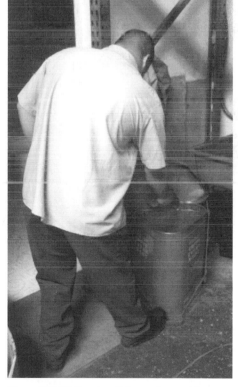

Figure 15.23 Combustible waste must be properly managed.

Figure 15.21 Some exit doors must have panic hardware.

Figure 15.25 Firefighters may be required to test built-in fire protection systems.

Figure 15.24 Company personnel may assist with plant safety planning.

ing built-in fire detection and suppression systems (Figure 15.25).

There is no substitute for the pre-inspection research that company-level personnel must do to prepare for the inspection of any occupancy that they are assigned. However, such preparation is even more important if the company is assigned to inspect some highly complex and very specialized occupancies. The inspection criteria peculiar to the most common of these occupancies are discussed in the following section.

Occupancy Classifications

In terms of fire and life safety inspections, NFPA 101® classifies buildings according to their intended use (occupancy). There are ten occupancy classifications:

- Assembly
- Educational
- Health care
- Detention and correctional
- Residential
- Mercantile
- Business
- Industrial
- Storage
- Special structures and high-rise buildings

Buildings within each of these occupancy classifications all have certain requirements in common, but each classification also has certain requirements that may be unique. All the occupancies covered by NFPA 101® have requirements relating to the means of egress, construction features, and building service and fire protection equipment. The following are some, but not all, of the more common code requirements for each of the occupancy classifications.

Assembly

These occupancies include buildings or portions of buildings where 50 or more persons gather for deliberation, worship, entertainment, eating, drinking, amusement, or to await transportation. Typical examples of assembly occupancies include auditoriums, bars, college classrooms, conference rooms, courtrooms, dance halls, exhibit halls, gymnasiums, libraries, mortuary chapels, motion-picture theaters, museums, airport and other transportation waiting rooms, churches and other religious gathering places, restaurants, and stadiums. Assembly rooms and other spaces with occupant loads of less than 50 and that are part of and incidental to another occupancy (for example, the room or area in a restaurant where people wait to be seated) are subject to the requirements applicable to that occupancy.

In addition to the general safety requirements for emergency lighting, fire extinguishers, etc., the requirements typical of assembly occupancies relate primarily to occupant loads and the means of egress from buildings with and without fixed seating. For example, the occupant load in a concentrated use without fixed seating, such as a dance hall or discotheque, is based on one person per 7 square feet (0.65 m²) of floor space; a less concentrated use such as a dining and/or drinking establishment is based on 15 square feet (1.4 m²) of floor space per occupant; bleachers and bench-type seating require 18 linear inches (45.7 linear cm) per occupant. These figures are used as the basis for determining the number, size, marking, and distribution of required exits. When an assembly occupancy shares a building with one or more other occupancies, the means of egress also may be shared, provided that the assembly and the other occupancies considered separately each have sufficient exiting.

Educational

These occupancies include buildings or portions of buildings where six or more persons gather for educational purposes through the twelfth grade for at least four hours per day or twelve hours per week (Figure 15.26). Typical examples of educational occupancies include schools

Figure 15.26 Educational occupancies may have large occupant loads.

and academies (religious or secular), kindergartens, nursery schools, and day-care facilities (regardless of occupant load). Where instruction is incidental to another occupancy, such as a small training/conference room in a business, the code requirements applicable to the business apply.

Code requirements typical of educational occupancies are similar to those for assembly occupancies. Their emphasis is on providing adequate means of egress. However, the requirements for educational occupancies also address construction features designed to separate the students from those areas most likely to become involved in fire, such as boiler rooms and equipment rooms. The requirements also address built-in fire detection and suppression systems as well as the means of notifying the fire department in case of a fire.

For day-care centers, the codes specify staff-to-client ratios based on the ages of the clients. For example, if the clients are two years old or under, a ratio of one staff member for every three clients (1:3) must be maintained. The number of clients allowed per staff member increases progressively with the age of the clients, up to a maximum of 1:15 for clients seven years old and older. Day-care centers that share a building with other occupancies must be separated from those other occupancies by a one-hour-rated fire barrier.

Health Care

These occupancies include buildings or portions of buildings used for the medical or other treatment of those who are suffering from physical or mental illness, disease, or infirmity — excluding dentists' offices. Also included in this classification are those facilities used for the care of infants, convalescents, or infirm elderly people. These occupancies provide sleeping facilities for four or more persons who are mostly incapable of caring for themselves because of age or because of physical or mental impairment. Typical examples of health care occupancies include hospitals, nursing homes, and health care centers for the ambulatory.

Code requirements for health care occupancies attempt to minimize the possibility that a fire emergency will require the evacuation of the occupants. The code requires that the building be designed, constructed, and compartmented so that a fire is likely to be confined to the room of fire origin. Fire detection, alarm, and extinguishment capabilities must also be provided. In addition, the staff must be trained in fire prevention, in programs for the isolation of fire, in the transfer of occupants to areas of safe refuge, and in the evacuation of the building. The code specifies minimum requirements for aisle, corridor, and ramp widths in various types of health care occupancies. When health care occupancies share a building with another occupancy of a different class, the occupancies must be separated by a two-hour-rated fire barrier.

Detention and Correctional

These occupancies are used to house those who are under varying degrees of restraint or security and, because of security measures beyond their control, who are mostly incapable of self preservation. Typical examples of these occupancies include adult and juvenile substance-abuse centers and work camps, adult and juvenile community residential centers, adult correctional institutions, and juvenile detention facilities and training schools.

Code requirements for detention and correctional occupancies attempt to minimize the possibility of a fire emergency. Because the occupants of these facilities are under some degree of restraint, their safety cannot be ensured solely by dependence on evacuation of the building. When security measures necessitate locking the means of egress, the facility staff must be capable of the supervised release of occupants at any time. Therefore, these facilities must be adequately staffed by personnel who are trained in fire prevention, the techniques of isolating fires, evacuating the occupants or transferring them to areas of safe refuge, or protecting them in place.

To assist in the provision of security to the degree necessary for the safety of the public and the occupants of the facility while still providing adequate and appropriate means of egress during an emergency, the code classifies these facilities by the degree of restraint imposed. There are five classifications or "use conditions":

- I — free egress
- II — zoned egress

- III — zoned impeded egress
- IV — impeded egress
- V — contained.

Staff must develop fire and life safety programs for any of these use conditions that exist within the facility. To be sure that the programs will function as designed, facility staff also must conduct periodic drills on the emergency procedures.

Residential

These occupancies include all buildings in which sleeping accommodations are provided for normal residential purposes, except those classified as health care or detention and correctional (Figure 15.27). This occupancy classification includes hotels, motels, and dormitories; apartment buildings; lodging and rooming houses; one- and two-family dwellings; and board-and-care facilities.

It is anticipated that the occupants spend a portion of their time asleep. Therefore, the code requirements for residential occupancies attempt to increase the likelihood of fires being confined to the room of origin, of occupants being alerted to the existence of a fire, and of the occupants being able to evacuate the building if necessary. The code prohibits certain construction features that would contribute to the spread of fire. For example, transoms, louvers, or ventilating grilles are not allowed in partitions or above doors that separate interior corridors from guest rooms (Figure 15.28). Where these features already exist, they are required to be permanently closed or covered. Each guest room door that opens into an interior corridor must be equipped with a self-closing device. The code also specifies the number, size, marking, and distribution of exits. It also specifies the number and type of smoke detectors required.

In board-and-care facilities, the occupants do not require chronic or convalescent medical or nursing care. However, the occupants are often aged and require daily attention and perhaps some level of assistance from staff. The code anticipates that assistance from staff may be needed with evacuations from the building. Therefore, the code recognizes three levels of evacuation capability by the occupants: prompt, slow, and impractical. The *prompt level* is the capability equivalent to that of the general population. The *slow level* anticipates that occupants can move to a point of safety in a timely manner, with some assistance from staff. At the *impractical level*, occupants are incapable of reliably moving to a point of safety in a timely manner, even with staff assistance. Staff must develop plans for the safety of all occupants, regardless of their individual and collective evacuation capabilities.

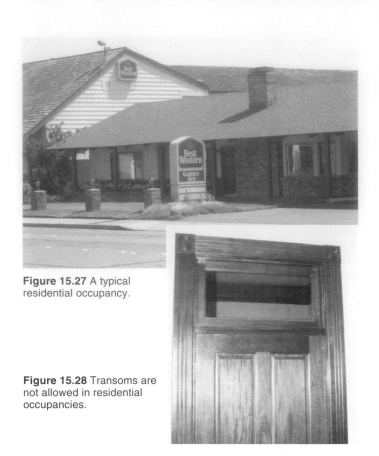

Figure 15.27 A typical residential occupancy.

Figure 15.28 Transoms are not allowed in residential occupancies.

Mercantile

These occupancies include buildings and portions of buildings used for the display and sale of merchandise (Figure 15.29). Typical examples of mercantile occupancies are auction rooms, department stores, drugstores, service stations, malls and shopping centers, and supermarkets.

Code requirements for mercantile occupancies vary based on the total amount of floor space within the occupancy. In general, the bigger the occupancy, the more restrictive the requirements because of the greater anticipated occupant load. However, the maximum allowable occupant loads vary also. They vary from 30 square feet (2.8 m^2) of floor space per person on the street floor and 60 square feet (5.6 m^2) on upper floors, to 100 square feet (9.3 m^2) in office space, and to 300 square feet (27.9 m^2) per person in storage or shipping and receiving spaces.

Means of egress requirements in mercantile occupancies are similar to those for assembly occupancies with comparable occupant loads. For instance, exit doors are generally required to swing open in the direction of exit travel (Figure 15.30). The maximum allowable travel distance to an exit in a particular class of mercantile occupancy can generally be doubled if the building is fully protected by an automatic sprinkler system. Covered malls and larger mercantile occupancies require emergency lighting; others do not. Exits from large mercantile occupancies must be marked appropriately, but in smaller mercantile occupancies where the exits are obvious, marking is not required.

Business

These occupancies are used for the transaction of business (other than those classified as mercantile), for maintaining business records and accounts, and for similar activities (Figure 15.31). Typical examples of business occupancies include government offices, college and university buildings (excluding assembly buildings), courthouses, doctors' and dentists' offices, insurance and real estate offices, restaurants and coffee shops with occupant loads of less than 50, and outpatient clinics for the ambulatory.

Code requirements for business occupancies include those for conventional business offices and buildings, but they also include requirements for buildings in which both business and residential occupancies exist. Business occupancies are allowed to have a dwelling unit above, provided that the exit from the dwelling unit does not have to pass through the business. However, multiple dwelling occupancies are not allowed above business occupancies. In most business buildings, or parts of buildings used for business, the occupant load is calculated on the basis of 100 square feet (9.3 m²) per person. When business occupancies share a building with a parking structure, the walls separating the business occupancy from the parking area must have a two-hour fire rating.

Industrial

These occupancies include factories of all kinds and properties devoted to processing, assembling, mixing, packaging, finishing, decorating, repairing, or otherwise producing a product or service (Figure 15.32). Typical examples of industrial occupancies include dry-cleaning plants, factories, food-processing plants, hangars for aircraft service and/or maintenance, laundries, power plants, pumping stations, refineries, mills, and telephone exchanges.

Figure 15.29 A typical mercantile occupancy.

Figure 15.30 Exit doors must swing in the direction of travel.

Figure 15.31 A typical business occupancy.

Figure 15.32 A typical industrial occupancy.

Code requirements for industrial occupancies are based on three subclassifications within this occupancy class — general, special purpose, and high hazard.

General. These industrial occupancies are ordinary- and low-hazard industrial operations conducted in buildings of conventional design suitable for various types of industrial processes. Included are multistory buildings in which floors are subject to being occupied by different tenants, with the possibility of a large employee population.

Special purpose. These industrial occupancies are those low- and ordinary-hazard industrial operations in buildings designed and suitable only for particular types of operations, characterized by a small employee population, and with the bulk of the floor space occupied by machinery or equipment.

High hazard. High-hazard industrial occupancies are those in which there are high-hazard materials, processes, or contents. However, incidental high-hazard operations in otherwise low- or ordinary-hazard occupancies is not justification to reclassify those occupancies.

Every high-hazard industrial occupancy, operation, or process must have automatic extinguishing systems or other protection that is appropriate to the particular hazard. An example of such protection might be explosion venting or suppression in an area with explosion potential in order to minimize danger to the occupants before they have time to use the exits to escape. In general, however, most of the fire and life safety requirements related to hazardous industrial materials, processes, or contents are found in other codes specific to those hazards.

The applicable requirements in NFPA 101® are related mainly to means of egress. For example, there must be no less than two means of egress from every story or section. Dead-end corridors must not exceed 50 feet (15 m) in length. Maximum allowable travel distance to an exit varies with the subclassification and whether the building is single story or multistory.

In addition to the *Life Safety Code®* requirements, in those occupancies where the hazards of the materials manufactured or stored there may not be readily apparent, the labeling requirements of NFPA 704, *Standard System for the Identification of the Hazards of Materials for Emergency Response,* also should be enforced (Figure 15.33). This labeling system can be critical to firefighter safety in the event of a fire or other emergency at the facility.

Storage

These occupancies are buildings or structures used primarily for storing or sheltering goods, merchandise, products, vehicles, or animals (Figure 15.34). Typical examples of storage occupancies include barns, bulk-oil-storage facilities, cold-storage plants, freight terminals, grain elevators, aircraft hangars (used for storage only), parking structures, stables, truck and marine terminals, and warehouses. Depending upon the nature of the materials stored within, these occupancies also may need to display the fire hazard labeling required by NFPA 704.

Because materials are not being processed in these occupancies, the code requirements relate primarily to the means of egress. There are specific requirements relating to the number and distribution of exits required in storage occupancies, but they vary depending upon the size and configuration of the buildings.

Special Structures and High-Rise Buildings

This classification relates more to the buildings than to the occupancies within. Included in this classification are the following:

- **Open structures** — Those that are not enclosed within a building's walls — such as in oil refineries, chemical plants, and power stations

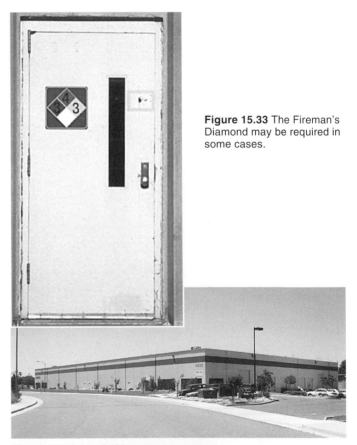

Figure 15.33 The Fireman's Diamond may be required in some cases.

Figure 15.34 A typical storage occupancy.

- **Towers** — Separate structures or portions of buildings that are used to support elevated equipment or that are occupied for observation, control, operation, signaling, and similar limited use and not open to general use

- **Underground structures** — Those in which the structure or a portion of it is below the level of the exit discharge

- **Certain types of vehicles** — Those vehicles, such as trailers, railroad cars, buses, streetcars, and other similar vehicles, that are immobile and attached to a building or are permanently affixed to a foundation

- **Certain types of vessels** — Those vessels, such as ships, barges, and other similar vessels, that are permanently affixed to a foundation or mooring and are incapable of navigating under their own power

- **Water-surrounded structures** — Those surrounded on all sides by water

- **Windowless structures** — Buildings or portions of buildings that do not have outside openings that may be used for ventilation or rescue

- **High-rise structures** — Those more than 75 feet (23 m) in height

Obviously, with this variety of occupancy classifications, the code requirements also vary considerably. However, because most of these structures are by definition unusual and because this characteristic often translates into unusually difficult access by emergency responders and egress by the occupants, the requirements emphasize increased fire protection for the occupants. Construction requirements are more stringent than for other occupancies, and in many cases, codes require automatic sprinkler coverage throughout. If assigned to inspect an occupancy within this classification, company members diligently must research the individual occupancy before conducting the initial inspection.

Mixed Occupancies

Where two or more classes of occupancy are housed in the same building or structure, they may be so intermingled that separate code requirements are impractical. In these cases, the means of egress, construction, facilities, fire protection, and other safeguards must comply with the most restrictive life safety requirements of the occupancies involved.

Hazard of Contents

In addition to the preceding categories of occupancy classification, NFPA 101® further classifies every individual occupancy according to the relative fire hazard of its contents. These classifications are based on a subjective evaluation of "the relative danger of the start and spread of fire, the danger of smoke or gases generated, and the danger of explosion or other occurrence potentially endangering the lives and safety of occupants of the building or structure." There are three contents-hazard classifications:

- *Low hazard* is the classification for contents of such low combustibility that a self-propagating fire cannot occur in them. Examples of such materials might include fiberglass insulation or minerals that do not contain hydrocarbons.

- *Ordinary hazard* is the classification for contents that are likely to burn with moderate rapidity or give off a considerable volume of smoke. Examples of these materials might include paper, cardboard, textiles, and some plastics.

- *High hazard* is the classification for contents that are likely to burn with extreme rapidity or from which explosions are likely. Examples of these materials might include flammable liquids or highly reactive substances.

Closing Interview

When the inspection tour has been completed, the team's findings should be discussed with the business owner or designated representative during a closing interview (Figure 15.35). If no violations were found, he should be congratulated. If any violations were found, these violations should be reviewed and discussed. As mentioned earlier, immediate threats to life safety, such as locked or obstructed exits, must be corrected immediately — before the inspection team leaves the premises. Other, less critical violations should be pointed out to the representative and the necessary corrective measures explained.

Figure 15.35 Inspection results should be discussed with the building representative.

A reasonable amount of time should be allowed for the corrections to be made. As discussed earlier in this chapter, the amount of time allowed varies depending upon the nature of the violations and the difficulty involved in their correction, but a date and time for a follow-up inspection should be established during the closing interview. If correcting the violations will take some time (installing a fire detection and alarm system, for example), a plan of correction should be developed with the representative. The plan should include reinspections at specified intervals to ensure that reasonable progress is made and that full compliance is eventually obtained.

Documentation

As with other fire department activities, documenting company-level inspections is extremely important. This documentation forms the inspection history of every individual occupancy that company members inspect. The documentation may be needed to force reluctant property owners to comply with the code requirements, or it may be needed as evidence should there be a fire in a particular occupancy. These data also may be needed for statistical purposes at the state or provincial level. Therefore, it is also extremely important that the documentation be as complete, accurate, and readable as possible.

Conducting Exit Drills

Company-level personnel may be required to conduct exit drills in some occupancies. Exit drills are particularly important in schools and similar occupancies. These drills are used to familiarize the occupants with the procedures to follow and the route to take when exiting the building in an emergency. In hospitals and nursing homes, only the staff should participate in these drills. Plans must be in place for evacuating the patients or moving them to an area of refuge. Because these facilities typically operate 24 hours a day, drills should be conducted with all shifts. Company-level personnel also may be involved in helping certain occupancies develop their emergency exit plans. Regardless of how well-written these plans may be, they should be tested periodically through a series of realistic exercises. From time to time, it may be appropriate to conduct these drills without prior notification.

Inspecting/Testing Fire Protection Systems

Depending upon local code requirements and department policy, company-level personnel may be responsible for inspecting and testing any built-in fire protection systems in the occupancies they inspect. Some occu-

Figure 15.36 The sprinkler system service tag should be checked.

pancies have a maintenance and testing contract with a local fire protection service firm. In these cases, all that is required of company-level personnel is to check the service tag to see that the system has been inspected and tested within the time interval specified in the code (Figure 15.36). In other cases, company-level personnel accompany fire-insurance or service-firm employees as they inspect and test these systems.

Regular inspection of fire protection systems is vital to firefighter safety. Communities that mandate regular testing of fire protection systems report a very high rate of fire protection system failures during the initial retesting period. A significant number of the failures are due to problems with the built-in system components. The most common problems encountered are inoperative fire alarm systems and inoperative fire pumps. With a regular retesting program, the failure rate of these systems drops significantly.

When inspecting these systems, company personnel should look for evidence of damage to any part of the system and for anything that might obstruct the system's operation. They also should look for any remodeling of the building or additions to it to be sure that newly created spaces are covered by the protective system.

There are several different types of systems that occupants may have installed to comply with local code requirements. The types most often inspected and tested by company-level personnel are fire detection/signaling systems, water supplies, stationary fire pumps, public fire alarm systems, standpipe systems, and fire extinguishing systems.

Fire Detection/Signaling Systems

Different types of fire detection and signaling systems are installed in various types of occupancies. Regardless of the type of system or the means of activation, each must meet the requirements of NFPA 72, *National Fire Alarm Code*, and company personnel must be familiar with how these systems operate and how to test them. The most common types of systems are local, auxiliary, remote station, proprietary, central station, and emergency voice/alarm communications.

Local Alarm Systems

Local alarm systems may be activated by a number of different means, but they all have one feature in common — they initiate an alarm signal only on the premises where they are installed. They do not transmit a signal to the fire department or to any other location. These systems primarily are intended to alert the occupants of the building to a fire so that they will leave the building. Secondarily, they are

Figure 15.37 Local systems may be activated in a variety of ways.

intended to alert passersby to a fire in the building so that they will call the fire department. These systems may be activated manually or by sensors that detect heat, smoke, or flame (Figure 15.37).

Auxiliary Alarm Systems

These systems are used only in communities that have municipal alarm box systems. Auxiliary alarm systems are installed within a building and are connected directly to a municipal alarm box. When the system is activated by a fire in the protected premises, the system transmits a signal to the fire department by the same means as an alarm from any other street box.

Remote Station Systems

These systems are similar to auxiliary systems in that they also are connected directly to the fire department communications/dispatch center. However, remote station systems transmit an alarm by some means other than the municipal fire alarm box circuits, usually over a leased telephone line. Where permitted, a radio signal on

a dedicated fire department frequency may be used instead. Commonly used in communities that are not served by a central station system, remote station systems may be of the coded or noncoded type. A noncoded system may be used where only one building is covered by the system; a coded system is necessary in occupancies consisting of buildings at different locations. Up to five buildings may be covered by one remote station system, and it may or may not have local alarm capability.

Proprietary Systems

A proprietary system is used to protect large commercial and industrial buildings, high-rise buildings, and groups of commonly owned buildings in a single location such as a college campus or an industrial complex. Each building in the complex is protected by a separate system connected to a common receiving point somewhere on the premises. The receiving point must be in a separate structure or in a part of a structure that is remote from any hazardous operations. It must be staffed constantly by a representative of the occupant who is trained in system operation and in what to do when an alarm is received (Figure 15.38). In addition to fire and life safety functions, some proprietary systems also are used to monitor plant security systems.

Central Station Systems

A central station system is basically the same as a proprietary system with two differences. First, the receiving point is not on the protected premises, and second, the

Figure 15.38 Alarms must be received by trained operators.

person receiving the alarm is not an employee of the owner of the protected premises. The operator works in a receiving point called a *central station* and is an employee of the alarm service company that contracts with the owner or occupant of the protected premises. When an alarm is received in the central station, the operator notifies the fire department and a representative of the property owner or occupant (Figure 15.39).

Because the central station may be located in another state, it is critically important that the operator provide the fire department with the correct address of the property and accurately identify what area of the protected property is affected. Some departments require that the central station provider be listed by Underwriters Laboratories (UL).

Emergency Voice/Alarm Communications Systems

These are supplementary systems installed in properties in addition to one of the other types of systems just discussed. Their purpose is to increase the capability of transmitting detailed information to occupants and/or firefighters who are on the premises. These systems may be separate from or integrated into the main fire detection/signaling system protecting the premises. They may be one-way communication systems in which information can be announced to but not received from the occupants; they may be two-way systems in which communications also can be received from the occupants.

Water Supplies

Company-level personnel may be assigned to inspect occupancies that have their own water supply to operate required sprinklers and/or standpipes. In the absence of a municipal water system, or if the pressure in the municipal system is too low to adequately supply the fire protection system, the owner or occupant may have installed a water tank on the roof of the building (Figure 15.40). In other cases, a freestanding water tank may have been installed (Figure 15.41). In either case, company-level personnel will not be involved in determining the adequacy of the system but only in how well it is maintained. They should look for signs of rust or corrosion around valves and fittings and should check the pressure readings of any gauges. Even though the occupant should have flow data available, company personnel may have to conduct flow tests to verify these figures (Figure 15.42). For more information on inspecting water supplies, see the IFSTA **Fire Inspection and Code Enforcement** manual.

Stationary Fire Pumps

In some occupancies where maintaining water storage for fire protection is impractical or impossible, stationary fire pumps may be installed. These installations must

Figure 15.39 The alarm operator notifies the fire department and the property owner.

Figure 15.40 Some buildings have rooftop water storage tanks.

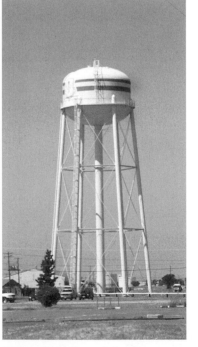

Figure 15.41 Some industrial occupancies have freestanding water storage tanks.

Figure 15.42 Flow tests may have to be conducted.

conform to NFPA 20, *Standard for the Installation of Centrifugal Fire Pumps*. The pumps are used to increase the pressure in the fire protection system when needed. They are almost always electrically-driven centrifugal pumps with a discharge capacity of from 500 to 4,500 gpm (2 000 L/min to 18 000 L/min). As with stored water supplies, company-level personnel usually are not required to test these pumps, but they may be. Company personnel should be familiar with the types of pumps installed in the occupancies they may be assigned to inspect. When inspecting these installations, they should check the occupant's pump maintenance and test records; NFPA 20 requires these pumps to be run for at least 30 minutes per week (Figure 15.43). Company personnel also should look for signs of water or oil leaks and for rust, corrosion, or damage to the pumps or associated piping (Figure 15.44). For more information on inspecting stationary fire pumps, see the IFSTA **Private Fire Protection and Detection** manual.

Public Fire Alarm Systems

Unlike the other fire protection systems discussed in this chapter, public fire alarm systems are usually owned and maintained by the municipality or other entity of which the fire department is a part. They may consist of a number of dedicated fire alarm circuits connected to street fire alarm boxes or consist of street boxes that are individual radio transmitters on a dedicated fire alarm frequency. These systems are classified as either Type A (manual retransmission) or Type B (automatic retransmission). In Type A systems, alarms received from the street boxes must be manually retransmitted to the affected fire stations by the alarm operator. In Type B systems, alarms received from the street boxes are auto-matically retransmitted to all fire stations within the jurisdiction. Type A systems are necessary in jurisdictions with a large call volume to keep the stations from being inundated with fire calls for which they are not part of the assigned initial response.

The routine maintenance and testing of these systems are often done by personnel other than those at the company level, but not always. In some cities, line personnel are assigned these duties. For more information on the installation, maintenance, and testing of these systems, see NFPA 1221, *Standard for the Installation, Maintenance and Use of Public Fire Service Communications Systems*.

Standpipe Systems

Standpipe systems are required on each floor and sometimes the roof of certain occupancies. Their purpose is to provide a quick and convenient source of water for fighting a fire. These systems must be installed according to NFPA 14, *Standard for the Installation of Standpipe and Hose Systems*, and to be effective, supplied with water in sufficient volume and at adequate pressure. NFPA 14 classifies standpipe systems as Class I, II, or III according to their intended use:

- *Class I systems* are intended to be used by firefighters and fire brigade members who are trained in handling heavy hose streams. They usually consist of strategically located valve-controlled 2½-inch (65 mm) outlets without hose (Figure 15.45).

- *Class II systems* are intended to be used by untrained building occupants until the arrival of the fire department or fire brigade. They are usually equipped with a rack or reel of 1½-inch (38 mm) fire hose (with nozzle) connected to a valve-controlled outlet.

Figure 15.43 The pump maintenance records should be checked.

Figure 15.44 The pumps and associated piping should be inspected.

Figure 15.45 A typical Class I standpipe.

Class III systems combine the features of both of the other classes and are intended to be used by firefighters, brigade members, and untrained occupants (Figure 15.46). This combination allows the occupants to apply water to a fire until firefighters or brigade members arrive, and it allows the trained firefighters to attack the fire with heavy hose streams.

When inspecting any of these systems, company personnel should check the hose cabinets to see that they are free of trash and debris. They should check the hose to see that it is not showing signs of deterioration—water stains, cuts, or abrasions on the surface of the hose. They also should feel the hose between the connection and the first fold to see whether water has accumulated in the hose (Figure 15.47). If it has, then this would indicate that the valve is partially open or is leaking. On 1½-inch (38 mm) hose connections, the hose should be disconnected and the valve tested by being opened to allow water to flow into a bucket held close to the outlet. While the hose is disconnected, the condition of the hose threads and gasket also should be checked (Figure 15.48). The hose nozzle also should be removed and its operation and gasket checked (Figure 15.49). On 2½-inch (65 mm) hose connections, the cap should be removed, the threads

checked, and a pressure gauge connected to the outlet so that the valve can be opened to test it. The fire department connection to the system also should be checked to make sure that the threads are undamaged and the inlets are free of debris (Figure 15.50). For more information on inspecting standpipe systems, see the IFSTA **Fire Inspection and Code Enforcement** manual.

Fire Extinguishing Systems

Company-level personnel may have to inspect and test a variety of fire extinguishing systems and equipment. The most common of these are automatic sprinkler systems, special-agent fixed fire extinguishing systems, and portable fire extinguishers.

Automatic Sprinkler Systems

An automatic sprinkler system consists of a water source, distribution piping, and one or more individual sprinklers (Figure 15.51). Depending on the particular situation, either a wet system or a dry system may be installed.

In wet-pipe systems, the piping is constantly full of water under pressure. Heat from a fire causes the one or more sprinklers to fuse (open) at a specified temperature allowing water to be discharged directly onto the fire (Figure 15.52). Wet-pipe systems can apply water onto a fire faster than dry systems, but the water in the piping is subject to freezing. Frozen distribution piping can burst and the linkage in individual sprinklers can be broken. When frozen piping thaws, water flows through the open sprinklers, possibly causing considerable water damage. Therefore, in cold-storage units and occupancies in cold climates, dry sprinkler systems are required.

In dry systems, the distribution piping is filled with air. This allows the system to remain functional during

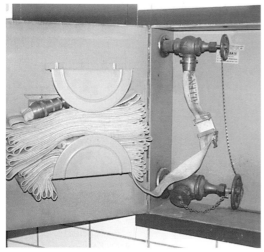

Figure 15.46 A Class III standpipe provides the most options for application.

Figure 15.47 The hose should be checked for water accumulation.

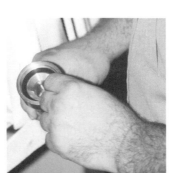

Figure 15.48 Hose threads and gaskets should be inspected.

Figure 15.49 Nozzle operation and condition should be checked.

Figure 15.50 The fire department connection should be inspected.

WET SYSTEM

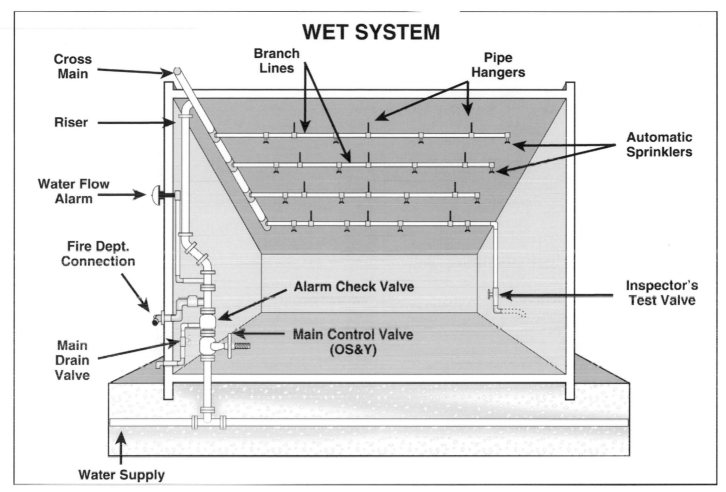

Cross Main

Branch Lines

Pipe Hangers

Riser

Automatic Sprinklers

Water Flow Alarm

Fire Dept. Connection

Alarm Check Valve

Inspector's Test Valve

Main Drain Valve

Main Control Valve (OS&Y)

Water Supply

Figure 15.51 A typical wet sprinkler system.

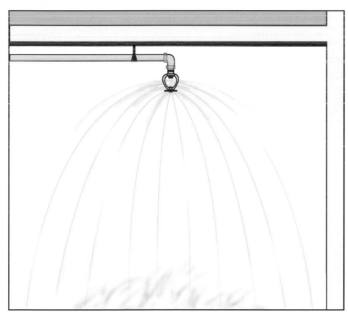

Figure 15.52 Sprinklers are designed to discharge directly onto an incipient fire.

freezing temperatures, but it delays the application of water onto a fire. There are three types of dry sprinkler systems — dry-pipe systems, pre-action systems, and deluge systems.

In *dry-pipe systems,* conventional sprinklers are installed in the distribution piping, which is filled with air under pressure. The air pressure in the piping is greater than the pressure of the water supplying the system, and so the air pressure keeps the main water control valve (dry-pipe valve) closed (Figure 15.53). When a sprinkler fuses because of a fire, the air within the piping is released, allowing water from the source to flow into the system. After the air in the piping has been discharged, water begins to be applied to the fire.

In *pre-action systems,* conventional sprinklers are used in combination with heat-sensing devices (Figure 15.54). When a fire starts, the heat-sensing devices allow water to enter the distribution piping and be discharged through those sprinklers that have fused due to the heat of the fire. These systems are used where preventing water damage is important.

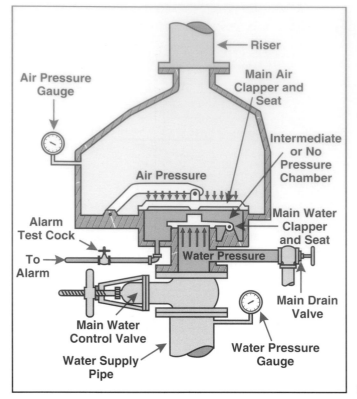

Figure 15.53 A typical dry-pipe system.

Figure 15.54 A heat sensor in a pre-action system.

Figure 15.55 Sprinklers are always open in deluge systems.

In *deluge systems*, heat-sensing devices are used to control the flow of water to the distribution piping in which the individual sprinklers are installed. However, in this type of system, all the sprinklers are open (Figure 15.55). Therefore, when any heat-sensing device activates, water discharges from all the sprinklers at once. Obviously, this type of system is used where overwhelming a fire with massive amounts of water is more important than preventing water damage.

Dry Chemical Systems

Dry chemical systems must conform to NFPA 17, *Standard for Dry Chemical Extinguishing Systems*. They are used in areas where a rapid knockdown of a fire is required but where reignition is unlikely. These systems may be either *engineered*, that is, specifically calculated and constructed for a particular occupancy, or *pre-engineered*, designed to protect a given amount of area in any type of occupancy.

These systems use the same fire extinguishing agents as portable dry chemical fire extinguishers. These agents are nontoxic and nonconducting, but they leave a very fine powdery residue that is extremely difficult to clean up. In some systems, the agent and expellent gas are stored in the same tank; in others, they are stored in separate tanks. There are two main types of dry chemical systems — local application and total flooding.

Local application is the most common type of dry chemical system. These systems are designed to dis-

charge agent directly onto a relatively small area such as the cooking surfaces in a commercial kitchen (Figure 15.56). If installed over a deep fryer or commercial range, these systems are designed also to shut off the flow of gas to the unit when the extinguishing system actuates (Figure 15.57). Company personnel inspecting these systems should perform the following checks:

- Check the discharge nozzles to see that they are not so heavily coated with grease or other material that they would not function as designed (Figure 15.58).

- Check the manual controls to see that the safety seals have not been broken (Figure 15.59).

- Check the fusible link(s) to see that they are clean and intact (Figure 15.60).

- Check the pressure gauge on the agent tank(s) to see that it is within the operating range, and check the service tag to see that the system has been serviced within the preceding year (Figure 15.61).

Total flooding dry chemical systems are installed in areas, such as spray booths, where a heavy cloud of agent is needed to fill the entire space when it is discharged. Like local application systems, total flooding systems may be actuated manually or automatically. Automatic actuation is by means of a fusible link holding a spring-loaded cable to the system controls. The same items that were listed for the local application systems should be inspected on total flooding systems.

Figure 15.56 A typical local-application dry chemical system.

Figure 15.57 Range-hood systems are designed to shut off the gas supply when actuated.

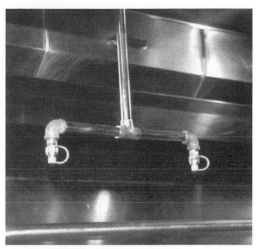

Figure 15.58 The discharge nozzles should be checked.

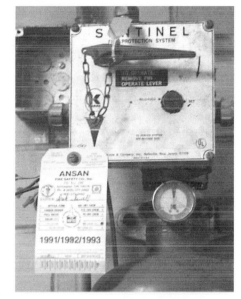

Figure 15.61 The pressure gauge and service tag should be checked.

Figure 15.59 The safety seal should be in place and unbroken.

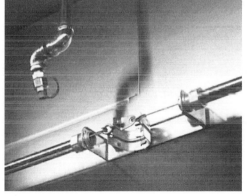

Figure 15.60 The fusible link should be inspected.

Wet Chemical Systems

These systems are designed to be installed in commercial range hoods, plenums, and ducts. They must conform to the requirements of NFPA 17A, *Standard for Wet Chemical Extinguishing Systems*. Similar to dry chemical systems in operation, wet chemical systems use an agent that is typically a mixture of water and either potassium carbonate or potassium acetate that is delivered in the form of a spray. Wet chemical systems are especially well-suited for cooking-related applications because the agent reacts to animal and vegetable oils by forming a noncombustible soap. This extinguishes a fire by denying it fuel. The components of a wet chemical system are essentially the same as dry chemical systems, as are the items to be inspected.

Carbon Dioxide Systems

The installation of these systems must conform to NFPA 12, *Standard on Carbon Dioxide Extinguishing Systems*. Like dry chemical systems, carbon dioxide (CO_2) systems are designed as either local application or total flooding systems; the type of system used in a particular area depends upon the situation.

Because CO_2 extinguishes fire by excluding oxygen (smothering), the total flooding systems can be hazardous to anyone in the room that is flooded. Therefore, total flooding CO_2 systems must have a predischarge alarm to warn anyone in the room of an impending discharge so that they can immediately leave the room (Figure 15.62). Both the automatic and normal manual operation activate the predischarge alarm before discharging the agent. But, in addition, these total flooding systems also have emergency manual operation that discharges (dumps) the agent into the room immediately and without warning (Figure 15.63). In the automatic mode, these systems are actuated by any type of detector — heat, rate-of-rise, smoke, or flame.

Local application CO_2 systems are usually supplied from one or more small cylinders, similar to portable extinguisher cylinders, located near the area to be protected (Figure 15.64). Total flooding systems are usually supplied by much larger tanks or a bank of cylinders (Figure 15.65). In either case, the agent is discharged through a system of piping from the supply to the point of discharge. The items to be inspected by company personnel are essentially the same as for types of fixed extinguishing systems.

Halogenated Agent Systems

The production of halogenated agents (halons) after the year 2000 is prohibited by the Montreal Protocol, but applications that are deemed essential, and for which no suitable alternative agents have been found, may continue to use halogenated agents after the agreement is in full effect. Even though the United States unilaterally stopped production of these materials in 1993, there are still many occupancies with systems that use halogenated agents. Their primary use is in "clean rooms" such as computer rooms, high-tech manufacturing facilities, and similar occupancies where extinguishing agent residue could do more harm than a fire (Figure 15.66). Because such facilities may be found in any business or commercial district, company personnel are very likely to be assigned to inspect occupancies that have these systems.

Like dry chemical systems, halon systems may be engineered or pre-engineered. Except for some local application systems, most halon systems are engineered for the particular occupancy in which they are installed. However, regardless of the design or installation, all halon systems have the same component parts: agent tanks and associated piping, valve actuators, nozzles, detectors, manual releases, and control panels. One feature unique to halon systems is an abort switch to cancel an inadvertent actuation of the system so that these very expensive agents are not wasted by being dumped accidentally (Figure 15.67).

Figure 15.62 A typical predischarge alarm.

Figure 15.63 A typical total flooding system dump valve.

Figure 15.63 Typical range-hood system cylinders.

Figure 15.66 Some "clean rooms" still have halon systems.

Figure 15.67 A typical halon system abort switch.

Figure 15.65 Typical total flooding system supply.

When inspecting these systems, company personnel should check the agent storage tanks for loss of agent — some systems have a dipstick-type gauge to indicate the amount of agent in the tank (Figure 15.68). Personnel should make sure that the detectors and discharge nozzles are not obstructed (Figure 15.69). Also, they should check the service tags to see that the system has been serviced by a licensed service firm within the time interval specified in the code.

Foam Systems

Foam systems are used in locations where the application of water alone, such as from a conventional automatic sprinkler system, may not be effective in extinguishing a fire. Such locations include facilities for the processing or storage of flammable or combustible liquids, aircraft hangars, and facilities in which rolled paper or textiles are stored (Figure 15.70). Foam systems may be designed to produce protein, fluoroprotein, film forming fluoroprotein (FFFP), or aqueous film forming foam (AFFF) in low-, medium-, or high-expansion ratios; the design in use depends on the hazards present in the particular occupancy. Systems designed to produce low-

expansion foam must conform to NFPA 11, *Standard for Low-Expansion Foam*; other systems must conform to NFPA 11A, *Standard for Medium- and High-Expansion Foam Systems*. Some systems are designed to produce ATC (alcohol-type concentrate) foams for polar solvents and other flammable liquids that are miscible with water. These various types and ratios of foam may be delivered through deluge nozzles or through special foam sprinklers (Figure 15.71). When company personnel inspect these installations, they should be guided by the foam and foam system manufacturers' recommendations and by the IFSTA **Private Fire Protection and Detection** manual.

Portable Fire Extinguishers

Part of the process of inspecting any occupancy involves checking the portable fire extinguishers on the premises. Regardless of the type of occupancy, all portable fire extinguishers must be installed and maintained according to NFPA 10, *Standard for Portable Fire Extinguishers*. Depending upon the types of flammable or combustible materials that are in the particular occupancy, a variety

Figure 15.68 Some halon tanks have dipstick gauges.

Figure 15.69 Detectors and nozzles should be inspected.

Figure 15.71 A typical deluge nozzle on a foam system.

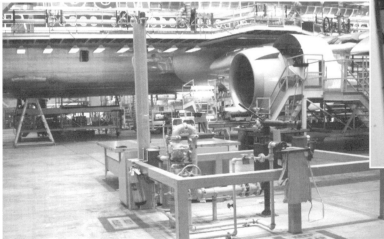

Figure 15.70 Some areas require foam systems.

of types and sizes of portable fire extinguishers may be present. Company personnel should check for the following:

- Clearly marked locations of extinguishers with unobstructed access (Figure 15.72)
- Signs of damage (Figure 15.73)
- Service tag and the safety seal (Figure 15.74).
- Pressure gauge (if so equipped) reading within the operational range.

In addition, personnel also should heft each one to see whether it feels as though it is full of agent. For more information on inspecting portable fire extinguishers, see the IFSTA **Fire Inspection and Code Enforcement** manual.

Summary

One of the most effective ways of preventing fires and other emergencies is through the adoption and enforcement of appropriate ordinances, codes, and standards to reasonably regulate the activities of the citizens of the jurisdiction. The enforcement of these regulations is often done at the company level through a conscientiously applied inspection program. Therefore, company officers must know how to use the laws and regulations that have been adopted to save lives, reduce injuries, and protect property through the enforcement of these requirements.

Figure 15.72 Extinguishers should be easy to locate in an emergency.

Figure 15.73 Portable extinguishers should be inspected for damage.

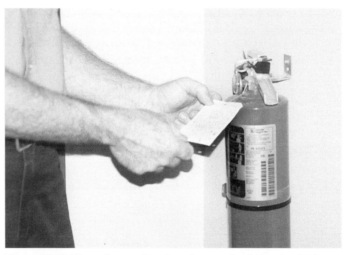

Figure 15.74 The safety seal and service tag should be checked.

This chapter provides information that will assist the reader in meeting the following job performance requirements from NFPA 1021, *Standard for Fire Officer Professional Qualifications*, 1997 edition. The colored portions indicate the topics addressed in the chapter. The numbers of the job performance requirements are also noted directly in the sections of text where they are addressed. Those in the following list that are denoted with an asterisk (*) are global in nature and are covered by reading the chapter in its entirety.

Fire Officer I

2-5.1   Evaluate available information, given a fire incident, observations, and interviews of first-arriving members and other individuals involved in the incident, so that a preliminary cause of the fire is determined, reports are completed, and, if required, the scene is secured and all pertinent information is turned over to an investigator.

(a) *Prerequisite Knowledge:* Common causes of fire, fire growth and development, and policies and procedures for calling for investigators.

(b) *Prerequisite Skills:* The ability to determine the basic fire cause and the ability to conduct interviews and write reports.

2-5.2   Secure an incident scene, given rope or barrier tape, so that unauthorized persons can recognize the perimeters of the scene, are kept from restricted areas, and all evidence or potential evidence is protected from damage or destruction.

(a) *Prerequisite Knowledge:* Types of evidence, the importance of fire scene security, and evidence preservation.

(b) *Prerequisite Skills:* The ability to establish perimeters at an incident scene.

Fire Officer II

3-5.2   Determine the point of origin and preliminary cause of a fire, given a fire scene, photographs, diagrams, pertinent data and/or sketches, to determine if arson is suspected.

(a) *Prerequisite Knowledge:* Methods used by arsonists, common causes of fire, basic cause and origin determination, fire growth and development, and documentation of preliminary fire investigative procedures.

(b) *Prerequisite Skills:* The ability to communicate verbally and in writing and to apply knowledge using deductive skills.

Fire Investigation

In addition to their other duties at fires, company officers are responsible for securing the fire scene and protecting possible evidence until the cause of the fire has been determined. In many departments, they are also responsible for making the preliminary cause determination. These requirements dictate that company officers have a good understanding of fire behavior, investigation techniques, and the importance of documentation.

This chapter discusses the company officer's responsibilities regarding fire cause determination, scene security, and evidence preservation. In addition, the investigation of accidental, natural, and incendiary fires and how to properly document the results of the investigation are also discussed.

Fire Investigation

Company officers must be able to make a preliminary determination of the cause of any fire to which they respond. When the situation or department policy requires, they must be able to secure the scene to preserve any evidence or potential evidence of the fire cause and call for a fire investigator.

CAUTION: One of the most important aspects of fire cause determination is an awareness by company officers and their crews of the importance of preserving evidence. Fire crews must be careful during suppression operations not to needlessly disturb or destroy potential evidence of the fire cause. In addition, company officers must not allow the overhaul or mop-up process to begin before the cause of the fire has been determined and any evidence protected.

At the company level, the fire investigation involves three major components: (1) locating the point of origin, (2) securing the scene, and (3) determining the cause of the fire. Company officers are responsible for making sure that these things are done — and done correctly.

Locating the Point of Origin

[NFPA 1021; 3-5.2]

The first step in the fire investigation process is to locate the point of origin. Some of the most important sources of information about the point of origin are those who reported the fire and those who fought it (Figure 16.1). The reporting party and any other witnesses should be interviewed to determine where the fire was burning when they first saw it. The initial-attack firefighters also should be asked the same sorts of questions.

In the absence of meaningful eyewitness information, by applying the principles of basic fire behavior, company officers can estimate where, in general, the fire started. However, this part of the process can be very different depending upon whether the fire being investigated is a structure fire, a vehicle fire, or a fire in the wildland. Even though the chemistry and physics involved are exactly the same, there are different environmental influences on fires burning within a confined space and those burning outdoors. Outdoor fires are affected by topography where interior structure fires are

Figure 16.1 The reporting party and first-in crew should be interviewed.

not, and outdoor fires are influenced by weather to a much greater degree than interior fires. Regardless of whether a fire was inside a structure or out in the wildland, the burn pattern left by the fire is the first indicator of the point of origin.

A fire inside a structure also behaves in predictable ways, and the burn pattern it leaves is one of the most important indicators of the point of origin. Because there is usually no wind to influence how the fire spreads, burn patterns tend to be vertical from the point of origin and are often V-shaped (Figure 16.2). If accelerants were used, their characteristic burn pattern is often obvious (Figure 16.3). Just as in the wildland, the deepest char on structural members appears on the side from which the fire spread. Also, because the fire burns longer at the point of origin, it is usually the area of greatest fire damage (Figure 16.4).

Fires in vehicles behave according to the same physical laws as any other fire, and they may present the same challenges to those investigating them. In general, vehicle fires fall into one of two broad categories — those that occur while the vehicle is being driven, and those that occur while the vehicle is parked.

Fires that occur while a vehicle is being driven are most often due to mechanical or electrical malfunctions, or to carelessness with smoking materials — but not always. Fires that result from a mechanical malfunction are usually rather easily traced to their source. They occur most often in the engine compartment, in the exhaust system, or in the wheel-and-brake assembly (Figure 16.5). These fires often result from fuel leaks, combustibles too close to catalytic converters, or friction from overheated brakes or worn-out bearings and drive

belts. Fires caused by electrical malfunction are most likely to be in the engine compartment or under the dashboard. Fires that result from carelessness with smoking materials often occur when someone inside the vehicle attempts to throw out lighted material but the wind blows the material back into the vehicle. This may go unnoticed by the vehicle occupants until a fire starts in the upholstery or seat cushions. On rare occasions, fires may start inside a moving vehicle when reactive materials are accidentally mixed by the motion of the vehicle — perhaps the violent motion resulting from the vehicle being involved in an accident. For example, if a soft drink containing sugar mixes with swimming pool chemicals, the resulting chemical reaction can generate enough heat to ignite adjacent combustibles.

Vehicle fires that occur when the vehicle is parked may simply be the delayed result of something that happened while the vehicle was being driven. The driver may park the vehicle and leave it unattended with smoking material smoldering in the back seat. Malfunctioning mechanical or electrical components that had been kept below their ignition temperature by the cooling effect of the wind while the vehicle was in motion may overheat and cause a fire when the vehicle is parked. However, if a fire starts in a vehicle that has been parked for several hours or days, the likelihood of the fire being of incendiary origin increases significantly.

In general, a wildland fire spreads away from the point of origin in predictable ways — it spreads faster uphill than down, it spreads faster with the wind than against it, and it spreads faster in fine fuels, such as grass, than in heavier fuels, such as timber. Therefore, the point of origin is almost always nearer the heel of the fire than the head (Figure 16.6). The remains of fence posts, trees, and

Figure 16.2 A typical V-shaped burn pattern.

Figure 16.3 Flammable liquids leave a distinctive burn pattern. *Courtesy of Bill Lellis.*

Figure 16.4 The deepest char is usually at the point of origin.

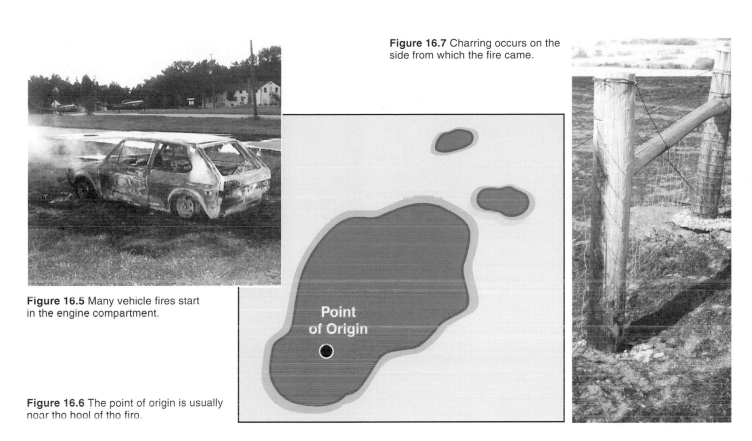

Figure 16.5 Many vehicle fires start in the engine compartment.

Figure 16.6 The point of origin is usually near the heel of the fire.

Point of Origin

Figure 16.7 Charring occurs on the side from which the fire came.

stumps show the deepest char on the side that was exposed to the advancing flame front (Figure 16.7). So, the depth of char indicates the direction *from which* the fire spread. For more information on wildland fire investigation, see the IFSTA **Fundamentals of Wildland Fire Fighting** manual.

Regardless of whether a fire occurred inside a structure, in a vehicle, or in the wildland, once the point of origin is located, the company officer must protect that part of the fire scene until the specific cause of the fire is determined — and perhaps longer if further investigation is warranted.

Securing the Scene

[NFPA 1021: 2-5.2]

Just as there are similarities and differences in how the point of origin is located in structure fires, vehicle fires, and wildland fires, there are also similarities and differences in how the respective scenes are protected. In all cases, a secure perimeter must be established within which only those responsible for determining the fire cause are allowed. Rope or some form of barrier tape may be used to establish a perimeter (Figure 16.8). Evidence or possible evidence of the fire's cause may need to be protected by additional means until it can be properly investigated. Depending upon the size of the evidence and the nature of its surroundings, it may be possible to protect it by covering it with a salvage cover or a cardboard box (Figure 16.9).

If it is necessary to call an investigator, company personnel should secure the scene and preserve any evidence until the investigator arrives. They should not move or handle evidence unless it is absolutely necessary in order to preserve it. However, there may be times when it is necessary because of the immediate unavailability of an investigator or to avoid destruction of the evidence.

The most thorough investigation to determine the cause of a fire can be wasted completely if the chain of evidence is broken because the scene was not secured properly. If an investigator is not immediately available, the property must remain under the control of the fire department until all evidence has been collected. All evidence must be marked, tagged, and photographed before the scene is released by the fire department because a search warrant or written consent from the owner may be needed for investigators to reenter the property.

In most cases, the fire department has the authority to deny access to any building during fire fighting operations and for as long afterward as deemed reasonably necessary. However, company officers should be aware of any local laws pertaining to the right of access by owners, occupants, or members of the news media.

No one, including the property owner or occupant, should be allowed to enter the premises for any reason before it is released unless they are accompanied by a fire officer or firefighter. A written log of any such entry

Figure 16.8 The area around the point of origin should be cordoned off. *Courtesy of Bill Lellis.*

Figure 16.9 Evidence should be protected.

should be kept, showing the person's name, times of entry and exit, and a description of any items moved or taken from the scene.

Determining the Cause of the Fire

[NFPA 1021: 2-5.1]

Once the point of origin has been located and any obvious evidence protected, company officers also must apply their understanding of basic fire behavior to determine the specific cause of the fire. Company officers and their crews must work together in this process. For example, as the company officer searches for any physical evidence, one firefighter may assist by taking notes while another makes a sketch of the scene and another photographs the evidence found (Figure 16.10). If the company officer cannot determine the specific cause, he must follow department policy with regard to listing the cause as *undetermined* or calling for an investigator. If the fire appears to be the result of a malicious or negligent act, an investigator should be called. However, in order to determine the cause of a fire and to decide when to call an investigator, company officers must be familiar with the most common causes of fire.

The cause of any fire may be classified as accidental, natural, incendiary, or undetermined. *Accidental fires* are those that did not result from intentional and malicious human activity, but they still may result in litigation if negligence is alleged. *Natural fires* are those that result from phenomena such as lightning strikes and earthquakes and not from human activity. *Incendiary fires* are those that are deliberately set with malicious intent.

Fire cause determination requires the identification of the circumstances and factors that were necessary for the fire to have occurred. These circumstances and fac-

Figure 16.10 Company members can work together as a team. *Courtesy of Bill Lellis.*

tors include, but are not limited to, a competent ignition source, the material first ignited, and the actions that brought them together.

The mere presence of a readily ignitable fuel and a competent ignition source does not establish a fire cause. The fire cause is the sequence of events that allowed the fuel and the source of ignition to come together.

If doubt about the cause of a fire exists, the investigator first must eliminate all possible accidental or natural causes before concluding that the fire was a result of incendiarism. The term *suspicious* should not be used as a fire cause classification. Mere suspicion concerning a fire's cause is an unacceptable level of proof, and it should not be used in fire reports. As mentioned earlier, if the cause cannot be determined with a reasonable degree of certainty, it should be listed as *undetermined.*

Accidental Fires

Many accidental fires are started by human activity, but they differ from incendiary fires in that there was no malicious intent on the part of the person who started the fire. Some accidental fires start as what the fire insurance industry calls *friendly fires*. These are fires that are started intentionally but for a legitimate purpose such as burning leaves, prunings, or other refuse but that get out of control and spread to adjacent combustibles. If someone started such a fire on a windy day or during an official ban on outside burning, that person may be subject to prosecution for negligence.

Other common accidental fire causes are such things as people falling asleep while smoking, refueling gasoline-powered equipment near a source of ignition such as a pilot light, placing combustibles too close to a furnace register or other heat source, or putting fireplace ashes into a paper bag, cardboard box, or combustible trash container. Sparks from welding and cutting operations also can start fires accidentally, as can those from unscreened fireplaces. There are countless ways in which fires start accidentally; however, a significant number of accidental fires involve electricity and electrical appliances (Figure 16.11).

Smoking-Related Fires

Many of these fires occur when the occupant inadvertently allows lighted smoking materials to come into contact with combustibles. This may be by dumping an ashtray into a wastebasket or allowing an unattended cigarette to fall from an ashtray onto bedding or upholstered furniture. Fatalities often occur in these fires if the occupant is incapacitated by alcohol or other drugs and either falls asleep or passes out. An ashtray, the metal parts of a cigarette lighter, or other evidence of smoking may be found in the ashes at the point of origin.

Pyrophoric Ignition

These fires occur under conditions that appear to be without a competent heat source. However, when wood or other cellulose material is more or less continuously subjected to a low level of heat over a long period, the material can be converted to pyrophoric carbon through pyrolysis (Figure 16.12). As this conversion takes place, the ignition temperature of the material is gradually lowered until autoignition occurs. The following items are common heat sources for pyrophoric ignition and may be found near the point of origin:

- Steam pipes
- Flues pipes (wood-burning stoves and fireplaces)
- Fluorescent light ballasts

Electrical Fires

Electrical conductors (wiring) and appliances rarely cause fires if they are used as intended and are protected by functioning fuses or circuit breakers of the appropriate size. The mere presence of electrical wiring or appliances near the point of origin does not necessarily mean that the fire was electrical in nature. However, heat generated by electrical wiring and equipment can ignite adjacent combustibles, so it should be considered along with other possible sources of ignition.

Perhaps the most common cause of electrical fires involves misuse of the electrical system by the building occupants. This often involves the use of lightweight extension cords, sometimes called "zip cords." Electrical fires also commonly result from the use of a multiple-outlet device commonly called an "octopus" (Figure 16.13). When all the appliances that are plugged into the device are operated simultaneously, the wiring and/or the fixture can overheat and eventually catch fire (Figure 16.14).

Figure 16.11 Electricity is a frequent cause of fires *Courtesy of Bill Lellis.*

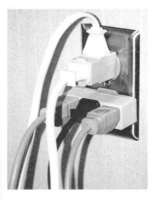

Figure 16.12 Over time, the ignition temperature of combustibles can be lowered. *Courtesy of Bill Lellis.*

Figure 16.13 An obviously overloaded electrical outlet.

Figure 16.14 Multiple-outlet devices can be dangerous. *Courtesy of Bill Lellis.*

Another very common scenario involves an automatic coffeemaker or similar appliance inadvertently being left on when the occupants leave the premises. As long as liquid remains in the unit, evaporation keeps it from overheating. However, after a few hours all the liquid evaporates, and the unit begins to overheat. If the automatic temperature control within the unit fails, the plastic parts of the unit will eventually reach their ignition temperature and catch fire. If the unit is sitting on or near combustible materials, they may become involved and spread the fire. Therefore, one of the most important things to check during the fire cause investigation is the position of the power switch on any electrical appliance found at the point of origin.

Clothes dryers, both electric and gas, sometimes start fires because of a failure of the high-temperature control or the timing mechanism. If a malfunction of either of these devices occurs, abnormal heat buildup can result, possibly igniting clothing or accumulated lint. However, fires in clothes dryers may simply be the result of accumulated lint ignited during normal operation of the machine.

Another common scenario in which electricity is the fire cause involves improperly installed wiring and/or equipment. Homeowners and business owners who lack the training to properly install electrical wiring and fixtures sometimes try to save money by doing the work themselves instead of calling a licensed contractor or electrician. The results can be far more expensive than the cost of paying a trained professional (Figure 16.15). Interviewing the property owner often confirms improper installation as the real cause of the fire.

Natural Fires

Nature can cause fires in a variety of ways. Fires may result from lightning strikes, earthquakes, and other natural phenomena. One of the most common of these is a lightning strike.

Lightning-Related Fires

When lightning strikes a building, it can instantly overload the building's entire electrical system by introducing several thousand volts into it and thus cause multiple fires. It can destroy television sets, stereo sound systems, and other appliances that normally remain plugged in all the time. In these fires, the main fuses or circuit breakers may be melted (Figure 16.16). If a lightning strike cannot be confirmed by a witness or by finding an obvious point of contact, the fire scene must be examined carefully for evidence of a strike. However, there are incidents where lightning strikes have produced no visible damage. Some of the most likely contact points are as follows:

- Roof peaks with metal flashing
- Any metal object of significant size, such as tanks, blowers, and air-handling units, on or near the top of the structure
- Antennas affixed to and serving the structure
- Electrical service weather head

Earthquake-Related Fires

Earthquakes occur daily in some parts of North America, but they may occur anywhere at any time. When major earthquakes occur, structures may suffer serious damage or may even collapse (Figure 16.17). The movement

Figure 16.15 Improper wiring has started many fires. *Courtesy of Bill Lellis.*

Figure 16.16 A lightning strike can virtually melt a circuit breaker panel.

Figure 16.17 Structural damage is common in seismically active areas. *Courtesy of Barry Gaab.*

can break gas pipes and cause electrical equipment and systems to short out. This resulting combination of abundant fuel and a competent ignition source often results in fires starting — sometimes in numerous locations simultaneously (Figure 16.18). These sometimes catastrophic events can also start fires by causing chemical containers to fall from shelves and break. When several different chemicals mix on the floor of a damaged building, such as a hospital's pathology lab, a fire is just one of the hazardous possibilities. However, the resulting fires usually occur immediately, and the cause is rather obvious. Other earthquake-related fires are not so obvious.

Earthquakes can sometimes do damage that is not obvious in a cursory inspection but that can cause a fire later. For example, if the terra-cotta flue liner in a fireplace chimney is cracked by earthquake movement, a subsequent fire started in the fireplace may ignite combustibles adjacent to the chimney. An unusual amount of investigation may be required to determine the cause of these fires.

Other Natural Fires

While fires caused by lightning strikes and earthquakes may be the most common and most spectacular of those caused by natural forces, they are not the only ones. Other examples include fires caused by wind damage to electrical conductors and transmission lines. The wind also can cause fires by blowing electrical lines into contact with tree limbs. An obscure but not uncommon natural cause of fires is the heat generated by the friction between dehydrating logs piled on a sawmill log deck. If rain water dampens powdered swimming pool chemicals, the reaction can generate enough heat to ignite adjacent combustibles. Company officers may have to do an unusual amount of investigation to determine the fire cause in these situations.

WARNING

Company-level personnel and other fire investigators should consider any exposed electrical wiring or equipment as energized unless the power has been shut off by utility company personnel.

Incendiary Fires

Incendiary fires are caused by the same combination of a competent ignition source and an ignitable material that causes accidental and natural fires, but the most obvious difference between these types of fires is that incendiary fires are started intentionally and with mali-

Figure 16.18 Fires are a common result of earthquakes. *Courtesy of Bill Lellis.*

cious intent. When the company officer has eliminated accidental and natural causes for a particular fire having started, he must consider the possibility that the fire is of incendiary origin. In many cases, this conclusion is the obvious one. Other differences between these fires and those of accidental or natural origin are that the firesetters often do one or more of the following:

- Use accelerants to increase the rate at which the fire develops and spreads

- Disable fire detection systems and equipment to delay the fire being reported

- Disable fire suppression systems and equipment to allow the fire to develop

- Employ some means of delaying ignition

- Employ some means of delaying the fire department's response

Some other indicators that a fire was of incendiary origin are the following:

- **Multiple points of origin** — Separate fires in different rooms or areas.

- **Timing devices** — Cigarette-match combinations and candles are frequently used timing devices. Wax from a candle often soaks into the floor and can be detected on the scene or by a laboratory test. The spot beneath the candle often is not burned as badly as the surrounding floor. Alarm clocks are not often used but should not be discounted. The metal parts of alarm clocks and similar devices are seldom destroyed by fire.

- **Trailers** — Materials used to spread the fire from one area of a structure to another or from one floor level to another (Figure 16.19). They are usually ordinary combustibles often soaked with flammable liquids. Items used to make trailers may include the following:

  — Toilet paper

  — Newspapers

- Gunpowder
- Wax paper
- Excelsior
- Blasting fuse
- Oil-soaked string, cord, or rope
- Cotton, wool, and similar materials

- **Chemicals** — Phosphorous, metallic sodium, potassium permanganate, or glycerin.

- **Matches** — They are not always consumed by the fire, and even if they are, the staple from a matchbook will remain if the matchbook was left at the scene. Unburned matchbook covers may yield fingerprints, so they must be handled carefully.

- **Flammable liquids** — Gasoline, kerosene, solvent, alcohol, carbon disulfide, paint thinner, acetone, ether, and other accelerants.

- **Bottles** — These often are used to make Molotov cocktails. Unburned cloth may be found in the bottle's neck. Some remains of the bottle almost always can be found.

- **Rubber items** — Balloons, condoms, hot-water bottles, and similar rubber items used to hold flammable liquids or phosphorous and water sometimes can be recovered at the scene (Figure 16.20).

- **Other containers** — Those that may have held flammable liquids often can be found in or around the scene.

- **Glass** — Sometimes used to focus the sun's rays on combustible materials, glass may be found at the scene, especially in wildland fires.

- **Butane lighters** — Even if the plastic fuel reservoir is consumed, the metal parts of the lighter are usually identifiable (Figure 16.21).

- **Altered heating equipment** — Improperly adjusted draft controls, deliberate breaks in flue and stove pipes, or oil or gas lines deliberately damaged.

- **Electrical appliances** — Lamps or heating equipment intentionally placed in contact with combustibles; deliberate overloads on circuits.

- **Tools** — Those used for forcible entry, such as crowbars, screwdrivers, hammers, etc. (Figure 16.22).

- **Oily rags** — The ash from an oily rag retains its shape and may be identifiable.

- **Newspapers** — These often are used as the initial fuel. Undisturbed ash may still be readable, and headlines, dates, etc., can be photographed.

- **Burn patterns** — They may be consistent with the use of flammable liquids.

- **Highway flares (fusees)** — Striker can be used to trace the source of the flare and may yield fingerprints. The nail contained in some highway flares also may be located (Figure 16.23).

- **Financial papers** — Demands for payments, etc., may have been left intentionally where they would burn.

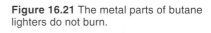

Figure 16.21 The metal parts of butane lighters do not burn.

Figure 16.19 A typical trailer.

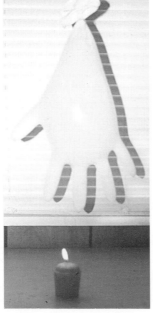

Figure 16.20 Rubber containers are often used by arsonists.

Figure 16.22 Tools left at the scene may have been used by the perpetrator.

Figure 16.23 The remains of a road flare.

- **Valuable items replaced with cheaper ones** — Sometimes valuable furnishings are listed on the inventory, but only inexpensive furnishings are found in the debris.

- **Items present/missing** — Things that should not be there, but are; things that should be there, but are not. A gasoline can in a bedroom closet requires explanation. Outbuildings and storage areas may contain valuable items or those with sentimental value that were removed from the building before the fire.

- **Signs of forced entry** — Jimmy marks on doors or windows, doors broken in.

- **Anything unusual or out of place** — Combustibles arranged in a way that makes them more susceptible to ignition; items in rooms where they are not normally found — for example, a gasoline can in a bedroom closet.

- **Bridges or access roads blocked, damaged, or destroyed; address numbers removed or obliterated; gates or doors locked or barricaded** — Anything that might impede the response of the fire department.

- **Smoke/heat detectors removed or disabled, or automatic sprinklers shut off.**

- **Windows covered or blacked out to delay discovery of the fire**.

If any of these conditions are found at the scene, a more thorough investigation is warranted, and the company officer must follow departmental protocols for calling an investigator. Pending the arrival of the investigator, the company officer's responsibilities are to control the scene, protect the evidence, and inform the investigator of what has been found. For more information about fire and arson investigation, see the IFSTA **Introduction to Fire Origin and Cause** manual or NFPA 921, *Guide for Fire and Explosion Investigations*.

Even after a fire investigator arrives on scene and assumes control of the investigation, the company officer's job is not finished. The company officer and his subordinates may be asked to assist with the investigation. If so, this is a tremendous opportunity for them to learn about the art and science of fire investigation. But even if company personnel are not included in the investigation, they still have work to do — they still must write the required reports on the incident.

[NFPA 1021: 2-5.1]

The company officer at least must submit a company-level incident report (sometimes called a "run report") to his supervisor. Even though this report may be only one of several that make up a comprehensive report on that incident, it may be used in a variety of ways. At the very least, it will become part of the statistical data reflecting the jurisdiction's fire history for that period. It also may be used to help the department choose where and how to focus fire prevention and public education efforts. It ultimately may be used as evidence in court, and if so, its credibility may be judged by how it is written. Therefore, the company officer's report must be complete, clear, and above all, factual.

Completeness. The report must describe all pertinent details of the company's involvement in the incident — from the time of alarm until the company was released from the incident. This can sometimes be a challenge, but it is a very important part of the report's credibility. If any salient point is omitted, the obvious question that follows is, "What else has been left out?" If necessary, the company officer should use a checklist to make sure that all important points have been addressed.

Clarity. Even if the report is very comprehensive, if it is written in a way that intentionally or unintentionally obscures important information, its value will be greatly diminished, and its veracity may be challenged. The company officer must use words and phrases that are least likely to be misinterpreted or misunderstood. Keeping a dictionary and thesaurus handy when writing reports is a good habit for company officers to develop.

Factuality. While the other two writing characteristics are important, they pale in comparison to the factuality of the report. In this context, factuality has nothing to do with the writer's honesty; it has to do with assumptions and interpretations.

In writing their incident reports, company officers must avoid making assumptions. For example, if on arrival at the fire, the company officer noticed that all the windows in the building were broken. He must not assume that they were broken out by someone trying to provide more oxygen to the fire and accelerate its spread. The windows may have been blown out by an explosion within the building or may have been broken by the heat of the fire. The report should describe what the company officer and the firefighters saw, not what they may have assumed because of what they saw.

Equally important to the report's factuality is that the company officer not interpret the facts. He may interpret certain behavior exhibited by someone at the scene to mean one thing, while in reality, it means something else. For example, motorists who have driven through a cloud of chlorine gas can exhibit the same behavior as some who is intoxicated from excessive alcohol consumption. Therefore, it is very important that when documenting their involvement in an incident, company officers only report the facts and not attempt to interpret them.

Summary

Company officers are responsible for securing the fire scene and protecting possible evidence until the cause of the fire has been determined. In many fire departments, company officers are also responsible for making the preliminary cause determination. These requirements dictate that company officers have a good understanding of fire behavior, investigation techniques, and the importance of documentation.

Section VI • Emergency Service Delivery

Chapter 17 • Job Performance Requirements

This chapter provides information that will assist the reader in meeting the following job performance requirements from NFPA 1021, *Standard for Fire Officer Professional Qualifications*, 1997 edition. The colored portions indicate the topics addressed in the chapter. The numbers of the job performance requirements are also noted directly in the sections of text where they are addressed. Those in the following list that are denoted with an asterisk (*) are global in nature and are covered by reading the chapter in its entirety.

Fire Officer I

2-6.1*   Develop a pre-incident plan, given an assigned facility and preplanning policies, procedures, and forms, so that all required elements are identified and the appropriate forms are completed and processed in accordance with policies and procedures.

(a) Prerequisite Knowledge: Elements of a preincident plan, basic building construction, basic fire protection systems and features, basic water supply, basic fuel loading, and fire growth and development.

(b) Prerequisite Skills: The ability to write reports, to communicate verbally, and to evaluate skills.

Pre-Incident Planning

Every emergency incident is, to a greater or lesser extent, an uncontrolled situation. For the emergency personnel involved in trying to bring that situation under control, the fewer things they have to think about and the fewer on-scene decisions they have to make, the more they can concentrate on the decisions involved in mitigating the emergency itself. Therefore, the success or failure of emergency operations often depends upon the amount of knowledge that the emergency personnel have about the environment in which they are operating and on the amount of pre-incident planning that was done. Pre-incident planning allows the fire department to anticipate the resources and procedures needed to meet special demands within its jurisdiction. A current and well-written pre-incident plan gives the company officer and the members of his company the information needed to devise and implement a successful incident action plan.

This chapter discusses the nature and purposes of pre-incident surveys and how to conduct them. Also discussed are what to look for in various types of occupancies as well as developing pre-incident plans and managing pre-incident data.

The Pre-Incident Survey

Although gathering information about a particular building or occupancy during a pre-incident survey is often referred to as pre-incident planning, information gathering is only one part of the process. Pre-incident planning is the entire process of gathering and evaluating information, developing procedures, and keeping the information current.

Company officers, and their department administrations, also need to understand the difference between pre-incident surveys and code enforcement inspections. Pre-incident surveys and code enforcement inspections

are sometimes conducted by the same personnel because departments require their companies to perform both functions in one visit. But pre-incident surveys and code enforcement inspections are conducted for entirely different purposes and should *not* be combined. When company-level personnel conduct a code enforcement inspection, of course they become more familiar with the occupancy simply by being there, but their attention is focused on the code requirements for that occupancy. They are there to see that the occupant has done everything that the code requires to prevent fires from occurring and that will allow the occupants to get out if and when a fire does occur.

On the other hand, pre-incident surveys are conducted to provide the emergency response personnel with information about the occupancy that they will need should a fire or other emergency develop on the premises. During the survey they concentrate on where and how fires are most likely to occur and how those fires are likely to behave. Their focus is on what is likely to happen and what they will need in order to mitigate those contingencies. They also focus on any potential hazards to firefighter safety that may exist on the premises — hazardous materials or processes, high-voltage equipment, unprotected openings, and extreme elevation differences, to name a few. In short, they are there to determine what firefighters will need to know about the occupancy in order to function there safely when their vision is totally obscured by darkness and/or smoke. They are also there to determine whether the department is adequately prepared to deal safely and successfully with the emergencies that are most likely to occur in that occupancy. They are there to answer such questions as *"Are current strategic plans and tactical procedures appropriate, or do new ones need to be developed?"* and *"Does the initial alarm assignment include sufficient resources, or will additional resources or mutual aid be needed?"* and other similar questions.

In some jurisdictions, the sheer number of commercial, multifamily residential, and industrial occupancies in each district make it virtually impossible for the responsible companies to conduct pre-incident surveys in all of them; therefore, companies must prioritize the occupancies to be surveyed. The priorities are normally based on the life safety risk (including the risk to firefighters), the property values at risk, and the likelihood of fires or other emergencies occurring. Once these *target hazards* (occupancies with the highest priority) have been identified, the responsible companies can focus their efforts on those occupancies.

As mentioned earlier, pre-incident planning involves more than just the pre-incident survey. Pre-incident planning actually consists of three separate functions:

- Conducting the pre-incident survey (Figure 17.1)
- Developing pre-incident plans (Figure 17.2)
- Managing pre-incident data (Figure 17.3)

Facility Survey Equipment

Before a survey can be conducted, the company must be provided with the proper tools and equipment, and the survey visit must be scheduled. The personnel conducting the survey must have the tools and equipment needed to gather and document the information necessary to develop a complete pre-incident plan. The equipment needed may vary depending upon what is specified in the department's guideline and the nature of the occupancy to be surveyed (Figure 17.4). However, most pre-incident survey kits include the following:

- Writing equipment (tablet, pens, pencils, pencil sharpener, eraser, clipboard, and any department facility survey forms)
- Drawing equipment (engineering or graph paper, straightedge, and a copy of the NFPA standard symbols or those used by the department)

Other equipment (flashlight, water-pressure gauge, camera, and a 50- or 100-foot [15 m or 30 m] measuring tape)

The members of the survey team will need at least one portable radio if they will remain in service during the survey (Figure 17.5). They will also need appropriate personal protection such as helmets, eye protection, gloves, and hearing protection if ambient noise is excessive (Figure 17.6).

Scheduling Pre-Incident Surveys

In some fire departments, company officers are required to schedule their own pre-incident survey visits; in others, scheduling is done by someone else, and the company officer is merely informed of the arrangements. Either approach will work. The former allows the company officer more control over the company's schedule, and the latter allows for departmentwide coordination of effort. Regardless of who makes the arrangements, the visits should be scheduled at times that are convenient for the building occupants. For example, it would be counterproductive to schedule a pre-incident survey at a large retail store during the Christmas shopping season. If the occupants are not unduly inconvenienced by the visit, they are more likely to be cooperative with the survey team and more likely to be positively impressed with the effort. However, even at the risk of inconveniencing the occupants, the visits should be scheduled at times that will allow the survey team to get a realistic picture of the activities that normally take place in the building and of the normal number of occupants at various times of the day and night.

Another consideration regarding the scheduling of pre-incident survey visits relates to the department's fire prevention and code enforcement program. It would be unwise to schedule a pre-incident survey visit to any building that has had a recent code enforcement inspec-

Figure 17.1 The survey helps crews become more familiar with the occupancy.

Figure 17.2 The information gathered is converted into a plan.

Figure 17.3 Managing the data is an ongoing problem.

Figure 17.4 Typical survey tools and equipment.

Figure 17.5 The crew will need at least one radio.

Figure 17.6 PPE may be needed.

tion — especially if the same personnel perform both functions — because the occupants may perceive the survey visit to be another inspection. This misperception can make the occupants feel as though they are being harassed, so it is important that this situation be avoided. For the same reason, it is very important that the company officer carefully explains to the occupants the reasons for the pre-incident survey, the planning process, and how the occupants will benefit from them.

Public Relations During the Survey

Much of the success of the departmental pre-incident planning program relies on the manner in which the pre-incident survey team members conduct themselves and on the image they project. To be successful, facility survey teams must present a positive public image. Throughout the survey, the team members should stay together and conduct themselves in a businesslike manner. The company officer is responsible for seeing that this is done.

Team members should be in a uniform appropriate to the situation. In mercantile and office buildings, clean, crisp station uniforms are usually appropriate (Figure 17.7). In other occupancies, coveralls and safety equipment (helmets, safety glasses, etc.) may be needed. The mode of dress should be the uniform equivalent of what the occupants wear.

Conducting the survey in a courteous but businesslike manner is also critically important. The team is on the premises to do a job—not to socialize among themselves or with the employees of the business. Team members should be friendly but not familiar. They should courteously answer any questions that they are asked, but they should avoid engaging in extended conversations that might keep employees from their work.

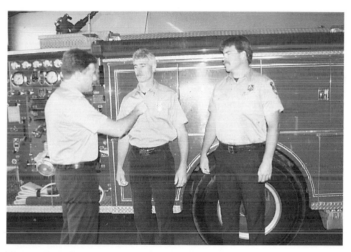

Figure 17.7 Company members should look sharp.

Conducting the Pre-Incident Survey

The most common method of obtaining the information on which to base pre-incident plans consists of sending one or more companies to a selected site to survey the facility (Figure 17.8). As mentioned earlier, the survey team's focus during the facility survey is dictated by the department policy as set forth in guidelines for pre-incident planning, and company officers are responsible for knowing and following these guidelines. Pre-incident surveys are usually conducted by company-level personnel for the following reasons:

- To allow firefighters to become familiar with the building, its physical layout and design, any built-in fire protection systems, and any hazards that may exist

- To allow firefighters to visualize and discuss how fire is likely to behave in the occupancy and how existing strategies and tactics might apply to an incident there

- To allow firefighters to identify critical conditions that were not noted during or that have changed since any previous facility surveys

Considering these points, pre-incident surveys serve a twofold purpose: information gathering and training. As the personnel conduct the survey to gather information, they also have an opportunity to consider various scenarios and to discuss the tactics and resources that would be needed to safely and effectively deal with each of these contingencies. For example, the members of the survey team can discuss how the situation would change if the occupant load is significantly different during the day and at night. They can also discuss how to make the best use of built-in fire protection systems, such as automatic sprinklers, and how building features, such as fire walls, can be used to confine a fire to one section of the building (Figure 17.9). Additionally, they can discuss how to deal with obstacles such as metal-clad doors or overhead power lines (Figure 17.10).

Some departments require that upon arrival at the survey location, company members remain at the apparatus while the company officer contacts the occupant, confirms the appointment, and reviews the survey procedure (Figure 17.11). The officer should inform the occupant of how many company members will be involved in the facility survey and request any assistance the team may need from the occupant. The company officer should also explain that, while the facility survey is not a code enforcement inspection, any serious fire or life safety hazards found will have to be corrected. When serious hazards are found, the best approach is to attempt to obtain an on-the-spot correction and to follow up with a memo to the fire prevention bureau.

After initial contact with the occupant, company members can begin the exterior facility survey of the building. Primarily, the exterior facility survey focuses on obtaining the necessary information for the plot plan. The building should be measured and its dimensions recorded, including distances from it to exposures. The location of fire hydrants and valves, utility shutoffs, fences, landscaping, power lines, obstructions, sprinkler and standpipe connections, and any underground tanks should be noted on the plot plan. During the exterior survey, information about any exposures should be gathered. The building height can be determined while doing the exterior facility survey; however, the exterior of the building is not a good vantage point for gathering construction information. Many buildings are faced with brick or stone or are covered with aluminum siding (Figure 17.12). Any ornamental facings, awnings, or marquees should be noted during the exterior facility survey (Figure 17.13). The locations of doors, windows, and fire escapes should also be noted (Figure 17.14).

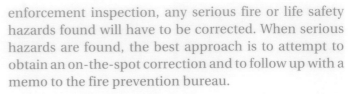

Figure 17.8 A company arrives for a pre-incident survey.

Figure 17.11 In some departments, the crew waits while the company officer makes contact.

Figure 17.9 Crew members can become familiar with building features that would be useful during a fire.

Figure 17.10 Potential forcible entry problems are identified.

Figure 17.12 Some buildings have false fronts that may fall in a fire.

Figure 17.13 Awnings and marquees should be noted.

Figure 17.14 Means of entry and egress should be noted.

Figure 17.15 Potential hazards to firefighters are identified.

Figure 17.16 Fire protection systems should be noted.

After the exterior has been surveyed, the company may move either to the roof of the building or to the lowest floor. Unless dictated by department policy, the starting point is a matter of personal preference, but most people prefer to start on the roof. Then personnel conduct the interior survey systematically working downward, drawing a floor plan of each floor that shows the location of permanent walls, partitions, fixtures, and machinery. Furniture should not be included in the floor plan because its location is not fixed. The locations of any vertical shafts and horizontal openings should be noted (Figure 17.15). The location of any fire protection equipment should be included on the floor plan, as should any life safety information (Figure 17.16).

During the survey, company officers must remain focused on the major considerations involved. These considerations are *life safety, fire control,* and *property conservation.* The first priority of the facility survey is to identify life safety concerns. Life safety information is collected in two basic areas: the protection and evacuation of occupants and the protection of the firefighters. Information about occupant protection that should be gathered and recorded includes the following:

- Location and number of exits
- Location of escalators and elevators
- Location of windows and other openings suitable for rescue access
- Special evacuation considerations such as disabled occupants, very old or very young occupants, and large numbers of occupants
- Location of areas of safe refuge
- Flammable and toxic interior finishes or processes

As firefighters gather and record information about occupant life safety, they should also be gathering information about conditions in the building that may threaten or enhance their own safety (Figure 17.17). Some of the potential life hazards to the firefighters are the following:

- Flammable and combustible liquids
- Toxic chemicals
- Explosives
- Reactive metals
- Radioactive materials
- Processes performed in the building that are inherently dangerous

In addition to gathering and recording information about the contents of the building, physical conditions of the structure that may be hazardous during a fire should be noted. Such conditions include:

- Structural components that may fail during a fire
- Construction materials that might lose their strength when exposed to fire (unprotected steel, for example)
- Ornamental building fascia, awnings, and marquees
- Unsupported partitions or walls
- Roof construction
- Conditions in the building that can become dangerous during a fire
- Stacked or high-piled storage
- Heavy objects on the roof that can cause roof collapse
- Heavy equipment that may fall through a floor or cause the floor to collapse
- Building features that may confuse or trap firefighters during a fire

Figure 17.17 The survey may reveal especially hazardous areas.

- Large open areas
- Dead-end corridors or hallways
- Open vats, pits, or shafts
- Openings into underground utility shafts or tunnels
- Multilevel floor arrangement
- Mazelike room divisions or partitions
- Alterations that disguise the original construction

Basic Building Construction

Some of the most useful information that company officers can and should gather during a pre-incident survey is how the building is constructed. Because each type of building construction behaves differently under fire conditions, company officers must be able to identify the various types during pre-incident surveys. Knowing how stable or unstable different materials and assemblies are under fire conditions allows appropriate plans and procedures to be developed that will allow firefighters to do their jobs with the greatest level of safety.

Types of Building Construction

Each building code classifies building construction in different terms. In general, construction classifications are based upon materials used in construction and upon hourly fire-resistance ratings of structural components. Most building codes have the same five construction classifications but may use different terms to describe each classification. For the purposes of this manual, the terms used will be those from NFPA 220, *Standard on Types of Building Construction,* which are consistent with those used in the National Fire Incident Reporting Systems (NFIRS). This standard uses Roman numerals to designate the five major classifications (Type I through

V). Each classification is further broken down into subtypes using a three-digit Arabic number code or several letters, such as Type I-443, in which:

- The first digit refers to the fire resistance rating (in hours) of the exterior bearing walls.
- The second digit refers to the fire resistance rating (in hours) of structural frames or columns and girders that support loads of more than one floor.
- The third digit indicates the fire resistance rating (in hours) of the floor construction.

The various types of construction and the degree of fire resistance of each is shown in Table 17.1. Construction classifications are further explained in the following sections:

Type I construction. Also called *fire-resistive construction* in some codes, Type I construction consists of structural members, including walls, columns, beams, floors, and roofs, that are made of noncombustible or limited combustible materials (Figure 17.18). Buildings of this type were originally designed to confine any fire and its resulting products of combustion to a given location. Because of the limited combustibility of the materials of construction, the primary fuel load is the contents of the structure. The ability of Type I construction to confine the fire to a certain area can be compromised by openings made in partitions and by improperly designed and dampered central heating and air-conditioning systems.

Type II construction. Also called *noncombustible* or *noncombustible/limited combustible construction,* Type II construction is similar to Type I except that the degree of fire resistance is lower (Figure 17.19). In some cases,

Figure 17.18 Type-I construction.

Figure 17.19 Type-II construction.

Table 17.1
Fire Resistance Requirements for Type I Through Type V Construction

	Type I		Type II			Type III		Type IV	Type V	
	443	332	222	111	000	211	200	2HH	111	000
Exterior Bearing Walls —										
Supporting more than one floor, columns, or other bearing walls	4	3	2	1	0^1	2	2	2	1	0^1
Supporting one floor only	4	3	2	1	0^1	2	2	2	1	0^1
Supporting a roof only	4	3	1	1	0^1	2	2	2	1	0^1
Interior Bearing Walls —										
Supporting more than one floor, columns, or other bearing walls	4	3	2	1	0	1	0	2	1	0
Supporting one floor only	3	2	2	1	0	1	0	1	1	0
Supporting roofs only	3	2	1	1	0	1	0	1	1	0
Columns —										
Supporting more than one floor, bearing walls, or other columns	4	3	2	1	0	1	0	H^2	1	0
Supporting one floor only	3	2	2	1	0	1	0	H^2	1	0
Supporting roofs only	3	2	1	1	0	1	0	H^2	1	0
Beams, Girders, Trusses & Arches —										
Supporting more than one floor, bearing walls, or other columns	4	3	2	1	0	1	0	H^2	1	0
Supporting one floor only	3	2	2	1	0	1	0	H^2	1	0
Supporting roofs only	3	2	1	1	0	1	0	H^2	1	0
Floor Construction	3	2	2	1	0	1	0	H^2	1	0
Roof Construction	2	1½	1	1	0	1	0	H^2	1	0
Exterior Nonbearing Walls	0^1	0^1	0^1	0^1	0^1	0^1	0^1	0^1	0^1	0^1

Those members listed that are permitted to be of approved combustible material.

[1] Requirements for fire resistance of exterior walls located in close proximity to property lines, other buildings, or exposures, the provision of spandrel wall sections and the limitation of protection of wall openings are not related to construction type. They need to be specified in other standards and codes, where appropriate, and may be required in addition to the requirements of this standard for the type of construction.

[2] "H" indicates heavy timber members; see text for requirements.

Reprinted with permisson from NFPA 220, *Standard on Types of Building Construction,* Copyright© 1995, National Fire Protection Association, Quincy, MA 02269. This reprinted material is not the complete and official position of the National Fire Protection Association, on the referenced subject which is represented only by the standard in its entirety.

materials with no fire-resistance rating, such as untreated wood, may be used. Again, the primary fuel load is the contents of the building. The heat buildup from a fire in the building can cause structural supports to fail. Another potential problem is the type of roof on the building. Type II construction buildings often have flat, built-up roofs (Figure 17.20). These roofs may contain combustible felt (tar paper) and roofing tar. Fire extension to the roof can eventually cause the entire roof to become involved and fail.

Type III construction. Commonly referred to as *ordinary construction,* Type III construction consists of exterior walls and structural members that are of noncombustible or limited combustible materials (Figure 17.21). Interior structural members, including walls, columns, beams, floors, and roofs, may be completely or partially constructed of wood. The wood used in these members is of smaller dimensions than required for Type IV, heavy timber construction. The primary fire concern specific to Type III construction is the problem of fire and smoke spread through concealed spaces between the walls, floors, and ceiling. Heat from a fire may be conducted to these concealed spaces through finish materials, such as drywall or plaster, or the heat can enter the concealed spaces through holes in the finish materials. From there, the heat, smoke, and gases may be communicated to other parts of the structure. If enough heat is present, the fire may actually burn within the concealed spaces and feed on the combustible construction materials in the space. These hazards can be reduced if fire-stops are placed inside the concealed spaces to limit the spread of the combustion by-products.

Type IV construction. Also called *heavy timber construction*, Type IV construction consists of exterior and interior walls and their associated structural members that are of noncombustible or limited combustible materials (Figure 17.22). Other interior structural members, including beams, columns, arches, floors, and roofs, are made of solid or laminated wood with no concealed spaces. These wooden members must be of large enough dimensions to be considered heavy timber. The dimensions that qualify as heavy timber vary depending on the particular code being used, but it is usually defined as being at least 8 inches (200 mm) in its smallest dimension.

Type V construction. In this type of construction, exterior walls, bearing walls, columns, beams, girders, trusses, arches, floors, and roofs may be entirely or partially of wood or other approved combustible material. Just as in Type III construction, Type V construction differs from Type IV mainly in the smaller dimensions of the structural members. Buildings of Type V construction are typically wood frame structures used for many mercantile occupancies, most single-family and multifamily residences, and other free-standing structures up to about six stories in height (Figure 17.23).

Types of Roofs

The basic purpose of a roof is to protect the inside of a building from exposure to snow, wind, rain, etc. However, the roof also provides for a controllable interior

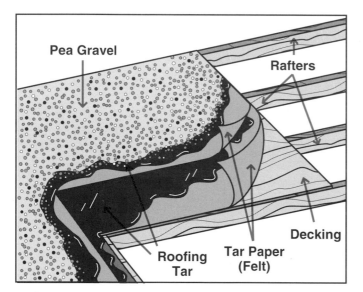

Figure 17.20 Some Type-II buildings have flat roofs.

Figure 17.22 Type-IV construction.

Figure 17.21 Type-III construction.

Figure 17.23 Type-V construction.

environment, enhances the architectural style of a building, and contributes to the functional purpose of the building. An example of a roof designed around function is a domed roof over a sports arena.

The primary concern for firefighter safety is a roof's susceptibility to sudden and unexpected collapse because of its supporting structure being weakened by the fire. Beyond that, the combustibility of the surface of a roof is a basic concern to the fire safety of an entire community. Roofs which can be easily ignited by flaming brands have been a frequent cause of major conflagrations. The danger of easily ignited roof coverings has been recognized for hundreds of years and some of the first fire regulations in America imposed restrictions on combustible roof materials.

Flat roofs. Most commonly found on commercial, industrial, and apartment buildings, flat roofs may or may not have a slight slope to facilitate water drainage. Flat roofs are often penetrated by chimneys, vent pipes, shafts, scuttles, and skylights. The roof may be surrounded and/or divided by parapets, and it may support water tanks, air-conditioning equipment, antennas, and other objects that add to the dead load of the building and that may interfere with ventilation operations (Figure 17.24).

The structural part of the flat roof is generally similar to the construction of a floor that consists of wooden, concrete, or metal joists covered with sheathing. The sheathing is often covered with a layer of insulating material and is always covered by a finish layer of some weather-resistant material. In some installations, flat roofs do not employ joist and sheathing construction but are constructed of poured, reinforced concrete or lightweight concrete, precast gypsum, or concrete slabs set within metal joists. Another form of flat roof, referred to as *lightweight construction* or *panelized roofing*, is discussed later in this chapter.

The best way to determine the material from which a roof is constructed is through pre-incident planning surveys while the building is still under construction. The materials used in flat roof construction dictate the type of equipment that will be needed to breach it.

Pitched roofs. These roofs have a peak along one edge or in the center, and the deck slopes downward from the peak to one, two, or all edges (Figure 17.25). The slope of a pitched roof may vary from gradual to steep, but it is always more pronounced than those of flat roofs. Pitched roof construction consists of timber rafters or metal trusses that run from the ridge to a wall plate on top of the outer wall at the eaves level (Figure 17.26). The rafters or trusses that carry the sloping roof can be made of various materials. Sheathing boards or panels are usually ap-

Figure 17.24 Some flat roofs carry heavy dead loads.

Figure 17.25 A typical pitched roof.

Figure 17.26 Typical pitched roof framing.

plied directly onto the rafters. Pitched roofs usually have a covering of roofing paper (felt) applied before shingles are laid. Shingles may be wood, metal, composition, asbestos, slate, or tile.

Pitched roofs on barns, churches, supermarkets, and industrial buildings are usually covered with shingles but may have roll felt applied over the sheathing, which then has been mopped with asphalt roofing tar. In other installations, instead of wood sheathing, gypsum slabs, approximately 2 inches (50 mm) thick, may be laid between metal trusses. These variations should be determined during pre-incident surveys.

Arched roofs. This type of roof is used on a wide variety of building types. One form of arched roof construction uses the bow-string trusses as the main supporting members (Figure 17.27). The lower chord of the trusses may be covered with a ceiling to form an enclosed cockloft or roof space. Such concealed, unvented spaces may contribute to the spread of a fire and early failure of the roof.

Trussless arched roofs, sometimes called *lamella roofs*, are made up of relatively short timbers of uniform length. These timbers are beveled and bored at the ends where they are bolted together at an angle to form an interlocking network of structural timbers. This network forms an arch of mutually braced and stiffened timbers. Being an arch rather than a truss, the roof exerts a horizontal reaction in addition to the vertical reaction on supporting structural components. In trussless arch construction, all parts of the underside of the roof are visible. A hole of considerable size may be cut or burned through the network sheathing and roofing any place without causing collapse of the roof structure, instead the loads are distributed to less damaged timbers around the opening.

Concrete roofs. The use of precast concrete is very popular in certain types of construction. Precast roof slabs are available in many shapes, sizes, and designs. These precast slabs are hauled to the construction site, ready for use. In other cases, the roof structure is formed and the concrete poured on site. Roofs of either precast or reinforced concrete are extremely difficult to breach, so another means of gaining access or ventilating the building should be used whenever possible. However, these roofs are virtually impervious to fire, so they are some of the most stable roof types.

A popular lightweight material made of gypsum plaster and portland cement mixed with fillers, such as perlite, vermiculite, or sand, provides a lightweight floor and roof assembly. This material is sometimes referred to as *lightweight concrete*. Lightweight precast planks are manufactured from this material, and the slabs are reinforced with steel mesh or rods. Lightweight concrete roofs are usually finished with roofing felt and a mopping of hot tar to make them weather-resistant.

Lightweight concrete roof decks may also be poured in place over permanent form boards, steel roof decking, paper-backed mesh, or metal rib lath (Figure 17.28). These lightweight concrete slabs are relatively easy to penetrate. Some types of lightweight concrete can be penetrated with a hammer-head pick, power saw with concrete blade, jackhammer, or any other penetrating tool. These roofs are also very stable under fire conditions.

Metal roofs. These roof coverings are made from several different kinds of metal and are constructed in many styles (Figure 17.29). Light-gauge-steel roof decks are most often supported on a framework of steel or wooden trusses. Other types of corrugated roofing sheets are made from light-gauge cold-formed steel, galvanized sheet metal, or aluminum. The light-gauge cold-formed steel sheets are used primarily for the roofs of industrial buildings. Metal roofs on industrial buildings often have numerous roof openings, such as skylights and hatches, that can be used for ventilating a fire. Generally, metal roofs are lighter in weight per unit area than other types of roofs. Therefore, unless the supporting structure is weakened by a fire, metal roofs may be less prone to collapse than other types of roofs.

Lightweight Construction

Roof and floor construction in many commercial buildings no longer includes conventional construction materials and designs. Conventional construction – traditionally, assemblies made of lumber — has been replaced with what has come to be called *lightweight construction*. In this type of construction, plywood panels (called *panelized roofing*) are supported by purlins between laminated wooden beams or gusseted wooden trusses that span from outside wall to outside wall (Figure 17.30). Conventional subfloor construction has been

Figure 17.27 A typical arched roof.

Figure 17.28 Lightweight concrete roofs often have metal decking.

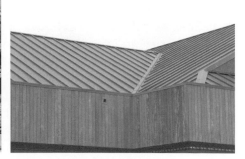

Figure 17.29 A typical metal roof.

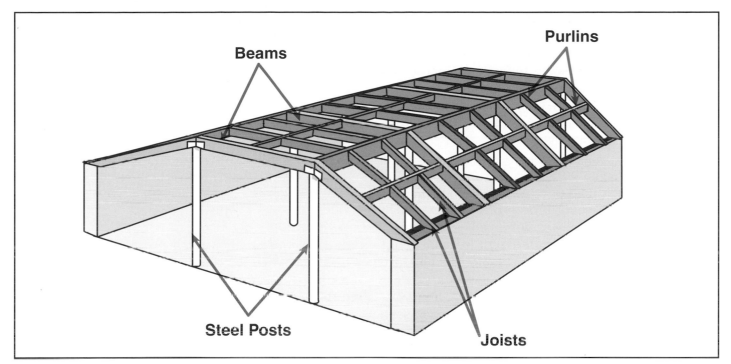

Beams **Purlins**

Steel Posts **Joists**

Figure 17.30 A panelized roof system.

replaced by open web trusses or wooden I-beams (Figure 17.31). Compared to conventional construction, these systems are much lighter per unit area and are generally less prone to collapse. However, roof or floor systems supported by open web trusses *are* prone to sudden and unexpected collapse if the unsupported bottom chord is subjected to downward force, such as when firefighters inadvertently pull on them when pulling ceiling panels with pike poles.

Fuel Loading

Because the materials used in the construction of most modern commercial and mercantile buildings contribute relatively little fuel to a fire, the major source of fuel is the furnishings and other contents of the building (Figure 17.32). The contents of a building represent the bulk of the fuel available to burn — its *fuel load*. When company officers assess the fuel load of buildings during pre-incident surveys, and subsequently devise plans for dealing with the fires that may feed on this load, they are primarily addressing the fire control considerations of pre-incident planning.

Because different materials behave differently during a fire, different fire control procedures may have to be used depending upon what is burning. Therefore, knowing what combustibles a building contains can have a profound effect on firefighter safety and on the tactics and strategies employed during a fire. And, because it may be impossible to identify the building's contents after a fire starts, it is imperative that this information be

Figure 17.31 Many floor assemblies are supported by open web trusses.

Figure 17.32 Some buildings contain a heavy fuel load.

gathered beforehand—during pre-incident surveys. This is especially important in buildings in which toxic, highly flammable, or explosive materials are stored or used. During pre-incident surveys, company officers should be sure to document the existence of large quantities of plastics, aerosols, compressed gases, explosives, flammable liquids, combustible liquids, combustible dusts, and corrosive materials (Figure 17.33).

Fire Protection Systems

Another important item to be checked during the pre-incident survey is any built-in fire protection equipment and systems. Because this is not a code enforcement inspection, there is no need for the survey team to test this equipment, but rather merely to note its presence and condition and to evaluate its usefulness during a fire in the premises. Naturally, if the team observes some condition that would reduce the effectiveness of such equipment, such as stock piled in a way that blocked one or more sprinklers, they should report it to the occupant and suggest the corrective action needed. However, during the survey, they should remain focused on their primary mission — gathering the information that will be needed by the fire suppression forces during a fire or other emergency on the premises.

For purposes of developing a pre-incident plan for the premises, the survey team should pay particular attention to the presence and condition of *fixed extinguishing systems, standpipe systems*, and *fire detection and alarm*

systems. Fixed extinguishing systems (automatic sprinklers, CO_2 or dry chemical flooding systems, etc.) may reduce the need for interior attack lines but increase the need for system support (Figure 17.34). Standpipe systems may allow firefighters to carry hose packs into the building rather than lay long attack lines from an engine outside (Figure 17.35). Fire detection and alarm systems may allow fires to be detected and reported sooner, the first-in unit to arrive sooner, and firefighters to face smaller fires than might develop in the absence of such systems.

Water Supply

Another critically important aspect of pre-incident planning relates to water supply (Figure 17.36). Because water is still the cheapest, most widely available extinguishing agent, it will be the primary extinguishing agent used in most cases. Assessing the availability and reliability of the water supply is a key element in the development of any pre-incident plan. The pre-incident survey of any given occupancy should gather the following water supply information:

- Required fire flow
- Available fire flow
- Location(s) of supply
- Reliability of supply
- Auxiliary supply

Figure 17.35 Functioning standpipes may reduce the need for long attack lines.

Figure 17.33 Some buildings contain highly flammable materials.

Figure 17.34 A functioning sprinkler system may mean that fewer hoselines will be needed.

Figure 17.36 The amount of water available should be determined.

- Water system interconnections
- Water supply utilization methods

Given this information, critical decisions about the number and types of other needed water supply resources can be reflected in the pre-incident plan. If a reliable water supply of sufficient quantity is available on-site, personnel and equipment that might otherwise be needed to shuttle water will be available for rescue, fire attack, or other duties. On the other hand, if the water supply is marginal, the plan must anticipate the need for additional personnel and equipment to make up for the deficiency.

The pre-incident survey should identify the exact location of fire hydrants and the amount of water available from them (Figure 17.37). The sizes and locations of water mains serving the occupancy should be determined. If hydrant systems and water mains are not available, pre-incident plans must include provisions for using alternative sources to deliver sufficient water to the scene by long supply hoses, pumpers with large tanks, or water tenders (Figure 17.38).

Property Conservation

Another major consideration to be addressed during pre-incident surveys is *property conservation*. While conducting facility surveys, company officers and their subordinates should continuously ask themselves what can be done before a fire occurs and while one is being fought

in order to reduce property loss. They should start by identifying the building's contents with the highest value. Depending upon the occupancy, these high-value items may include files and records, electronic equipment, machinery, merchandise, antiques, or any irreplaceable items (Figure 17.39). Such items may require that special salvage procedures be developed.

A major property conservation consideration that should be addressed during pre-incident surveys is the use of water as the primary extinguishing agent. Regardless of whether the water is likely to be delivered by an automatic sprinkler system or by fire department hoselines, its possible effects must be assessed. In many cases, the water used to extinguish a fire can do more damage than the fire itself. In addition to the damage that can be done to papers, books, and electronic equipment, if a large quantity of water is absorbed by materials in the building, the weight of the water can threaten the building's structural integrity. Dealing with this potentially significant safety consideration, as well as the property conservation considerations, can require careful planning if some extremely undesirable outcomes are to be avoided. The building may contain features that will help prevent the accumulation of water, such as floor drains, scuppers, or other drains (Figure 17.40). Stairways, halls, and other passages through which large volumes of water (including contaminated runoff) may be channeled to the outside should be noted during these surveys.

Figure 17.38 Water for fire fighting may have to be hauled in. *Courtesy of John Hawkins.*

Figure 17.37 In some cases, flow tests should be done.

Figure 17.39 Some occupancies may contain many high-value items.

Figure 17.40 Floor drains can help prevent excessive property damage.

Developing Pre-Incident Plans

[NFPA 1021 2-6.1]

Upon completion of the on-site visit, the company officer is responsible for processing the information gathered — either using it to develop a pre-incident plan or forwarding it to those responsible for developing the plan. Even though pre-incident planning may involve a collective effort by all levels within the department, it begins with the company performing the on-site facility survey. The success of the entire pre-incident planning process depends upon the ability of the company to conduct adequate pre-incident surveys and the company officer's ability to forward complete, accurately written reports and information.

There are two general schools of thought about what should and should not be included in a pre-incident plan. Each of these approaches has certain advantages and disadvantages. The first approach assumes that all interior structure fires behave in generally the same way — and that this behavior is predictable unless there is something in the fire environment to make it behave differently. Those who subscribe to this approach do not want a large volume of data about the building and its contents. Beyond certain essential information, such as the basic floor plan and the locations of utility controls, they only want to know what will make this fire behave differently than any other fire in a similar structure. This approach has the advantage of being simple to develop, use, and maintain. Some incident commanders prefer this type of plan because they do not have to filter the essential information they need from many pages of extraneous data. The key to using this approach successfully is making sure that the plan contains all essential data and enough additional information to make it complete (Figure 17.41). However, even with this "essentials-only" approach, the larger the structure and the more complex the occupancy, the more data will be needed to develop a complete plan.

The other approach to pre-incident plan development is much more involved and much more structured. It is more involved in that the volume of information gathered on every structure and occupancy surveyed is extensive. It is more structured in that the same items of information are gathered on every structure and occupancy surveyed, regardless of how similar or different the structures are from each other. The main advantage of this approach is that the likelihood of some critical item of information being omitted from the plan is extremely low. However, it may take the incident commander a considerable amount of time and effort during an emergency to find the critical information within a large mass of data.

One advantage to using this approach to pre-incident planning is that there are some well-developed national standards that can be and usually are followed. One of these is NFPA 903, *Fire Reporting Property Survey Guide*, and the other is NFPA 1420, *Recommended Practice for Pre-Incident Planning for Warehouse Occupancies*. These standards provide the information needed to conduct thorough pre-incident surveys and the sample forms needed to develop comprehensive pre-incident plans from the information gathered during the facility surveys. Even though NFPA 1420 was written for use in warehouse occupancies, its general principles can be applied to any type of occupancy as long as the individual occupancy's unique features are considered.

Facility Survey Drawings

While some of the information gathered during a pre-incident survey should be compiled in the form of a written report, information about the building layout is more effectively described by a drawing or series of drawings that are included in the pre-incident plan. There are three general types of drawings used to show building information: *plot plans, floor plans*, and *elevations*. Plot plans are used to indicate how the building is situated with respect to other buildings and streets in the area (Figure 17.42). Floor plans show the layout of individual floors and the roof (Figure 17.43). Elevations are used to show the number of floors in the building and the grade of the surrounding ground (Figure 17.44).

Most building details can be shown on a floor plan drawing. When surveying relatively small buildings, all the information can often be shown on one drawing, but as the building size or complexity increases, the number of drawings needed to show the necessary detail clearly

Figure 17.41 Some prefer simple, concise plans.

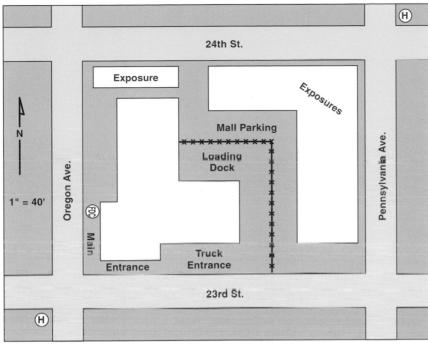

Figure 17.42 A typical plot plan drawing.

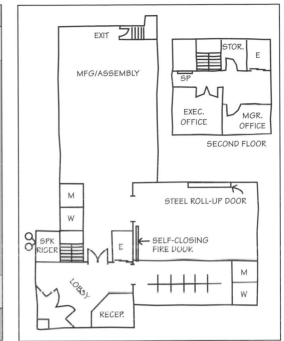

Figure 17.43 A typical floor plan drawing.

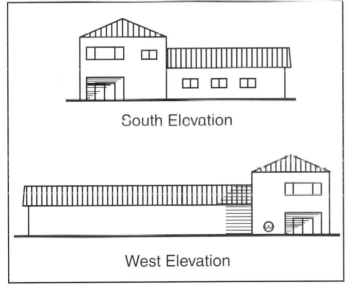

Figure 17.44 A typical elevation drawing.

Figure 17.45 A rough sketch should be made of the building.

will also increase. Every drawing or page of a set should be labeled with a title that clearly indicates the type of information that is included. Producing the three types of drawings is a two-step process: making *field sketches* and creating *report drawings*.

Field Sketches

The field sketch is a rough drawing of the building prepared during the facility survey (Figure 17.45). This drawing should show general information about building dimensions and such other related outside information as the locations of fire hydrants, streets, water tanks, and the distances to nearby exposures. All the basic information for the report drawing should be shown on the field sketch, but all the details need not be included.

Making the field sketch on graph paper makes it easier to draw it to scale (Figure 17.46). Drawing to scale is not absolutely necessary but it does help to keep the drawing in proportion. This will make it easier to transfer the information onto the report drawing.

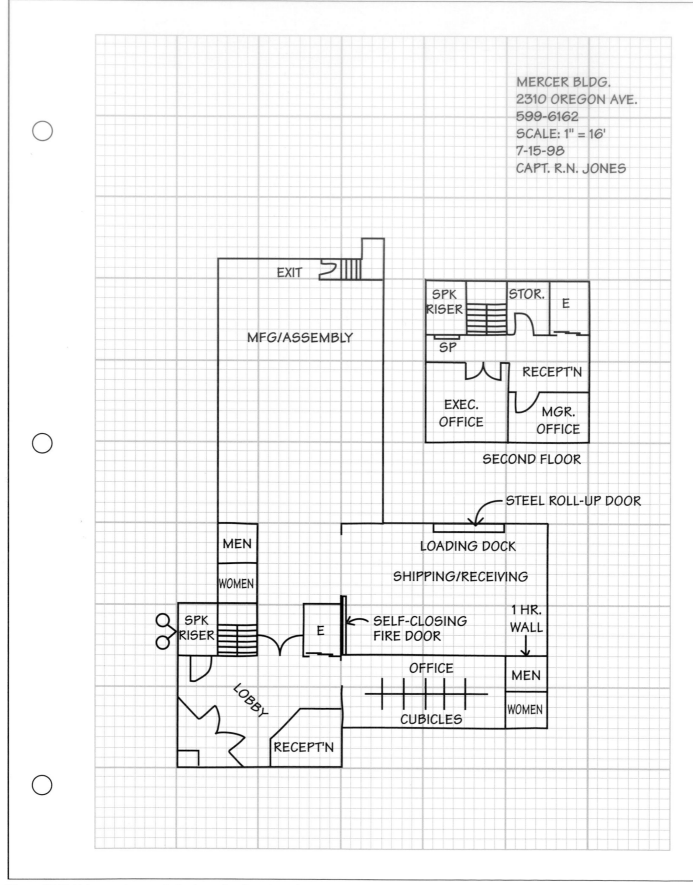

Figure 17.46 Using graph paper helps keep drawings to scale.

Report Drawings

Report drawings are "polished" versions of the field sketches, and they must be drawn to scale showing the essential details of the building and its surroundings. The details should be shown using the standard mapping symbols adopted by the department (Figure 17.47). If a drawing is not labeled, a legend explaining the symbols must be included. If an item must be included for which there is no standard symbol, it should be indicated by a circled numeral. The numeral is then identified and explained in the legend.

Photography

Some departments choose to supplement their pre-incident plan drawings with photographs. Using photographs can provide some distinct advantages over drawings alone. Taking a photo is much faster than making a drawing if the subject is at all complicated (Figure 17.48). Also, a photograph will capture every visible detail, leaving nothing out. On the other hand, a photograph may capture too much detail and actually obscure the essential information in the picture. Whether and when to use photography in the pre-incident planning process is a departmental decision.

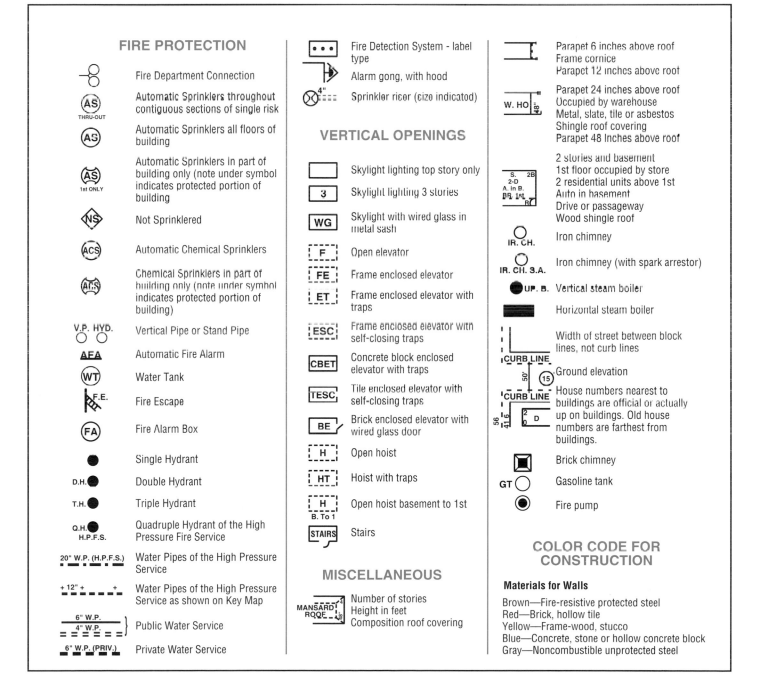

Figure 17.47 Standard map symbols.

Figure 17.48 Photographs sometimes make plans clearer.

Written Report

After all drawings and any photographs have been compiled and labeled, a clear but concise written report must also be prepared. In most cases, the cover of the report includes such basic information as the address of the building or occupancy, the date of the facility survey, the type of building, and the name of the submitting officer. The form and content of the written report will be dictated by departmental policy. As mentioned earlier, if department policy dictates that pre-incident plans be very streamlined and contain only information that indicates how this occupancy is different from others, then the written report should reflect that. If, on the other hand, department policy dictates that the same information be included about every occupancy surveyed (as outlined in NFPA 903 and NFPA 1420), the written report should reflect that.

Managing Pre-Incident Data

Systems must be developed for managing the data that is gathered during site surveys, and that is used to produce pre-incident operational plans. Some departments use computer programs such as CAMEO℠ to manage data regarding hazardous materials. There is similar software designed to assist in planning for other types of emergency responses. Programs such as FIREHOUSE® software and Firesoft® can be used to store and retrieve data relating to particular occupancies. For departments that have the necessary hardware, these programs can make the process of managing large quantities of pre-incident planning data much easier and make the information much more accessible when it is needed during an emergency. Information such as directions to the scene, cross streets, hydrant and other water supply locations and flow rates, unusual hazards on site, emergency phone numbers, and other essential data can be transmitted from the communications center to MDTs or MDCs in apparatus responding to or on the scene (Figure 17.49). However, even these sophisticated programs are only as good as the data they contain. If the data is current, they can be extremely useful tools for incident commanders and company officers. But if the data is inaccurate or out-of-date, it may not only be useless, but it may even be dangerous.

Other departments use hard-copy systems that usually consist of one or more binders filled with loose-leaf pages that contain essential information on the target hazards within the district (Figure 17.50). They may be indexed by street address, business name, or some other method. These systems may be based on NFPA 1470, *Standard on Search and Rescue Training for Structural Collapse Incidents,* or a similar planning guide, but just as with the computer-based programs, these hard copy systems must also be kept current to be most useful.

There are three major problems with any pre-incident plan — gathering the data, entering the data, and keeping the data current. Businesses remodel or expand their facilities, add or eliminate equipment or processes, increase or reduce the amount of materials on the premises, or they move to a different location. Any of these changes can invalidate existing pre-incident plans on these occupancies unless the plans are updated to reflect the changes.

In some areas, the business license and/or building permit processes help fire departments stay informed of business activity in their districts. When someone wants to start a business, they are supposed to apply for a business license. The application process is supposed to identify the type of business to be conducted, as well as provide information regarding materials and processes that will be part of the operation. The licensing agency is supposed to review the application to make sure that the type of business is allowed in the proposed location and

Figure 17.49 Some departments can retrieve pre-incident plans electronically.

Figure 17.50 Some departments keep pre-incident plans in a loose-leaf binder.

Figure 17.51 Ideally, business license applications require fire department approval

that all zoning, environmental, health, fire protection, and safety requirements have been met. The same is true for individuals applying for a building permit. The responsible agency is supposed to review the building plans to make sure that all code requirements are met. Both business license and building permit applications should be reviewed by the fire department so that information about new businesses and structures within the district can be obtained (Figure 17.51). However, there is no completely reliable system for tracking these activities.

One of the best ways of identifying changes in any business or building within the district is by having the local fire companies document and report any changes they observe in the course of the daily activities. These changes can then be reflected on any pre-incident plans that may have been developed for an affected occupancy.

Summary

The safety and effectiveness of the fire department's emergency operations can be greatly enhanced if the emergency responders have comprehensive and up-to-date information about the occupancies in which they will be required to operate. The more information they have, and the more reliable that information is, the better. The best way for this information to be gathered and transformed into a plan that will be useful during a fire or other emergency is through a pre-incident planning process that involves company officers and the members of their companies.

This chapter provides information that will assist the reader in meeting the following job performance requirements from NFPA 1021, *Standard for Fire Officer Professional Qualifications*, 1997 edition. The colored portions indicate the topics addressed in the chapter. The numbers of the job performance requirements are also noted directly in the sections of text where they are addressed. Those in the following list that are denoted with an asterisk (*) are global in nature and are covered by reading the chapter in its entirety.

Fire Officer I

2-1.1 **General Prerequisite Knowledge**. The organizational structure of the department; departmental operating procedures for administration, emergency operations, and safety; departmental budget process; information management and record keeping; the fire prevention and building safety codes and ordinances applicable to the jurisdiction; incident management system; socioeconomic and political factors that impact the fire service; cultural diversity; methods used by supervisors to obtain cooperaiton within a group of subordinates; the rights of management and members; agreements in force between the organization and members; policies and procedures regarding the operation of the department as they involve supervisors and members.

2-1.2 **General Prerequisite Skills**. The ability to communicate verbally and in writing, to write reports, and to operate in the incident management system.

Incident Scene Communications

Effective communication is critically important if emergency scene activities are to be conducted safely and efficiently. Company officers play a very important role in a fire department's incident scene communications because they transmit and receive the majority of all incident scene messages. Whenever the situation allows, the preferred method of communication is direct, face-to-face voice communication. However, the variety of environments in which firefighters must attempt to communicate usually makes it necessary for them to use some form of electronic communications. Because each form of emergency scene communication has certain advantages and disadvantages, no one method or system is optimally effective in every situation. This means that emergency scene communications may involve everything from face to face oral communication to the use of very sophisticated satellite communications systems.

This chapter is intended to acquaint company officers with the types of communications equipment they will be expected to use and with the proper procedures for using this equipment. Discussed in this chapter are fire departments radios, pagers, and alternative communications methods. Also discussed are advanced technology communications systems and communications procedures.

Communications Equipment

To be most effective at communicating on the emergency scene, company officers must be adept at using the communications equipment they have at their disposal and know the standard communications procedures used by their jurisdiction. This section highlights some of the common types of communications equipment that company officers are expected to operate.

Radios

Communications using some type of radio equipment is one of the most common forms of emergency scene communication (Figure 18.1). Radios provide instantaneous communication among fire fighting units, between fire units and the communications center, and between fire units and the rest of the emergency-scene organization through the chain of command. Properly operated and monitored radio communication provides the following advantages:

- The incident can be quickly surveyed and evaluated.
- All parties involved in handling the incident can be informed or consulted.
- Orders, plans, and information can be quickly given or received to meet changing conditions.
- Personnel accountability can be maintained.

The communications center is the focal point for all emergency scene radio communications (Figure 18.2). The resources (personnel and equipment) needed to operate at emergency scenes are dispatched by the communications center (Figure 18.3). In general, the communications center keeps track of all apparatus assigned to an incident and may be responsible for initiating a move-up or call-back system to provide coverage for

Figure 18.1 Radio communications is the most common form of communication during emergencies.

Figure 18.2 The communications center is a vital part of emergency communications.

Figure 18.3 Units are dispatched and monitored from the communications center.

districts left unprotected. In order for the system to function as designed, the communications center must be kept apprised of each unit's status at all times. There are a variety of means by which the communications center may dispatch and keep track of the department's resources. Most modern communications centers use some form of computerized system with an audio tape backup to manage their activities. These systems are commonly called computer-aided-dispatch (CAD) systems. The complexity of the CAD system in any jurisdiction is usually directly related to the size and activity level of that department or jurisdiction.

Radio Frequencies

While a relatively small-scale emergency operation can work effectively using a single radio frequency, this is not recommended. When the number of units from one agency assigned to a given incident increases or when units from several different agencies are assigned to one incident, the use of additional frequencies is usually necessary. Radio frequencies cannot be arbitrarily assigned and must not be unilaterally assumed by any operating unit during an incident. The assignment of frequencies reflects both pre-incident planning and the communications element of the incident action plan for that particular incident. Agencies that commonly work together should have written or working agreements for mutual frequency use and sharing. The number of frequencies needed on any given incident depends on the number of resources involved and the size of the management organization. On large incidents, there may be as many as five major uses for radio communications. Each of the following areas may require one or more radio frequencies on large incidents:

- Command
- Tactical operations

- Support operations
- Air-to-ground communications (airport crash/rescue, wildland, or medical evacuation operations)
- Air-to-air communications (wildland operations)
- Medical

Fire departments may have anywhere from one to ten or more radio frequencies available for their use. Small, rural fire departments that handle a low-call volume normally function on a single frequency. Larger fire departments, or a group of smaller fire departments that operate through the same communications center, require a number of frequencies to operate efficiently. In many cases, all emergency dispatch functions are on one frequency, routine operations are handled on a second frequency, and additional frequencies are available for large-scale incidents. At the incident commander's discretion, all communications at a large-scale incident may be switched to one of the extra frequencies to avoid interference from routine transmissions on the primary frequency. Extremely large incidents may require multiple frequencies assigned to that incident. For example, all Command section functions may be carried out on one channel, Operations section communications carried on a second channel, and Logistics functions on yet a third channel.

All agencies that routinely work together on emergency incidents must have the ability to communicate with each other by radio on common or mutual aid frequencies. In some cases, it may be necessary to provide mutual aid companies with portable radios once they are on the scene so that they may communicate with first-due companies (Figure 18.4).

Three types of radios may be used at an emergency scene, depending on the magnitude of the incident:

- Base radios
- Mobile radios
- Portable radios

Radios in aircraft may also be used on special incidents such as large-scale wildland fires, airport operations, or medical evacuations (Figure 18.5). However, because few if any company officers are expected to be able operate aircraft radios, and those that are must be specifically trained to do so, it is beyond the scope of this manual to cover their use.

Base Radios

Base radios are normally operated from the jurisdiction's communications center. However, on large-scale incidents that are expected to be of relatively long duration, a base radio may be set up at a fixed location such as the command post (CP) or the incident base (Figure 18.6). While these radios are typically scaled-down versions of the base radios found in a communications center, they must be capable of monitoring and transmitting on all the frequencies used on that particular incident. Depending on the area involved in the incident and the required range for radio communications, the base radio may need to be equipped with a sizable exterior antenna (Figure 18.7). If pagers or similar alerting devices are used at the incident, the base radio must be capable of activating these devices as well.

Mobile Radios

Mobile radios are those mounted in vehicles. While most mobile radios are designed to be operated from the front seat of the vehicle cab, some pumping apparatus also allow the driver/operator to operate the mobile radio from the pump panel area. Regardless of the operator's position, he speaks through a handheld microphone or through a headset that is part of a vehicle intercom system (Figure 18.8). As with base stations, these radios should be capable of communicating on any frequency used on an incident. At the very least, apparatus given specific functional or geographic assignments should be capable of communicating with each other and with their supervisor. Most modern mobile radios are capable of scanning, transmitting, and receiving on hundreds of frequencies. This capability is critical when working as part of a large incident organization with units from jurisdictions that operate on different frequencies than local units.

Portable Radios

Portable radios, sometimes referred to as *walkie-talkies* or simply "portables," are handheld radios that allow firefighters to remain in contact with each other, other units, and their supervisor when they are away from the mobile radio in the apparatus (Figure 18.9). Most portable radios have a very limited amount of transmitting and receiving power, usually only 1 to 5 watts (compared to the 100 to 150 watts of a typical mobile radio). Therefore, portable radios have a very limited range. When communicating from portable to portable, the range may be less than 1 mile (1.6 km). Communications distances between portable radios and mobiles or base stations vary depending on the capability of the mobile or base.

Figure 18.4 Mutual aid units may need portable radios with local frequencies.

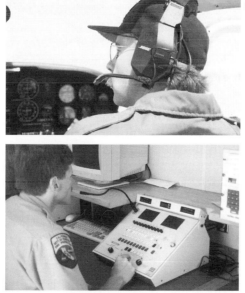

Figure 18.5 Aircraft communicate with ground units by radio.

Figure 18.6 Base radios may be set up on large incidents.

Figure 18.7 Base radios may require large antennas.

Figure 18.8 Driver/operators may be able to use the mobile radio from the panel.

Figure 18.9 Typical modern portable radios. *Courtesy of National Interagency Fire Center.*

Figure 18.10 Repeaters may be fixed or portable. *Courtesy of National Interagency Fire Center.*

The range of portable radios may be extended using a repeater system. The repeater system receives the signal from the portable, boosts its power, and then transmits the signal to the intended receiver. Two primary types of repeater systems are in common use. One type is part of the mobile radio in the apparatus assigned to the crew using the portable radio. When the crew member transmits on the portable radio, the repeater system in the mobile radio boosts the radio's signal to its optimum power and rebroadcasts the signal. The second type of repeater system is one in which fixed or portable repeaters are located throughout a particular geographical jurisdiction (Figure 18.10). These repeaters pick up signals from portable or mobile radios and boost their power so they are received by other portable, mobile, or base station radios.

As with mobile radios, portable radios may be operated on multiple channels. Newer portables can scan, transmit, and receive on hundreds of channels.

Pagers

Pagers are most often used to notify volunteers, paid-on-call and off-duty career firefighters, and staff officers to respond to the station or fire scene. Pagers are available in a wide variety of types and sizes and are capable of making contact with an individual or a group of individuals selectively. Some pagers are activated by simply dialing a specific telephone number. Most pagers used in the fire service are activated by a transmitter tone from the communications center. Pagers provide information to the wearer in one of two modes: a voice message or a written display message.

Many volunteer fire departments use pagers that allow the wearer to monitor radio traffic on the dispatch frequency at all times. It is a good standard practice to broadcast emergency evacuation messages to all firefighters over the dispatch frequency — in addition to the fireground frequency — as firefighters who do not have portable radios may be able to hear the command over their pagers.

Alternative Communications Methods

Because of the long duration of many large-scale emergency incidents, alternative communications systems may be used during these incidents. The use of each of the following methods depends on the level of preparedness of the agency or agencies involved in the incident.

- Citizens band (CB) radios
- Ham radios
- Land-based telephones
- Cellular telephones
- Facsimile (fax) machines
- Computer modems
- Satellite phones

Citizens Band (CB) Radios

Some small, rural jurisdictions rely on citizens band (CB) radios as their primary mode of mobile communication. This is primarily because CB radios are relatively inexpensive, and many of these small departments do not have the financial resources to purchase standard mobile radios for their apparatus. In addition to their low cost, CB radios offer several other advantages to these departments. These advantages include the following:

- They are better than having no radios at all.
- Most modern CB radios have 40 channels, which allows different parts of the organization to operate on their own frequency.
- Many personnel have CB radios in their personal vehicles, which can be a benefit when setting up a command structure.

In addition to these advantages, CB radios also have their disadvantages, including the following:

- Members of the public may be operating on the same frequencies.

- The quality of the radio transmission may not be as clear as with standard fire department mobile radios.

- The range of effective communication is generally less than that of standard fire department mobile radios.

- They are not intrinsically safe (may be a source of ignition).

Ham Radios

Ham radio clubs and individual operators have an extensive communications network. Through their base stations and mobile and portable radios, ham operators can access repeaters, satellites, and telephone systems. These operators and their equipment are often available on a volunteer basis, but it may take several hours to mobilize them. Drills should be held with ham operators to practice notification and mobilization procedures.

In some areas, organized groups of ham operators are available and equipped to supplement or aid official emergency radio systems when the need arises (Figure 18.11). Departments that have the access to a RACES chapter can usually mobilize an effective alternative radio system faster than those where individual operators must be notified one at a time. Operators in a RACES organization are also more likely to understand the needs of the emergency providers and to carry out these functions more efficiently and effectively.

Land-Based Telephones

Public telephones or field telephones are sometimes used as a means of communicating on large-scale incidents, high-rise incidents, and in shipboard and other confined space incidents. If radio communication breaks down, telephones may be an effective alternative. Even if radio communications are operational, it may be advantageous to communicate lengthy routine messages (ordering supplies, giving lengthy status reports, etc.) by telephone instead of tying up radio frequencies. Land-based telephones are most commonly used when the incident base or command post is located in a permanent structure that has telephone service. Temporary telephone service can also be run into a command post or other location by telephone company personnel if it appears that an incident will be a protracted operation.

Cellular Telephones

Advances in cellular telephone technology have made telephone service much more accessible to fire service

personnel working on emergency incidents. Cellular telephone service is now available in most geographical areas. Cellular phones may be handheld or mounted in a vehicle (Figure 18.12). They allow personnel access to the world telephone network, without being hard-wired into a local telephone system. Telephone messages are transmitted as radio signals between the cellular phone and repeater/downlink equipment ("cell sites") that enter the call into the telephone system.

However, cellular telephones are not foolproof. If the emergency scene is in an area that is not serviced by a cell site, no service is available. Even within a cell site area, there may be "dead spots" where reception is not available. Another major limitation is that incidents in densely populated areas tend to generate massive amounts of cellular telephone traffic from emergency providers and citizens alike. This increase in traffic can quickly overwhelm existing cell-site equipment and block further calls from being made. When this happens, the cellular phone provider can provide equipment to temporarily boost the system's capacity. They can also provide special cellular telephones that have priority programming to ensure that every call made to or from these phones goes through. Departments should confirm the availability of these services during pre-incident planning.

Satellite Telephones

On large-scale incidents, a satellite telephone system that is independent of land-based and cellular systems can be set up (Figure 18.13). With the requisite equip-

Figure 18.11 Volunteer radio operators can be extremely helpful during emergencies.

Figure 18.12 Cellular phones offer great mobility.

Figure 18.13 A typical satellite phone system.

ment, this wireless telephone system can provide a reliable communications system that is free of the limitations and interference that characterize the other types of telephonic communications.

Facsimile (Fax) Machines

On major emergency scenes, the incident command post and/or incident base may have one or more facsimile (fax) machines (Figure 18.14). Fax machines can be very useful for transmitting and/or receiving written documents such as situation status reports, building plans, hazardous chemical data, and weather updates. Fax machines normally transmit their signals over land-based telephone lines, but they may be operated through cellular telephone systems.

Computer Modems

A modem (modulator/demodulator) converts the signal produced by one type of device (computer) to a form compatible with another device (telephone). This allows a computer at the incident command post, incident base, or other location to access databases and computer networks over a telephone line. As with fax machines, computer modems may be attached to cellular or land-based telephone equipment.

Advanced Technology Communications Systems

Even though communications technology has made significant advancements because of research and development efforts in private industry in general, the aerospace industry in particular, and the military, much of this technology is still beyond the fiscal means of the majority of the fire service. However because this technology is likely to become more common, and therefore less expensive, it warrants at least a brief discussion in this manual.

Geographic Information System (GIS)

A GIS is designed to provide a computer-readable description of geographic features in a particular area. A built-in computer stores and, on command, displays data on specific segments of the area covered. In urban/suburban areas, addresses and occupancy information on individual structures may be stored in the GIS. This information may be useful to dispatchers, incident commanders, planning personnel, and technical specialists assigned to an incident.

Mobile Data Terminal (MDT)

Of the advanced communication technologies covered in this section, a mobile data terminal (MDT) is the one in most common use by the fire service. An MDT is a radio-operated data terminal that allows a communication center to transmit dispatch information, incident/patient status information, confidential messages not appropriate for verbal transmission over the radio, chemical information, and maps and charts. One style of MDT looks like a small personal computer mounted on a pedestal near the vehicle dashboard (Figure 18.15). Another style resembles a laptop computer that can be pulled from the vehicle and used in a remote location, if needed. Many MDTs are also equipped with status buttons that allow the communications center to stay apprised of the unit's status (en route, on scene, available, etc.) without the need for verbal radio transmissions.

Mobile Data Computer (MDC)

Mobile data computers have all the features of an MDT with the addition of a keyboard that allows two-way communication between the mobile units and the communications center (Figure 18.16). Instead of the status buttons that MDTs use to transmit their status, MDCs allow complete messages to be transmitted and

Figure 18.14 Fax machines are a vital piece of communications equipment. *Courtesy of National Interagency Fire Center.*

Figure 18.15 Many fire vehicles are equipped with MDTs.

Figure 18.16 Some fire vehicles have MDCs.

received in the vehicle. This facilitates two-way communications that are not appropriate for transmission over the radio.

Global Positioning System (GPS)

Originally developed by the United States military as a means of tracking troops in combat, the global positioning system (GPS) is now in use by the civilian emergency services. In a GPS, each vehicle is equipped with a radio transmitter. The signal transmitted bounces off a satellite and is received by an automatic vehicle locator (AVL) at the communications center. The position of the vehicle is then shown on a map of the jurisdiction using the system. These systems are generally capable of determining the location of a vehicle to within approximately 10 yards (10 m) of its actual position.

Global positioning systems are typically used in conjunction with computerized dispatch systems, MDTs, and global information systems. There are several uses for the GPS. Two of the most common uses are for tracking companies on the fire scene and dispatching the closest available companies to an emergency.

Communications Procedures

To company officers, more important than a familiarity with communications equipment is a thorough knowledge of the procedures for using that equipment. Most fire departments have a communications management policy that defines the procedures and language to be used during routine activities and emergency operations. By including communications in their standard operating procedures, communications protocols are applied much more consistently. The communications procedure must do two things:

- Establish the use of specific common terms (clear text) that mean the same thing to all emergency response personnel.

- Establish a system of transmitting periodic progress reports to keep all units current on the progress of the incident.

In clear text, there are specific terms that should be used to describe apparatus and standard operational modes and functions. For example, when a unit has been dispatched on an emergency call, the company officer transmits "Engine 7187 responding." The term *responding* is only used for emergency response but not for routine, nonemergency movements. Nor should *en route* or any other term be used instead of *responding* when responding to an emergency call. There are many other terms that have specific meanings and applications in clear text. Despite the fact that clear text has been in use

for decades, some of the most common misuse of radio terminology occur in the area of resource identification. Many departments refer to their engines as "trucks" even though a truck is a ladder company. These same departments refer to mobile water supply apparatus as "tankers" even though a tanker is an aircraft. Company officers have an obligation to learn and use correct radio terminology.

Radio Communications

The purpose of fire department radio communications is to allow units in the field to communicate with each other, with the communications center, and with the incident chain of command during emergency operations. Being able to exchange critical or pertinent tactical information allows all elements of the organization to monitor the status of other units and of the overall operation. The information exchanged can be task-related (for example, "Command, Engine 7; we need an additional supply line to support Truck 37's ladder pipe."), or the information can be a direct order based upon the decision of the incident commander (for example, "Communications, Penn Command; strike a third alarm. Have all companies report to Staging at 5th and Penn Streets").

Individuals who operate radio equipment should realize that all radio transmissions can be monitored by the news media, the public, and the Federal Communications Commission (FCC). Any communications transmitted via radio may be repeated on tomorrow's front page. Radio operators should always be careful to not transmit any message that might reflect badly on the department. Company officers are responsible for the radio conduct of their crews.

Basic Radio Communications

All emergency responders — not just company officers — should be trained in the use of whatever radio equipment their department has. Regardless of whether they have been issued a portable radio or whether they normally do not operate department radios, emergency responders need to be able to use radios effectively if and when they need to. Company officers are responsible for making sure that every member of their crew is trained on the following:

- Basic radio operation and maintenance (changing batteries, etc.)

- Radio frequency assignments and usage

- Departmental radio procedures

Obviously, it is important that all emergency responders be able to operate the radio equipment available to them. They should understand the operation of all the various controls on the radio, and be able to quickly select different channels as the situation requires. They should also be capable of performing any routine maintenance or care, such as keeping the radios clean and changing batteries.

Those who work in departments that use multiple radio frequencies must know which frequencies are used for various functions. They must be able to differentiate among dispatch, tactical, and command frequencies, and they must be sure that their radios are always on the correct frequency. This is especially critical in situations where personnel may be in mortal danger in fires or other emergencies.

CAUTION: Be sure that all personnel know the correct frequency to use for each function. Failure to use the correct frequency could result in no communication or in delay of assistance. Case histories show that in some instances help for trapped firefighters was delayed because their calls for help were transmitted over the wrong radio frequency and were not heard by units on the fireground.

Company officers must know and use their department's radio procedures. These procedures should be used on a daily basis during both routine and emergency activities. If all members of the department follow the established procedures on small, day-to-day incidents, using the procedures during major incidents will be routine.

Clear Text Versus Radio Codes

In the fire service, there are two basic methods of transmitting information over the radio — using clear text and radio codes. *Clear text*, as mentioned earlier, involves using certain standard English terms and phrases to convey information. Radio codes (also known as *10-codes* or *signal codes*) have been used since the earliest days of fire service radio communications. Historically, the use of coded language was a necessity because the quality of radio transmissions was often poor. A series of short, easy-to-understand codes were developed that could be used to transmit messages that would otherwise take many words to communicate. For example, the message "Your signal is read loud and clear" could be narrowed down to "10-2" (pronounced "ten-two").

However, a major problem with radio codes is that different jurisdictions developed different radio codes or modified existing ones to fit their particular needs. For example, in one community "10-23" might be the code for "Unit arriving on location," while in another community it might be the code for "Fire under con-

trol." The problems that these differences can create on mutual aid operations are obvious. Even if the various departments could receive and transmit on the same radio frequency, they could not communicate because they use different codes.

Modern radio equipment has eliminated the need for radio codes, and in most areas the use of radio codes is considered to be antiquated. Jurisdictions that still use them do so because of tradition — not necessity. Most fire departments now use clear text which eliminates the problems associated with radio codes.

Transmitting Essential Information

One potential problem with the use of clear text is that some radio operators may become lax and begin to ramble when they are transmitting. Company officers should monitor their crews' radio usage and see that their personnel follow procedures and keep radio messages short and to the point. Only essential information should be transmitted, and proper radio format should be used. For example, when an engine arrives at the emergency scene, the company officer should simply transmit, "Engine 3581 at scene." When calling the communications center or another unit, the company officer identifies the unit being called and then identifies the calling unit. For example, "Communications, Engine 7582." After the other units acknowledges ("Go ahead 7582."), the company officer transmits the message.

Direct Orders

An example of a direct order is, "Ladder 65, Operations — ventilate the roof." A direct order can be made more explicit by adding extra information such as who is to carry out the task and why, how, when, and where it must be done. The officer issuing the order must decide how specific to make the order by considering the urgency of the task and the capabilities of the individual or unit to which the order is given.

Directives

As discussed in Chapter 14, "Fire Department Communications," a directive is similar to a request but has almost the same effect as a direct order. For example, if a company officer asks one crew member to help another with some task, it is a request that serves as a directive. Requests are appropriate in nonemergency situations but not during emergency operations.

The Five Cs of Communication

At an incident scene, there is no time for company officers to think about the correct method of communicating. Therefore, they must use good communications procedures in day-to-day operations so these skills will become second nature. There are five Cs of communication that every fire officer should practice:

- Conciseness
- Clarity
- Confidence
- Control
- Capability

Conciseness

Numerous functions must be performed at an incident scene, and many will involve some form of communication. Therefore, communications must be kept as concise as possible or the assigned frequencies will become too congested with traffic to be of any use. To ensure conciseness, company officers must learn to plan their transmissions before keying the microphone. They should do the following:

- Make messages task-oriented.
- Direct messages to companies and not individuals.
- Match the message to the receiver.
- Keep messages specific.

Clarity

The clarity of a message adds to the overall effectiveness of all incident communications. Company officers should use standard terms and everyday language when possible. When planning their transmissions, company officers should also strive to combine clarity with simplicity. To remain simple, good orders should communicate only one task at a time and have the unit report back for additional tasks. Orders issued to different units must be sufficiently spaced to avoid any question that separate orders are being transmitted. Emergency orders should be well timed because many operations can be anticipated by an experienced company officer/incident commander, but the order that assigns units to those operations should not be issued until those operations are ready to be undertaken.

Confidence

Especially during emergency operations, company officers must show confidence when using communication equipment. When confidence is communicated, receiving units react with confidence. Company officers can communicate confidence by using a calm, natural tone and by speaking at a controlled rate.

Control

Communications can break down if they are not managed. Of most importance in controlling communications at the company level are the dispatcher and the officer in charge. These key individuals should set a positive example for all units on the scene by following this procedure: Before transmitting, units must identify who they are calling and identify themselves before transmitting; and the receiver of the message should repeat or paraphrase the essence of the message back to the sender.

Requiring the receiver to acknowledge a message by repeating it reduces the chances of misunderstanding. This tells the sender that the message was understood as transmitted, or it alerts the sender that the message was not understood correctly and further clarification is necessary.

Capability

Effective communication depends on capable (well-trained) senders and receivers. But capability is not limited to technical proficiency; it also includes an ability to communicate. This means that company officers must be capable of effective listening as well as initiating messages. To do this, company officers must be able to exercise the emotional control needed to remain calm under stress and the emotional maturity to set a positive example by following established communication procedures.

Summary

Effective emergency scene communication is an essential part of operational effectiveness and safety. Company officers play a pivotal role in the communications process during these incidents. Not only do they transmit and receive most of the radio messages initiated during an incident, their crew members look to them for an example of how to use communications equipment properly and effectively. To fulfill their role, company officers must know what communications equipment is available to them, how to use it effectively, and how to be a positive role model for their crew members.

This chapter provides information that will assist the reader in meeting the following job performance requirements from NFPA 1021, *Standard for Fire Officer Professional Qualifications*, 1997 edition. The colored portions indicate the topics addressed in the chapter. The numbers of the job performance requirements are also noted directly in the sections of text where they are addressed. Those in the following list that are denoted with an asterisk (*) are global in nature and are covered by reading the chapter in its entirety.

Fire Officer I

2-5.2   Secure an incident scene, given rope or barrier tape, so that unauthorized persons can recognize the perimeters of the scene, are kept from restricted areas, and all evidence or potential evidence is protected from damage or destruction.

(a) *Prerequisite Knowledge:* Common causes of fire, fire growth and development, and policies and procedures for calling for investigators.

(b) *Prerequisite Skills:* The ability to determine basic fire cause and the ability to conduct interviews and write reports.

Reprinted with permission from NFPA 1021, *Standard for Fire Officer Professional Qualifications*, Copyright © 1997, National Fire Protection Association, Quincy, MA 02269. This reprinted material is not the complete and official position of the National Fire Protection Association on the referenced subject which is represented only by the standard in its entirety.

Chapter 19

Incident Scene Management

The safe and efficient handling of any emergency incident requires that emergency responders gain control of the incident scene and maintain that control throughout the incident. What seems like a relatively minor part of mitigating an emergency can sometimes be extremely difficult. Emergency scenes may encompass a wide and diverse area. There may be numerous victims, witnesses, and curious bystanders milling about the scene. It may be difficult for the first-arriving company officer to tell the victims from the bystanders and to address the needs of the victims and the safety of both groups. Overcoming these difficulties and successfully controlling the incident scene are critically important to the successful outcome of the incident.

This chapter discusses the objectives and phases of incident scene management, including scene assessment and scene control. The methods by which traffic is controlled, a perimeter is established, crowds are controlled, witnesses are managed, and evacuations are conducted are also discussed. Finally, the procedures for terminating an emergency incident are discussed.

Objectives of Scene Management

The objectives of incident scene management should always reflect the overall incident objectives. Scene management is not separate from but is an integral part of successfully disposing of the problem. Therefore, the objectives of incident scene management are the following:

- Life safety
- Incident stabilization
- Property conservation

Life Safety

One of the most important ways that scene control supports the life safety objective is that it helps in the implementation of a personnel accountability system. By establishing control zones and by maintaining control over who enters and leaves these zones, it is easier to keep track of personnel in high hazard areas. Because emergencies tend to attract large numbers of spectators, maintaining control of the scene makes it easier to maintain safety and provide information. Controlling the movements of nonemergency personnel near a high-hazard area can certainly contribute to life safety on the scene. One of the most important ways of protecting the lives of the emergency responders, and perhaps the victims as well, is protecting a roadway scene from oncoming traffic.

Incident Stabilization

Perhaps the most important way that scene control can support the incident stabilization objective is by allowing the emergency responders to work in a controlled area that is free of interference from nonemergency personnel and free from many other distractions. Working within a controlled area also allows emergency responders to have their vitally needed tools and equipment readily available. Having the command post within a controlled area certainly creates a more calm, quiet area where the incident commander (IC) can make critical decisions and the command staff can function without distractions.

Property Conservation

Scene control can help emergency responders confine the problem to a smaller area, and this may keep other property from becoming involved. Anything that helps the emergency responders function better contributes to a more efficient operation, and this can translate into a faster mitigation of the problem. The faster the problem is mitigated, the less property is at risk. Maintaining control of the scene can also save property by preventing looters from taking advantage of the situation. Controlling the scene can also protect property that may later be needed as evidence.

Phases of Scene Management

Incident scenes can vary considerably in size, configuration, and nature. Some emergency scenes involve extreme differences in elevation. Others involve confined areas with limited access, contaminated atmospheres, and little, if any, natural light. Some involve mangled and twisted metal and the very real threat of spilled fuels being ignited. Still, others involve fire, smoke, and the threat of structural collapse. Regardless of the size of the scene and what is involved, there are two phases of scene management that always apply:

- Scene assessment
- Scene control

Scene Assessment

Assessing the emergency scene is one of the first steps in the process of sizing up an incident (Figure 19.1). It is the part of a size-up that is made while approaching the scene and immediately after arrival. As described in Chapter 20, "Size-Up and Incident Plans," a complete size-up is broader and deeper than merely assessing the scene. Assessing the scene is part of the *location* step in the three-step method of size-up. It is part of defining the problem; however, the scene assessment focuses on a narrower range of concerns than a full size-up. Two of the most important concerns in the scene assessment are the *nature* of the incident and its *size*.

Nature of the Incident

Determining the nature of the incident helps emergency responders decide how closely they can approach the source of the problem and how they must make their approach (Figure 19.2). If the problem is a rapidly spreading wildland fire, the assessment may indicate that certain highway intersections need to be closed in order to keep nonemergency traffic away from the danger area and to keep the roads near the fire clear for emergency vehicles. If the problem is a hazardous materials release, the assessment may indicate the need to approach from upwind of the release and that those assigned to scene control need to be encapsulated while setting up barricades. If the problem is a trench collapse, the assessment may indicate the need to limit the approach of heavy fire apparatus. If the problem is a motor vehicle accident, the assessment may indicate the need for fire protection because of spilled fuel. If the problem is a working structure fire, then the possibility of a wall collapse, and perhaps falling debris, must be considered.

Size of the Incident

How big or how small an incident is may determine how scene control can be established and maintained. In the case of a wildland fire, the sheer size of the involved area may dictate that scene control can best be achieved by controlling the highway intersections surrounding the fire. In the case of a hazardous materials release, it may be possible to control the scene by simply closing certain interior doors and denying access to that part of the building. Or, scene control may be achieved with simple barricades or fireline tape if the incident is somewhat less confined. Otherwise, access to a relatively large area downwind and/or downhill of the release may have to be controlled or evacuated — perhaps with the assistance of law enforcement personnel. In the case of a trench collapse, the area immediately surrounding the collapse must be controlled as well as enough additional area as is necessary to provide working room for the rescuers and support functions. This can usually be accomplished with fireline tape. In the case of a structure fire, the area immediately surrounding the fire building must be controlled — usually with fireline tape. In addition, the intersections at both ends of the block in which the building is located should be controlled to limit access to the street in front of the building. If the fire building is large, or if more than one building is involved, the entire block may need to be controlled.

Elements of Scene Management

The methods by which scene control can be established and maintained vary almost as much as the incidents themselves. However, experience by fire department personnel operating at countless emergency incidents has identified some scene control elements that apply to a greater or lesser degree in most emergency incidents. These fundamental elements are traffic control, perimeter control, crowd control, witness control, occupant services, and in some cases, evacuation.

Figure 19.1 Scene assessment begins upon arrival.

Figure 19.2 Determining the nature of the incident drives other decisions.

Traffic Control

A very important part of maintaining safety around an emergency scene is the control of vehicular traffic. Controlling the flow of traffic makes operations at the scene run more smoothly and allows for more efficient access and departure of emergency vehicles. Although law enforcement personnel usually handle traffic control, in some cases fire department personnel may have to perform this function. Some volunteer departments that are located in areas with a limited number of law enforcement personnel have volunteers called "fire police" who are trained in traffic/crowd control and empowered to arrest anyone refusing to leave the scene when ordered, etc. These trained volunteers are members of the fire department who perform crowd and traffic control, secure the scene, and perform similar functions that would normally be handled by law enforcement personnel. Company officers should see that their firefighters are trained in the basics of traffic direction and safety.

As mentioned earlier, to provide maximum protection for emergency crews when traffic must be allowed to continue, emergency vehicles should be positioned so that they provide a barrier between the traffic and the personnel working at the scene. If it is not necessary to close all lanes of traffic, the lane in which the accident occurred as well as the lane next to it should be closed (Figure 19.3). In such incidents it is also extremely important that firefighters wear protective clothing that is brightly colored (fluorescent orange, canary yellow) and/or has reflective striping (Figure 19.4).

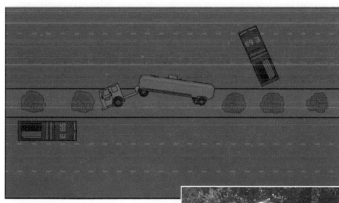

Figure 19.3 An additional traffic lane should be closed to protect rescuers.

Figure 19.4 Firefighters working near moving traffic should be highly visible.

Emergency incidents often do not involve vehicles nor are they always located on a street or roadway. They often occur inside buildings or in areas well off the roadway. In these cases, it is important to park emergency vehicles in a way that will not interfere with the normal flow of traffic. Emergency vehicles parked out of traffic lanes should shut down their emergency lights and headlights so that passing motorists will not be distracted or blinded by them nor react to them. Shutting down the lights will also reduce the number of spectators drawn to the scene.

Proper placement of apparatus on the emergency scene is also an important part of scene management and safety. The goal is to get the vehicles that need to be closest to the operation into that position. Some emergency vehicles need to be closer to the scene than others. For example, at some incidents, vehicles that are used to supply electrical power, operate hydraulic tools, etc., need to be close enough to operate effectively. Those that do not need to be close to the incident scene should be positioned to allow room for later-arriving vehicles that are needed to mitigate the problem. The following sections give general guidelines for apparatus placement at emergency scenes.

Fire Scene

When operating at a fire scene, vehicles directly involved in fire fighting (engines, trucks, etc.) should be positioned in a location that supports the fire fighting operations while providing for access, rescue, escape, relocation, protection from collapse, etc. Nonfire vehicles should be positioned where they will not interfere with fire fighting operations but where their equipment will still be readily available. Tools and equipment that might be needed from nonfire vehicles can be carried to the scene. Parking some distance from the fire building also provides a good location for treating victims or firefighters and makes it easier to coordinate with ambulances. It would be counterproductive to try to treat people in a rescue vehicle parked in the middle of the smoke.

Rescue Scene

Proper placement of emergency vehicles at nonfire scenes depends upon a number of variables. Placement is generally opposite that normally found at a fire scene. For example, at a rescue scene, rescue vehicles should be positioned nearest the incident. This is necessary because the rescue and extrication equipment may be most important in the situation and should be most readily available.

As mentioned earlier, the placement of emergency vehicles at the scene can either help or hinder the operation. The following are some general guidelines for the placement of emergency vehicles:

- Park emergency vehicles between the scene and oncoming traffic to protect rescuers if the incident is on the roadway (Figure 19.5).

- Park emergency vehicle(s) close enough to the incident to make their equipment readily available with a minimum carrying distance.

- Do not position emergency vehicles close enough to be in the way or to expose victims or emergency workers to vehicle exhaust, vibration, or noise.

- Park emergency vehicles upwind and uphill from the scene whenever possible (Figure 19.6).

- Position emergency vehicles well away from downed power lines, damaged transformers, or escaping flammable gas.

- Do not drive heavy vehicles near an open trench because the vibration could cause additional trench wall collapse.

- Do not block the scene. Allow access for ambulances and other emergency vehicles, and allow for the normal flow of traffic if the incident is not in the roadway.

- Coordinate closely with law enforcement officials on-scene to address safety issues/concerns for emergency personnel, bystanders, and other traffic.

Perimeter Control

There are numerous reasons to control the perimeter of an incident scene. As mentioned earlier, controlling the perimeter facilitates the use of a personnel accountability system (Figure 19.7). It also helps in accounting for victims and in keeping the scene clear of curious spectators and potential looters. Because it is an effective way to establish and control the perimeter of an incident scene, setting up *control zones* is also the most common way.

The most common method of organizing an emergency scene is to establish three operating zones. These zones are commonly labeled "hot," "warm," and "cold" (Figure 19.8). There is no specific distance or area that should be cordoned off. The zone boundaries should be established by taking into account the amount of area needed by emergency personnel to work, the degree of hazard presented by elements involved in the incident, wind and weather conditions, and the general topography of the area. The zones can be cordoned off with rope or fireline tape tied to signs, utility poles, parking meters, or any other objects readily available (Figure 19.9). The three zones can be described as follows:

Restricted (hot) zone. This is the area where mitigating the problem is taking place — fires are fought, hazardous materials releases are controlled and contained, vehicle extrication is done, etc. Only personnel who are directly involved in disposing of the problem are allowed into the hot zone. This limits crowding and confusion at the most critical area of the scene. The size of the hot zone may vary greatly depending upon the nature and extent of the problem.

Limited access (warm) zone. This is the area immediately outside the hot zone — the area for personnel who are directly supporting those in the hot zone. The warm zone is where those who are handling hydraulic tool power plants, providing emergency lighting, and providing fire protection would be. In hazardous materials incidents, the warm zone is where the decontamination station is normally set up. Access to this zone should be limited to personnel who are not needed in the hot zone but who are closely supporting the work being performed there.

Support (cold) zone. This is the area immediately surrounding the previously described zones. This area may include the command post (CP), the information officer's

Figure 19.5 Emergency vehicles can be used to form a protective barrier.

Figure 19.6 Emergency vehicles should be parked uphill and upwind.

Figure 19.7 Perimeter control makes personnel accountability easier.

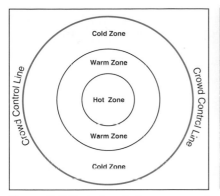

Figure 19.8 Typical control zones around an incident.

Figure 19.9 Barrier tape can be secured to any fixed object.

Figure 19.10 If available, law enforcement personnel should be used for crowd control.

(PIO) location, and staging areas for personnel and portable equipment. Backup personnel should remain in this zone until needed in the warm or hot zones. This is the area where witnesses and family members of victims should be gathered. The outer boundary of this area should be the control line for the general public — the *crowd control line.*

Crowd Control

In smaller incidents, where no evacuation is necessary, cordoning off the area as just described will keep bystanders a safe distance from the scene and out of the way of emergency personnel. Once the area has been cordoned off, the boundary should be monitored to make sure people do not cross it. If large-scale evacuations are not needed and if there is no need for extensive traffic control, law enforcement personnel may be available to monitor the crowd control line (Figure 19.10).

It is preferable for law enforcement personnel to perform this function because of their training in dealing with crowds and because of their power to make arrests if necessary. Another reason that it is preferable to use law enforcement personnel for crowd control is that members of the news media can sometimes be overzealous in their pursuit of a story. While they have a right to gather the facts, they sometimes put themselves at great risk and even interfere with the work of emergency personnel. The rights of legitimate media representatives are interpreted differently in different jurisdictions, so law enforcement should be allowed to handle that situation. Besides the media, many private citizens now carry video camcorders with them in their vehicles. These individuals may simply be curious, or they may hope to get footage that they can sell to the media. In either case, they can be so intent on taping the incident that they stray into hazardous areas or interfere with emergency personnel. For their protection, it is important that company officers know what the ground rules are in their particular area.

If law enforcement personnel are not available for crowd control, firefighters or other department personnel may have to perform this function. Using firefighters for crowd control may be necessary, but it should be avoided if possible (Figure 19.11). Firefighters who are busy with crowd control are not available to help mitigate the problem that brought them to the scene. In addition, when dealing with the crowd, firefighters are placed in a position for which most have little or no training. If firefighters must perform this function, they should quickly establish a line and two collection points on one side of the line. They should move everyone behind the line and then direct those in the crowd who say they were involved in the incident to cross the line and go to one of the collection points. They should then ask anyone in the crowd who witnessed the incident to cross the line and go to the other collection point. The groups at the collection points should not be allowed to converse among themselves, nor should the witnesses be allowed to talk to each other.

All these people should be assessed by emergency medical personnel before being released (Figure 19.12). Without a local protocol to the contrary, anyone who refuses treatment or transportation should be asked to sign a release-of-liability form (Figure 19.13).

Reasons for controlling those individuals who were involved in some way with the incident include the following:

* To keep them from wandering the scene
* To keep the uninjured from getting injured
* To provide a method of accounting for everyone involved in the incident
* To obtain information from those involved in the incident
* To separate witnesses from each other to prevent them from discussing what they saw and perhaps influencing each other to coordinate their stories

Figure 19.11 Firefighters may have to be used for crowd control.

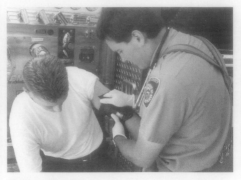

Figure 19.12 Those involved in the incident should be medically evaluated.

Figure 19.13 Anyone refusing evaluation and/or treatment should sign a release.

Even in the most remote locations, bystanders or spectators are often drawn to emergency scenes. Bystanders are often quite curious and try to get as close to the scene as possible. All bystanders should be restrained from getting too close to the incident for their own safety and for that of victims and emergency personnel.

Emergency scenes tend to be emotional situations that should be handled with care. This is particularly true when friends or relatives of the victims are at the scene. These particular bystanders are often difficult to deal with, but emergency responders should treat them with sensitivity and understanding. Relatives and friends of victims should be gently but firmly restrained from getting too close to the incident, and they should be kept some distance from the actual incident but still within the cordoned area. While they may console each other, they should not be left entirely on their own. A firefighter or other responsible individual should be assigned to stay with them until the victims have been removed from the scene (Figure 19.14).

Witness Control

As mentioned earlier, witnesses should be separated from those who were involved in the incident *and* from each other. Experience in countless emergencies — large and small — has shown that if witnesses are allowed to remain together, they inevitably talk among themselves about what they saw. In other words, they compare notes (Figure 19.15). Witnesses can be influenced by what other witnesses say, and some may subconsciously modify or color their perception of the incident to agree with what the others say they saw. Through this mutual support and reinforcement, the witnesses often develop a consensus version of the event that may or may not be accurate. In any case, this consensus version will be more biased and less spontaneous than versions from individual witnesses whose perceptions have not been influenced by others.

To accomplish the required separation and isolation of witnesses while they are waiting to be interviewed,

they should be collected in the cold zone. A firefighter or other responsible person should be assigned to each witness, and these pairs should be dispersed within the zone. If there are numerous witnesses, staff officers and other support personnel should be paired with the witnesses to avoid depleting the ranks of those directly involved in mitigating the problem.

Members assigned to individual witnesses should be attentive to what the witnesses volunteer about what they saw, but they should also be careful not to ask the witnesses leading questions that might influence their perceptions. Leading questions contain one or more conclusions within them. For example, a leading question might be, "Did you see the bus cross the center line before it hit the car?" This question assumes that the bus crossed the center line before the collision, which may or may not be true. It also assumes that both vehicles were moving before the collision, which may or may not be true. Leading questions tend to be closed-end questions — those that only require a "yes" or "no" answer. On the other hand, open-ended questions require a more expressive response. For example, an open-ended question might be, "Where were you when the accident occurred?"

Another extremely important element in the control of an incident scene is how to effectively and sensitively deal with those directly and indirectly involved. In some departments, this concern has come to be called *occupant services.*

Occupant Services

Occupant services involves firefighters seeing beyond the obvious physical impact of the incident on those directly and indirectly involved — the victims and the witnesses — and being aware of and sensitive to the mental and emotional impact as well. Of course, displaced victims should be medically evaluated and treated as needed and given shelter from the elements (perhaps in a department vehicle), and the appropriate relief agen cies should be called (Figure 19.16). But in addition, firefighters should help those directly involved to notify relatives, etc. — perhaps by making a department cellular phone available to them. Firefighters should also be aware of what those at the scene may see or may have seen — seriously injured or dead victims, major property losses (perhaps irreplaceable items), and firefighters doing things that the observers do not understand (forcible entry, ventilation, taking what seems like an extraordinarily long time to stabilize a victim instead of rushing them off to the hospital, etc.). It is an important part of occupant services to provide those at the scene with a reasonable explanation of why the firefighters are doing what they are doing (Figure 19.17). They should also be given accurate and timely information about the progress of the incident and an estimate of if and when they might be able to reoccupy their property. If it is safe to do so, property owners should be escorted through the damaged area so they can see it for themselves.

If those at the scene witnessed deaths and/or serious injuries, a CISD team may be called to the scene to deal with the victims and witnesses. In addition — and this cannot be overemphasized — firefighters must be aware that their every action is being observed. Innocent jokes, laughter, horseplay, or even high-fives for a job well done can be misunderstood by those at the scene (Figure 19.18). These seemingly innocuous gestures can make the firefighters appear uncaring and callous. Years of goodwill can be destroyed in a single moment.

A sometimes critically important part of controlling an emergency scene is the need to protect those nearby who might be at risk. In general, there are two ways to accomplish this objective — *evacuation* and *sheltering in place*.

Evacuation

Evacuation of a building or neighborhood may be necessary during an emergency operation. Depending on the number of people involved and their condition, evacuation can be a relatively simple or a very complex operation. After it has been determined that evacuation is necessary, the next thing that must be determined is what area needs to be cleared. In the case of a structure fire, moving the occupants either out of the involved building or to a safe haven within the building (sheltering in place) may be all that is needed. However, in the case of a hazardous materials incident or a major wildland fire, a large number of people may have to be moved a considerable distance to ensure their safety.

One important element in a successful large-scale evacuation is pre-incident planning. If the department has a pre-incident plan for various levels of evacuation from target hazards within the jurisdiction, the chances for an efficient and timely evacuation are greatly enhanced. Working with other local agencies, the fire department should develop contingency plans for small-, medium-, and large-scale evacuations. An effective means of notifying people when to evacuate is

Figure 19.14 Family members should not be left alone at the scene.

Figure 19.15 Witnesses should not be allowed to compare notes.

Figure 19.16 Those involved should be sheltered from the weather.

Chapter 19 • Incident Scene Management **265**

Figure 19.17 Fire suppression activities should be explained to the property owner.

Figure 19.19 Law enforcement personnel can assist in evacuation notifications.

Figure 19.18 Firefighters' actions can be misinterpreted by others.

Figure 19.20 Large public buildings may be used as relocation centers.

also needed. Arrangements should be made with local television and radio stations to broadcast evacuation orders and information.

Law enforcement and emergency preparedness (civil defense) personnel can be extremely helpful in large-scale evacuations. Law enforcement personnel can patrol an area and make announcements over public-address systems. Both law enforcement and emergency preparedness personnel can conduct door-to-door evacuation notifications if necessary (Figure 19.19). Evacuees should be given clear directions as to where they should relocate and approximately how long they will be displaced. Those who cannot leave the area and relocate on their own should be assisted in doing so. Some people may refuse to leave their homes or businesses. Depending on the reason for the evacuation and on local protocols, they may be either allowed to stay or placed in protective custody (arrested) by law enforcement personnel and forced to leave.

Before people are asked to leave, some adequate place to temporarily relocate them should be identified, and security for their unoccupied homes and businesses must be provided. If an incident involves only a few people, they may go or be taken to the homes of friends or family. Large-scale evacuations may require the use of churches, schools, auditoriums, municipal buildings, or hotels/

motels (Figure 19.20). The cooperation of those in charge of these facilities, as well as of the Red Cross and similar organizations, should be enlisted during pre-incident planning. Provisions should also be made to feed the anticipated number of displaced people, if necessary. Evacuees should be checked in when they arrive at a relocation center and checked out when they leave.

In most evacuations, the majority of those displaced will be ambulatory and can provide their own transportation to relocation centers; however, some will be nonambulatory and without personal transportation. Of the nonambulatory, most will be in wheelchairs, but some will be completely bedridden. Some will be on full-time oxygen or other life-support systems. These exceptional needs must be anticipated and provisions made for them during pre-incident planning.

Air Evacuation

If helicopters are to be used to transport injured or uninjured people, company-level personnel may be responsible for setting up the landing zone (LZ). They should identify a large open area that is close to the scene but out of the danger zone. Appropriate landing sites might include empty parking lots, open fields, parks, golf courses, highways, or median strips. The unobstructed open area should be at least 70×70 feet (21 m by 21 m), with no more than a 2 percent slope (Figure 19.21). Helicopters rarely land straight down or take off straight up, so the area surrounding the landing zone should be clear of tall obstructions. The landing zone should be well-marked so that it can be easily seen by the pilot. For this purpose, any objects that will not be blown about by the downdraft and that contrast starkly with the color of the landing surface may be used. Some jurisdictions allow flares to be used if there is no danger of them starting fires; others do not. The use of flares to mark the LZ, as well as other protocols and requirements, should be verified with helicopter personnel and made a part of the department's training for helicopter operations. Hand lights or vehicle headlights may be used to mark the LZ at night.

CAUTION: During night operations, personnel should *never* shine lights toward an operating helicopter, whether it is aloft or on the ground.

Sheltering in Place

The theory of sheltering in place (also called *safe haven*) is that if there is too little time to conduct a full-scale evacuation, it may be just as effective to simply have the occupants remain inside the protective cocoon of the building until the danger has passed. In response to the Americans with Disabilities Act (ADA), many new buildings and those that have undergone major renovation now include what are called *areas of rescue assistance.*

These areas have certain minimum structural requirements (including a means of communication) and fire protection features that effectively isolate them from the rest of the building. They provide a safe haven for the occupants without them having to leave the building. In case of a fire in the building, those occupants who cannot exit the building can simply go to one of these areas and await rescue by firefighters. It is important that these areas be identified during pre-incident surveys and clearly indicated on pre-incidents plans.

A rather common application of the theory of sheltering in place is in fires in the wildland/urban interface. Firefighters and others who are in danger of being overrun by a fast-moving wildland fire can take refuge in a structure until the flame front passes. Even if the structure catches fire and eventually burns to the ground, it will protect the occupants long enough for them to survive the wildland fire, and they can escape the structure before it is completely consumed (Figure 19.22). They will then be in a burned over area that is relatively safe.

Another use of this concept is in the release of airborne contaminants in hazardous materials incidents. If the release has been stopped and all that remains is a windborne cloud of toxic vapor or gas, those inside buildings downwind of the release may be safer if they simply close all doors, windows, and vents, shut down HVAC, and remain inside until the cloud passes.

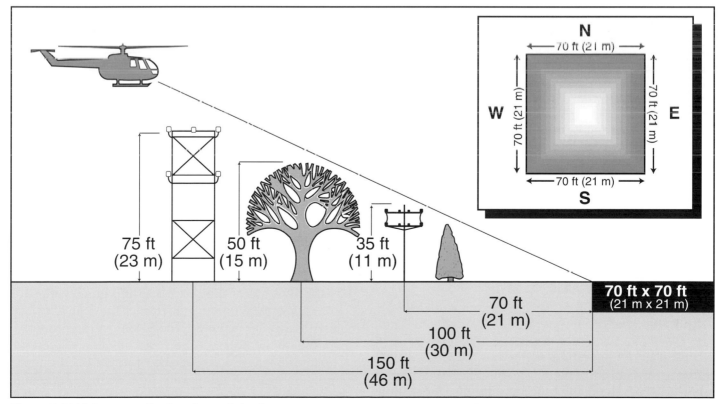

Figure 19.21 Minimum specifications for a safe landing zone.

Figure 19.22 Firefighters can take refuge in threatened structures.

Company officers should participate in their department's planning for how to deal with large numbers of people at risk because of some approaching threat to their safety. They should be aware of the advantages and disadvantages of both evacuation and sheltering in place.

As soon as the emergency is stabilized (earlier if personnel are available on scene), department personnel should make contact with all those who were displaced during the incident to determine their status and needs. See Occupant Services section earlier in this chapter.

However, the need for scene control does not end with evacuating those who were threatened by the emergency. An emergency scene must be controlled until the emergency responders have mitigated the problem — and sometimes for a considerable period of time thereafter. Therefore, the final period of incident scene control extends through the termination of the incident and the release of the scene.

Termination of the Incident

The termination phase of an emergency operation involves such obvious elements as retrieving pieces of equipment used in the operation. It also involves less obvious elements such as investigating the cause(s) of the incident, releasing the scene to those responsible for it, and conducting critical incident stress debriefings (CISD) with personnel who were directly involved with the victims.

Equipment Retrieval

Depending on the size, complexity, and length of time involved in the operation, the job of retrieving all the various pieces of equipment used may be very easy, or it may be very difficult and time-consuming. Under some circumstances, it can also be quite dangerous.

Collecting Equipment

The process of identifying and collecting pieces of equipment assigned to the various pieces of apparatus on-scene is much easier if each piece of equipment is clearly marked (Figure 19.23). However, it may be necessary for the driver/operators of emergency apparatus on the scene to conduct an inventory of their equipment prior to leaving the scene. If the operation was large enough to require the establishment of a demobilization unit, that unit will coordinate the recovery of loaned items, such as portable radios, and documenting lost or damaged pieces of apparatus and equipment.

Abandonment

In some cases, the environment within the emergency scene may be too hazardous to justify sending personnel back to retrieve pieces of equipment — even expensive ones. Rather than putting personnel at risk to retrieve tools and equipment in the hazard zone, they simply abandon the equipment in place. It may be retrievable after the scene has been restored, or it may be possible to recover the cost of replacing the abandoned equipment from the owner of the property, insurance, or government assistance. The process of recovering the costs of abandoned equipment, and the need to replace lost or damaged equipment quickly, underscores the need to fully document every emergency incident.

Investigation

All incidents should be investigated at some level. At the very minimum, a departmental investigation should be conducted for purposes of reviewing and critiquing the operation. However, if several members were injured or if one or more were killed in the incident, the incident will be investigated by the Occupational Safety and Health Administration (OSHA) and perhaps by other entities such as the jurisdiction's insurance carrier. Obviously, if the emergency was the result of a crime, such as a bombing, law enforcement agencies will also investigate the incident (Figure 19.24). Company officers must communicate and cooperate fully with incident command to support this phase of the operation.

Release of Scene

Once firefighters respond to an emergency scene, they assume control of the scene and the immediate surrounding area. Within certain limits, they can deny access to anyone, including the owner of the property. Legitimate members of the news media have certain constitutionally protected rights of access, but the interpretation of these rights vary from state to state and from country to country. Firefighters should be guided

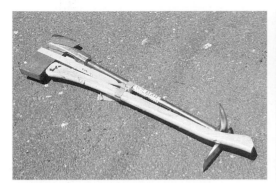
Figure 19.23 All equipment should be clearly marked.

Figure 19.24 Some incident scenes are also crime scenes. *Courtesy of Mike Wieder.*

Figure 19.25 The property owner may be required to provide security.

by local protocols, but at the very least, they should communicate with incident command to maintain safety and ensure coordinated and accurate information being released.

The process of releasing control of the scene back to the owner or other responsible party is sometimes not as straightforward as it might seem. The owner or responsible party should be escorted on a tour of the scene, or as close to it as possible consistent with safety, and should be given an explanation of any remaining hazards. If the scene is still too hazardous to leave unattended, the owner may be required to post a security guard, erect a security fence around the hazard area, or do both (Figure 19.25). Before the scene is released, the department may require the owner to sign a written release that describes the hazards and stipulates the conditions the owner must meet. This, too, is a part of occupant services referred to earlier in this chapter.

Critical Incident Stress Debriefing

Because the injuries suffered by the victims in some incidents can be extremely gruesome and horrific, the firefighters and any others who had to deal directly with the victims should be *required* to attend a critical incident stress debriefing (CISD) process. Because individuals react to and deal with extreme stress in different ways — some more successfully than others — and because the effects of unresolved stress reactions tend to accumulate, participation in this type of process should not be optional.

The process should actually start *before* personnel enter the scene if it is known that conditions exist there that are likely to produce psychological or emotional stress for those involved. This is done through a *prebriefing* process wherein the personnel who are about to enter the scene are told what to expect so that they can prepare themselves.

If personnel will be required to work more than one shift in these conditions, they should go through a minor debriefing, sometimes called "defusing," at the end of each shift. They should also attend the full debriefing process within 72 hours of completing their work on the incident.

Summary

Controlling an emergency scene can be one of the most important elements in the successful disposition of an incident. Effective scene control can support the life safety objective by protecting emergency responders from traffic hazards, by facilitating a personnel accountability system, by preventing curious bystanders from wandering into hazardous areas, and by removing (evacuating) people from potentially hazardous areas. It also supports other incident objectives by keeping the incident scene free of distractions, prevents interference with emergency responders, and prevents property from being looted. Company officers who are assigned to scene control should not feel that they are being left out of the action — rather they should feel proud to have been given such an important assignment.

This chapter provides information that will assist the reader in meeting the following job performance requirements from NFPA 1021, *Standard for Fire Officer Professional Qualifications*, 1997 edition. The colored portions indicate the topics addressed in the chapter. The numbers of the job performance requirements are also noted directly in the sections of text where they are addressed. Those in the following list that are denoted with an asterisk (*) are global in nature and are covered by reading the chapter in its entirety.

Fire Officer I

2-6.2 Develop an initial action plan, given size-up information for an incident and assigned emergency response resources, so that resources are deployed to control the emergency.

(a) *Prerequisite Knowledge:* Elements of a size-up, standard operating procedures for emergency operations, and fire behavior.

(b) *Prerequisite Skills:* The ability to analyze emergency scene conditions, to allocate resources and to communicate verbally.

Fire Officer II

3-6.1 Produce operational plans, given a hazardous materials incident and another emergency requiring multi-unit operations, so that required resources, their assignments, and safety considerations for successful control of the incident are identified.

(a) *Prerequisite Knowledge:* Standard operating procedures; national, state/provincial, and local information resources available for the handling of hazardous materials under emergency situations; basic fire control and emergency operation procedures; and incident management system; and a personnel accountability system.

(b) *Prerequisite Skills:* The ability to implement an incident management system, to communicate verbally, and to supervise and account for assigned personnel under emergency conditions.

In addition to all their other duties, company officers are responsible for taking charge of any emergency at which they are the first-arriving officer. This can sometimes be a heavy responsibility and a daunting task. If there is a roaring fire with billowing smoke, the temptation to develop tunnel vision and focus exclusively on the fire can be quite strong. If there are multiple casualties (especially children), the urge to focus on relieving their pain and suffering to the exclusion of the rest of the situation can be almost overwhelming. However, in these stressful and sometimes chaotic situations, the company officer's first and most important duty is to protect himself and his crew. Life safety includes those activities that reduce the threat of death or serious injury — to the emergency personnel as well as civilians. In many respects it is more important to protect emergency personnel than civilians because if the emergency personnel become victims themselves, they cannot help anyone else. Addressing the life safety issue may include evacuation, limiting exposure to the hazards, or simply requiring full protective gear. Life safety must always remain the first and highest priority.

The first-in officer's next most important duty is to answer one question: Are the resources at scene and en route sufficient to handle this situation? The reason that this question is so important is *reflex time*. Also called *lead time*, reflex time is the amount of time it takes for additional resources to be requested, to be dispatched, to reach the scene, and to achieve fireground objectives — apply water to the fire, ventilate, evacuate, set up exposure protection, etc. If the call for these resources is delayed because of a company officer's indecision, the resources may arrive at scene too late for them to be effective. Then, even more resources may have to be requested. In order for first-in officers to be able to determine what resources are needed, they must be able to quickly assess the situation and decide on resource needs. If there is any doubt about what resources will be needed,

these officers should request any and all resources that *might* be needed. If any of the additional resources are subsequently deemed unnecessary, they can be canceled while still en route or after they arrive at the scene. To make these critical decisions, company officers must be able to perform a competent size-up of the situation.

If the initial size-up confirms that there is a legitimate emergency in progress, the first-in officer is also responsible for initiating the proper command mode, developing and implementing an incident action plan, and maintaining control of the incident unless and until relieved. Regardless of whether the incident is small enough to require only the first-in unit or is large enough to require massive numbers of various types of resources, an incident command/management system must be used. (See Chapter 21, "Action Plan Implementation," for discussion of command modes.)

This chapter discusses the importance of size-up, the elements of size-up, and the step-by-step process that is involved. Also discussed are two different approaches to sizing up an emergency situation. The relationship of size-up to the priorities involved in fighting fires and handling other types of emergencies is also examined. Finally, the various types of incident plans are discussed.

Size-Up Defined

Size-up — an evaluation or assessment of the situation — has been defined by numerous authors writing about emergency operations. While each author may take a slightly different view of the process or use slightly different words to describe it, the process is essentially the same in all cases. For purposes of this manual, the following definition will be used: *Size-up* is the ongoing process of evaluating a situation to determine what has happened, what is happening, what is likely to happen, and what resources will be needed to resolve the situation.

Obviously, there are many different ways to fulfill the requirements of this definition.

Traditional Size-Up

Lloyd Layman and others have written extensively about the size-up process. Decades after Layman wrote his seminal work *Fire Fighting Tactics*, its principles are as valid today as ever. In his book, Layman described a five-step process for analyzing any emergency situation. The steps he described are:

1. Facts

2. Probabilities

3. Own situation

4. Decision

5. Plan of operation

Facts

The facts of the situation are those things that are known about it. Some of these items are time (month, day, hour), location (address, business name, landmarks), nature of the emergency (fire, hazardous materials release, structural collapse, motor vehicle accident [MVA] , etc.), life hazard (occupants and firefighters), exposures (adjacent uninvolved property), building or buildings involved (or vehicles, etc.), fire (or other emergency), weather (wind, temperature extremes, humidity, etc.). All these items can and should be factored into the company officer's thought processes regarding the emergency.

Probabilities

Obviously, probabilities are things that are not known for sure, but based on the facts that are known, probabilities are things that are *likely* to happen. In which direction is the fire likely to spread, given existing wind and topography? Are exposures likely to become involved? Are explosions likely? Is a secondary collapse likely? Is an evacuation of those downwind likely to be needed? Are additional resources likely to be needed? If so, what types and how many? These are just some of the questions that must be answered regarding the probabilities of the situation.

Many of the decisions involved in the probabilities phase of a size-up can be made easier and the result more accurate if the officer making the decisions has some knowledge of the following:

- Fire behavior (from training and education)

- The building or topography involved (from pre-incident planning)

This knowledge is especially important if the building involved has lightweight trusses and/or built-in fire protection. Many modern wood-frame buildings have lightweight truss components that have a tendency to fail early in a fire—creating a significant risk of early collapse for first-in crews. Also, knowledge of any built-in fire protection systems — and how they are inspected and maintained — can suggest how much first-in crews can rely on them. Unless these systems (automatic sprinklers, standpipes, etc.) are regularly inspected and tested, they may not perform as designed.

Own Situation

The first-in officer's own situation is one set of facts that is known about the overall situation. Among these facts are the number and types of resources already at the scene. Also known are what additional resources are available immediately, with some delay, and with considerable delay. Knowing the capabilities and limitations of these resources are important factors in the development of an incident action plan. Also to be considered in this phase is the officer's assessment of his own ability to deal with the situation based on his training and experience.

Decision

Even though Layman labeled this step in the singular, he went on to identify two or more separate decisions that must be made in the ongoing size-up process—an initial decision and one or more supplemental decisions. Even the initial decision may be seen as three. The first involves deciding whether the resources at the scene and those en route are adequate for the situation; the second, how to deploy the resources already at the scene in a way that will accomplish the most; and the third is what to do with the resources that arrive (immediate deployment, Level I or Level II staging?). Obviously, if lives are threatened, this is the first and highest priority. Company officers should not forget that the life hazard also includes themselves and their crews. If lives are not in immediate jeopardy, the initial decision may be to use the members of his crew to establish a command structure with which to manage the balance of the incoming resources (Figure 20.1).

As the incident progresses and the situation changes, other decisions will have to be made. For instance, the incident commander (IC) needs to decide whether the initial deployment of the resources is still producing the desired results or whether the plan needs to be changed. Also, on very protracted incidents, decisions have to be made regarding relief crews, additional supplies, etc. The longer the incident goes on, the more supplemental decisions will be required.

Plan of Operation

The information gathered in the size-up process serves no purpose unless it is used as a basis for making decisions about how to handle the incident. Depending upon the nature and scope of the incident, the incident action plan may be simple or complex. On relatively small, routine incidents, those that do not involve more than the initial assignment, the plan need not be in writing — but there *must* be a plan. Larger, more complex incidents will require a written incident action plan, often with numerous annexes (Figure 20.2). The incident action plan normally covers a single operational period, usually 12 hours.

Three-Step Process

Another way to conform to the size-up definition given earlier involves using a three-step process. Evaluating any emergency, regardless of its specific nature, can be done with the following general steps:

1. Locate
2. Isolate
3. Mitigate

Locate

The *location* step is the process of defining the problem — identifying its location, nature, and scope. It includes everything from getting the correct address or location of the incident, to defining the incident's limits. This could mean everything from estimating the extent of a wildland fire's perimeter, to determining how fast and in what direction it is spreading, and to identifying what lies in the path of the fire (Figure 20.3). It could also mean determining whether a fire inside a structure has spread beyond the room of origin, area of origin, or floor of origin. It would also include determining whether all occupants have left a burning and/or collapsed building or whether a search and rescue operation is necessary. Another example of this step would be the initial survey of a vehicle accident scene to make sure that all victims — not just the obvious ones — are located and their condition assessed. Other examples are taking a patient's medical history and doing a total body exam (Figure 20.4).

Isolate

The second step in this process, *isolation*, involves identifying what will be needed to interrupt the dynamic nature of the incident. By definition, an *emergency* is a situation that is "emerging." In other words, the situation is getting worse and will continue to do so unless and until something is done to stop it — or it runs out of fuel, the patient dies, etc. A wildland fire will continue to spread (and consume valuable property and put more lives at risk) until it is contained. A structure fire will burn until nothing but the foundation remains — and may spread to adjacent structures unless these exposures are protected and the original fire is controlled. Contaminated runoff water will continue to spread the contamination until the water is dammed or diked. Injured MVA victims will continue to deteriorate until they are treated for shock, any bleeding is stopped, and any injuries are treated. The isolation step is where the IC determines how to stabilize the situation — to stop it from getting worse — until the resources needed to mitigate the problem can be brought to bear. This may

Figure 20.1 Organizing for an attack may be the best use of personnel.

Figure 20.2 Large incidents require a written action plan.

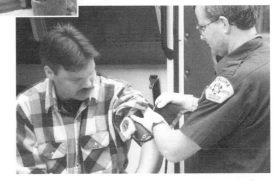

Figure 20.3 Determining the extent of involvement is part of the location step.

Figure 20.4 Assessing a patient is part of defining the problem.

include a decision of whether to operate in a defensive, offensive, or rescue mode.

Mitigate

The third and final step in this process is *mitigation*. This means determining what will be needed to eliminate the problem. It may mean deciding whether additional strike teams, heavy equipment, and/or air attack will be needed to extinguish a wildland fire (Figure 20.5). It may mean striking additional alarms to get more personnel and equipment to the scene of a structure fire (Figure 20.6). It may mean obtaining additional ambulances or a medevac helicopter to transport seriously injured patients (Figure 20.7). It may mean that one or more tow trucks will be needed to remove damaged and disabled vehicles.

Company officers must use the size-up method adopted by their department. However, considering that any emergency situation can be evaluated using this simple three-step process, departments may want to consider adopting this method of performing an initial size-up.

Application

The size-up process actually begins before an incident is reported and continues through the fire department's arrival at the scene and throughout the incident. This section discusses the application of size-up theory to those time periods.

Pre-Incident

The size-up process not only begins before an incident is reported, but it begins well before—perhaps even months or years before. The information gathered in the pre-incident planning process, discussed in Chapter 17, "Pre-Incident Planning," can be an extremely important part of the size-up process (Figure 20.8). This information is gathered at a time when there is no reason to hurry, and the data can be carefully reviewed and analyzed. When decisions are made regarding resources that will be needed to mitigate certain hypothetical incidents at specific locations, these decisions can and should be translated into operational plans for those anticipated incidents. Doing so can reduce the number of decisions that personnel have to make during an incident at any of the surveyed locations.

Regardless of whether pre-incident plans have been developed, the size-up process still begins before an alarm is sounded. Each day as company officers and their firefighters travel to work, they should begin a general size-up of the situation that day (Figure 20.9). They should review the weather forecast and ask themselves how and to what extent the weather might affect any emergency to which they are called. Will response time be slowed because rain or ice has made the roads slick and dangerous? Will detours be necessary because of construction

Figure 20.7 Transporting patients is part of mitigating a mass casualty incident.

Figure 20.5 Calling for air attack is part of mitigating a wildland fire.

Figure 20.6 Ordering more resources is part of mitigating a large incident. *Courtesy of National Interagency Fire Center.*

Figure 20.8 The information gathered during pre-incident surveys is used in size-up.

or other factors — parades, demonstrations, etc.? Will ventilation crews be at additional risk because of wet or icy roofs? Will the wind combine with high temperature and low humidity to increase the likelihood of wildland fires? Will these conditions make wildland fires burn more intensely and make them more difficult to extinguish? Will extreme weather adversely affect trapped and injured victims? Are there any extremes of temperature that could make it more difficult and perhaps dangerous for firefighters working outside? Firefighters performing strenuous work while wearing protective clothing in hot weather can be vulnerable to heat-related illnesses such as heat exhaustion or even heatstroke (Figure 20.10). Company officers should be aware of the possible effects of weather and other factors (crew strength, inexperienced members, etc.) on their companies' ability to perform effectively and safely.

And when an alarm is sounded, the size-up process should continue during the response. Company officers should consider the time of day when the alarm is received. Is it in the morning when burning conditions will become more extreme as the day goes on? Or is it already late afternoon or evening and the burning conditions can be expected to moderate? Is it during a time of day when the address at which the incident was reported is likely to be heavily occupied? Are the occupants likely to need help getting out of the building? Is it the middle of the night when the occupants may be sleeping? Is it during school hours on a weekday? How are the month, day of the week, and time of day likely to affect traffic congestion along the response route? How will the incident be affected? Company officers should continue to evaluate such variables as they respond to the scene of a reported incident.

Additionally, company officers should factor in any other data that they can gather before arriving at the scene of an emergency. For example, they can observe cloud formations and be able to anticipate the weather's possible effects on fire behavior (Figure 20.11). They can observe the amount, color, pressure, and movement of any smoke produced by the fire (Figure 20.12). This information, combined with a knowledge of fire behavior and of the building or area where the fire is burning, can help company officers better assess resource needs. Company officers should also evaluate any additional information provided by the communications center over the radio during the response.

Figure 20.9 Firefighters should begin assessing conditions as they travel to work.

Figure 20.11 Company officers should continue to evaluate the situation as they respond.

Figure 20.10 The effects of weather on personnel must be considered.

Figure 20.12 Amount, color, pressure, and movement of smoke should be observed. *Courtesy of National Interagency Fire Center.*

On Arrival

The most intense part of the size-up process may occur at the time of arrival at the emergency scene. As mentioned earlier, the first-in officer may come upon a scene of utter chaos. In addition to the problem and those involved in it, there may be numerous spectators wandering the scene making it difficult to distinguish them from the occupants. There may be hysterical bystanders screaming for the fire crew to do something! And, yes, there may be photographers jostling for the best camera position.

The first-in officer must resist the urge that is sometimes called the "candle/moth syndrome," which is to focus exclusively on the fire. Unless the scene is extremely large, as in a huge wildland fire, the first-in officer should take a quick walk around the incident to view it from all angles. He must focus on the job at hand — answering the question discussed earlier, "Can the resources at the scene and en route handle this situation?" If the answer is "no," or even "maybe," then he must request additional resources *immediately* (Figure 20.13). Addressing this critical question is why the initial size-up sets the tone for the balance of the incident. If the size-up is accurate and the needed resources are either at the scene, en route, or requested early in the incident, the incident should be handled successfully and in a timely manner. However, if there are not enough resources initially and the request for additional ones is delayed, the crews are likely to start the incident "behind the curve" and may never catch up. In that case, the problem wins, and the firefighters lose. Then, the best the fire forces can do is fight a holding action until the problem resolves itself by burning itself out, by all the hazardous material escaping and dissipating into the atmosphere, or by the victims expiring. These are not the desired outcomes, so it is critically important for the initial size-up to be done quickly and well.

An additional, but no less important, decision that must be made initially is whether to operate in a defensive, offensive, or rescue mode. This decision will usually be driven by the nature and scope of the problem and by

Figure 20.13 If additional resources are needed, they should be ordered immediately.

the number and types of resources on-scene or immediately available. If the situation is beyond the capabilities of the initial alarm resources, then a defensive mode of operations is probably most appropriate until additional resources arrive. Even if the initial alarm resources are insufficient to control and mitigate the problem, if they are capable of attacking the problem safely and can make a positive difference in the ultimate outcome, then an offensive mode may be appropriate.

During the Incident

Once past the initial phase of the incident, fire crews will be busy carrying out their assignments and, hopefully, making progress toward resolving the problem. This phase (between arrival and problem resolution) can be relatively short, or it may last for a considerable length of time. If the problem is relatively small and/or the crews get ahead of the curve early, the problem may be resolved in a few minutes. If not, they may be on the scene for days. During this phase, the situation will change as it either gets worse or gets better. In either case, the decisions that were based on the initial size-up may or may not remain valid. The IC must continue to size up the situation and make changes to the incident action plan as needed. For example, if the situation continues to deteriorate, the IC may need to request additional resources or decide to switch the mode of operation from offensive to defensive. If the situation is gradually improving but will take a long time to resolve, the IC may need to plan for crew reliefs, logistical needs, etc. (Figure 20.14). As the situation improves, the IC should continually reassess (size up) the resource needs and release those that are no longer needed as soon as possible.

Just as when making an initial size-up, as the incident progresses the IC must remain focused on the priorities in the situation. The following section discusses the priorities that are common to all types of emergencies.

Figure 20.14 Protracted incidents require additional resources and logistical support.

In every emergency situation, whether it is a fire, rescue, vehicle extrication, or whatever, the priorities are basically the same. These priorities are:

- Life safety

- Incident stabilization

- Property conservation

While the terms may be slightly different in various types of emergencies, the actual priorities remain the same. Life safety is always the first and highest priority, although rescue may not be the first *action* taken by the first-in crews. In some cases, it is necessary to control the fire before attempting a rescue. The second priority is to isolate and/or mitigate the problem. If a fire can be controlled or a hazardous materials release contained, then both the situation will be stabilized and the third priority — conserving property (which includes protecting the environment) — can be addressed. Once the problem is stabilized and contained, it is no longer a threat to adjacent properties.

RECEO

Layman also recognized the need for identifying priorities in emergency situations. Even though his list of priorities is couched in fire control terms, he also acknowledged that the same priorities could be applied to any type of emergency. Layman's list of priorities are represented by the acronym RECEO (ree-cee-oh). Layman also included two other functions that are almost exclusively related to structure fires — *ventilation* and *salvage.* Since Layman intended RECEO to be both a list of priorities *and* a sequence of operations, he did not include ventilation and salvage in the list because they are not needed in every fire, and they are not always performed at the same point in the fires where they are used. However, RECEO always applies, and those initials stand for the following:

- Rescue

- Exposures

- Confinement

- Extinguishment

- Overhaul

Rescue

This is the term that Layman used to identify the life safety aspect of fireground priorities. In most departments, the term is taken to include humans, pets, and livestock. However, the term is not limited to the occupants; it also includes the firefighters. In fact, it can be argued that the firefighter's life safety is the most important. As discussed earlier in this chapter, the basis for this idea is that if a firefighter is disabled by an injury, he cannot rescue the occupants who may be depending upon him (Figure 20.15). Whether this position is valid or not, clearly the firefighters' life safety is at least as important as the occupants'. Therefore, company officers should neither expect nor allow their firefighters to sacrifice themselves by taking unnecessary risks on the fireground.

Being the first and highest priority, life safety takes precedence over any and all other considerations. This means that, *if necessary*, a building may be allowed to burn to the ground in order to facilitate a rescue. The same is true regarding firefighters — they should not be ordered into buildings that are already lost nor ordered into life-threatening situations to recover a body. Most buildings and their contents are insured, and even if they are not, they can usually be replaced. Of course there are irreplaceable items, but no mere object is worth a human life.

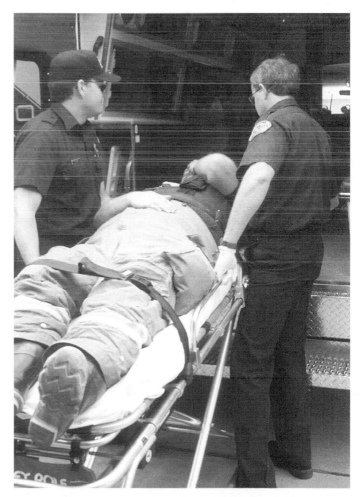

Figure 20.15 Injured firefighters cannot help others.

Addressing the rescue or life safety priority can place the IC in one of the most stressful situations in any emergency. As mentioned earlier, firefighters should not be ordered into life-threatening situations to recover a victim's body. While any trapped victim should be given the benefit of the doubt, the IC must decide (based on the best information available) whether it is reasonable to expect that anyone remaining in the situation is still viable and, therefore, that firefighters should be ordered in to conduct a search and rescue operation. There is no clear, unequivocal answer to this dilemma.

Exposures

This is the term that Layman used to describe the need to limit the fire or other emergency to the property of origin. Similar to the idea of sacrificing a building to facilitate a rescue, limiting the problem to the building or property of origin means, *if necessary*, allowing the building of origin to burn in order to save adjacent buildings that are uninvolved or only slightly involved. If the first-arriving unit(s) have only enough resources to begin to resolve the problem or to keep it from spreading — but not both — then they should focus their efforts on keeping the problem from spreading to uninvolved properties. It may be that attacking the source of the problem is the best way to protect the exposures, but if not, attacking the source of the problem is of a lower priority than protecting the adjacent but uninvolved properties. Stopping oncoming traffic to protect the scene of a vehicle accident from being hit by other vehicles and thereby compounding the situation could be seen as addressing this priority (Figure 20.16).

Confinement

This is the term that Layman used to describe the need to confine the fire or other problem to the smallest possible area within the property of origin. In the case of a structure fire, the priority is to confine the fire to the room of origin, if possible. Failing that, it should be limited to the area or floor of origin; failing that, the building of origin. The principle can be applied to other types of emergencies as well — limiting a hazardous materials problem to the smallest area of the property in which it originated, for example.

Extinguishment

Even though Layman used this fire-specific term, the concept can be applied to any type of emergency. The concept is that of mitigating the problem. It could mean extinguishing a fire, performing a rescue, stopping the flow of a hazardous material, or packaging and extricating the victims of a vehicle accident. This is the phase of the operation in which the incident action plan that was based on the initial size-up is implemented. If the size-up was accurate and the plan was sound, the incident can usually be resolved successfully and in a timely manner.

Overhaul

Layman carried his list of priorities beyond mitigating the problem. He also included restoring the scene to as nearly normal as possible. In this phase of the operation, holes that were cut for access or ventilation are covered to protect the property from further damage by the elements (Figure 20.17). After a fire has been knocked down, any and all hidden fire must be found and extinguished. After a hazardous materials release has been stopped, liquids must be cleaned up and packaged for proper disposal, and any residues neutralized. Following a vehicle accident, the roadway must be cleared, any spilled liquids picked up or neutralized, and traffic flow restored. This phase of the operation can be made much easier if the proper resources were called to the scene based on an accurate initial or supplemental size-up.

Incident Plans

In order for the resources assigned to an incident to work together effectively and in a coordinated effort, they must all work from the same plan. Each resource, whether an individual fire company or an entire strike team, must know what the strategic goals and tactical objectives are for the incident and what their individual roles are in achieving those objectives. This level of coordination requires a clearly defined plan for all to follow. NFPA 1021 requires company officers to be able to develop an "initial action plan" and produce "operational

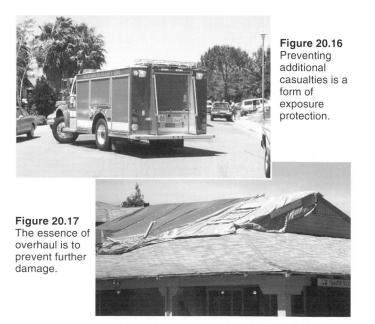

Figure 20.16 Preventing additional casualties is a form of exposure protection.

Figure 20.17 The essence of overhaul is to prevent further damage.

plans." The term *initial action plan* means the same thing as *incident action plan* (IAP), which is the term used in both the Incident Command System (ICS) and the Incident Management System (IMS). An *incident action plan* is a written or unwritten plan for the safe and efficient disposition of an emergency incident. According to the IMS, which is based on NFPA 1561, *Standard for Fire Department Incident Management System*, an incident action plan identifies "the strategic goals, tactical objectives, and support requirements for the incident." Neither command/management system defines or uses the term *operational plan*.

During an incident, the information on which an IAP is based comes from the information gathered in the initial size-up made by the first-in officer. The size-up attempts to determine what has happened, what is happening, what is likely to happen, and what resources are needed to safely and effectively handle the situation. In some cases, at least part of the information on which the initial size-up is based was gathered during a pre-incident survey well in advance of the incident.

Pre-Incident Survey Data

As described in detail in Chapter 17, "Pre-Incident Planning," fire companies should identify the target hazards (occupancies with the highest potential for the loss of lives or property) in their response districts. They should survey these occupancies to gather information about the buildings and their contents, any extraordinarily hazardous materials or processes, any impediments to access/egress, any built-in fire protection devices or systems, and anything that would affect fire behavior or fire suppression and/or rescue efforts in the buildings (Figure 20.18). These data are then analyzed and translated into operational plans for the buildings surveyed.

Figure 20.18 Information gathered during pre-incident surveys becomes part of incident plans.

Operational Plans

[NFPA 1021 3-6.1]

Operational plans are described in NFPA 1021 as those that "identify the required resources, their assignment(s)

and safety considerations for the successful control of a hazardous materials incident or other emergency requiring multi-unit operations." In most fire departments, operational plans (also called "pre-fire plans," "pre-incident plans," or "strategic plans") identify the specific resources needed to successfully deal with a variety of hypothetical incidents at a particular location or occupancy. The incident scenarios analyzed are those that are considered to be the most likely to occur at the location in question. For example, if an occupancy uses or stores large quantities of toxic or highly flammable materials, scenarios involving these materials are created and analyzed. Likewise, if an occupancy houses a large number of elderly or infirm residents, scenarios that require the evacuation of these residents or moving them to areas of safe refuge are created and analyzed. This process is applied to as many target hazards as time and staffing allow.

Operational plans often include possible resource deployments. In the most likely scenarios at a given location, possible options for deploying the initial alarm resources are studied, as well as options for the deployment of those resources that would respond only if called. Scenarios based on increasingly larger and more complex hypothetical incidents help planners to identify the resources that may be needed and to identify how they can be deployed to the best advantage.

In addition, operational plans often include provisions for a number of possible contingencies. Typical contingencies might include unusually severe weather conditions that could greatly increase the potential for wildland fires starting and increase the likelihood of these fires spreading at a greater-than-normal rate. Considering these variables, an operational plan might specify an increase in the initial alarm resources at certain points on the daily burning index. Operational plans might specify different initial alarm resource levels for a given occupancy if the number of people normally in the building is significantly different at different times of the day or night. For example, the operational plan for an elementary school might specify that the initial alarm assignment be doubled if an alarm is received from the school during the hours when it is normally in operation. However, it might also specify that a lesser response be dispatched at other hours. The operational plans for occupancies that store large quantities of flammable liquids might specify that crash/rescue vehicles from the local airport be a part of the initial alarm assignment so that their foam-making capabilities are immediately available if needed (Figure 20.19). The operational plans for large industrial complexes might specify that the first-arriving unit is to respond directly to the fire alarm

Figure 20.19 Plans may include a need for specialized vehicles to respond.

panel or the plant security station but that other responding units are to stage at the facility gates and await directions from the first-in unit.

In essence, the data gathered at any particular target hazard is used to project the strategic and tactical possibilities and probabilities at that location. Based on these scenarios, the resources needed are compared to the resources available in the department. If resources indicated are more than or different from what the department has, planners can then recommend the purchase of the needed resources or the development of mutual aid or automatic aid agreements with nearby departments that do have the needed resources.

Incident Action Plans
[NFPA 1021 2-6.2]

Given the information obtained in the initial size-up, and any other information available in an operational plan, the IC can devise a plan for the safe and efficient disposition of an incident. As mentioned earlier, on relatively small, routine incidents, the plan need not be in writing, but there *must* be a plan, and it must be communicated throughout the on-scene organization. On larger, more complex incidents, the plan should be in writing, and it must be distributed to the leaders of all units assigned to the incident and communicated to all incident personnel. Because subsequent litigation is a possibility with every incident, it is also important to have a written record of what was done during the incident. Every incident requires its own action plan, and all IAPs have certain common elements. However, because the factors that they address vary in importance from one incident to the next, every IAP is unique. The incident action plan specifies the strategic goals and tactical objectives for the next operational period, usually 12 hours.

Strategic Goals

Strategic goals are the overall plan for controlling the incident. They are broad, general statements of the overall outcomes to be achieved. Prior to an incident occur-

ring, strategic goals should be translated into departmental SOPs. These goals are dictated by the three overall priorities mentioned earlier in the discussion of size-up. These priorities are:

- Life safety
- Incident stabilization
- Property conservation

These three priorities should always guide the development of the incident action plan. Deciding how to meet them dictates the tactical objectives for the incident. Strategic goals and tactical objectives must be constantly evaluated/reevaluated to ensure that they are being accomplished. This is done by the continual process of size-up. As goals and objectives are met, the situation changes — and as the situation changes — so do the priorities. Company officers must be flexible enough to cope successfully with a rapidly changing situation.

Tactical Objectives

Achieving tactical objectives leads to the completion of goals. Tactical objective statements are less general and more specific than strategic goal statements. Tactical objectives are statements of measurable outcomes. Examples of some common tactical objectives are:

- Provide for the safety of firefighters, occupants, and others.
- Contain the incident to a specified geographic area.
- Mitigate the problem.
- Restore the scene.

How these objectives are achieved is determined by how the plan is implemented. The implementation of an incident action plan is discussed in Chapter 21, "Action Plan Implementation."

Summary

The ability to quickly and accurately size up an emergency situation is a critical skill for company officers. Because they are in charge of the units most often first to arrive on the scene, they must be able to remain calm in the midst of chaos. They must be able to do this in order to identify the nature and scope of the problem, assess the current and future resource needs, and gather the information needed to develop an incident action plan. Having done that, they need to be able to develop and implement a plan for the safe and efficient disposition of the problem.

This chapter provides information that will assist the reader in meeting the following job performance requirements from NFPA 1021, *Standard for Fire Officer Professional Qualifications*, 1997 edition. The colored portions indicate the topics addressed in the chapter. The numbers of the job performance requirements are also noted directly in the sections of text where they are addressed. Those in the following list that are denoted with an asterisk (*) are global in nature and are covered by reading the chapter in its entirety.

Fire Officer I

2-6.3* Implement an action plan at an emergency operation, given assigned resources, type of incident, and a preliminary plan, so that resources are deployed to mitigate the situation.

(a) *Prerequisite Knowledge:* Standard operating procedures, resources available, basic fire control and emergency operation procedures, an incident management system, and a personnel accountability system.

(b) *Prerequisite Skills:* The ability to implement an incident management system, to communicate verbally, and to supervise and account for assigned personnel under emergency conditions.

Action Plan Implementation

When company officers are the first officers on the scene of an emergency (as is usually the case), they must immediately perform a series of critical functions. They must continue the size-up process that was begun even before the alarm was received. As described in Chapter 20, "Size-Up and Incident Plans," company officers must use whatever information is available to them to assess the situation as it exists and to project how it is likely to change so that they can develop a plan of action (incident action plan) for safely and efficiently dealing with the emergency. However, regardless of how well-conceived an incident action plan is, if the emergency is to be disposed of, the plan must be implemented.

This chapter discusses the implementation of an incident action plan. The discussion includes modes of operation and incident command/management. Personnel accountability is also discussed.

Action Plan Implementation

Once an incident action plan has been developed, it must be implemented. That is, the available resources must be deployed in a way that will do the most good. The first step in this process is to communicate the plan to all on-scene personnel. This usually starts with the first-in officer transmitting a report on conditions over the radio and formally assuming command of the incident. This is done by naming the incident and specifying the location of the command post or by using one of the other command options discussed later in this chapter (Figure 21.1). For example, an initial alarm assignment (perhaps two engines, a truck, a rescue squad, and a chief officer) is dispatched to a reported structure fire. After performing an initial size-up, the first-in company officer might transmit the following:

Company officer: Dispatch, Engine 7185.

Alarm operator: Go ahead, 7185.

Company officer: We have a working fire involving one ground floor apartment of a four-story, wood frame apartment building in the 1500 block of Maple Street. Engine 7185 is Maple command, and the command post is at the corner of Maple Street and 15th Avenue. Strike a second alarm.

Alarm operator: Copy. 7185 is Maple command, and you want a second alarm. Channel 2 is tactical.

This brief exchange accomplishes several things. It confirms that the call on which the units have been dispatched is, in fact, an emergency — a working structure fire in an occupied (as opposed to abandoned) building where there is a potential life safety hazard if the residents are at home. Depending upon the time of day, day of the week, month of the year, and other variables, there may be many residents to evacuate or there may be none. In any case, other incoming units will know that a search of the building will be necessary. They will also know to switch their radios to Channel 2 for incident traffic (Figure 21.2). This gives the units assigned to the incident a clear radio channel on which to communicate and keeps the primary channel clear for other traffic.

Figure 21.1 A company officer assumes command of an incident.

Figure 21.2 The radios on all units should be switched to the assigned channel.

Depending upon department policies and procedures, if the first-in engine did not lay a supply line from the nearest hydrant (or otherwise ensure a water supply), one of the other incoming units will have to do this (Figure 21.3). Again depending upon department policy, this may be automatic, or it may have to be assigned by the incident commander (IC). In the latter case, providing the water supply would be a part of the incident action plan and is one more thing that the first-in officer must consciously decide.

However, the first and most important part of the incident action plan — and the part that must be implemented as soon as possible — is that dealing with life safety. Addressing life safety will involve a series of decisions by the IC. One of the first decisions relates to the mode of operation. Essentially, there are three possible modes of operation — *defensive, offensive,* and *rescue.* In general, defensive and offensive modes should *not* be mixed. The offensive mode often involves rescues, but these are done in addition to the coordinated fire attack. In the rescue mode, sometimes called "all-hands rescue," search and rescue are the *primary* activity — fire attack is performed only to protect the rescuers and is incidental to the rescue operation. The IC must communicate to all company officers what each one's assignment is in implementing the life safety and other parts of the incident action plan (Figure 21.4).

Upon the arrival of the first-in unit, if an occupied building is fully involved in fire and the fire is threatening to involve other nearby buildings, then a defensive mode may be most appropriate. In this case, the occupants of the burning building either have escaped on their own or did not get out, and as difficult as the decision is, the IC may decide that the best use of the available resources is to protect the threatened exposures while allowing the original building to burn. On the other hand, if the building is heavily involved (but not fully involved), and there are enough resources on scene, then the IC may decide that an offensive mode is possible and that some firefighters can safely conduct a search, others fight the fire, and a rapid intervention crew stands by outside (Figure 21.5). If the first or second floor of a fully occupied four-story apartment building is totally involved in fire, the first-in company officer may decide that the limited resources on scene would do the most good (save the most lives) by declaring an all-hands rescue.

Defensive Mode

Essentially, operating in a defensive mode is intended to isolate or stabilize the incident — to keep it from getting any worse or any bigger. In the case of a structure fire, a defensive mode may mean sacrificing a building that is on fire to save others that are not burning. A defensive mode is usually (but not always) an exterior operation that is chosen because there are not enough resources available to conduct a safe and effective offensive attack. For example, a defensive mode may reflect a decision by the IC that the burning building is not worth the risk to firefighters to order an aggressive interior attack. This may be because the burning building is an abandoned derelict. It may be because the building is so heavily involved in fire that it is not reasonable to expect that anyone inside could still be alive, so it would not be prudent to put firefighters in mortal jeopardy by ordering them inside (Figure 21.6). It may also reflect an assessment by the IC that there are too few resources at the scene to mount an effective attack.

In this case, the IC might assign the first available engine companies to apply water to the exterior of the exposures. If resources are extremely limited, as they often are, the IC may decide to allow the building of

Figure 21.3 The second-in engine may have to provide a water supply. *Courtesy of Barry Gaab.*

Figure 21.4 The IAP must be communicated to all units.

Figure 21.5 If there are enough resources at the scene, an offensive mode may be indicated.

Figure 21.6 If the firefighters' lives are the only ones at risk, a defensive mode may be prudent. *Courtesy of Barry Gaab.*

Figure 21.7 Firefighters should not be put in jeopardy to recover a body.

Figure 21.8 In the offensive mode, truck personnel have specific responsibilities.

origin to burn until additional resources arrive. When additional resources arrive, master streams can be set up to attack the fire in the burning building from the outside.

Another example of a defensive mode of operations is a body recovery (Figure 21.7). If the IC determines that it is not reasonable to expect that anyone in the building is likely to have survived a fire, it would not be prudent to order firefighters into the building until the fire has been controlled. Likewise, if a swimmer or boater has not been seen for several hours, the search should be conducted in a defensive mode — that is, slowly and carefully — and without putting personnel at undue risk. If the victim of a trenchwall cave-in has been under tons of debris for so long that the likelihood of his survival is extremely remote or if the trench filled with water after the cave-in, the operation should probably be conducted as a recovery and not a rescue. These are very stressful and difficult decisions, but they must include a recognition that the firefighters' lives are as important as those of the victims. It does no good to sacrifice firefighters in a futile attempt to save a building that is already lost or to recover the body of someone who is already dead.

This concept is clearly stated in the decision-making model developed by the Phoenix (AZ) Fire Department (PFD). The model is a departmental SOP that is used to help PFD officers in making sound emergency response decisions. The essence of the model is as follows:

- Each emergency response is begun with the assumption that "they can protect lives and property."

- They will "risk their lives a lot, if necessary, to save savable lives."

- They will "risk their lives a little, and in a calculated manner, to save savable property."

- They will "NOT risk their lives at all to save lives and property that have already been lost."

In a still emerging incident, such as a working fire, the IC may be forced to use a defensive mode in the early stages because of resource limitations (too few personnel for two-in/two-out, for example). But as additional resources arrive at the scene, it will be possible at some point to switch from a defensive to an offensive mode of operation.

Offensive Mode

This is the mode of operation with which firefighters are most comfortable. It involves taking direct action to mitigate the problem, whatever that may be. It may be fighting a fire, performing a rescue, stopping a hazardous materials release, or extricating the occupants of a wrecked vehicle. Just as in the defensive mode, the IC must decide how to deploy the available resources in a way that will do the most good. These decisions translate into an important part of the incident action plan.

In a structure fire, the offensive mode usually means an aggressive interior attack by one or more engine companies — attacking the fire from the unburned side. In the meantime, truck personnel are assigned to perform forcible entry, initial search, utility control, and ventilation (Figure 21.8). There are countless possible variations on this scenario depending upon the size of the structure, the amount of fire involvement, whether the fire is on the ground floor or an upper floor, whether the building is occupied, whether the building contains toxic or explosive materials, whether the building has built-in fire protection systems, the proximity of the burning building to uninvolved exposures, the number of resources at the scene and the number that are available with some delay, and other variables.

By talking to building occupants who have escaped the fire, or to neighbors or other witnesses, the IC may be able to determine whether there are any occupants still inside, and if so, whether there is a reasonable chance that any of them are still alive. If there are occupants still unaccounted for and that may be trapped inside but still be alive, then an offensive mode is indicated. If personnel resources permit, an aggressive fire attack would be started simultaneously with a search and rescue operation. If not, the search might have to be delayed until the fire is at least contained.

In a nonfire rescue incident, the offensive mode usually means deploying rescuers into the environment where the victim is trapped. It may mean assigning firefighters to rig a mechanical advantage system with which to raise or lower a victim. It may mean rappelling down the face of a building or a cliff to reach a stranded victim (Figure 21.9). It may mean installing emergency shoring in a collapsed trench to facilitate entry by rescuers. It may mean sending a rescue team into another type of confined space. It may mean sending rescuers into the water or onto the ice to rescue victims in danger of drowning. Regardless of what type of rescue is to be undertaken, safety and effectiveness dictate that the firefighters performing the rescue be fully trained and equipped for that type of operation. For more information on conducting these operations, see the IFSTA **Fire Service Rescue** manual.

Rescue Mode

As mentioned earlier, a third mode of operation at structure fires is the *rescue mode*. Sometimes called an "all-hands rescue" or "rescues in progress," this tactic focuses exclusively on the life safety priority. One of the most important requirements of an all-hands rescue is that it be declared over the radio to alert the communications/dispatch center and all other incoming units of the situation and the tactical decision. Search and rescue teams still take a charged line with them, but the line is only for their protection and that of those being rescued — not for fire extinguishment. Obviously, this is a drastic and infrequently used tactic that violates the two-in/two-out rule — but with lives at stake, violating the rule is justified. For more information on the two-in/two-out rule, see Chapter 22, "Firefighter Safety and Health."

Regardless of the nature of the incident, the incident action plan should anticipate the need for calling additional resources if it appears that the incident will be protracted or has the potential to be a long-term operation. These additional resources may be held in reserve, used to relieve first-in crews that have become fatigued, or assigned tactical objectives on the incident.

If additional resources are called, one or more staging areas may have to be established. On relatively small incidents, the IC can often manage the staging function

by having incoming units stage at *Level I*. Level I staging is when incoming units, other than the first-due unit, stop (stage) at the last intersection in their route of travel before the reported incident location (Figure 21.10). This is used when the actual location, nature, and scope of the incident are not yet confirmed. Staging in this way allows for a maximum of deployment flexibility. However, on any incident large enough or complex enough to warrant a designated staging area (Level II), the IC may appoint an Operations Section Chief. Among his other duties, "Operations" is responsible for designating where the staging areas are to be located and for appointing a manager for each area (Figure 21.11).

On all incidents, some level of fireground organization will have to be developed to implement the incident action plan. Some system should be used to manage the assigned resources and provide for incident safety. Especially if the nature and/or scope of the incident will require a large number of resources to meet the objectives specified in the incident action plan, an incident command/management system will be needed.

Incident Command

It is important to use an incident command/management system on all incidents, no matter how small or how large. Using such a system on the small, day-to-day, incidents gives company officers an opportunity to practice using the system so that when it is absolutely essential (on large or complex incidents), the system will not seem foreign to them.

The larger and more complex the incident, the more it is important to use a command/management system. Whether the system used is the Incident Command System (ICS), the Incident Management System (IMS), or another system, everyone in the department, especially company officers, must be familiar with the system and well-versed in its application. In addition, all agencies with whom mutual aid or automatic aid agreements are in force should know and use the same system. This may require extensive cross-training at all organizational levels among units of the participating agencies, but especially at the company level. An incident action plan is an integral part of these systems, and implementing the plan will affect how the emergency resources are organized.

Regardless of which incident command/management system is used, certain characteristics are common to all:

- Common terminology
- Modular organization
- Common communications
- Unified command structure

Figure 21.9 Rappelling down to a stranded victim is operating in an offensive mode.

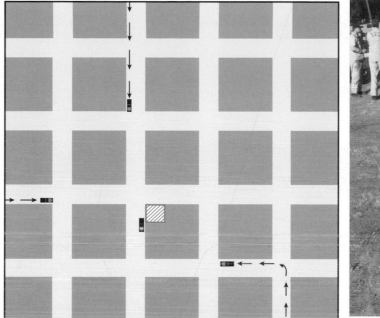

Figure 21.10 Units in Level I staging.

Figure 21.11 The Operations Chief may appoint a manager for Level II staging on large incidents.

- Incident action plans
- Manageable span of control
- Predesignated incident facilities
- Comprehensive resource management

Common Terminology

Common terminology is essential for any command/management system, especially one that will be used by units from more than one agency. Both the ICS, which grew out of the California FIRESCOPE system, and the Phoenix Fire Department's Fireground Command (FGC) system use common terminology for resources and incident facilities; however, they use different terminology for certain organizational functions. While the terms used for most of the organizational functions are the same in both systems, some of the company-level functions have different names.

In ICS, a *division* corresponds to a geographical area. For example, the perimeter of a fire is subdivided with alphabetical letters identifying each section. Beginning at the heel of a wildland fire or the front of the building in a structure fire, the nearest area is designated Division A, and working clockwise around the perimeter, the next section is designated Division B, and so on around the entire perimeter (Figure 21.12). In a multistory structure, each floor is a different division. For example, the ground floor is designated Division 1, the second floor Division 2, etc. (Figure 21.13).

A *group* identifies a functional assignment. For example, in a large structure fire, one or more companies may be assigned to the roof of the building. The entire roof area is designated the Roof Division and is the responsibility of the Roof Division Supervisor — usually one of the company officers. If the roof should need to be ventilated, one or more of the roof companies may be designated as the Ventilation Group. One of the company officers becomes the Ventilation Group Supervisor, who reports to the Branch Director, or to the Operations Section Chief if branches have not been formed. When the ventilation operation is completed, the group reverts to being part of the Roof Division or is reassigned to another division or function. If one or more companies have been assigned to Division 5 (fifth floor), one or more additional companies may be assigned to search that floor as the Search Group. ICS does not use *sector* for any organizational designation.

In FGC, the term *sector* is used interchangeably for both geographical areas and functional assignments. In the same situation as described for ICS, the company or companies assigned to the roof of a building in FGC would be designated the Roof Sector. Likewise, the company or companies assigned to ventilate the roof would be designated the Ventilation Sector.

In IMS, which is a blend of the ICS and FGC systems, any of the terms *division*, *group*, or *sector* can be used interchangeably as long as they are used consistently and all personnel are trained in how they are to be used. This

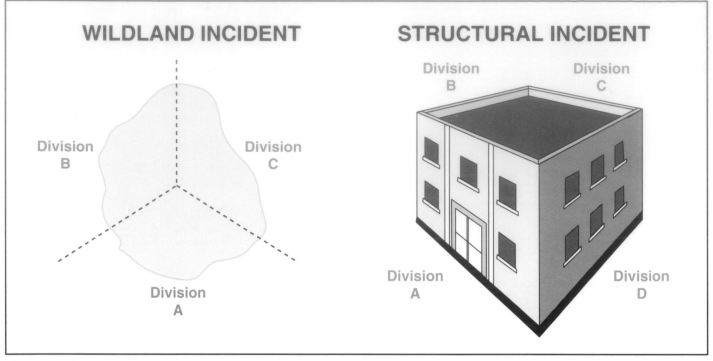

WILDLAND INCIDENT

Division B
Division C
Division A

STRUCTURAL INCIDENT

Division B
Division C
Division A
Division D

Figure 21.12 Exterior divisions are usually designated alphabetically.

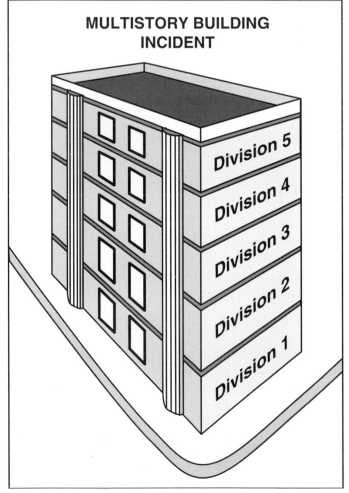

MULTISTORY BUILDING INCIDENT

Division 5
Division 4
Division 3
Division 2
Division 1

Figure 21.13 Interior divisions are usually designated numerically.

makes for a more flexible system, especially among departments or jurisdictions that have adopted a different system than is used by those with whom they must function from time to time.

Modular Organization

Both ICS and IMS provide for *modular organization*. This means that in both systems, the organization develops in a modular fashion based on the nature and scope of the incident (Figure 21.14). In most cases, the first-in company officer becomes the IC and directs both the strategic and tactical operations. The initial IC remains in charge of the incident until properly relieved or the problem is mitigated and the incident terminated. Regardless of who is in command, as the incident grows, so must the fireground organization; however, it should only grow as much as is needed to maintain span of control — and no more. Only those organizational positions that are necessary to manage the incident and bring it to a timely and successful conclusion need be staffed.

Common Communications

A common means of communication is essential to maintaining control, coordination, and safety (Figure 21.15). This means that all units must use clear text (specified phrases in plain English) rather than the 10-Code or any other agency-specific radio codes. Incident command/management systems provide a common communica-

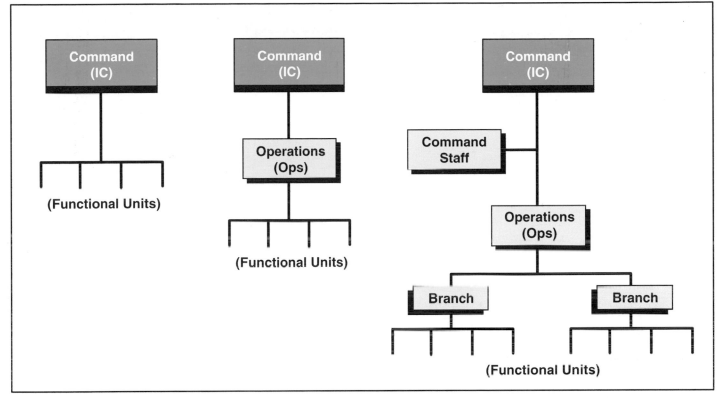

Figure 21.14 Both ICS and IMS provide for modular organization.

tions plan that identifies different channels (frequencies) to be used exclusively for specified organizational functions. Channels may be assigned for the following functions:

- Command
- Safety
- Tactical
- Support
- Ground-to-air
- Air-to-air

As part of the check-in procedure on an incident, all unit leaders should be given a copy of the communications plan for the incident. One of the most critical pieces of information to be passed on is the number of the safety channel. Someone in each unit should be designated to monitor this channel.

To avoid the chaos that would result from all units attempting to receive and transmit on the same channel, the incident communications plan assigns specific channels to specific functions or units. While most modern mobile and portable radios are capable of scanning, receiving, and transmitting over dozens — if not hundreds — of channels, not every department is equipped with the latest communications equipment. If mutual aid units are not equipped with radios that can receive and transmit on the channels assigned to them in the plan, they must be issued portable radios that will function on those channels.

Unified Command Structure

A unified command structure is necessary when, as is often the case, an incident involves or threatens to involve more than one jurisdiction or agency. For example, a fire that originates near the edge of a city may spread to an adjacent suburb, or vice versa (Figure 21.16). However, these multijurisdictional incidents are not limited to fires. A release of a hazardous vapor or gas may be carried by the wind into the neighboring jurisdiction. Likewise, if a flammable or toxic liquid enters a sewer or storm drain in one jurisdiction, it may flow into the next.

A unified command may also be appropriate within a single jurisdiction if multiple agencies are affected. For example, a hostage situation may be primarily a law enforcement incident, but if there is the possibility of a fire or explosion being involved, the fire department also has a legitimate interest in influencing the strategic and tactical decisions relating to the incident.

In a unified command structure, representatives of all affected entities share the command responsibilities and decisions (Figure 21.17). They jointly arrive at the strategic goals for the incident and agree on the tactical objectives that must be achieved. In some entities, legal authority to act is vested in those occupying certain positions of responsibility. Unified command allows these individuals to interface with those who have the operational expertise required to dispose of an incident.

CLEAR TEXT TERMINOLOGY

WORDS AND PHRASES	APPLICATION
Unreadable	Used when signal received is not clear. In most cases, try to add the specific trouble. Example: "Unreadable, background noise."
Loud and Clear	Self-explanatory
Stop Transmitting	Self-explanatory
Copy, Copies	Used to acknowledge message received. Unit radio identifier must also be used. Example: "Engine 2675, copies."
Affirmative	Yes
Negative	No
Respond, Responding	Used during dispatch - proceed to or proceeding to an accident. Example: "Engine 5176, respond..." or "St. Helena, Engine 1375 responding."
Enroute	Normally used by administrative or staff personnel to designate destinations. Enroute is *NOT* a substitute for responding. Example: "Redding, Chief 2400 enroute RO II."
In-quarters, with Station Name or Number	Used to indicate that a unit is in a station. Example: "Morgan Hill, Engine 4577 in-quarters, Sunol."
Uncovered	Indicates a unit is not in-service because there are no personnel to operate it.
Out-Of-Service	Indicates a unit is mechanically out-of-service. Example: "Auburn, transport 2341, out-of-service." Note, when repairs have been completed, the following phrase should be used: "Auburn transport 2341, back-in-service, available."
In-Service	This means that the unit is operating, not in response to a dispatch. Example: "Fortuna, Engine 1283, in-service, fire prevention inspections."
Repeat	Self-explanatory
Weather	Self-explanatory
Return to	Normally used by ECC to direct units that are available to a station or other location.
What is Your Location?	Self-explanatory
Call____by Phone	Self-explanatory
Disregard Last Message	Self-explanatory
Stand-By	Self-explanatory
Vehicle Registration Check	Self-explanatory
Is____Available for a Phone Call?	Self-explanatory
At Scene	Used when units arrive at the scene of an incident. Example: "Perris, Engine 6183, at scene."
Available at Residence	Used by administrative or staff personnel to indicate they are available and on-call at their residence.
Can Handle	Used with the amount of equipment needed to handle the incident. Example: "Susanville Battalion 2212, can handle with units now at scene."
Burning Operation	Self-explanatory
Report on Conditions	Self-explanatory
Fire Under Control	Self-explanatory
Emergency Traffic Only	Radio users will confine all radio transmissions to an emergency in progress or a new incident. Radio traffic which includes status information such as responding, reports on conditions, at scene and available will be authorized during this period.
Emergency Traffic	Term used to gain control of radio frequency to report an emergency. All other radio users will refrain from using that frequency until cleared for use by ECC.
Rescue Normal Traffic	Self-explanatory

Figure 21.15 Common clear text words and phrases.

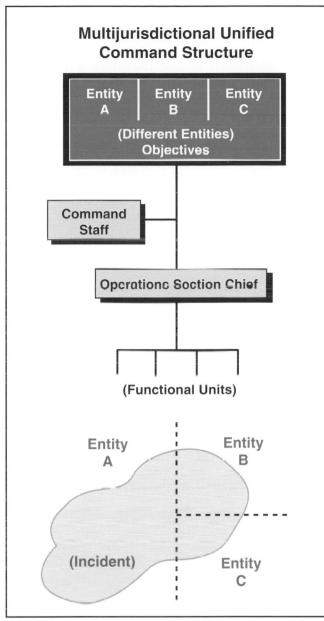

Multijurisdictional Unified Command Structure

Entity A	Entity B	Entity C
(Different Entities) Objectives		

Command Staff

Operations Section Chief

(Functional Units)

Entity A

Entity B

(Incident)

Entity C

Figure 21.16 A typical multijurisdictional incident.

Command Options

Of particular interest to company officers are the various options open to them when they are the first officer on the scene of an emergency. Beyond single or unified command, ICS does not define command options, but IMS does. Under IMS, the first-arriving officer has three optional modes available: nothing showing, fast attack, and command.

Nothing-showing mode. When the problem generating the response is not obvious to the first-in unit, the company officer should assume command of the incident and announce that nothing is showing. He should direct the other responding units to stage at Level I, accompany the crew on an investigation of the situation, and maintain command using a portable radio.

Figure 21.17 All affected entities are represented in a unified command structure.

Fast-attack mode. When the company officer's direct involvement is necessary for the crew to take immediate action to save a life or stabilize the situation, the officer should take command and announce that the company is in the fast-attack mode. Fast-attack mode usually lasts only a short time. The crew will remain in a fast-attack mode until one of the following occurs:

• The situation is stabilized.

• The situation is not stabilized, but the officer must withdraw to the outside to establish a command post. Depending upon the situation, the balance of the crew may be left inside if they can function safely and effectively *and* if they have radio communications capability.

• Command is transferred.

Command mode. Because of the nature and/or scope of some incidents, immediate and strong overall command is needed. In these incidents, the first-in officer should assume command by naming the incident and designating a command post, give an initial report on conditions, and request the additional resources needed. In addition, the company officer must decide how to use the balance of the crew. There are normally three options:

• Appoint one of the crew members as the acting officer, and give him a portable radio and an assignment (tactical objective).

• Assign the crew to work under the supervision of another company officer.

• Use the crew members to perform staff functions in support of command.

When there is a need for a company officer to transfer command of an incident to another officer, the transfer must be done correctly. Otherwise, there can be confusion about who is really in command of the incident. The officer assuming command must communicate with the officer being relieved by radio or face-to-face (face-to-face is preferred) (Figure 21.18). *Command should never be transferred to someone who is not on the scene.* When transferring command, the officer being relieved should brief the relieving officer on the following:

- Name of incident

- Incident status (fire conditions, number of victims, etc.)

- Safety considerations

- Action plan for the incident

- Progress toward completion of tactical objectives

- Deployment of assigned resources

- Assessment of the need for additional resources

Incident Action Plans

As described in Chapter 20, "Size-Up and Incident Plans," an incident action plan is a written or unwritten plan for the safe and efficient disposition of an emergency incident. According to the IMS, an incident action plan identifies "the strategic goals, tactical objectives, and support requirements for the incident."

Manageable Span of Control

Span of control relates to the number of direct subordinates that one supervisor can effectively manage. Variables such as proximity, similarity of function, and subordinate capability affect that number. If all subordinates are within sight of the supervisor and are able to communicate effectively with each other, the number of subordinates can be higher than when they are widely separated. Likewise, it is easier to supervise subordinates who are all performing the same or similar functions, so the number of subordinates can be higher than if they are all doing very different tasks. If all subordinates are skilled in performing the assigned task,

Figure 21.18 Command is best transferred face-to-face.

the number of subordinates can also be relatively high. In both ICS and IMS, an effective span-of-control ranges from three to seven subordinates per supervisor, depending upon the variables just discussed, with five being the optimum number (Figure 21.19). If an effective span of control is maintained, it is much easier for supervisors to keep track of their subordinates and to monitor their safety.

Predesignated Incident Facilities

There are several possible types of facilities that can be established in and around an incident. The types of facilities and their locations are determined by the requirements of the incident as outlined in the incident action plan. The most commonly used incident facilities are as follows:

- **Command post (CP)** — The location from which all incident operations are directed. There is only one CP per incident (Figure 21.20).

- **Incident base** — The location at which primary support functions are performed. There is only one base per incident, and its location remains fixed throughout the incident.

- **Camps** — Locations at which minor support functions are performed on very large wildland incidents. Camps are remote from the incident base, and they may be relocated as the needs of the incident dictate.

- **Staging** — The location(s) at which resources are held in reserve. On wildland fires and other incidents, units in staging are on a three-minute availability (Figure 21.21). In a high-rise fire, staging is located two floors below the fire floor.

- **Helibases** — The locations where helicopters are parked, serviced, maintained, and loaded. There may be more than one helibase on large incidents (Figure 21.22).

- **Helispots** — Temporary locations where helicopters can land, refuel, and be reloaded (Figure 21.23).

Comprehensive Resource Management

Depending upon the needs of the incident, as specified in the incident action plan, resources may be managed in three different configurations: single resources, task forces, and strike teams.

- **Single resources.** Single resources are individual pieces of apparatus (engines, trucks, water tenders, bulldozers, air tankers, helicopters, etc.) and the personnel required to make them functional (Figure 21.24). Single resources may also be personnel (hand crews, specialists, technicians, etc.).

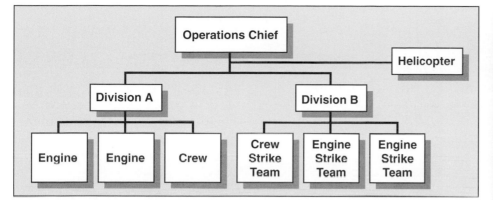

Figure 21.19 A span of control of 5:1 is optimum.

Figure 21.23 Reloading and refueling may be done at helispots.

Figure 21.21 A typical staging area on a major wildland incident. *Courtesy of Monterey County Training Officers.*

Figure 21.22 Major support is available at helibases.

Figure 21.20 A typical command post.

• **Task forces**. Any combination of up to five resources (engines, trucks, bulldozers, etc.) assembled for a specific assignment (Figure 21.25). There must be a task force leader, and all units in the task force must have common communications capability. Once a task force's tactical objective has been met, the task force is disbanded, and the individual resources reassigned or released.

• **Strike teams**. A set number of the same kind and type of resources (engines, hand crews, bulldozers, etc.) staffed with a specified minimum number of personnel (Figure 21.26). Strike teams must have a leader in a separate vehicle, and all units in the team must have common communications capability. Unlike task forces, strike teams remain together and function as a team throughout an incident.

To make the best use of all incident resources, each company officer must keep incident command apprised of their units' status. Three standard terms are used to report resource status:

• Assigned — Performing an active assignment

• Available — Ready for assignment (all resources in staging are available)

• Out-of-service — Not ready for assignment (unable to respond)

Resource status reports and other management devices, such as span-of-control, help incident command/management personnel and company officers fulfill one of their most important functions — personnel accountability.

Personnel Accountability

Firefighters are at some level of risk whenever they are on the fireground or other emergency scene. If conditions change suddenly and significantly, firefighters can be in mortal danger. Firefighters usually depend on their company officers to warn them of impending danger and to order them to leave a dangerous environment in time to escape to safety. However, if firefighters become separated from their unit, they may have to decide for themselves when and in which direction to escape. Those with little emergency experience may be unable

Figure 21.24 A typical single resource.

Figure 21.25 A typical dozer task force.

Figure 21.26 A typical engine strike team.

to make the decisions needed to save themselves. Therefore, it is critically important that some means be used to keep track of every firefighter on the incident. *Company officers are responsible for keeping track of their subordinates.*

All command/management systems provide various means of tracking the personnel resources assigned to a given incident. Personnel accountability includes all the following:

- **Check-in** — Requires all responders, regardless of agency affiliation, to check-in to receive their assignments

- **Incident action plan** — Identifies incident priorities and objectives, which dictate how tactical operations must be conducted

- **Unity of command** — Dictates that each firefighter has only one supervisor

- **Span of control** — Gives supervisors a manageable number of subordinates

- **Division/group/sector assignment list** — Identifies resources with active assignments in the Operations section

- **Resource status** — Ensures that each company officer reports resource status changes as they occur

- **Resource status unit** — Maintains status of all incident resources

When personnel at all levels in the emergency organization operate according to these principles and procedures, personnel accountability and safety are maximized. As an incident grows from an initial alarm assignment to a major incident, these basic principles and procedures must continue to be applied.

Summary

For every emergency incident, regardless of how large or how small, how simple or how complex, there must be an incident action plan. If it is to be effective, the plan must be communicated to all emergency personnel. Creating and implementing an incident action plan involves a series of sometimes very difficult decisions. Maintaining command and control of the resources needed to implement an incident action plan will require that some form of incident command/management system be used. If the system is used effectively and the incident action plan is implemented conscientiously, personnel accountability and safety will be maintained.

This chapter provides information that will assist the reader in meeting the following job performance requirements from NFPA 1021, *Standard for Fire Officer Professional Qualifications*, 1997 edition. The colored portions indicate the topics addressed in the chapter. The numbers of the job performance requirements are also noted directly in the sections of text where they are addressed. Those in the following list that are denoted with an asterisk (*) are global in nature and are covered by reading the chapter in its entirety.

Fire Officer I

2-7.1 Apply safety regulations at the unit level, given safety policies and procedures, so that required reports are completed, in-service training is conducted, and member responsibilities are conveyed.

(a) *Prerequisite Knowledge:* The most common causes of personal injury and accident to the member, safety policies and procedures, basic workplace safety, and the components of an infectious disease control program.

(b) *Prerequisite Skills:* The ability to identify safety hazards and to communicate verbally and in writing.

2-7.2 Conduct an initial accident investigation, given an incident and investigation forms, so that the incident is documented and reports are processed in accordance with policies and procedures.

(a) *Prerequisite Knowledge:* Procedures for conducting an accident investigation, and safety policies and procedures.

(b) *Prerequisite Skills:* The ability to communicate verbally and in writing and to conduct interviews.

Fire Officer II

3-7.1 Analyze a member's accident, injury, or health exposure history, given the case study, so that a report is prepared for a supervisor and includes actions taken and recommendations given.

(a) *Prerequisite Knowledge:* The causes of unsafe acts, health exposures, or conditions that result in accidents, injuries, occupational illnesses, or deaths.

(b) *Prerequisite Skills:* The ability to communicate in writing and to interpret accidents, injuries, occupational illnesses, or death reports.

Firefighter Safety and Health

Because of their position in the organizational structure, company officers are responsible for their own health and safety and that of each firefighter in their company. This means that company officers must know the requirements of the applicable safety standards, the department's safety policies and procedures, the potential threats to firefighter safety, and the means available to minimize those threats. Company officers must give the safety of their personnel the highest priority, so they must know what safety is and enforce good conduct for the safety of their crews. Because of their position in the organization, company officers are able to greatly influence how the firefighters perceive the department's safety policies and procedures and the extent to which they will comply with those policies and procedures. Therefore, company officers must set a good example by showing that they take safety issues seriously — by complying with the department's safety program themselves and by requiring that their subordinates do the same.

This chapter discusses the most commonly applied fire service safety standards, typical safety policies and procedures, workplace safety, and initial accident investigations. Also discussed are the causes of firefighter injuries, work-related stress, accidents, and accident analysis.

Safety Standards

[NFPA 1021 2-7.1]

Most departmental safety programs, policies, and procedures are based on applicable laws and standards that are recognized as being appropriate for the fire service. However, it is important to understand the difference between laws and standards.

Laws are legislative mandates that restrict the conduct of all who are subject to them. Those under the jurisdiction's authority are bound to obey these laws or be subject to penalties for not doing so. These penalties may include fines and/or imprisonment.

Standards are criterion documents that are developed to serve as models or examples of acceptable performance or behaviors. The standards' requirements are not legal mandates unless the standards are formally adopted by the authority having jurisdiction, in which case they become law. For example, if a fire department is in a state or province that has not adopted NFPA 1500, *Standard on Fire Department Occupational Safety and Health Program*, the local entity of which the department is a part may choose to formally adopt it. If neither authority has adopted the standard into law, the department may still choose to meet the standard but is not required to do so. However, if there is a firefighter injury or death, the courts may hold that the department should have followed the standard because its requirements represent what a reasonable person would have done under the circumstances.

OSHA Regulations

On April 28, 1971, the Williams-Steiger Occupational Safety and Health Act became federal law in the United States. Out of this law came the Occupational Safety and Health Administration (OSHA). Operating under the U.S. Department of Labor, OSHA sets out two duties for employers:

- Furnish to each employee a place of employment that is free from recognized hazards that are likely to cause death or serious injury.

- Comply with the occupational safety and health standards contained within the OSHA regulations.

As discussed in Chapter 3, "The Company Officer's Legal Responsibilities and Liability," federal OSHA authority and regulations apply mainly to the private sector — specifically to general industry, construction, shipyard, longshoring, marine terminal workplaces, and any other private enterprise doing business across state lines. The only exceptions are self-employed persons, farms on which only the farmer's immediate family members are employed, and workplaces protected by other federal statutes. Federal OSHA authority and regulations do not cover employees of state and local governments, including career and some volunteer firefighters.

Applicability to Firefighters

Federal OSHA standards apply only to federal employees who fight fires and to private-sector employees who fight fires (industrial fire brigades and incorporated volunteer fire companies). Although federal OSHA has no jurisdiction over public-sector firefighters, the 25 states operating OSHA-approved state plans do cover them. These state plans may differ from the federal standards but must provide equivalent protection. It is through these state plans that the "two-in/two-out rule" applies to state and local government firefighters in these states. Company officers must comply with the occupational safety and health regulations that apply in their particular jurisdiction.

Federal OSHA regulations are contained in Title 29 of the Code of Federal Regulations (CFR), which applies to labor. Chapter XVII of Title 29 contains the occupational safety and health requirements. Some of the more common OSHA regulations that fire departments and other emergency response agencies follow are:

- 29 CFR 1910.120, which covers hazardous materials emergency response

- 29 CFR 1910.134, which covers respiratory protection

- 29 CFR 1910.146, which covers confined space operations

- 29 CFR 1910.156, Subpart L, which covers fire brigades

- 29 CFR 1910.1030, which covers bloodborne pathogens and requires employers to provide employees with immunization against Hepatitis B

- 29 CFR 1910.1200, which covers hazard communication (material safety data sheets [MSDS])

- 29 CFR 1926, Subpart P, "Excavations," which covers operations in trenches

However, because of fiscal and staffing limitations, federal and state OSHA personnel cannot inspect every job site. Like other publicly funded entities, they must prioritize their activities and invest resources where and when they will do the most good. OSHA personnel prioritize and schedule their inspections on the following basis:

1. In response to worker fatalities or multiple hospitalizations (five or more)

2. In response to employee complaints

3. Random inspections of high-hazard industries

NFPA 1500

NFPA 1500, *Standard on Fire Department Occupational Safety and Health Program*, was originally approved in 1987. The standard contains the minimum requirements for a fire department safety and health program, and it may be applied to any fire department or similar organization, public or private. The standard requires fire departments to recognize safety and health as legitimate departmental objectives and to provide as safe and healthy a work environment as possible. The basic concept of NFPA 1500 is to establish a minimum level of safety in all fire service organizations regardless of the size or type. Because it is a minimum standard, it does not restrict any department or jurisdiction from exceeding the requirements specified in the standard.

NFPA 1500 is the benchmark by which all fire department safety and health programs are measured. The standard is very comprehensive and includes requirements in the areas of training and education, vehicles and equipment, protective clothing and protective equipment, emergency operations, facility (fire station) safety, medical and physical requirements for firefighters, and employee assistance programs. Company officers should be thoroughly familiar with the requirements of this standard.

Other Safety Standards

There are many other standards that address firefighter safety and health in one way or another. Safety-related standards are developed and published by several different organizations, including the National Fire Protection Association (NFPA), American National Standards Institute (ANSI), National Institute for Science and Technology (NIST), American Society for Testing and Materials (ASTM), and the National Institute for Occupational Safety and Health (NIOSH). As mentioned earlier, many states also have their own health and safety regulations.

Safety and Health Policies and Procedures

[NFPA 1021 2-7.1]

Departmental safety and health programs should begin with a declaration of policy from the highest ranking official within the department. Regardless of whether this individual is the fire chief, fire commissioner, public safety director, or whoever, he must actively support the idea of a safety and health program, or it is not likely to succeed. In some jurisdictions, it may be necessary to have the policy approved by the governing body (for example, the city council, city commission, or district board of directors) in order to satisfy legal and liability requirements. Even if not required, the approval of a policy by the governing body adds credence.

With this declaration of policy, the fire chief officially acknowledges the hazards associated with fire fighting and expresses a desire to reduce these hazards as much as possible. Following adoption of the safety and health policy statement, the fire department management should bring together representatives of each level within the organization (including the union, if any) to design the program. This process gives management an opportunity to display its genuine concern for the health and safety of all personnel and its commitment to safety. It also gives those at every level of the organization an opportunity to contribute to the program and to make sure that it addresses everyone's concerns. It is important for company officers to participate in this process to the fullest extent possible.

Safety and Health Program

A comprehensive departmental safety and health program must cover all anticipated hazards to which the members might be exposed. Besides the obvious hazards associated with fighting fires, the members may be exposed to hazardous materials spills, communicable diseases, energized electrical equipment, as well as the hazards of driving apparatus during emergency responses.

As mentioned earlier, company officers are responsible for seeing that their subordinates follow established safety policies and procedures. Many departmental safety policies and procedures are based on the requirements of NFPA 1500. Some of the things required by this standard are as follows:

- Inspection, maintenance, and repair of vehicles
- Properly worn and maintained protective clothing
- Proper use and maintenance of self-contained breathing apparatus (SCBA)
- Proper use and maintenance of personal alert safety system (PASS) devices
- Fire station safety
- Proper apparatus riding procedures

These are only a few of the requirements of NFPA 1500. Company officers are responsible for reviewing the entire standard and determining which aspects of the standard come under their direct supervision and control.

For those departments that provide emergency medical aid, one of the most important parts of the safety program is that dealing with infectious disease control.

Even though the following section is focused on infectious disease control programs, *the principles involved may be applied to any aspect of firefighter safety and health.*

Infectious Disease Control Program
[NFPA 1021 2-7.2.1]

A department's infectious disease control program is designed to protect the health of its members, but it also helps to protect the department against related liability. For these reasons, it is important to examine federal, state, provincial, and local statutes relating to infection control/environmental issues when designing the program. One of the most useful guides for an infection control program is NFPA 1581, *Standard for Fire Department Infection Control Program.* Regardless of what is required by the applicable statutes, all comprehensive infection control programs must have certain critical components:

- A written policy statement
- An exposure control plan
- Infection control SOPs
- An information management system
- A training/education program
- Compliance- and quality-monitoring processes
- A program evaluation system

Written Policy Statement

The department should have a written policy statement that clearly explains the intent, benefits, and purpose of the infection control program. This statement should define the department's philosophy on infection control, including such issues as treating those infected with human immunodeficiency virus (HIV) and/or other communicable diseases.

Exposure Control Plan

OSHA regulations require employers, including emergency response agencies, to establish an exposure control plan. The plan should identify how exposure will be limited. The three most effective ways of protecting firefighters from communicable diseases on the job are through immunizations, protective barriers, and proper disposal of contaminated materials. While it is beyond the scope of this manual to specify in detail what is required to protect emergency care providers in the field, it is the department's responsibility to provide these protections, and it is the company officer's responsibility to see that they are used.

Standard Operating Procedures (SOPs)

While the policy statement is intended to provide general guidance, the SOPs should provide specific direction for daily activities. Normally, the SOPs include the assignment of specific roles and responsibilities related to infection control, as well as procedural guidelines for all required tasks and functions.

Information Management

An effective infection control program generates a substantial amount of data, for example, member health records, training records, and so on. An efficient information management system that ensures appropriate confidentiality of medical information is an essential program requirement.

Training and Education

Department members must be trained in the proper use of personal protective equipment (PPE), exposure protection, post-exposure protocols, and other infection control subjects. Members also must receive education on diseases, modes of transmission, and related topics. All such training must be properly documented.

Compliance and Quality Monitoring

The program must include provisions for monitoring member compliance with established SOPs. Noncompliance must be documented and corrected.

Program Evaluation

A means of program evaluation allows analysis of program effectiveness, feedback for program improvement, and updating to reflect new medical or regulatory information. In fact, periodic review and updating of the infection control plan are required by OSHA.

Bloodborne and Airborne Pathogens

A major component of any comprehensive infectious disease control program is one dealing with protection from bloodborne and airborne pathogens. This component is intended to protect firefighters and members of the public from communicable diseases when they are exposed to blood, bodily fluids, or other potentially infectious materials.

Communicable diseases may be transmitted by bloodborne and airborne pathogens, such as viruses, bacteria, and other harmful organisms. Bloodborne pathogens are those contained in an infected patient's blood. Transmission occurs when an infected patient's blood enters openings in the noninfected person's skin. Airborne pathogens are spread when an infected patient breathes, coughs, or sneezes and tiny droplets are sprayed into the air. These droplets enter the noninfected person's eyes, mouth, or nose or are absorbed through the skin.

Firefighter Injuries

Fighting fires, performing rescues, and delivering other emergency services is inherently dangerous work. On average, more than 100,000 firefighter injuries are reported in the U.S. each year. These injuries range from those that are relatively minor to those that require admission to a hospital. Many firefighter injuries can be prevented by effective supervision, training, use of personal protective equipment, and high levels of physical fitness for firefighters. Physically fit firefighters are not only more productive but also less likely to suffer strains and sprains, which account for more than 30 percent of all firefighter injuries. Physical exercise is also a very effective way of reducing stress (Figure 22.1).

While the experience may vary from department to department, NFPA statistics show that the majority of serious injuries to firefighters, as well as the greatest number of injuries, occur at the scene of emergency incidents (Figure 22.2). Other injuries occur during nonemergency incidents, during training, while responding to or returning from an incident, and in various other activities while on duty.

Incident Safety

The National Fire Protection Association conducts an annual survey of accident locations and injury types. Table 22.1 illustrates the injuries by nature and the type of duty that were reported for 1995.

Figure 22.1 Physically fit firefighters are less likely to be injured.

Figure 22.2 The most serious injuries occur on the fireground.

Table 22.1
Firefighter Injuries by Nature of Injury and Type of Duty, 1996

Nature of Injury	Responding to or Returning From an Incident		Fireground		Nonfire Emergency		Training		Other On-Duty		Total	
	Number	Percent	Number	Percent	Number	Percent	Number	Percent	Number	Percent	Number	Percent
Burns (fire or chemical)	65	1.0	4,360	9.5	140	1.1	635	10.2	215	1.3	5,415	6.2
Smoke or gas inhalation	115	1.8	4,660	10.2	305	2.4	70	1.1	105	0.6	5,255	6.0
Other respiratory distress	45	0.7	740	1.6	210	1.6	75	1.2	125	0.8	1,195	1.4
Eye irritation	225	3.6	2,735	6.0	390	3.1	165	2.7	620	3.8	4,135	4.7
Wound, cut, bleeding, bruise	1,375	21.8	8,775	19.2	2,055	16.3	1,085	17.5	3,325	20.4	16,615	19.1
Dislocation, fracture	190	3.0	1,090	2.4	260	2.0	235	3.8	550	3.4	2,325	2.7
Heart attack or stroke	25	0.4	300	0.7	45	0.4	35	0.6	310	1.9	715	0.8
Strain, sprain, muscular pain	3,545	56.1	17,455	38.2	7,020	55.6	3,160	51.0	8,540	52.5	39,720	45.6
Thermal stress (frostbite, heat exhaustion)	60	1.0	2,720	5.9	185	1.5	260	4.2	100	0.6	3,325	3.8
Other	670	10.6	2,890	6.3	2,020	16.0	480	7.7	2,390	14.7	8,450	9.7
	6,315		45,725		12,630		6,200		16,280		87,150	

NOTE: If a firefighter sustained multiple injuries for the same incident, only the nature of the single most serious injury was tabulated.

Reprinted with permission from *NFPA Journal*®, (November/December, Vol. 91, No. 6) Copyright© 1997, National Fire Protection Association, Quincy, MA 02269.

NFPA Journal® is a registered trademark of the National Fire Protection Association, Inc., Quincy, MA 02269.

Table 22.2 illustrates the nature of firefighter injuries on the fireground. Along with local data, the National Fire Incident Reporting System (NFIRS) is another possible source of fireground injury statistics.

By knowing what injuries occur, where they occur, and why they occur, methods can be developed to recognize, reduce, and eliminate factors that could injure firefighters performing their duties. Regardless of how sophisticated the injury prevention methods are, their effectiveness depends upon company officers applying them conscientiously. There are several things that company officers can do to reduce the number of firefighter injuries:

- Having a personal commitment to reducing injuries
- Using and requiring all firefighters to use all personal protective equipment
- Delivering effective training for firefighters in critical areas such as:
  — Using self-contained breathing apparatus (Figure 22.3)
  — Recognizing inherent hazards in emergency operations
  — Practicing vehicle/equipment safety (Figure 22.4)
- Following all departmental safety and emergency SOPs including:

	At the Fireground			At Nonfire Emergencies	
Year	Injuries	Injuries per 1,000 Fire		Injuries	Injuries per 1,000 Incidents
1987	57,755	24.8		13,940	1.41
1988	61,790	25.4		12,325	1.13
1989	58,250	27.5		12,580	1.11
1990	57,100	28.3		14,200	1.28
1991	55,830	27.3		15,065	1.20
1992	52,290	26.6		18,140	1.43
1993	52,885	27.1		16,675	1.25
1994	52,875	25.7		11,810	0.84
1995	50,640	25.8		13,500	0.94
1996	45,725	23.1		12,630	0.81

Table 22.2
Firefighter Injuries at the Fireground and at Nonfire Emergencies, 1987-96

Reprinted with permission from *NFPA Journal* ®, (November/December, Vol. 91, No. 6) Copyright© 1997, National Fire Protection Association, Quincy, MA 02269.

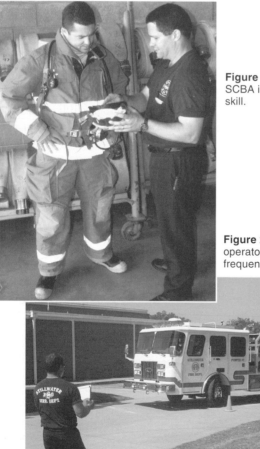

Figure 22.3 Use of SCBA is a critical skill.

Figure 22.4 Driver/ operators need frequent practice.

— Ventilation

— Hoseline placement

— Command

• Participating in physical fitness and weight control programs

• Promoting individual wellness including:

— Smoking cessation

— Nutrition

• Conducting an objective and thorough investigation of time-loss injuries to determine the following:

— Whether unsafe acts are being performed (which indicates the need for training)

— The existence of unsafe conditions

— Whether equipment is inadequate or inappropriate for the task

Two-In/Two-Out Rule

Another critically important aspect of incident safety in some confined spaces and during interior structural fire fighting is the "two-in/two-out" rule. Anytime firefighters are inside a space that has an oxygen-deficient or contaminated atmosphere (including burning buildings), then they are in a space with an atmosphere that is immediately dangerous to life and health (IDLH). Anyone entering an IDLH space must wear appropriate respiratory protection. In addition, both NFPA 1500 and 29 CFR 1910.134 (Respiratory Protection) specify that in these situations, the entrants must work in teams of two or more (remaining in visual and voice contact with each other) and there must be another two-person team (sometimes called a "rapid intervention team") outside of the space but immediately available and properly equipped to enter in case the first team needs assistance or rescue. "Properly equipped" means that the rescue/assistance team must wear at least the same level of personal protective clothing and equipment that the first team did.

Workplace Safety

[NFPA 1021 2-7.2.1]

There are certain safety hazards common to any fire station. NFPA 1500 requires that fire stations be inspected for safety at least monthly. In many agencies, the jurisdiction's insurance carrier also requires periodic inspection of the stations. There are also certain types of accidents that are not limited to any specific location within a station. Many firefighters are injured when they are either getting on or getting off their apparatus or when they are maintaining them. Improper lifting techniques and slip-and-fall accidents are two of the most common accidents that result in injury.

Lifting

Although back strains are the most common injuries related to improper lifting techniques, bruises, sprains, and fractures can also result from improper lifting and carrying techniques. Improper lifting techniques can result not only in personal injury but also in damage to equipment that is dropped or improperly handled in the process of lifting. Back injuries have been statistically proven to be the most expensive, single type of accident

in terms of workers' compensation claims, and they occur with disturbing frequency.

Every firefighter should be trained in safe lifting techniques, and company officers should insist that they use them. Without assistance, firefighters should not attempt to lift or carry any object that is too bulky or heavy for one person to safely handle. Lifting and carrying heavy or bulky objects without help can result in unnecessary strains and injuries. If it is big, bulky, or heavy, get help to lift it (Figure 22.5).

Safe lifting techniques include getting as close to the object as possible, getting a good grip on the object, keeping the back straight or slightly arched, and lifting with the legs, not the back. When lifting, firefighters should bend at the knees, not at the waist (Figure 22.6). However, not all lifting-related injuries are the result of firefighters failing to use the prescribed techniques. At least some of these injuries result from poorly designed procedures and equipment — insufficient attention to *ergonomics*.

Ergonomics

Also called "human engineering," *ergonomics* is the process of designing the workplace (and the tools and equipment therein) to allow the worker to perform efficiently and safely. This means designing apparatus so that firefighters do not have to overextend their reach, bend at the waist, or assume an awkward position when removing heavy tools (such as rolls of large diameter hose, hydraulic rescue tools, and portable monitors) from the apparatus (Figure 22.7). It may mean that heavy portable objects should be stored only in compartments that have roll-out trays or drawers. Ergonomic design may also

Figure 22.5 Firefighters should get help with bulky objects.

Figure 22.6 Firefighters should bend their knees, not their backs.

Figure 22.7 Firefighters should not have to reach for heavy objects.

mean purchasing safety equipment and clothing that are convenient to use; otherwise, firefighters may be tempted to take shortcuts with these items. It may also mean developing techniques and procedures that do not require firefighters to use unsafe movements. Firefighters who are physically fit and have sufficient upper body strength are less likely to suffer the types of injuries typically associated with lifting. This, too, is part of sound ergonomics.

Slip, Trip, and Fall Accidents

Another type of common accident is the slip, trip, and/or fall. Numerous factors contribute to these accidents, but they generally result from poor footing. This can be caused by improper footwear, slippery surfaces, objects or substances on walking surfaces, inattention to footing on stairs, uneven surfaces, and similar hazards. These accidents can easily result in minor and serious injuries as well as damaged equipment. To prevent such accidents, it is important that firefighters wear proper footwear that meets the requirements of NFPA 1977.

It is also important to stress good housekeeping. For example, floors must be kept clean and free from slipping hazards such as loose items and spilled liquids. Aisles must be unobstructed, and stairs should be well-lighted. In addition to walking surfaces (such as floors, stair treads, and aisles), items such as handrails, slide poles, and slides must also be maintained in good condition. The following sections highlight precautions that can be taken to prevent these types of accidents from occurring.

Floors. Traditionally, fire station floors have been smooth concrete or glossy tile surfaces that are easy to sweep. Firefighters generally keep these surfaces mopped and waxed to ensure a clean station and a to project a good image. When these smooth surfaces are wet, they can cause falls resulting in injuries to firefighters and visitors. Floors that are to be wet-mopped or waxed should be done in sections so that portions

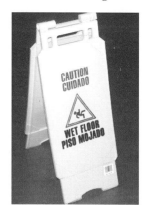

Figure 22.8 Warnings should be posted.

of the floor are dry for pedestrian traffic. Where practical, wet floors should be posted with warning signs to alert those who may need to walk through the wet areas (Figure 22.8).

Some fire departments have installed nonslip floor surfaces and all-weather carpet to reduce slipping problems. Flammability, smoke production, and static elec-

tricity production should be considered when departments select carpeting for their stations. Carpeting is generally not appropriate for the apparatus floor, but nonskid patches or strips can be installed where slipping is most likely. These strips should be inspected regularly and replaced when they start to deteriorate or peel. Another way to reduce the possibility of slipping on smooth apparatus floors is to score the floor's surface along designated walkways. These paths should also be outlined with colored striping to clearly define them (Figure 22.9).

Stairs. Stair treads should also have nonskid patches or strips to prevent slipping (Figure 22.10). These strips should be placed in the middle of the stair tread. The strips should be inspected regularly and replaced promptly when they become smooth or worn.

Stairways should be well-lighted at all times. As in any other means of ingress/egress, stairways should have emergency lighting in case of power failure. Stairways must always be kept free of obstructions and litter. Spilled liquids, grease, and oils should be cleaned up immediately. It should be the responsibility of every firefighter to keep all walking surfaces safe, even if it that means cleaning up after someone else.

Handrails must be maintained in good condition. They should be inspected regularly to make sure that they remain firmly attached and that their surfaces are smooth and free of splinters or burrs (Figure 22.11).

Slide poles. Many injuries have resulted from firefighters using slide poles in fire stations (Figure 22.12). Where possible, stations should be designed with the sleeping quarters on the ground level. Typical hazards related to slide poles include the lack of safety rails or enclosures around the access point, loose fittings at the top or bottom of the pole, the absence of energy-absorbing landing mats, and firefighter carelessness.

Slides. Some two-story fire stations have slides instead of brass poles (Figure 22.13). Most slides have handrails and rubber landing mats as extra safety features. Even though slides do not eliminate all the hazards associated with poles, they are generally safer than poles.

Housekeeping

Just as in every commercial or residential occupancy that firefighters inspect, basic housekeeping is an important safety consideration in the fire station (Figure 22.14). Besides making a fire station look bad, accumulations of litter can be a slip hazard as well as a fire hazard. Stepping on a piece of glossy paper on a smooth floor can cause a firefighter or a visitor to slip and fall. Accumulations of

Figure 22.9 Nonskid areas help prevent slipping.

Figure 22.10 Stair treads may need nonskid patches.

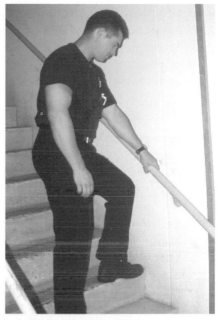

Figure 22.11 Handrails should be kept in good repair.

Figure 22.12 Many firefighter injuries are associated with slide poles.

Figure 22.13 Some departments have designed slides into their multistory fire stations.

Figure 22.14 Litter can be a safety hazard.

Figure 22.15 Ladders must be set properly.

paper, rags, or other combustibles can both obscure possible sources of ignition and provide fuel to any fire that should start.

When firefighters use ladders around the station, such as when they wash the windows or change lightbulbs, they should be as careful about ladder placement as on the fireground (Figure 22.15). They should not overreach, even if it means that their ladders will have to be moved frequently. Firefighters should not be allowed to stand on chairs, tables, or other objects when a ladder is needed.

Stress

During emergency operations — often life-and-death situations — firefighters are subjected to a significant amount of stress. Stress is simply an adjustment to change. The change can be good or it can be bad. In psychology, good stress is called *eustress* and bad stress is called *distress*. Because distress is the most harmful, this chapter only deals with this form of stress.

When uncontrolled, stress can build to dangerous levels that affect a firefighter's health and ability to function. These adverse effects occur when the stressor, or demanding stimulus, is beyond the firefighter's ability to adjust to it. However, some individuals adjust to stress better than others. Stress can be acute (short term) or chronic (long term). Current theory holds that most forms of acute stress do not cause permanent damage. On the other hand, chronic stress can lead to significant permanent damage.

Dr. Hans Selye developed a theory that he called the General Adaptation Syndrome to explain why chronic stress affects our health and acute stress does not. Dr. Selye broke the physiological response to a stressor into three distinct stages:

- **Stage 1.** *Alarm reaction* stage is the initial reaction to the stressor. The body responds with a massive release of hormones, including adrenaline. During this stage, blood is drawn away from the digestive organs and is concentrated in the brain, heart, lungs, and muscles in preparation for the next stage.

- **Stage 2.** The *resistance* stage has also been called the "fight/flight response." In this stage, the body prepares to defend itself or remove itself from the presence of the stressor. During this stage, the body may seem to be adapting quite nicely; however, energy needed to continue is being depleted. When the adaptational energy is gone, the body passes to the third and final stage.

- **Stage 3.** The final stage is called the *exhaustion* stage. This is the stage where permanent damage to the system occurs. The damage may be large or small, but if the stressor is not removed during this stage, death may result.

Chronic stress, that most associated with the exhaustion stage, has been linked to insomnia, ulcers, heart disease, and cancer. It is obviously a serious health threat. Fires and other emergency operations are inherently stressful, but firefighters can manage this stress if they are given the proper support (discussed later in this chapter). Company officers should see that they get it.

Physical, Environmental, and Psychological Stressors

Fighting fires and delivering other emergency services often requires extreme physical exertion, sometimes in inclement weather. Exertion is a physical stressor and weather is an environmental stressor. Psychological stressors are slightly more difficult to identify. Some psychological stressors associated with being a firefighter are the following:

- The sound of the alerting system
- Interruption of meals and sleep
- The need for speed when responding to alarms
- The potential dangers at the scene

All these stressors can have profound and damaging effects on the body, especially on the cardiovascular system.

Besides the severe environmental conditions of extremely high and extremely low temperatures are the problems of high humidity, contaminated atmospheres, and high noise levels. These all cause stress on the body and are capable of causing permanent damage. For example, exposure to high temperature in humid conditions results in fatigue and can have adverse effects on the cardiovascular system.

Firefighters also are exposed to psychological stressors that are not exclusive to their profession. Some of these stressors are:

- Poor work relationships
- Poor work atmosphere
- Lack of promotions
- Lack of support or recognition by superiors
- Difficult work roles

Psychological stressors from firefighters' personal lives can also affect their health and work performance. Some common sources of off-the-job stressors are divorce or separation, death or illness of a family member, and financial difficulties. It is sometimes difficult for the company officer to determine whether stress is caused by factors on the job or off; this is so even for the individual experiencing the stress. Company officers should consider stress as a possible source of a firefighter's unusual behavior on the job.

Reducing Physical and Environmental Stress

By supporting and enforcing sound safety and health care policies, company officers can do a great deal to help maintain firefighters' health. Use of personal protective equipment will help reduce the effects of physical and environmental stressors (Figure 22.16). Positive-pressure self-contained breathing apparatus will provide clean air to breathe, and protective clothing will insulate the body from temperature extremes. A policy requiring training in and the proper use of personal protective clothing and equipment should be implemented and strictly enforced in every fire department. In most departments, the task of implementing and enforcing these policies is delegated to company officers.

In addition to the use of protective clothing and equipment, company officers should support the department's physical fitness program, and they should set a good example by keeping themselves in top physical condition (Figure 22.17). These programs are designed to reduce the damaging effects of stress by increasing the functional capability of the cardiovascular system. There are other programs designed to decrease the risks associated with coronary heart disease and to reduce firefighter injuries in general. These programs include:

- Annual medical checkups
- Fitness evaluations
- Weight-control programs
- No-smoking regulations
- Prescribed blood-pressure medications

Psychological Stress — Signals and Reduction

Company officers are responsible for recognizing when one of their firefighters may be suffering from the effects of stress (Figure 22.18). Some of the more noticeable signs that indicate that stress may be building to dangerous levels are:

- General irritability
- Emotional instability
- Inability to concentrate
- Fatigue
- Insomnia and restless sleep

- Loss of appetite
- Alcohol and drug use

It is important to respond to any of these signs as quickly as possible. In some cases, individuals may not realize they are suffering from stress, and just pointing out their behavior may help them realize that they need some professional assistance. If the individual is in a stressful situation, the company officer needs to be understanding. The firefighter may just need to talk to someone (Figure 22.19). This one-to-one communication sometimes allows the firefighter to see things in a different perspective. If this does not seem to help, the individual may need professional help, and the company officer should refer them to whatever counseling services that are available through the member assistance program. It is important for the company officer to show genuine concern and understanding for the firefighter's problem and to support the decision to seek professional help. In situations where the firefighter may have become a danger to himself or others but refuses to seek help voluntarily, the company officer has the responsibility to take appropriate action (which may be to relieve the firefighter from duty) and inform the administration of the situation.

Figure 22.18 Company officers should recognize when crew members are stressed.

Figure 22.16 Company officers should set a good example by wearing proper PPE.

Figure 22.17 Company officers should keep themselves in top shape.

Figure 22.19 Sometimes, a firefighter just needs to talk to someone.

Company officers can help themselves and their firefighters to reduce the effects of psychological stress by recognizing the need for stress reduction. Some of the most common methods of stress reduction are:

- Getting adequate rest
- Exercising regularly
- Eating a balanced diet
- Taking a vacation
- Taking "quiet times"
- Laughing
- Relaxing or slowing down

Critical Incident Stress

A type of stress that deserves special attention is the stress that occurs as a result of a particularly traumatic or disturbing incident. This type of stress is called *critical incident stress*. Critical incident stress can be very detrimental to both a firefighter's professional life and personal life. Some examples of incidents that may cause critical incident stress are those that involve the following:

- Multiple casualties
- People sustaining extraordinarily gruesome injuries
- A firefighter being seriously injured or killed
- Children being injured or killed
- The death of a victim because of a failed search and rescue operation
- A fatality occurring despite extraordinary efforts by department personnel

Not all firefighters suffer from critical incident stress after responding to a major incident because different people react differently to the same situation. However, the majority of the firefighters who are involved with a particularly traumatic incident experience some type of reaction. This reaction (critical incident stress) is a normal response to a very abnormal situation. While company officers can take steps to mitigate critical incident stress, they cannot entirely prevent it and neither can anyone else.

Symptoms of Critical Incident Stress

There are many symptoms that may indicate that a firefighter is suffering from critical incident stress. These symptoms can appear during an incident or hours, days, weeks, or even months afterward. Some of the more common symptoms *during* an incident are:

- Denial of the situation (thinking that this cannot be happening)
- Anger
- Doubts about personal performance ability
- Anxiety
- Frustration
- Sense of hopelessness

As mentioned earlier, some of the common symptoms of critical incident stress may not appear until well after the incident. Some of the more common *delayed* symptoms are:

- Feelings of guilt
- Restlessness
- Irritability
- Drug or alcohol abuse
- Sleep disturbances
- Flashbacks of the incident
- Decreased appetite

Also as mentioned earlier, critical incident stress is not entirely preventable. However, company officers can do a great deal to reduce the long-term effects of critical incident stress by teaching their crews that these reactions and symptoms are entirely normal. In fact, anyone who did not experience at least some of these reactions might be psychologically unsuited to this type of work.

In the fire service, one factor that contributes to critical incident stress is the image of the "macho" firefighter. Firefighters who feel that they must live up to this unrealistic image can suffer guilt feelings when they experience or show any of the critical incident stress symptoms. By denigrating this unhealthy image, company officers can relieve some of their firefighters' unnecessary stress-caused guilt feelings. There is no reason to feel guilty about experiencing critical incident stress symptoms. Company officers should remember that they themselves are not immune to critical incident stress or the feelings of guilt when experiencing the symptoms.

There are several things that company officers can do to help alleviate the immediate reactions to a critical incident. One is to make sure that the company gets proper rest after the incident. Another important thing that company officers can do is talk with their crews about the trauma of the emergency. This informal discussion, sometimes called *defusing*, is usually all that is necessary after most emergency calls. However, after particularly stressful incidents, company officers should request that the company be placed out of service temporarily and that a critical incident stress debriefing (CISD) be conducted.

Critical Incident Stress Debriefings (CISD)

As is clear from the previous discussion, critical incident stress can be very damaging to firefighters and costly to their department. A good way to help reduce this damage is with an established stress management program that includes critical incident stress debriefings. These debriefings are group sessions with a trained debriefer (usually a psychologist) in which company members are encouraged to talk about the incident and their feelings about it. Ideally, these debriefings should be conducted immediately after the company returns to quarters — in extreme cases, before the company is placed back into service. If one or more members of the crew are suffering from the effects of an especially stressful event, it would be counterproductive and perhaps dangerous to immediately send them out on another call. To place these individuals in a position where they might have to make life-and-death decisions when their judgment is impaired by psychological stress would not be prudent. If necessary, and if the members of the company can remain out of service, CISD can be delayed for up to 72 hours after an extraordinarily traumatic incident. However, the sooner that intervention is started, the better.

In some cases, individual counseling on a long-term basis may be necessary. Left untreated, the effects of critical incident stress may lead to a serious condition known as *post-traumatic stress disorder* (PTSD). PTSD can produce some of the very debilitating conditions discussed earlier in this section. Some of these conditions may be career threatening, or even worse.

Substance Abuse

High levels of stress, both on and off the job, may cause some people to turn to alcohol or drugs as an escape. In addition, since fire departments tend to be a reflection of the society of which they are a part, the abuse of alcohol and other drugs are also problems in the fire service. The work performance of someone under the influence can be unpredictable — and in the emergency services, that is entirely unacceptable.

Because of the investment made in training a firefighter and because of humanitarian considerations, fire departments should not arbitrarily terminate a firefighter who has developed a substance abuse problem. Obviously, no one can be allowed to remain on duty while under the influence. They should be relieved of duty and be required to participate in a substance abuse treatment program. Their continued membership in the de-

partment should be made contingent upon successful completion of the program. Most medical insurance policies and employee assistance programs will pay for this type of treatment. From a purely economic standpoint, it is less expensive to help a trained firefighter overcome a substance abuse problem than to terminate the individual and have to hire and train a replacement. The fire department will get a better return on its investment if it can retain a trained and seasoned firefighter who is drug and alcohol free.

Even though the majority of firefighter injuries are associated with emergency incidents and the stress they produce, firefighters also suffer injuries in their normal day-to-day activities in the fire station. The following section focuses on the causes and prevention of injuries in the workplace.

Accident Investigations

[NFPA 1021 2-7.2]

Accidents occur as a result of a sequence of events — sometimes called the *domino effect* — and the confluence of a number of contributing factors. In day-to-day activities, workers (including firefighters) do things that are unsafe, and nothing bad happens — they "get away with it." This happens because one or more of the factors needed to cause an accident is missing. However, if an unsafe act is repeated often enough, all the necessary factors eventually come together, and an accident occurs — perhaps with tragic results.

There are many good reasons for conducting competent and thorough investigations of accidents involving firefighters — this is how dangerous procedures, equipment, and conditions are identified. Then, steps can be taken to minimize or eliminate them. It is critically important that all line of duty accidents be thoroughly and properly investigated — especially those that involve firefighter fatalities. Section 8-4.3 of NFPA 1500 recommends that autopsy results, if available, be recorded in the health and safety database. In addition, a thorough and timely investigation is necessary to determine eligibility under the federal Public Safety Officer Benefit Act of 1976 (PSOB), which provides a benefit of up to $100,000 dollars to "the survivors of public safety officers found to have died as the direct and proximate result of a personal injury sustained in the line of duty, and to claimant public safety officers found to have been permanently and totally disabled as the direct result of a catastrophic injury sustained in the line of duty." For more information on the eligibility requirements for the PSOB, refer to 28 CFR 32 and the USFA publication *Firefighter Autopsy Protocol* (FA-156).

Conducting Accident Investigations

[NFPA 1021 2-7.2]

When an accident does occur, an investigation should be conducted to determine exactly what transpired — what was the *root cause*. Such investigations should be objective, impartial, and directed toward fact-finding, not fault-finding. There are several reasons to investigate workplace accidents:

- To identify the behavior or condition that caused the accident (root cause)

- To identify previously unrecognized hazards

- To identify additional training needs

- To identify improvements needed in safety policies and procedures

- To identify facts that could have a legal impact on an accident case

- To determine eligibility for the PSOB death benefit

When a workplace accident investigation is conducted, all principals and witnesses should be interviewed and all relevant factors documented. Prominent among these is the human factor. To conduct a thorough and comprehensive investigation, the investigators must have some knowledge of human behavior.

Understanding Human Factors

It has been shown that in industry, accidents happen frequently to some personnel and infrequently to others. This means that accidents are not distributed uniformly throughout the workforce. Workers who fail to control the factors leading to an accident because of mental, psychological, or physical reasons will be involved in accidents more often than other workers — they are said to be "accident prone." This can be explained in terms referred to as human factors.

Human factors are an individual's attributes or personal characteristics that cause this individual to be involved in more or fewer accidents than other individuals. In most cases, an organization can mitigate negative human factors through motivation, training, or technical revision. Human factors that often contribute to accidents have been classified into three broad categories:

- **Improper attitude**. This includes willful disregard, recklessness, irresponsibility, laziness, disloyalty, uncooperativeness, fearfulness, oversensitivity, egotism, jealousy, impatience, obsession, phobia, absentmindedness, excitability, inconsideration, intolerance, or mental unsuitability in general. Readjusting any of these faulty attitudes or personality traits through

counseling, training, or discipline can lead to accident reduction (Figure 22.20).

- **Lack of knowledge or skill**. This includes insufficient knowledge, misunderstandings, indecision, inexperience, poor training, or failure to recognize potential hazards. These problems can be reduced or eliminated through training (Figure 22.21).

- **Physically unsuited**. This includes problems of hearing, sight, weight, height, illness, allergies, slow reactions, disabilities, intoxication, or physical limitations in general. Correcting these physical limitations can often reduce accident rates. If they cannot be corrected, the personnel should not be assigned to tasks where their limitations might create a hazard or be potentially dangerous to themselves or others.

An organization's effectiveness in mitigating the human factors that lead to accidents often depends upon a number of other factors. Some of these factors include time and effort committed to developing and implementing policies and procedures for training and certification on the safe use of equipment. The training must be documented and the policies and procedures enforced.

Figure 22.20 Company officers can help their crew members develop a positive attitude.

Figure 22.21 Company training is an important component of safety.

For more information on accident causes, prevention, and investigation, see the IFSTA **Fire Department Occupational Safety** manual.

In addition to being able to conduct an initial accident investigation, company officers are also required by NFPA 1021, *Standard for Fire Officer Qualifications*, to be able to analyze accident/injury reports they receive from others. The following section discusses accident/health exposure analysis.

Analyzing Accident/Injury Reports

[NFPA 1021 3-7.2]

After all data have been compiled following an accident, the information must be analyzed. A careful analysis of an accident/injury report can have some very positive effects on workplace safety in the future. However, just as with the initial investigation, the analysis must be conducted in an objective and impartial way. The point is to glean useful information from the report to determine the root cause and not to find fault or fix blame. The report should be carefully scrutinized to see whether any patterns emerge or whether there were common elements in the sequence of events leading to the accident.

All workplace accidents are the result of either unsafe acts, unsafe conditions, or both. The point of the accident analysis is to determine how these factors combined to create one root cause and what can be learned from the particular incident. Unsafe acts may result from inadequate training and supervision or from improper attitudes of the individual(s) involved. Unsafe acts may be the result of a well-intentioned attempt to save time by "cutting corners." Or, they may result from a careless attitude that reflects the low morale of those involved. Unsafe conditions are common on the fireground and at other emergency scenes. Most departments have SOPs designed to reduce the risks to firefighters in these situations. However, if the circumstances were beyond those anticipated in the SOPs, the guidelines may be inadequate.

In conducting an analysis of an individual accident/injury report, company officers should attempt to find answers to a number of basic questions. Some of these questions are:

• Who was involved?

• What was involved?

• What were the circumstances?

• What was the root cause?

Who Was Involved?

Is this the first time this individual has been involved in an accident, or is this just the latest in a series? Is this individual accident-prone? Was this individual assigned a task that was beyond his or her capabilities/limitations? Is there a need for more/different training?

What Was Involved?

Was the individual operating machinery or equipment? If so, was it being operated according to the manufacturer's recommendations and established policies and procedures? If not, why not? Did the situation justify not following established procedure? Does the procedure need to be changed, or is a new procedure needed? Was the equipment adequate for the job, or is more/better/different equipment needed?

What Were the Circumstances?

Was inclement weather or darkness a contributing factor? Is more/better lighting or other equipment needed? Did a drug/alcohol screening determine the presence/absence of these substances? Did the accident occur during an emergency or during routine activities? If during an emergency, was the accident reasonably preventable? Accidents occurring during routine, nonemergency activities should be assumed to be preventable until proven otherwise. Is there a need for more training or for more aggressive enforcement of established procedures?

What Was the Root Cause?

Was the accident the result of equipment failure? Do preventive maintenance procedures need to be changed? Was operator carelessness or negligence the cause? Was excessive speed involved, and if so, was it justified? Is more training on the operation of the involved equipment needed? Was the accident caused by a breakdown in communications? Is more/better/different communications equipment needed? Are the established communications procedures adequate? Are different communications procedures needed?

Conclusions

What conclusions can be drawn from this report? Are there any recognizable patterns? Were the same personnel involved in a number of accidents or near misses? Was the same equipment involved? Were the same operations/evolutions involved? What can be done to prevent similar accidents in the future?

A number of different solutions or partial solutions to accident prevention problems may emerge from this sort of analysis. For example, there may be a need for more personnel, more and better equipment, or more training. However, not every safety problem can be solved by spending more money. A certain amount of risk is inherent in fire fighting and other emergency work. Beyond that, much of the success or failure of the department's safety program is the direct result of the attitudes and behavior of those doing the job — the firefighters themselves. And no one has more influence over the firefighters' attitudes than their company officer. Especially in the area of safety, company officers have a responsibility to take action — discipline or other corrective action for accidents that were caused by negligence or not following procedure. But if a company officer fails to wear the proper safety gear, he cannot expect his firefighters to wear theirs. As the company officer goes, so go the firefighters. For more information on accident investigation and analysis, refer to the IFSTA **Fire Department Occupational Safety** manual, or contact the National Safety Council at P.O. Box 558, Itasca, IL, 60143-0558, or call (800) 621-6244.

Wellness Programs

Wellness programs are designed to help maintain the occupational health of a fire department's most important resource—its personnel. Wellness programs should include a means of monitoring the personnel and maintaining confidential records on each firefighter's health and fitness. These records should include the following information:

- Results of medical exams
- Results of physical fitness tests
- Occupational illnesses
- Occupational injuries
- Exposures (confirmed or suspected) to hazardous materials
- Exposures (confirmed or suspected) to communicable diseases

The overall wellness program should be comprehensive. Typically, these programs are composed of three subprograms:

- Medical program
- Physical fitness program
- Member or employee assistance program (EAP)

Medical Program

All routine and injury- and illness-related medical tests and physical examinations are conducted as part of the medical program (Figure 22.22). The results of these tests are used to determine whether firefighters are physically capable of performing their assigned duties. All such tests and examinations should be conducted by the fire department physician, and the records should be kept strictly confidential.

Physical Fitness Program

Fighting fires, performing rescues, and delivering other emergency services are often very physically demanding. While modern tools and equipment have made some parts of the job easier, safety requires that those who are doing the job be in top physical condition — in strength, endurance, and flexibility. All fire department personnel, regardless of rank or assignment, should be physically fit enough to safely perform every duty that is included in their job description. Company-level personnel must be in top physical condition because of the types of tasks that they must routinely perform (Figure 22.23). Command-level officers must have strong cardiovascular systems to handle the stresses associated with incident command and other critical decision-making functions.

The department's physical fitness program should follow the requirements of NFPA 1500 and should be administered by the department physician. The program should be used to help firefighters and other department personnel achieve and maintain the required levels of physical fitness through appropriate exercise and weight training. Weights, exercise equipment, and

Figure 22.22 Medical screenings are a part of a safety program.

Figure 22.23 Fire fighting duties demand a high level of physical fitness.

facilities should be provided, and their use should be encouraged or required. Such programs can also help personnel speed their recovery from occupational illnesses and injuries.

Member Assistance Program

The member assistance program, also known as *employee assistance programs* (EAP), assists members with problems resulting from stress, substance abuse, and personal matters. These programs usually offer a variety of professional counseling services at little or no cost to the member. To be most effective, these programs should be available to all fire department personnel and their families.

Summary

There are many factors that influence firefighter safety and health. Some of these are inherent dangers of the job. Others are controllable conditions that a conscientious company officer can recognize and take action to mitigate. To do this, the company officer must be aware of all aspects of company safety. By realizing where accidents are occurring and what the major causes are, company officers can help prevent unnecessary injuries by setting a good personal example and by teaching firefighters to be safety and health conscious.

Stress and substance abuse problems should be addressed as soon as they are discovered in order to preserve the health of the affected firefighter and to keep the fire fighting team intact. The effectiveness of a fire fighting team (company) will eventually be compromised if a member's stress or substance abuse problem goes unresolved. The company officer can do more than anyone else in the organization to help maintain a healthy fire fighting team.

A

ADA — Abbreviation for Americans With Disabilities Act.

Administrative Law — Rules and regulations adopted by government agencies to implement the laws that these agencies are charged with enforcing.

Affirmative Action — Administrative law adopted by the Equal Employment Opportunity Commission to implement the requirements of Title VII of the Civil Rights Act of 1964. Affirmative action programs are designed to make a special effort to identify, hire, and promote special populations where the current labor force in a jurisdiction or labor market is not representative of the overall population.

American National Standards Institute (ANSI) — Voluntary standards-setting organization that examines and certifies existing standards and creates new standards for a wide variety of materials, products, processes, and procedures.

American Society for Testing and Materials (ASTM) — Voluntary standards-setting organization that sets standards for systems, materials, and services.

Americans With Disabilities Act (ADA) — 1990 federal law intended to eliminate discrimination against people with permanent disabilities.

ANSI — Acronym for American National Standards Institute.

Assembly — Components fitted together to make a complete machine, structure, or unit.

ASTM — Abbreviation for American Society for Testing and Materials.

Autocratic Leadership — Leadership style in which the leader makes decisions independently of others, informing others only after the decision has been made.

Automatic Sprinkler System — System of pipes, discharge nozzles, and control valves designed to automatically activate during a fire and discharge water or foam to control or extinguish the fire. Also called Sprinkler System.

B

Base Radio — Fixed (nonmobile) radio at a central location.

Bureaucratic Leadership — Leadership style in which the leader has a low degree of concern for workers and production.

C

CABO — Abbreviation for Council of American Building Officials.

Capital Budget — Budget intended to fund large, one-time expenditures such as those for fire stations, fire apparatus, or major pieces of equipment.

Carbon Dioxide System — Extinguishing system that uses carbon dioxide as the primary extinguishing agent; designed primarily to protect confined spaces because the gaseous agent is easily dispersed by wind.

Case Law — Laws based on judicial interpretations and decisions rather than created by legislation.

CISD — Abbreviation for Critical Incident Stress Debriefing.

Citizens Band (CB) Radio — Low-power radio transceiver which operates on frequencies authorized by the Federal Communications Commission (FCC) for public use with no license requirement.

Civil Liability — Legal responsibility for fulfilling a specified duty or behaving with due regard for the rights and safety of others.

Coercive Power — Power to punish or impose sanctions on those who fail to behave in a prescribed manner.

Command — Act of directing, ordering, and/or controlling resources by virtue of explicit legal, agency, or delegated authority.

Common Law — Law not created by legislative action but based on certain commonly held customs, traditions, and beliefs within a particular culture.

Communication — Exchange of ideas and information that conveys an intended meaning in a form that is understood.

Confinement — Fire fighting operations required to prevent fire from extending from the area of origin to other uninvolved areas within the property of origin.

Constitutional Law — Law based on the constitution; all state/provincial laws must be consistent with the respective federal constitution.

Control Zones — System of barriers surrounding designated areas at emergency scenes intended to limit the number of persons exposed to the hazard, and to facilitate its mitigation. At a major incident there will be three zones — restricted (hot), limited access (warm), and support (cold).

Corrective Maintenance — Maintenance or repairs that are performed as a result of a breakdown or mechanical failure; reactive in nature.

Council of American Building Officials (CABO) — Umbrella organization for BOCA (Building Officials and Code Administrators), ICBO (International Conference of Building Officials), and SBCCI (Southern Building Code Congress International).

County/Parish — Political subdivision of a state, province, or territory for administrative purposes and public safety.

Criminal Law — Law intended to protect society by identifying certain conduct as criminal and by specifying the sanctions to be imposed on those who engage in criminal activity.

Critical Incident Stress Debriefing (CISD) — Counseling designed to minimize the effects of psychological/emotional trauma on those at fire and rescue incidents who were directly involved with victims suffering from particularly gruesome or horrific injuries.

Crowd Control — Limiting access to an emergency scene by curious spectators and other nonemergency personnel.

D

Defensive Mode — Deployment of resources to limit the growth of an emergency incident rather than mitigating it.

Delegation — Providing subordinates with the authority, direction, and resources needed to complete an assignment.

Democratic Leadership — Leadership style in which the leader is team-oriented and gives authority to the group; the group makes suggestions and decisions; also called participative leadership.

Directive — Authoritative instrument or order issued by a superior officer.

Direct Order — Command or assignment to a subordinate that specifies the desired behavior or outcome.

Discipline — To maintain order through training and/or the threat or imposition of sanctions; setting the limits or boundaries for expected performance and enforcing them.

Division of Labor — Breaking down an assignment into its constituent parts in order to equalize the workload and increase efficiency.

Drilling — *See* Training.

Dry Chemical Systems — Extinguishing system that uses dry chemical powder as the primary extinguishing agent; often used to protect areas containing volatile flammable liquids.

Dual-Issue Leadership — Leadership style in which the leader has a high degree of concern for both workers and production.

E

Egress — Place or means of exiting a structure.

Evacuation — Process of leaving or being removed from a potentially hazardous location.

Expert Power — Sufficiently strong perception that a leader's expertise, knowledge, and abilities will produce a desirable outcome so others willingly follow that leader.

Exposure — (1) Adjacent structure or separate part of the fireground to which a fire could spread. (2) People, property, systems, or natural features that are or may be exposed to the harmful effects of a hazardous materials release.

Extinguish — To put out a fire completely.

F

Factory Mutual System (FM) — Fire research and testing laboratory that provides loss control information for the Factory Mutual System members and others who may find it useful.

Fast Attack — When the first-arriving unit at a fire initiates a quick offensive attack on the fire.

FM — Abbreviation for Factory Mutual System.

Foam System — Extinguishing system that uses a foam such as aqueous film forming foam (AFFF) as the primary extinguishing agent; usually installed in areas where there is a risk of flammable liquid fires starting.

Fuel Loading — Amount of fuel present expressed quantitatively in terms of weight of fuel per unit area; may be available fuel (consumable fuel) or total fuel and is usually calculated in dry weight.

Functional Supervision — Organizational principle that allows workers to report to more than one supervisor without violating the unity of command principle; workers report to their primary supervisor for most of their activities but report to a second supervisor for activities that relate to an assigned function only, and both supervisors coordinate closely.

G

Global Positioning System (GPS) — System for determining position on the earth's surface by calculating the difference in time for the signal from a number of satellites to reach a GPS receiver on the ground.

GPS — Abbreviation for Global Positioning System

H

Halogenated Agent System — Extinguishing system that uses a halogenated gas as the primary extinguishing agent; usually installed to protect highly sensitive electronic equipment.

I

Identification Power — That which stems from the human tendency to follow or mimic those who are admired or respected.

Incident Action Plan — Written or unwritten plan for the disposition of an incident; contains the overall strategic goals and tactical objectives and support requirements for a given operational period. When written, the plan may have a number of forms as attachments.

Incident Command System — System by which facilities, equipment, personnel, procedures, and communications are organized to operate within a common organizational structure designed to aid in the management of resources at emergency incidents.

Indirect Attack — Directing fire streams toward the ceiling of a room or building in order to generate a large amount of steam. Converting the water to steam absorbs the heat of the fire and cools the area sufficiently for firefighters to safely enter and make a direct attack on the fire.

Industrial Fire Department — Fire prevention/suppression force that operates within the confines of a given plant or industrial complex; usually trained to deal with the hazards associated with the particular industrial operations conducted in the facility.

Isolate — (1) To set apart. (2) Second of three steps (locate, isolate, mitigate) in one way of sizing up an emergency situation.

J

Judicial System — System of courts set up to interpret and administer the laws and regulations.

Jurisdiction — (1) Legal authority to operate or function. (2) Boundaries of a legally constituted entity.

L

Legitimate Power — That which stems from any or all of three sources: shared values, acceptance of social structure, or the sanctions of a legitimizing agent.

Line-Item Budget — Budget that details the department's proposed expenditures line by line; the most common type of fire department budget.

Local Alarm System — Fire alarm system designed to alert the occupants of the existence of a fire so that they can safely exit the building and call the fire department.

M

Management by Objectives — Planning and control device used to organize resources and motivate personnel toward the fulfillment of specified objectives.

Middle-of-the-Road Leadership — Leadership style characterized by a moderate degree of concern for both production and workers.

Military Fire Department — Fire prevention/suppression unit operated by the Department of Defense; jurisdiction is usually limited to the confines of a military base or installation.

Mitigate — (1) To make less severe or intense. (2) Third of three steps (locate, isolate, mitigate) in one way of sizing up an emergency situation.

Mixed Occupancy — Where two or more types or classes of occupancy exist in the same building or structure. Separate requirements are often impractical so the most restrictive fire and life safety requirements apply.

Mutual Aid — Prearranged plan or contract whereby separate fire protection agencies assist each other on a reciprocal basis.

N

National Fire Protection Association (NFPA) — Nonprofit educational and technical association devoted to protecting life and property from fire by developing fire protection standards and educating the public.

National Institute for Occupational Safety and Health (NIOSH) — U.S. government agency that helps ensure the safety of the workplace and associated equipment by conducting investigations and making recommendations.

Negligence — Conduct that fails to meet the standard of care required by the law or that would be expected of a reasonable and prudent person under like circumstances.

NFPA — Abbreviation for National Fire Protection Association.

NIOSH — Acronym for National Institute for Occupational Safety and Health.

O

Occupational Safety and Health Administration (OSHA) — U.S. federal agency that develops and enforces standards and regulations for safety in the workplace.

Offensive Mode (Offensive Attack) — Aggressive fire attack that is intended to control or extinguish a fire before it spreads to other uninvolved property.

Operating Budget — Budget intended to fund the day-to-day operations of the department or agency; usually includes the costs of salaries and benefits, utility bills, fuel, and preventive maintenance.

Outside Aid — Assistance from agencies, industries, or fire departments that are not part of the agency having jurisdiction over the incident.

Overhaul — Searching for and extinguishing any hidden or remaining fires once the main body of fire has been extinguished.

P

Paid-On-Call — System in which firefighters or emergency personnel are paid on an hourly or per-call basis.

Performance Budget — Form of program budgeting in which the cost of each unit of performance (fire call, EMS call, code enforcement inspection, plan review, etc.) is identified, and total funding is based on projected performance levels.

Performance Evaluation — Evaluation of an individual's job performance as measured against one or more objective performance criteria.

Perimeter Control — Establishing and maintaining control of the outer edge or boundary of an incident scene.

Personnel Record — Account of an individual employee's work history; includes personal data (name, address, date of employment, job classification, etc.) citations, commendations, promotions, performance evaluations, letters of reprimand or other disciplinary documentation, and medical history.

Plan of Operations — Clearly identified strategic goal and the tactical objectives necessary to achieve that goal. Included are assignments, authority, responsibility, and safety considerations.

Preventive Maintenance — Routine maintenance performed according to a schedule; designed to prevent breakdowns or malfunctions, not to repair or replace damaged or worn-out components.

Program Budget — Budgetary system in which each major program (administration, suppression, prevention, EMS, training, etc.) is funded independently of the other departmental programs. The overall department budget is a composite of the individual program budgets.

R

Reasonable Accommodation — Legal requirement (under Title VII of the Civil Rights Act of 1964) that employers make *reasonable* adjustments to an employee's work schedule or other job requirements to accommodate employee differences such as religion, gender, and/or physical or mental disability.

Reward Power — Based on the subordinate's perception of the leader's ability to grant rewards such as salary increases, promotions, and bigger budgets.

S

Scene Assessment — Initial observation and evaluation of an emergency scene; related more to incident stabilization than to problem mitigation.

Scene Management — Those elements of incident management that include keeping those not involved in the incident from entering unsafe areas and protecting those in potentially unsafe areas through evacuation or sheltering in place.

Sexual Harassment — Unwanted and unwelcome sexual behavior toward a worker by someone who has the power to reward or punish the worker.

Shelter in Place — Locating those at risk from a rapidly approaching hazard (fire, hazardous gas cloud, etc.) inside a structure that can protect them from the hazard until it passes.

Single-Issue Leadership — Leadership style that is characterized by an overriding concern for either production or people.

Span of Control — Number of subordinates that one individual can effectively supervise. This number ranges from three to seven individuals or functions, with five generally established as optimum.

Sprinkler System — *See* Automatic Sprinkler System.

Statutory Law — Law promulgated by legislative action.

T

Theory X — Style of leadership in which the leader believes that the average worker prefers to be directed and will avoid responsibility due to a general lack of ambition.

Theory Y — Style of leadership in which the leader believes that the average worker enjoys work, performs well with minimal supervision, will both seek and accept responsibility if given the opportunity, and will subscribe to organizational objectives if he associates those objectives with direct rewards.

Theory Z — Management style based on the belief that involved workers are the key to increased productivity and that there is a mutual loyalty between the company and the workers that often translates into life time employment and a close relationship between work and social life.

Title VII — Part of the Civil Rights Act of 1964 that prohibits discrimination based on race, color, religion, national origin, or gender.

Tort Liability — Liability for a civil wrong or injury; noncriminal acts or failures to act that result in physical and/or monetary damages.

Traffic Control — Important function of scene management that helps to control scene access and vehicular traffic in and out of the area. This function is generally handled by law enforcement personnel.

Training — Supervised activity that helps workers develop and maintain required skills; also called Drilling.

Type I Construction — That which has structural members, including walls, columns, beams, floors, and roofs, made of noncombustible or limited combustible materials; also known as fire-resistive construction.

Type II Construction — Similar to Type I except that the degree of fire resistance is lower; also known as noncombustible or limited combustible construction.

Type III Construction — That which has exterior walls and structural members made of noncombustible or limited combustible materials, but with interior structural members (walls, columns, beams, floors, and roofs) completely or partially constructed of wood; commonly referred to as ordinary construction.

Type IV Construction — Heavy timber construction with exterior and interior walls and their associated structural members that are of noncombustible or limited combustible materials.

Type V Construction — That which has exterior walls, bearing walls, floors, roofs, and supports made completely or partially of wood or other approved materials of smaller dimension than those used for Type IV construction, also called wood frame construction.

U

Underwriters Laboratories Inc. (UL) — Independent fire research and testing laboratory.

Unified Command — In the Incident Command System, a shared command role that allows all agencies with responsibility for the incident, either geographical or functional, to manage the incident by establishing a common set of incident objectives and strategies. There is a single incident command post and a single operations chief at any given time.

Unity of Command — Organizational principle in which workers report to only one supervisor in order to eliminate conflicting orders and the confusion that would result.

W

Wet Chemical System — Extinguishing system that uses a wet chemical solution as the primary extinguishing agent; usually installed in range hoods and associated ducting where grease may accumulate.

Z

Zero-Base Budget — Budgetary system in which each department, function, or program theoretically terminates with the budget and must justify its existence in order to receive funding in the new budget.

Zoning Commission — Division of local government that is responsible for managing land use by dividing the area within the jurisdiction into zones in which only certain uses (residential, commercial, manufacturing, etc.) are allowed.

Index

A

abilities of company officer, 8-11
access and egress (inspection category), 196, 197
accessible means of egress, defined, 196
accidental fires, 220-222
accident/injury reports, analyzing, 311-312
accident investigation, 309-311
accidents. *See also* injuries, firefighter
   slip, trip, and fall, 304, 305
   workplace, 309-312
accountability
   centralized, 29
   personnel, 293-294
accreditation system, 114, 115
action plan, 78
   incident, 279, 280, 292, 294
action plan implementation, 283-294
   communication for, 283-284
   defensive mode, 276, 284-285
   incident command/management system, 286-293
   job performance requirements, 282
   life safety and, 284
   offensive mode, 276, 284, 285-286
   personnel accountability and, 293-294
   rescue mode, 276, 284, 286
activity records, 169-171, 172-173
administrative law, 33-34
agencies
   of local governments, 102
   of state and provincial governments, 104-106
   U.S. federal, involved in fire protection, 108-111
airport fire departments, 17
alarm systems
   auxiliary, 205
   local, 205
   public fire, 207
all-hands rescue, 276, 284, 286
American Arbitration Association, 145
American Federation of State, County, and Municipal Employees (AFSCME), 141
American Federation of Labor (AFL), 117, 140
American Federation of Labor/Congress of Industrial Organizations, 117
American National Standards Institute (ANSI) standards, 42-43
Americans with Disabilities Act (ADA), 40-41, 180, 267
apparatus
   as capital budget item, 152
   maintenance of, 81
   proper placement on emergency scene, 261
application step in four-step method of instruction, 89

arbitration, 145-146
area of refuge, 196
areas of rescue assistance, 267
assembly occupancies, 198
audiovisual equipment, 184
authority
   delegation of, 24, 29, 75, 78
   for fire and life safety inspections, 189-190
   to implement, 29
autocratic leadership, 64
automatic aid, 19-20
automatic sprinkler systems, 208-210
auxiliary alarm systems, 205

B

bargaining, collective, 142-143
bargaining procedures, 141
bloodborne pathogens, 300
"blue flu" tactic, 146
body recovery, 285
breach of duty, 35
budgeting, 10, 151-157
   budget process, 154-157
   capital budgets, 151-153
   grants and gifts and, 157
   inflating budget requests, 153
   job performance requirements, 150
   operating budgets, 153-154, 155
   techniques for extending budget, 19
Building and Fire Research Laboratory (BFRL), 118
building construction, 234-239
   lightweight construction, 238-239
   roofs, types of, 236-238
   types of, 234-236
bureaucratic leadership, 62
Bureau of Alcohol, Tobacco, and Firearms (BATF), 111
Bureau of Land Management (BLM), 110
business occupancies, 201

C

CAMEO, 246
Canada, government in
   federal, 111-114
      agencies creating laws, 33
      agencies involved in fire protection, 112-114
      lawmaking process of, 112
      structure of, 111-112
   municipal, 98
   provincial and territorial, 104
Canadian Centre for Occupational Health and Safety, 113
Canadian Constitution, 112
Canadian Defense Department, 17
Canadian Labor Congress, 117
Canadian Transportation Commission, 33
capital budgets, 151-153

capital improvement plans (CIPs), 151
carbon dioxide systems, 211-212
career counseling, 3, 85
career (full-time) personnel, 17
case law, 34
casualties, incident report on, 163
cause of fire, determining, 220
centralized authority, 29
central station systems, 205-206
chain of command, 22, 23
check-in, 294
civil actions (suits), 34, 35
civil law, 34
civil liability, 34-36
class action suits, 34
class I-III standpipe systems, 207, 208
clear text terminology, 256, 288, 290
closing interview, 203-204
code enforcement inspection, 229
Code of Federal Regulations, 37
   "Protection of Environment" chapter, 37-38
   Title 29 of, 298
code requirements
   for assembly occupancies, 198
   for business occupancies, 201
   for detention and correctional occupancies, 199
   for educational occupancies, 199
   for health care occupancies, 199
   for industrial occupancies, 202
   for mercantile occupancies, 200
   for residential occupancies, 200
   for special structures, 203
   for storage occupancies, 202
cold zone, 262-263
collective bargaining, 142-143
combination department, 18
command/management system. *See* incident command/management system
command mode, 291-292
command post (CP), 262-263, 292
commercial fire protection services, 17
common law, 33
communication(s)
   for action plan implementation, 283-284
   conflict, 145
   defined, 134
   effective, 9
   fire department, 176, 177-186
   for incident command/management system, 288-289, 290
   incident scene, 249-257
   nonverbal, 179
   as supervisory skill, 79-80
   written, 159-169, 179
communications center, 249-250
communication skills, 79-80, 134-135

community, education programs within, 10, 11. See also public education
community awareness, 120, 121-122, 123
company-level training, 87-94
  education, 87-89
  job performance requirements, 86
  standard for, 80
  training, 87, 89-94
company officer
  assuming role of, 7-11
  duties of, 1-3
  pivotal position in labor/management dichotomy, 69
  responsibilities of, 1, 75-77, 190-191. See also legal responsibilities and liability
  roles of, 49
  transition from firefighter to, 7-8
company organizational structure, 29-30
complaints, handling citizen, 123-125
comprehensive resource management, 292-293
computer-aided dispatch (CAD) systems, 250
computers, 171-175
confinement of problem, 278
conflict communication, 145
conflict resolution, 145-149
Congressional Fire Services Caucus, 114
Congressional Fire Services Institute, 114
Congress of Industrial Organizations (CIO), 117, 140
Consumer Product Safety Commission (CPSC), 111
Continuum of Leadership Behavior, 72-73
control zones, 262
corrective action/activities, 83-84, 93
corrective maintenance, 169, 170
counseling, 3, 85
criminal actions (prosecutions), 34
criminal law, 34
criminal liability, 34
critical incident stress, 308-309
critical incident stress debriefing (CISD), 269, 309
cross training, 25
crowd control, 263-264
customer service, 123-127

D

daily logs, 171, 172-173
damages, punitive, 35
data
  electronic data storage/retrieval, 159, 171-175
  managing pre-incident, 246-247
debriefing, critical incident stress (CISD), 269, 309
decentralized authority, 29
decision-making authority, 29
decision-making model, 79
decision making skills, 78-79
decision step in traditional size-up, 272
defensive mode of operation, 276, 284-285
defusing, 269, 308
delegation of authority, 24, 29, 75, 78
deluge sprinkler systems, 210
Deming, W. Edwards, 73
democratic leadership, 64

Department of Agriculture, Canadian, 113
Department of Consumer and Corporate Affairs, Canadian, 113
Department of Finance, Canadian, 113
Department of Insurance, 113
Department of Labour, Canadian, 113
Department of Public Works, Canadian, 113
Department of the Environment, Canadian, 113
Department of the Solicitor General, Canadian, 113
Department of Transport, Canadian, 113
Department of Transportation (DOT), 110-111
detention and correctional occupancies, 199-200
directives, 181, 256
direct orders, 256
discipline, 7, 82-84
  contract clauses on procedures for, 142
  main purpose of, 82
  negative, 82-83
  as organizational principle, 25-26
  positive, 82
  progressive, 83-84
discrimination, sexual harassment as, 39
distress, 306
division, use of term, 287
division/group/sector assignment list, 294
division of labor, 24-25
Drucker, Peter, 71
dry chemical systems, 210, 211
dry-pipe sprinkler systems, 209, 210
dry sprinkler systems, 208-210
dual issue leadership, 63
duty to act, 190

E

educational occupancies, 198-199
egress, means of. See means of egress
electronic data storage/retrieval, 159, 171-175
elevation drawing, 242, 243
emergency management, FEMA and, 108-110
Emergency Management Institute (EMI), 109, 110
emergency medical service (EMS) reports, 164
Emergency Medical Services (EMS), 117
emergency medical technician-basic (EMT-B), 117
emergency vehicles, placement for, 262
emergency voice/alarm communications systems, 206
employee assistance programs (EAP), 313
employment regulations, ADA, 41
English Common Law, 31, 33
environmental protection agency, state, 105
Environmental Protection Agency (EPA), 33
  regulations, 37-39
environmental stress, 306-307
Equal Employment Opportunity Commission (EEOC), 33
  regulations, 39-40
equipment
  abandonment of, 268
  facility survey, 230

for incident scene communications, 249-255
for inspections, 192
personal protective, 306-307
retrieval and collection at termination of incident, 268
equipment maintenance, 81
ergonomics, 303-304
esprit de corps, 49
esteem needs, 53, 54
ethics, conduct while on duty and, 56
eustress, 306
evacuation, 265-267
evacuation capability of occupants, levels of, 200
evaluation
  formative, 93
  in four-step method of instruction, 89
  of infection control program, 300
  performance, 164
  of public education program, 135-136
  summative, 93
  by supervisor, 75-76
exit doors, 196, 197
exit drills, conducting, 204
expectancy theory, 54-55
exposure control plan, 299
exposures, protecting, 278
exterior facility survey, 232
extinguishment phase, 278

F

facility survey drawings, 242-245
facility survey equipment, 230
Factory Mutual Research Corporation (FMRC), 117-118
Fair Labor Standards Act (FLSA), 41, 140, 180
Farmers' Home Administration, 110
fast-attack mode, 291
Federal Communications Commission (FCC), 255
Federal Emergency Management Agency (FEMA), 108-110
Federal Fire Prevention and Control Act (1974), 108
federal government, 106-114
  Canadian, 33, 111-114
  U.S., 106-111
Federal Labor Relations Council, 141
federal laws, 37-41
Federal Mediation and Conciliation Service, 141, 147
field sketches, 243, 244
fire and life safety education program. See public education
fire and life safety inspections. See inspections, fire and life safety
Fire and Thermal Burn Program, CPSC, 111
fire chiefs association, 105
fire department(s), 13-30
  job performance requirements in, 12
  organizational principles, 21-26
    discipline, 25-26
    division of labor, 24-25
    span of control, 23-24, 292, 294
    unity of command, 21-23
  organizational structure, 9, 14-15, 26-30

personnel, 15, 17-18, 19
public image of, 121-127
purpose of, 18-19
types of, 13-17
    private, 13, 16-17
    public, 13-16
fire department communications, 176, 177-
    186
fire detection and alarm systems, pre-
    incident survey of, 240
fire detection/signaling systems, 205-206
fire district, 15-16, 101
fire extinguishing systems, 208-214
firefighter-officer relationships, 182
firefighters association, 105
firefighter unions, 141
fire investigation. *See under* investigation
Fireman's Rule, 36
fire protection district, 14, 16
fire protection systems
    inspecting/testing, 204-214
    pre-incident survey of, 240
fire-resistive construction, 234, 235
fire training programs, state and provincial,
    104
five-step planning process for public
    education program, 130-136
fixed extinguishing systems, pre-incident
    survey of, 240
floor plan
    for inspection tour, 194
    from interior survey, 233
floor plan drawing, 242, 243
follow-up inspection, 190-191
forest fire management, 110
formal communications, 180-181
formative evaluation, 93
four-step method of instruction, 88-89
French, John, 59
frequencies, radio, 250-251, 289
fuel loading, 239-240
functional supervision, 23, 26-29

G
general industrial occupancies, 202
geographic information system (GIS), 254
global positioning system (GPS), 255
government immunity, 31-32
government structure, 9, 97-114
    federal, 106-114
        Canadian, 33, 111-114
        U.S., 106-111
    local, 97-101
        county/parish government, 100-101
        fire districts, 101
        impact on fire protection agencies, 101-
            103
        municipal (city) government, 97-100
        township government, 100
    provincial and territorial, 104-106
    state, 103-104
grievance procedures, 142
groups, 47-57
    cultural diversity and, 56
    defined, 47-48
    formal, 47
    group dynamics, 48-52
    job performance requirements in working
        with, 46

H
halogenated agent systems, 212-213
hazard of contents, 203
hazardous materials, labeling requirements
    for, 202
hazardous materials incidents
    assessment of, 260
    release of airborne contaminants in, 267
health care occupancies, 199
heavy timber construction, 236
helibases, 292
helicopters, landing zones for, 266-267
helispots, 292
Herzberg, Frederick, 70-71
Hewlett Packard, 70
high hazard classification for contents, 203
high-hazard industrial occupancies, 202
high-rise structures, 203
hot zone, 262
house captain, 80
Human Relations Theory, 70
human resources management, 9
hygiene theory, 70-71

I
immediately dangerous to life and health
    (IDLH) space, 302-303
immunity, government, 31-32
incendiary fires, 220, 223-225
incident action plan, 279, 280, 292, 294. *See
    also* action plan implementation
incident command/management system,
    286-293
    common communications, 288-289, 290
    common terminology, 287-288
    comprehensive resource management,
        292-293
    manageable span of control, 292
    modular organization, 288, 289
    pre-designated incident facilities, 292
    unified command structure, 288-292
Incident Command System (ICS), 279, 286-
    293
Incident Management System (IMS), 279,
    286-293
incident plans, 270, 278-280
incident reports, 160-164
    company-level, 225-226
incident safety, 300-303
incident scene communications, 249-257
    equipment for, 249-255
    five C's of, 257
    job performance requirements, 248
    procedures for, 255-257
incident scene management. *See* scene
    management
industrial fire departments, 16-17
industrial occupancies, 201-202
infectious disease control program, 299-300
information gathering, pre-incident survey
    for, 232
information management, 159-175
    electronic data storage/retrieval, 159, 171-
        175
    job performance requirements, 158
    record keeping, 3, 76-77, 169-171
        activity records, 169-171, 172-173
        inspection records, 191

maintenance records, 169, 170
personnel records, 171
written communications, 159-169, 179
    letter writing, 164-169
    report writing, 3, 76-77, 159-164, 165,
        246
injuries, firefighter, 300-305
    accident/injury reports, analyzing, 311-
        312
    incident safety and, 300-303
    reducing number of, 301-302
    workplace safety and, 303-305
inquiries, handling public, 125-127
inspections, fire and life safety, 2, 10, 189-
    214
    authority for, 189-190
    company-level responsibilities for, 190-
        191
    exit drills, conducting, 204
    fire protection systems, inspecting/
        testing, 204-214
        fire detection/signaling systems, 205-206
        fire extinguishing systems, 208-214
        public fire alarm systems, 207
        standpipe systems, 207-208
        stationary fire pumps, 206-207
        water supplies, 206
    follow-up, 190-191
    job performance requirements, 188
    preparing for, 191-193
    purpose of, 191
instruction, four-step method of, 88-89. *See
    also* training
Insurance Services Office (ISO), 20, 80
Interagency Fire Center, 110
interior survey, 233
Internal Revenue Service (IRS), 33
International Association of Arson
    Investigators (IAAI), 115-116
International Association of Black
    Professional Fire Fighters (IABPFF), 116
International Association of Fire Chiefs
    (IAFC), 116-117
International Association of Fire Fighters
    (IAFF), 117, 141-142
International Brotherhood of Teamsters,
    141
International City Management Association
    (ICMA), 1, 75
International Fire Code Institute, 189
International Fire Service Accreditation
    Congress (IFSAC), 114
International Fire Service Training
    Association (IFSTA), 114
International Municipal Signal Association
    (IMSA), 114-115
International Society of Fire Service
    Instructors (ISFSI), 115
interview
    closing, during inspection, 203-204
    media relations, 184-185
investigation
    accident, 309-311
    fire, 10-11, 217-226
        accidental fires, 220-222
        determining cause of fire, 220
        documentation of, preparing, 225-226
        incendiary fires, 220, 223-225

job performance requirements, 216
locating point of origin, 217-219
natural fires, 220, 222-223
securing scene, 219-220
training and education in, 115-116
at termination of incident, 268
ISO Grading Schedule requirement, 93
isolation step in size-up process, 273-274

J

job actions, 146-147
job analysis, 25
job breakdown, 70
job description, 25
jurisdiction of public fire department, 13-16

L

labor relations, 139-149. *See also*
  supervision/management
  conflict resolution, 145-149
  contracts and agreements, 139, 142-145
  defined, 139
  history of, 139-141
  job performance requirements, 138
  public sector unions and, 141-142
labor team in collective bargaining, 142-143
laissez-faire leadership, 65-66
Landrum-Griffin Act (1959), 141
law enforcement agencies
  local, 102
  state of provincial police, 105
lawmaking process
  of Canadian federal government, 112
  of local governments, 101-102
  of U.S. federal government, 107-108
Layman, Lloyd, 272, 277-278
leadership, 59-67
  dimensions of, 65-66
  gender and, 66-67
  job performance requirements, 58
  leading by example, 8
  styles of, 64-65
  theories of, 61-63
  types of power in, 59-60
leadership continuum, 72-73
legal responsibilities and liability, 9-10, 31-43
  civil liability, 34-36
  criminal liability, 34
  federal laws, 37-41
  Fireman's Rule, 36
  government immunity and, 31-32
  national standards, 36, 41-43
  sources of law, 33-34
liability. *See also* legal responsibilities and
  liability
  civil, 34-36
  criminal, 34
  personal, 9-10, 36
life safety
  action plan implementation and, 284
  as first and highest priority, 271, 277-278
  scene management for, 259
life safety information, facility survey for, 233
life safety skills, mastery learning for, 90-93
lightweight construction, 238-239
limited access (warm) zone, 262, 264

line and staff organization, 26-29
line-item budgets, 153-154
local alarm systems, 205
local application CO_2 systems, 212
local-application dry chemical system, 210, 211
local government, 97-101
  county/parish government, 100-101
  fire districts, 101
  impact on fire protection agencies, 101-103
  municipal (city) government, 97-100
  township government, 100
location step in size-up process, 273
low hazard classification for contents, 203

M

McGregor, Douglas, 61, 62, 71, 84
mainframe computers, 171-174
maintenance
  corrective, 169, 170
  of fire stations, 80
  preventive, 169, 170
  skill, 2, 89-90
  of vehicles, 80-81
maintenance records, 169, 170
management. *See also* leadership; scene
  management; supervision/management
  scientific theory of, 69-70
  by walking around, 70
Management by Objectives (MBO), 71-72
management rights and prerogatives,
  contract clauses on, 142
management team in collective bargaining,
  142
managerial grid, 62-63
Manufactured Housing and Construction
  Standards Division, 110
Maslow, Abraham, 52-54, 143
Maslow's hierarchy of needs, 52-54, 143
mastery learning, 90-93
Mayo, Elton, 70
means of egress, 193, 196, 197
  for assembly occupancies, 198
  defined, 196
  for detention and correctional
    occupancies, 199-200
  for industrial occupancies, 202
  in mercantile occupancies, 200-201
media programs, 122-123
media relations, 184-185
mediation, 145
member assistance program, 313
mercantile occupancies, 200-201
Metropolitan Committee of the IAFC (Metro
  Chiefs), 117
MFD model, 148-149
middle-of-the-road leadership, 63
military fire departments, 17
Ministry of State for Science and
  Technology, Canadian, 113
mission statement, 26, 27, 54
mitigation step in size-up process, 274
mixed occupancies, 203
mobile data computer (MDC), 254-255
mobile data terminal (MDT), 254
mobile radios, 251, 252
modern management, 73-75

modes of operation
  defensive, 276, 284-285
  offensive, 276, 284, 285-286
  rescue, 276, 284, 286
modular organization, 288, 289
morals, conduct while on duty and, 56
motivation
  building company members', 2-3
  hygiene theory and, 71
  Maslow's hierarchy of needs and, 52-54, 143
  as supervisory skill, 77-78
Mouton, 61, 62
multijurisdictional unified command
  structure, 289, 291
municipal fire department, 14-15
mutual aid, 20-21

N

National Board on Fire Service Professional
  Qualifications (NBFSPQ), 115
National Electrical Code (NEC), 190
National Emergency Training Center
  (NETC), 109
National Energy Board (Canada), 99
National Fire Academy (NFA), 109-110
National Fire Incident Reporting System
  (NFIRS), 234, 301
  report forms, 160-163
National Fire Protection Association
  (NFPA), 20
National Fire Protection Association
  standards, 42, 115
  NFPA 10, *Standard for Portable Fire
    Extinguishers*, 213
  NFPA 11, *Standard for Low-Expansion
    Foam*, 213
  NFPA 11A, *Standard for Medium- and
    High-Expansion Foam Systems*, 213
  NFPA 12, *Standard on Carbon Dioxide
    Extinguishing Systems*, 211
  NFPA 14, *Standard for the Installation of
    Standpipe and Hose Systems*, 207
  NFPA 17, *Standard for Dry Chemical
    Extinguishing Systems*, 210
  NFPA 17A, *Standard for Wet Chemical
    Extinguishing Systems*, 211
  NFPA 20, *Standard for the Installation of
    Centrifugal Fire Pumps*, 207
  NFPA 72, *National Fire Alarm Code*, 205
  NFPA 101®, *Life Safety Code®*, 190
  NFPA 220, *Standard on Types of Building
    Construction*, 234
  NFPA 704, *Standard System for the
    Identification of the Hazards of Materials
    for Emergency Response*, 202
  NFPA 903, *Fire Reporting Property Survey
    Guide*, 242
  NFPA 1420, *Recommended Practice for
    Pre-Incident Planning for Warehouse
    Occupancies*, 242
  NFPA 1470, *Standard on Search and
    Rescue Training for Structural Collapse
    Incidents*, 246
  NFPA 1500, *Standard on Fire Department
    Occupational Safety and Health
    Program*, 10, 37, 297, 298, 299

NFPA 1561, *Standard for Fire Department Incident Management System*, 279
NFPA 1581, *Standard for Fire Department Infection Control Program*, 299
National Industrial Recovery Act (NIRA) of 1933, 140
National Institute of Occupational Safety and Health (NIOSH), 109
National Institute of Standards and Technology (NIST), 118
National Labor Relations Board (NLRB), 140
National Professional Qualifications Board (NPQB), 115
National Registry of Emergency Medical Technicians (NREMT), 117
national standards, 36, 41-43
National Volunteer Fire Council (NVFC), 115
Natural Resource Atomic Energy Commission (Canada), 33
negligence, 35-36
  current status of governmental immunity laws on, 32
  defined, 35
  standard of care and, 36
negotiations
  conflict resolution during, 145-149
  contracts, 142-145
NFPA. *See* National Fire Protection Association (NFPA)
NFPA Inspection Manual, 191-192
noncombustible or noncombustible/limited combustible construction, 234-235
nonprofit fire departments, private, 17
Norris-La Guardia Act (1932), 139-140

O
objectives
  of scene management, 259
  tactical, 280
occupancy classifications, 192, 198-203
occupant load, 198
occupant services, 264-265
Occupational Health and Safety (OH&S) (Canada), 33
Occupational Safety and Health Administration (OSHA), 33, 110, 268, 297
  regulations, 37, 297-298
offensive mode of operation, 276, 284, 285-286
office of emergency preparedness, local, 103
office of emergency preparedness or civil defense, state, 106
Office of the Comptroller General, Canadian, 113
officer determined training (ODT), 94
operating budgets, 153-154, 155
operating zones, 262
operational plans, 273, 279-280. *See also* pre-incident planning
orders, 181
  direct, 256
  instruction, 93
  production, 93
ordinances, 189-190
ordinary construction, 235-236
ordinary hazard classification for contents, 203
organizational principles, 21-26
  discipline, 25-26
  division of labor, 24-25
  span of control, 23-24
  unity of command, 21-23
organizational structure, fire department, 9, 26-30
  municipal fire department, 14-15
origin, locating point of, 217-219
Ouchi, William G., 61, 74
outdoor fires, 217-218
  wildland fires, 218-219, 260, 267
outside aid, 21

P
paid-on-call firefighters, 18
parish fire department, 15
patient care report, 164, 165
performance, tracking, 73. *See also* job performance requirements, NFPA
performance budgets, 154, 155
performance evaluations, 164
performance standards, 92, 94
perimeter control, 262-263
personal computers, 174-175
personal liability, 9-10, 36
personal protective equipment, 306-307
personal services in line-item budget, 153-154
personnel, fire department, 15, 17-18, 19
personnel accountability, 293-294
personnel costs (personal services), 153
personnel records, 171
personnel reports, 164
Phoenix (AZ) Fire Department
  decision-making model of, 285
  Fireground Command (FGC) system, 287
physical fitness, 300, 302
physical fitness program, 307, 312-313
physical stress, 306-307
physiological needs, 52
plan of operation, 273
plot plan drawing, 242, 243
point(s) of origin
  locating, 217-219
  multiple, incendiary fire indicated by, 223
policies, 180
  safety and health, 298-300
portable fire extinguishers, 213-214
post-traumatic stress disorder (PTSD), 309
power, types of, 59-60. *See also* leadership
pre-action sprinkler systems, 209, 210
prebriefing process, 269
precedent, legal, 34
pre-designated incident facilities, 292
Pregnancy Discrimination Act of 1978, 40
pre-incident planning, 10, 229-247
  developing plans, 242-246
  evacuation and, 265-267
  job performance requirements, 228
  managing pre-incident data, 246-247
  pre-incident survey, 229-241
  probabilities based on, 272
  size-up and, 274-275
prescriptive training, 91, 94
presentation(s)
  to community group, 122
  in four-step method of instruction, 88-89
  for public speaking, 184
pretest/posttest approach to feedback, 135
preventive action, 83
preventive maintenance, 169, 170
priorities, size-up and, 277-278
prioritizing assignments, 81-82
private and professional organizations, 114-118
private fire department, 13, 16-17
Professional Air Traffic Controllers Organization (PATCO) strike (1981), 141
professional counseling services, 85
program budgets, 154, 155
progressive discipline, 83-84
property conservation, 241, 259
proprietary systems, 205
provincial government, 104-106
proximate cause, 35
psychological stress, 306, 307-308
public accommodations, ADA regulations affecting, 40
public education, 122-123
  community programs, 10, 11
  program development and implementation, 129-136
    company-level participation in, 129-130
    five-step planning process, 130-136
    job performance requirements, 128
public fire alarm systems, 207
public fire department, 13-16
public information officer (PIO), 184
public information officer (PIO) location, 262-263
public relations, 122-123
  handling citizen concerns, 123-125
  handling public inquiries, 125-127
  job performance requirements, 120
  during pre-incident survey, 231
public safety department, 15
  personnel, 18, 19
Public Safety Officer Benefit Act of 1976 (PSOB), 309
public sector unions, 141-142
punitive action, 84
punitive damages, 35
pyrophoric ignition, 221

Q
quality circles, 74
quality management, total, 73-74

R
radio codes, 256
radio communications
  common, 288-289, 290
  incident scene communications, 249-253
  procedures, 255-256
radio frequencies, 250-251, 289
rapid intervention team, 303
reasonable accommodation, 39-40, 41
RECEO, 277
record keeping, 3, 76-77, 169-171
  activity records, 169-171, 172-173
  inspection records, 191
  maintenance records, 169, 170
  personnel records, 171
"red-hot stove rule," 84

reflex time, 271
relationship-by-objectives (RBO), 147-148
release-of-liability form, 263, 264
release of scene, 268-269
relocation centers, 266
remote station systems, 205
report drawings, 245
report writing, 3, 76-77, 159-164, 165
  accident/injury reports, 311-312
  functions of, 159-160
  incident reports, 160-164, 225-226
  personnel reports, 164
  for pre-incident plan, 246
rescue, 277-278
rescue mode, 276, 284, 286
residential occupancies, 200
resource management, 80-81
  comprehensive, 292-293
resources
  defensive mode with limited, 285
  deployment of, in operational plans, 279
  efficient use of, 19
  size-up of, upon arrival at scene, 276
response considerations, 19-21
  outside aid, 21
  automatic aid, 19-20
  mutual aid, 20-21
response report, EMS, 164
response time, pre-incident size up of, 274
responsibilities of company officer, 1
  for fire and life safety inspections, 190-191
  legal. See legal responsibilities and liability
  supervision/management, 75-77
restricted (hot) zone, 262
right-to-work laws, 141
risk, fire-related, 131
role expectations, 49-51
roles
  of company officer, 49
  within group, 49
roofs, types of, 236-238
  panelized roofing, 238-239
Royal Canadian Mounted Police, 113
rules
  departmental, enforcement of, 2
  group, 51
  informal, 51
run report, 163, 225

S

safe haven, 267-268
safety and health, firefighter, 2, 76, 297-313
  accident/injury reports, analyzing, 311-312
  accident investigation, 309-311
  injuries, 300-305
    incident safety and, 300-303
    workplace safety and, 303-305
  job performance requirements, 296
  policies and procedures, 298-300
  safety standards, 297-298
  stress, 305-309
    critical incident, 308-309
    physical and environmental, 306-307
    psychological, 306, 307-308
    substance abuse, 309
    wellness programs, 312-313
safety and health program, 299

safety and security needs, 52
safety standards, 297-298
scalar organizational structure, 26
scene assessment, 260
scene management, 259-269
  elements of, 260-268
  job performance requirements, 258
  objectives of, 259
  phases of, 260
  termination of incident, 268-269
Schmidt, Warren, 72
scientific theory of management, 69-70
sector, use of term, 287
securing scene, 219-220
security, job, 144-145
selection of public education objectives, 131-132
selective duty, 146-147
self-actualization needs, 53
self-directed work teams (SDWT), 74-75
self-discipline, 82
self-esteem, 53
sensitive rooms, inspection of, 193-194
sexual harassment, 39
sheltering in place, 267-268
sick-outs, 146
signal codes, 256
single-issue leadership, 62-63
size-up, 260, 271-279
  application of, 274-276
    during incident, 276
    pre-incident, 274-275
    upon arrival, 276
  defined, 271-274
  job performance requirements, 270
  priorities and, 277-278
  three-step process, 273-274
  traditional, 272-273
"Skelly Rules," 83
skill development/maintenance training, 2, 89-90
skills
  accidents due to lack of, 310
  communication, 134-135
  of company officer, 8-11
  developing member, 76, 77
  supervisory, 77-86
social needs, 52-54
Society of Fire Protection Engineers (SFPE), 118
software, 171, 174
sovereign immunity doctrine, 31-32
span of control, 23-24, 292, 294
special purpose industrial occupancies, 202
staging areas, 286, 287, 292
standard operating procedures (SOPs), 21, 22, 181
  infection control, 300
standards, 189-190
  for company-level training, 80
  defined, 297
  national, 36, 41-43
  performance, 92, 94
  safety, 297-298
Standards Council of Canada (SCC), 43
standpipe systems, 207-208, 240
state government, 103-104
state laws, 37

status needs, 53, 54
statutory law, 33
storage occupancies, 202
strategic goals, 280
strategic plans, 279-280
stress, 305-309
  critical incident, 308-309
  physical and environmental, 306-307
  psychological, 306, 307-308
stress debriefing, critical incident (CISD), 269, 309
strikes, 141, 147
strike teams, 293
summative evaluation, 93
Superfund Amendments and Reauthorization Act (SARA) of 1986, 101
supervision/management, 9, 69-85
  functional supervision, 23, 26-29
  job performance requirements, 68
  modern management, 73-75
  responsibilities in, 75-77
  supervision, defined, 69
  supervisory skills, 77-86
    coaching and counseling, 3, 84-85
    communication, 79-80
    decision making, 78-79
    delegation, 78
    discipline, 82-84
    motivation, 77-78
    resource management, 80-81
    time management, 81-82
    training, 80
  theories of, 69-73
support (cold) zone, 262-263
Supreme Court, Canadian, 112
Supreme Court, U.S., 33, 106, 107, 108, 112, 140
survey, pre-incident, 229-241
  code enforcement inspection vs., 229
  conducting, 231-241
  equipment for, 230
  public relations during, 231
  purpose of, 232
  scheduling, 230-231

T

tactical objectives, 280
Taft-Hartley Act (1947), 140-141
Tannenbaum, Robert, 72
target hazards, 230
task forces, 293
Taylor, Frederick Winslow, 64, 69, 71
10-codes, 256
termination of incident, 268-269
Theory X, 61, 62-63, 64, 71
Theory Y, 61, 63, 71
Theory Z, 61-62, 74-75
third-party mediation, 145
time management, 2, 81-82
  work sheet, 81-82
Title VII, 39-40
tort claims, governmental immunity from, 32
tort liability, 35
total flooding CO_2 systems, 212
total flooding dry chemical systems, 210
Total Quality Management (TQM), 73-74
traffic control, 261-262

training
  company-level, 87-94
  cross, 25
  fire investigation, 115-116
  infection control and, 300
  state and provincial fire training
    programs, 104
  as supervisory skill, 80
transferring command, 291-292
two-in/two-out rule, 37, 298, 302-303
type I construction, 234-236

U

Underwriters Laboratories Inc., 117
Underwriters' Laboratories of Canada
  (ULC), 43, 117
unfair labor practices, 140
unified command structure, 288-292
Uniform Building Code (UBC), 190
Uniform Fire Code (UFC), 189, 192
unions, 139-142
United Auto Workers (UAW), 140
U.S. Constitution, 112
U.S. Department of Agriculture (USDA), 110
U.S. Department of Defense, 17
U.S. Department of Housing and Urban
  Development (HUD), 110
U.S. Department of Labor (DOL), 110
U.S. Department of the Interior (DOI), 110
U.S. Department of the Treasury, 111
U.S. Department of Transportation (DOT),
  110-111
U.S. federal government, 106-111
  agencies involved in fire protection, 108-
    111

lawmaking process of, 107-108
structure of, 106-107
U.S. Fire Administration (USFA), 33, 108-
  109
U.S. Forest Service, 110
U.S. Postal Service strike (1970), 141
unity of command, 21-23, 294

V

V.I.E. (valence, instrumentality, expectancy)
  Theory of motivation, 54-55
value systems, 66
  common values in group, 49, 50
vehicles, 203
  emergency, placement for, 262
  maintenance of, 80-81
  mobile radios in, 251, 252
ventilation, 277
vessels, 203
victims
  communicating with, 183
  occupant services for, 265
volunteer personnel, 18
Vroom, Victor, 54-55

W

Wagner, Robert, 140
Wagner-Connery Act, 140
warm zone, 262, 264
water supplies
  inspecting, 206
  pre-incident survey of, 240-241
  providing, 284

wellness programs, 312-313
Western Electric's Hawthorne plant,
  productivity experiment at, 70
wet chemical systems, 211
wet-pipe sprinkler system, 208, 209
wildland fire
  assessment of, 260
  locating point of origin in, 218-219
  sheltering in place from, 267
Williams-Steiger Occupational Safety and
  Health Act, 297
witness control, 264
witnesses, occupant services for, 265
work area safety and health, 76
work improvement plans, 164, 166
workplace accidents, 309-312
  analyzing accident/injury reports of, 311-
    312
  investigating, 309-311
workplace safety, 303-305
work schedule, 144
work teams, self-directed (SDWT), 74-75
work-to-rule, 146
written communication, 159-169, 179
  letters, 164-169
  reports, 3, 76-77, 159-164, 165, 246
written policies and procedures, 180-181

Y

yellow-dog contracts, 139

Z

zero-base budgets (ZBB), 154, 155